# AFTER THE HUMAN

*After the Human* provides a comprehensive overview of how a range of philosophical, ethical, and political ideas under the framework of posthumanism have transformed humanities scholarship today. Bringing together a range of interdisciplinary scholars and perspectives, it puts into dialogue the major influences from philosophy, literary study, anthropology, and science studies that set the stage for a range of new questions to be asked about the relationship of the human to other life. The book's central argument is that posthumanism's challenge to and disruption of traditional humanist knowledge is so significant as to presage a sea change from the humanities into the posthumanities. *After the Human* documents the emergence of posthumanist ideas in the fractures within traditional disciplines, examines the new objects of analysis that thus came into prominence, and theorizes new interdisciplinary methods of study that followed.

SHERRYL VINT is a leading scholar of speculative fiction, whose research focuses on embodiment, posthumanism, and biopolitics. She has published widely, including *Bodies of Tomorrow* (2007), *Animal Alterity* (2010), *The Futures Industry* (2015), *Science Fiction: The Essential Knowledge* (2020), and *Biopolitical Futures in Twenty-First Century Speculative Fiction* (2021).

T0381674

# AFTER SERIES

This series focuses on the legacy of several iconic figures, and key themes, in the origins and development of literary theory. Each book in the series attempts to isolate the influence, legacy and the impact of thinkers. Each figure addressed not only bequeathed specific concepts and doctrines to literary study, but they effectively opened up new critical landscapes for research. It is this legacy that this series tries to capture, with every book being designed specifically for use in literature departments. Throughout each book the concept of "After" is used in three ways: After in the sense of trying to define what is quintessential about each figure: "What has each figure introduced into the world of literary studies, criticism and interpretation?" After in a purely chronological sense: "What comes after each figure?," "What has his/her influence and legacy been?" and "How have they changed the landscape of literary studies?" Lastly, After in a practical sense: "How have their respective critical legacies impacted on an understanding of literary texts?" Each book is a collaborative volume with an international cast of critics and their level is suited for recommended reading on courses.

## Published Titles

*After Foucault: Culture, Theory and Criticism in the 21st Century*
*Edited by* Lisa Downing
University of Birmingham
*After Derrida: Literature, Theory and Criticism in the 21st Century*
*Edited by* Jean-Michel Rabaté
University of Pennsylvania
*After Lacan: Literature, Theory, and Psychoanalysis in the Twenty-First Century*
*Edited by* Ankhi Mukherjee
University of Oxford
*After Said: Postcolonial Literary Studies in the 21st Century*
*Edited by* Bashir Abu-Manneh
University of Kent
*After Queer Studies: Literary Theory and Critical Interpretation*
*Edited by* Tyler Bradway and E. L. McCallum
SUNY Cortland and Michigan State University

# AFTER THE HUMAN

*Culture, Theory, and Criticism in the 21st Century*

EDITED BY

SHERRYL VINT

*University of California, Riverside*

# CAMBRIDGE
## UNIVERSITY PRESS

University Printing House, Cambridge CB2 8BS, United Kingdom

One Liberty Plaza, 20th Floor, New York, NY 10006, USA

477 Williamstown Road, Port Melbourne, VIC 3207, Australia

314–321, 3rd Floor, Plot 3, Splendor Forum, Jasola District Centre, New Delhi – 110025, India

79 Anson Road, #06–04/06, Singapore 079906

Cambridge University Press is part of the University of Cambridge.

It furthers the University's mission by disseminating knowledge in the pursuit of education, learning, and research at the highest international levels of excellence.

www.cambridge.org
Information on this title: www.cambridge.org/9781108836661
DOI: 10.1017/9781108874427

© Cambridge University Press 2020

First published 2020

*A catalogue record for this publication is available from the British Library.*

*Library of Congress Cataloging-in-Publication Data*
NAMES: Vint, Sherryl, 1969– editor.
TITLE: After the human : culture, theory and criticism in the 21st century / edited by Sherryl Vint.
DESCRIPTION: Cambridge ; New York, NY : Cambridge University Press, 2020. | Series: After series | Includes bibliographical references and index.
IDENTIFIERS: LCCN 2020025096 | ISBN 9781108836661 (hardback) | ISBN 9781108874427 (ebook)
SUBJECTS: LCSH: Humanism. | Philosophical anthropology. | Human body (Philosophy)
CLASSIFICATION: LCC B821 .A38 2020 | DDC 001.3–dc23
LC record available at https://lccn.loc.gov/2020025096

ISBN 978-1-108-83666-1 Hardback
ISBN 978-1-108-81916-9 Paperback

# Contents

*List of Contributors*                                          *page* vii
*Acknowledgments*                                                       x

    Introduction                                    1
    *Sherryl Vint*

PART I  AFTER HUMANISM

1  Historicizing Posthumanism                                15
    *Veronica Hollinger*

2  Poststructuralism and the End(s) of Humanism              31
    *Stefan Herbrechter*

3  Postmodernism                                             44
    *Jonathan Boulter*

4  Embodiment and Affect                                     58
    *Michael Richardson*

5  Requiem for a Digital Humanist                            72
    *Marcel O'Gorman*

PART II  NEW OBJECTS OF ENQUIRY

6  Machines, AIs, Cyborgs, Systems                           91
    *Bruce Clarke*

7  Animals                                                  105
    *Susan McHugh*

8  Life "Itself"                                            120
    *Nadine Ehlers*

9    The Anthropocene                                              134
     *Gerda Roelvink*

10   The Inorganic                                                 147
     *Magdalena Zolkos*

PART III POSTHUMANITIES

11   More-than-Human Biopolitics                                   161
     *Sonja van Wichelen*

12   New Materialisms                                              177
     *Stacy Alaimo*

13   Speculative Realism: The Human and Nonhuman Divide            192
     *Brian Willems*

14   Race and the Limitations of "the Human"                       206
     *Mark Minch-de Leon*

15   Speculative Fiction                                           220
     *Sherryl Vint*

16   Aesthetic Manipulation of Life                                236
     *Ionat Zurr and Oron Catts*

*Collective Works Cited*                                           252
*Index*                                                           277

# Contributors

STACY ALAIMO is Professor of English and Core Faculty Member in Environmental Studies at the University of Oregon. Her books include *Undomesticated Ground: Recasting Nature as Feminist Space* (2000), *Bodily Natures: Science, Environment, and the Material Self* (2010), and *Exposed: Environmental Politics and Pleasures in Posthuman Times* (2016).

JONATHAN BOULTER is Professor of English at Western University. He is the author of *Posthuman Space in Samuel Beckett's Short Prose* (2019), *Parables of the Posthuman* (2015), *Melancholy and the Archive* (2011), *Beckett: A Guide for the Perplexed* (2008), and *Interpreting Narrative in the Novels of Samuel Beckett* (2001).

ORON CATTS AND IONAT ZURR are artists, researchers, and curators who formed the internationally renowned Tissue Culture & Art Project in 1996. Catts is the cofounder and Director of SymbioticA: The Centre of Excellence in Biological Arts at the University of Western Australia, and Zurr is a researcher and lecturer at the School of Design, University of Western Australia, and SymbioticA's academic coordinator. They are considered pioneers in the field of biological arts; they publish widely and exhibit internationally. Catts and Zurr's ideas and projects reach beyond the world of art and are often cited as inspiration in diverse areas such as new materials, textiles, design, architecture, ethics, fiction, and food.

BRUCE CLARKE is the Paul Whitfield Horn Professor of Literature and Science in the Department of English at Texas Tech University. His research focuses on systems theory, narrative theory, and ecology. Clarke coedits the book series Meaning Systems, published by Fordham University Press, and the website Gaian Systems (www .gaian.systems).

NADINE EHLERS teaches in the Department of Sociology and Social Policy at the University of Sydney. Her research broadly focuses on the sociocultural study of the body, law, and biomedicine to examine racial and gendered governance. Her most recent book is *Deadly Biocultures: The Ethics of Life-making* (with Shiloh Krupar).

STEFAN HERBRECHTER is a former Reader in Cultural Theory at Coventry University and a Professor of English and Cultural Studies at Heidelberg University. He has published widely on literature, culture, and media. His *Posthumanism – A Critical Analysis* (2013, first published in German in 2009) is one of the founding texts of critical posthumanism. For more information, see http://criticalposthumanism.net and http://stefanherbrechter.com.

VERONICA HOLLINGER is Emerita Professor of Cultural Studies at Trent University in Ontario. She is a long-time coeditor of *Science Fiction Studies* and coeditor of four academic collections. Most recently, she has published on posthumanism, on cyberculture and the climate crisis, and on gender and sexuality in contemporary science fiction.

SUSAN MCHUGH is Professor of English at the University of New England. Her books include *Animal Stories: Narrating across Species Lines* (2011) and *Love in a Time of Slaughters: Human-Animal Stories against Genocide and Extinction* (2019). She is coeditor of the forthcoming volume *Posthumanism in Art and Science: A Reader*.

MARK MINCH-DE LEON is an Assistant Professor of English at the University of California, Riverside. He works at the intersections of Indigenous Studies, Rhetorical Theory, and Narrative and Visual Studies. His current project looks at the anticolonial, non-vitalist dimensions of California Indian intellectual and cultural resurgence.

MARCEL O'GORMAN is University Research Chair, Professor of English, and Founding Director of the Critical Media Lab at the University of Waterloo. O'Gorman has published widely about technoculture, including the books *E-Crit*, *Necromedia*, and *Making Media Theory*. He is also a practicing artist with an international portfolio of exhibitions and performances.

MICHAEL RICHARDSON is a Senior Research Fellow in the School of the Arts & Media, UNSW. His transdisciplinary research investigates witnessing and the intersection of affect, power, and violence in culture, media, and politics. He is the author of *Gestures of Testimony: Torture, Trauma and Affect in Literature* (Bloomsbury, 2016).

GERDA ROELVINK is an interdisciplinary scholar at Western Sydney University. Her research expertise is in diverse economies, social movements, climate change, and affect studies. She is the author of the book *Building Dignified Worlds* (University of Minnesota Press, 2016) and has published work in a range of journals and books.

SONJA VAN WICHELEN is Associate Professor with the Department of Sociology and Social Policy at the University of Sydney and Director of the Biopolitics of Science Research Network. Her latest book is *Legitimating Life: Adoption in the Age of Globalization and Biotechnology* (Rutgers University Press, 2018).

SHERRYL VINT is Professor of Media and Cultural Studies at the University of California, Riverside, where she directs the Speculative Fictions and Cultures of Science Program. She has published widely on speculative fiction and cultural politics, including more recently the book *Science Fiction* for MIT Press's Essential Knowledge series and *Biopolitical Futures in Twenty-First Century Speculative Fiction* (Cambridge University Press, 2021).

BRIAN WILLEMS is Associate Professor of Literature and Film Theory at the University of Split, Croatia. He is most recently the author of *Speculative Realism and Science Fiction* (Edinburgh University Press, 2017) and *Shooting the Moon* (Zero Books, 2015).

MAGDALENA ZOLKOS is a political theorist and Humboldt Research Fellow at Goethe University, focusing on memory politics, reconciliation, and historical justice. She is the author of *Reconciling Community and Subjective Life: Trauma Testimony as Political Theorizing in the Work of Jean Amery and Imre Kertesz* (Continuum, 2010).

# *Acknowledgments*

I want to thank a number of people without whom this volume would not have been possible. First, my editor Ray Ryan for inviting me to conceptualize and edit this volume in the first place, and for his tremendous patience with how long it took for me to find a place for this work on my schedule. Second, I want to thank my contributors for their excellent work on this volume, contributors who represent exciting new ways to conceptualize and work within this field, in chapters that have pushed and revitalized my own thinking. The list of colleagues and friends (some of them contributors here as well) whose work in the broad area of study defined as "after the human" is too long to enumerate them all here, but I am grateful to the research communities to which I belong and to the generosity of scholars within these fields. Colin Milburn deserves special mention as a very helpful interlocutor in framing this project. I want to thank Brittany Roberts for her conscientious work as an excellent RA. Finally, I owe a huge debt of gratitude to Veronica Hollinger, who assisted me in this project both intellectually and with editorial assistance in the final assembly of the manuscript. But beyond this, Veronica has been a wonderful mentor, a valued colleague, and an inspiration for what it means to be a scholar. I thank her for her assistance, her example, and her friendship.

# Introduction

*Sherryl Vint*

What does it mean to think after the human? Before we might begin to answer that question, the meanings of both "after" and "the human" must be clarified. As the essays collected here demonstrate, although there may be some consensus that knowledge in the humanities and beyond needs urgently to take account of the more-than-human world and to redefine its concepts and methods beyond anthropocentricism, precisely how these goals are best achieved remains a matter of considerable debate. This volume, *After the Human*, provides an overview of how theory and criticism have been changed by the recognition that the human as theorized in western, liberal tradition can no longer serve as the center for intellectual enquiry in the humanities. Rather than attempting to answer definitively what should emerge in its place, this book strives instead to map a number of ongoing conversations across established and emerging fields, thereby to illuminate what is at stake in the project of theory and criticism after the human. Who and what "counts" as human today, and what is at stake in doing such counting?

Despite the divergences and tensions among these approaches, a few core ideas are evident across the chapters, marking why the twenty-first century can be described as the critical moment after the human. First is a pervasive sense that too much of the world has been left out of the picture by previously hegemonic epistemologies – great numbers of people never recognized as fully human due to colonialism, racism, and sexism, to name only the most evident discriminatory systems of western thought; but also other species, the living world that sustains all life including human life, material objects, and complex systems combining several of these neglected others, such as the climate. Even an anthropocentric viewpoint still primarily concerned with the future of the human species must now admit that its survival cannot be disentangled from the more-than-human world, and many of the approaches documented here eschew anthropocentrism as well as critique the historical limitations of the term "the human." Second is a sense of the timeliness of asking such questions, driven by multiple crises that include ongoing mass extinction, pervasive climate change, and the inadequacy of western humanism to provide ethical and political frameworks sufficient to respond to growing economic and other inequality and to the largescale human migrations that are a consequence of how colonialism and capitalism have carved up the world to privilege a select subset of humans, what Sylvia Wynter calls the overrepresented Man of western modernity.[1] Not all of the projects described in this volume would embrace the term "posthuman"[2] – although it can function as a rubric under which to collect them together and put them into conversation – and this refusal to acknowledge "the posthuman" as a universal is important too: if so much of what is wrong with "the human" lies in its claims to represent all while ignoring so much, it is fitting that approaches to posthumanism are multiple, even at times contradictory: what is required is a conversation, not a fixed concept.

Equally fraught is the question of what is "post," including contentions that the periodization implied by the prefix is part of the problem. As Stefan Herbrechter argues in Chapter 2, there is a sense of belatedness about this "post," which is also always a before; to push this idea even further, as Mark Minch-de Leon contends in Chapter 14, perhaps the "post" still concedes too much to "the human" and what is needed is not a working through and beyond this figure, but rather its suspension. Various philosophies, interdisciplinary formations, and new objects of study that emerge from what we might call "posthumanism" have equally divergent origin points as well as ends, as Veronica Hollinger maps out in Chapter 1. Some of the traditions represented here seek to continue the project of philosophy, whether this be in the deconstructive tradition inaugurated by Derrida, the refusal of fixed identities pursued by those following Deleuze, or the epistemological critique of what "the human" both enables and obscures implicit in Foucault's work. Other chapters initiate or extend projects of political and social critique, and Rosi Braidotti points out that we should recognize the emergence of fields such as women's studies, ethnic studies, postcolonial studies, queer studies, and the like as protests against the narrowness of authorized western knowledge systems that are part of the longer intellectual history from which posthumanism emerges.[3]

An equally important context is the widespread saturation of daily life by science and technology, both the hegemony of western scientific epistemologies and the degree to which daily life is substantially mediated by – and to a large extent, is dependent upon – science and technology. As Marcel

O'Gorman explores in his provocative analysis of how posthumanist thought intersects with the digital humanities in Chapter 5, there are profound questions to be asked about what it means to be a tool-using /tool-making species, including whether it is even possible to conceive of "the human" without such prosthetics. Thus, a range of posthumanist approaches engage with questions of media and information technology, including the possibility that capacities once deemed exclusive to "the human" may soon be shared by machinic, AI beings. Even more influential, however, has been the sea change in the life sciences since the mid-twentieth century, from the mapping of the genome through to synthetic biology, all of which have rewritten philosophical notions of "life itself," prompting new questions about our relationship with nonhuman species, our ethical and political ways of managing life across multiple embodiments. The framing of our contemporary era as the Anthropocene – a widely used, if also contested designation – is only the most recognizable of new intellectual formations that urge us to rethink the humanities in dialogue with the sciences.

Thus, scholarship referred to collectively as science and technology studies (STS) is as important to the emergence of posthumanism as are philosophical critiques of humanism. Evaluations of the knowledge-making practices of western scientific tradition – especially those by feminist and decolonial scholars – are central to the project of rethinking concepts, including the meaning of "the human," in the western world. Indeed, such critiques of the discourse and practice of science have often opened up the intellectual space into which discussions of the posthuman emerged, apparent in the indispensable role of Donna Haraway's thought to all of feminist science studies, the posthumanist conversation that followed from her influential "Cyborg Manifesto," and the emergence of scholarship on human-animal relations.[4] Although not as frequently labelled posthumanist, Karen Barad's *Meeting the Universe Halfway*, a feminist retheorization of knowledge through quantum physics that insists that ontology, epistemology, and ethics are necessarily coproduced, all part of the intra-actions of matter that make the world, including humanity, is similarly central to STS scholarship premised on paying attention to matter as agential and thus conceptualizing meaning and culture as always more-than-human.[5]

Other STS and cultural studies theorists have addressed in myriad ways how changing quotidian practices related to developments in science and technology have demanded that we rethink humanist assumptions, from Andrew Pickering's and Andrew Ross' respective works on technoculture,[6] to work on the implications of genomics and biotechnologies by scholars such as Sarah Franklin and Eugene Thacker,[7] to work about the intersections of scientific practice, media, and quotidian life, epitomized by N. Katherine Hayles and Colin Milburn.[8] Hayles in particular has been as influential as Haraway, if in a different sphere, charting the path for posthumanist scholarship about human-machine interfaces and co-evolution that has generated significant new ways of framing how we understanding consciousness, agency, and cognition. Her work has shaped conversations about representation and mediation, in conjunction with technologies of meaning-making, and forged a connection between the fields of posthumanism and media studies. At the same time, STS work in the life sciences, including that in the emergent field of the medical humanities, frequently reflects the insights of posthumanism, although it does not always use this language, reflected in scholarship about how notions of "life itself" intersect with the biopolitics of population management. Research on the biopolitics of health and governance is necessarily in dialogue with the decentering of a particular history of the human that has long been hegemonic in western thought. Such thinking about life, health, and technology after the human takes up issues of decolonization and antiracism, crucial topics that have been neglected in the philosophical tradition of posthumanist thinking until recently.[9]

As this brief overview already begins to suggest, there is more than one posthumanism and, while there are several key figures who are cited repeatedly in this volume, there are also distinct traditions that frequently do not refer to one another. In addition to Haraway and Hayles, another central figure is Rosi Braidotti, who has long worked in a Deleuzean tradition to develop a feminist practice of non-hierarchical, in-flux, and ethically oriented becoming that she refers to as nomadic subjectivity. In her most recent work, she has embraced the figure of the posthuman as a way to conceptualize necessary transformations in western thought, arguing for an affirmative posthumanism as an opportunity to remake ourselves and our ethics. Her recent *Posthuman Knowledge* includes a sustained analysis of how the humanities can and should transition into the posthumanities, thereby overcoming the historical limitations and omissions of "the human," as well as reinvigorating research cultures to rise to the challenges of contemporary crises which demand a non-anthropocentric mode of analysis.[10] Other central figures whose work has been important to shaping distinct modes of thinking after the human include Claire Colebrook, Timothy Morton, and Cary Wolfe.

Crucially, it is often the points of tension or disagreement among these traditions that are most productive for thinking today, pushing scholarship after the human beyond a critique of western humanities and into territories not even conceivable from its vantage point. Not everyone using the term posthuman means the same thing by it, which is true not only today but also throughout the philosophical history from which today's theory emerged out of diverse roots. All of the scholarly traditions represented in *After the Human* respond in some way to perceived limitations of humanist tradition – intellectual, political, and practical; they do not always agree, however, on how best to redress such failings. Interest in human/machine couplings expressed in transhumanism, for example, is often seen as intensifying rather than ameliorating the hierarchical way of thinking that has characterized human exceptionalism. Many of the approaches represented here prioritize questions of ethics vis-à-vis living beings, concerned with animals, microbes, plants, and the ecosystems that sustain the possibility of life at all, but others suggest that the life/nonlife binary, too, is a barrier to transitioning fully into non-anthropocentric thought. Some scholars seek to deconstruct or otherwise revise existing discourses from new perspectives, while others want to invent entirely new ways of thinking. Both Susan McHugh's chapter on Animals (Chapter 7) and Stacy Alaimo's chapter on New Materialisms (Chapter 12) draw attention to resistance within their respective fields to the term posthuman. Two kinds of tension are evident. On the one hand, there exists within these fields a sense that posthumanism remains too complicit in the anthropocentrism of humanism, too much an abstract philosophical discourse insufficiently committed to political praxis. On the other, those most immersed in philosophical traditions of posthumanism sometimes see scholarship about entities such as animals or ecosystems as insufficiently rigorous, which perhaps betrays a reflexive privileging of anthropocentric frameworks even as the project of humanism is critiqued. Other differences abound: the deconstructive project of critical posthumanism emphasizes the constitutive role of human language, the tradition of speculative realism attempts to escape such hermeneutics into what it argues is an objective realm of things-for-themselves, and the affirmative tradition championed by Braidotti critiques both for their failure to be sufficiently attentive to entangled bodies and their affects.

Such disagreements do not fall simply into differences between modes of critique versus more radical approaches to change, as Michael Richardson's chapter on Embodiment and Affect (Chapter 4) and Mark Minch-de Leon's chapter on Race and the Limitations of "the

Human" (Chapter 14) make clear. Both chart necessary interventions in the discussion of thinking after the human and yet also document significant reasons why scholars committed to rejecting "the human" as a racialized concept remain wary of (some discourses of) posthumanism. As Richardson puts it, understanding "after the human" as a movement "beyond the human" is often seen as a step in the wrong direction to those bodies – black, crip, queer, colonized, Asian – that have never fully been afforded the category of human in the first place.[11] Minch-de Leon thus insists that when we assess posthumanist knowledge production and its capacity to transform scholarship and practice, the most important question to ask is, "Have [such discourses] combatted a white supremacist racialized regime or contributed to it?" There is still much to overcome regarding the historical operation of "the human" as an ideal.

By documenting these tensions and the range of responses to the question of what the practices and politics of knowledge production after the human might be, this volume strives both to provide a map of the existing terrain and to open up space for further research that will follow from moments of convergence and from points where various posthumanisms disagree. *After the Human* documents research that begins from the premise that there is much to be gained from paying critical attention to objects and domains of knowledge that have traditionally not been considered appropriate to the humanities. All are committed to ethical and political projects of remaking knowledge – and thereby the world – by interrogating and in diverse ways refusing the hierarchical binaries that have grounded western thought and the privileged position "the human" occupies within them. A few key motifs recur across the chapters, suggesting something of an emergent frame of reference for posthumanist investigation. First, economic critique and the role of capitalism as a force that, hand-in-glove with humanism and colonialism, has produced a world beset by threats of extinction, including perhaps our own. Second, new conceptualization of subjectivity and agency, as well as a questioning of their relative importance as grounding rubrics for being, given that discourses which previously attributed specific capacities as the sole province of "the human" can no longer hold. Third, a sense of absence or omissions that must be ameliorated, apparent in the language of ghosts and hauntings across several chapters, as well as in the new objects and methods of study that are invented as ways of renewing the project of ethics. Importantly, this is not simply a case of bodies/subjects that have been left out of the humanist frame, but those who actively have been excluded by a process of dehumanization. If one thing can be claimed as central to all the chapters collected here, it is the recognition that "the human" is always coproduced with an abjected nonhuman.

In terms of criticism and theory after the human, we see a repeated emphasis as well on questions of representation and narrative, on how – if – we might interact with and create knowledge about the more-than-human world. As we move away from chapters documenting the critique of humanism and toward those seeking to install something else in its place, we see a shift away from concerns with signification and toward issues of process and relationality. Yet strategies for making the more-than-human world perceptible remain key, evident in the fables and stories to which theorists often turn to concretize their assertions, and in the collective conviction that there is a politics implicit in whose stories are told, by whom, and in the ontological weight we allow stories. This is why each of speculative fiction (Chapter 15) and the biological arts (Chapter 16) recur as examples in many other chapters as well.

Yet the most important thing that unites the scholarship collected here is a sense that posthumanism is an ethical and political project – even if there is no consensus on precisely what its interventions should be. What the scholarship analyzed in *After the Human* reminds us again and again is that not all beings are fostered and valued in existing systems, and that the human has been a major technology in producing such divisions historically. This is not to assert that all beings should necessarily be regarded as "equal" in some kind of undifferentiated vitalism, but it is to remind us that "the human" has never been a neutral term – it is coproduced with racism, ableism, sexism, and classism, and the like – and more rigorous ways of thinking through what we value, and why, and by which logics, are urgently needed. The myopic vision inherited via a western metaphysics obsessed with individualism and agential subjectivity is at an end. What remains to be decided – indeed, is a vibrant field of ongoing enquiry – is how to ensure that the posthuman does not become the next iteration of a privileged subject that continues to render invisible its abjected outside and other. Undoubtedly, new ethics are needed, but the work that remains is collectively to negotiate what they might be, from a perspective of solidarity that simultaneously leaves space for difference. This is neither an easy nor a self-evident task but it is a necessary one.

*After the Human* contributes to this work by documenting the range of conversations shaping the field right now, thereby to point toward places where new conversations might emerge. Part I contextualizes the field in terms of a long history of posthumanist thought, often ideas in circulation before the term became prevalent. It includes an overview of the field's emergence from multiple strains of western philosophy (Chapter 1); an analysis of the relationship between the linguistic turn in critical theory and the posthuman (Chapter 2); an analysis of the centrality of questions of representation and narrative practice to the project of rethinking subjectivity (Chapter 3); an engagement with Deleuzean and related traditions that followed, resisting the (over)emphasis on language to turn to queer posthumanism (Chapter 4); and, finally, a theorization of the relationship between meaning making and technological extensions of human capacities, which opens on to another way this philosophical history might have unfolded (Chapter 5). As a whole, this part charts the origin of posthumanist concepts in western philosophical skepticism, but also reveals that this line of thought has ended up at quite unanticipated destinations.

Part II foregrounds the new objects of analysis and new methods of study that emerged following the critique of humanist concepts and their ways of framing research agendas. As Braidotti argues in *Posthuman Knowledge*, such scholarship is not only an attempt to think beyond anthropocentrism, but also redefines the human "as materially embedded and embodied, differential, affective and relational" (11). This requires not merely new ways of thinking and reading, but of relating, being, perceiving, inter- and intra-acting with the world: once we change what is considered a proper object of knowledge, we also bring into question how to conduct research and thus introduce the possibility of collaborative methods that do not reduce the more-than-human world to a resource for human projects. The perspectives highlighted in this part are AIs, robots, machines, and systems (Chapter 6); animals (Chapter 7); life understood as distinct from its embodiment in specific living organisms (Chapter 8); the world conceived of as a system of intrinsic value for multiple agents, not as a space of rightful human dominion (Chapter 9); and a critique of how the life/nonlife binary has been foundational to western thought, which anticipates some of the critiques of "the human" from non-western points of view (Chapter 10).

Finally, Part III explores in greater details some new sites of knowledge formation and transformations of existing modes of enquiry that are attendant upon the emergence of posthumanist frames of reference. It asks how the human is co-entangled with other entities and it explores genealogies of thought neglected in anthropocentric, western tradition. It includes an analysis of how the biopolitical governance of life is significantly reshaped by the erosion of human exceptionalism (Chapter 11); an argument for new kinds of environmental politics enabled by thinking through new materialist frameworks that refuse to see matter as inert

(Chapter 12); an overview of how and why speculative realism attempts to think fully outside of human concepts (Chapter 13); an argument for decolonializing posthumanism through a politics of refusal that suspends the divisions that have been wrought by "the human" (Chapter 14); and analyses of new ways of making culture and meaning in the light of the turn toward the more-than-human world in humanities scholarship as manifested in speculative fiction (Chapter 15) and in the biological arts (Chapter 16).

Braidotti cautions that

> Statements like "we humans", or even "we posthumans", need to be grounded carefully on materially embedded differential perspectives, for "we-are-in-*this*-together-but-we-are-*not*-one-and-the-same". "We" are immanent to, which means intrinsically connected to, the very conditions we are *also* critical of. The posthuman convergence is a shared trait of our historical moment, but it is not at all clear whose crisis this actually is. Because we cannot speak of an undifferentiated humanity (or an undifferentiated "we") that is allegedly sharing in a common condition of both technological mediation and crisis and extinction, extra work is required of critical thinkers. (157)

The scholarship collected here begins this necessary, urgent work, attentive to its difficulty and to the multiplicity of neglected voices it adds to the conversation, to the diversity of "answers" being provided to ongoing crises. *After the Human* does not seek to be the final, definitive statement on criticism and theory after the more-than-human turn, but it does assert that they can no longer remain as they once were, in this light of rethinking the human.

## Notes

1. Sylvia Wynter, "Unsettling the Coloniality of Being/Power/Truth/Freedom: Towards the Human, After Man, Its Overrepresentation – An Argument," *CR: Centennial Review*, 3 (3) (2003): 257–337.
2. Among my reasons for using this term to collect these approaches together, despite tensions among them, is my conviction that there is much to be gained from a dialogue among them. Too often scholarship fragments, with scholars striving to introduce a multiplicity of terms such as the ahuman (J. Paul Narkunas, *Reified Life: Speculative Capital and the Ahuman Condition* [New York: Fordham University Press, 2018]) or the infrahuman (Megan H. Glick, *Infrahumanisms: Science, Culture, and the Making of Modern Non/Personhood* [Durham: Duke University Press, 2018]), to name only two I have recently encountered – and intellectual work seals itself off into unproductively

narrow conversations. To be clear, I do understand the resistance that some scholars express toward using the term given that early posthumanist conversations failed to engage colonialism and antiracism in a meaningful way. Moreover, I do not mention Narkunas or Glick to critique the ideas expressed in their work. Rather, my concern is that an opportunity to further decolonize posthumanist scholarship is missed when such important correctives are positioned as being parallel to rather than part of a broader conversation. I do, however, think it is important to differentiate between a range of posthumanist approaches that rethink knowledge outside of the structures of domination that have been the hallmark of humanism, versus transhumanism as a project of uber-human transcendence.

3. Rosi Braidotti, *Posthuman Knowledge* (Cambridge: Polity Press, 2019), 104.
4. Donna Haraway, "A Cyborg Manifesto: Science, Technology, and Socialist-Feminism in the Late Twentieth Century," in *Simians, Cyborgs, and Women: The Reinvention of Nature* (New York: Routledge, 1991), 149–81.
5. Karen Bard, *Meeting the Universe Halfway: Quantum Physics and the Entanglement of Matter and Meaning* (Durham: Duke University Press, 2007).
6. See Andrew Pickering, *The Cybernetic Brain: Sketches of Another Future* (Chicago: University of Chicago Press, 2011) and Andrew Ross, *Strange Weather: Culture, Science and Technology in the Age of Limits* (New York: Verso, 1991).
7. See Sarah Franklin, *Dolly Mixtures: The Remaking of Genealogy* (Durham: Duke University Press, 2007) and Eugene Thacker, *The Global Genome: Biotechnology, Politics and Culture* (Cambridge: MIT Press, 2006).
8. To name only their most cited texts, see N. Katherine Hayles, *How We Became Posthuman: Virtual Bodies in Cybernetics, Literature, and Infomatics* (Chicago: University of Chicago Press, 1999) and Collin Milburn, *Mondo Nano: Fun and Games in the World of Digital Matter* (Durham: Duke University Press, 2015).
9. Important examples of such STS scholarship include Neda Atanasoski and Kalindi Vora, *Surrogate Humanity: Race, Robots, and the Politics of Technological Futures* (Durham: Duke University Press, 2019) and Michelle Murphy, *The Economization of Life* (Durham: Duke University Press, 2017).
10. See Braidotti, *Posthuman Knowledge*. Crucially, Braidotti sees in the Critical Posthumanities not just new ways to do humanities research in the absence of "the human" as a guiding object of analysis, but also a way such scholarship could resist the neoliberal transformation of the university into an engine of capitalist accumulation: "Politically, the Critical PostHumanities represent both an alternative to the neo-liberal governance of academic knowledge, dominated by quantitative data and control, and a re-negotiation of its terms" (102). With Maria Hlaajova, Braidotti has also put together an encyclopedic *Posthuman Glossary* (London: Bloomsbury, 2018) which catalogues an

impressive range of concepts, thinkers, and schools of thought that are relevant to rethinking and remaking the humanities today.

II. In a series of essays and her book, Zakiyyah Iman Jackson does important work bridging the fields of posthumanism, animal studies, and queer-of-color and decolonial critique. See *Becoming Human: Matter and Meaning in an Antiblack World* (New York: New York University Press, 2020).

# PART I

# *After Humanism*

CHAPTER I

# Historicizing Posthumanism

## Veronica Hollinger

The stories that make us feel most human are no longer the stories that tell us the truth.[1]

There will be a time of the non-human, or the no-longer human.[2]

## 1.1 Post/Humanisms

In the second century BCE, there was a kind of common sense to the Roman playwright Terence's conviction that *Homo sum, humani nihil a me alienum puto*, or, "I am human, and I think nothing human is alien to me." In spite of its generosity, this recognition of a self-evident, universal humanity implicitly depends upon an equally commonsensical demarcation between humanity and everything else, situating the Earth and its nonhuman inhabitants as *alienum*. In the seventeenth century, Descartes' Enlightenment humanism valorized the rational mind (the *cogito*) over the body, so that the body too has tended to be positioned as *alienum* in western cultures, aligned with an objectified feminine "nature" rather than a glorified masculine "culture." Descartes also drew rigorous boundaries between human beings and nonhuman animals, on the one hand, and machines, on the other, relegating both to an unreasoning ontological outside. It is no coincidence that contemporary posthumanisms emphasize exactly how entangled the human has always been in interrelations both with the "natural" world and with the world of technoscientific "second nature." It has become increasingly difficult to defend the idea of human ontological self-sameness.

Our contemporary version of humanism has its roots in the industrialization/modernization of the eighteenth and nineteenth centuries and in the increasing expansion of market-driven capitalism. (Neo)liberal humanism is today's commonsense ideology of the subject. Briefly, in N. Katherine Hayles' words, it espouses "a coherent, rational self, the

15

right of that self to autonomy and freedom, and a sense of agency linked with a belief in enlightened self-interest."[3] As usual, there is a distinction to be made between rational humanity and everything else, and so (neo) liberalism easily sustains the philosophical boundaries earlier proposed by both Terence and Descartes.

The eighteenth- and nineteenth-century colonialist projects of western liberal humanism, influenced by Darwinian theory, hierarchized not only gender but also race, so that there were also distinctions to be made between more and less evolutionarily advanced races. Not surprisingly, and in large part supported by its advanced technologies, the "white" race considered itself to be the most advanced and therefore the most fully human. In his foundational work in animal studies, Cary Wolfe has argued that we should support rights for animals because so many oppressions are excused when human beings are first "reduced" to the status of animals: "We all, human and nonhuman alike, have a stake in the discourse and institution of speciesism; it is by no means limited to its overwhelmingly direct and disproportionate effects on animals."[4] Jacques Derrida's decon-struction of the human/animal divide in "The Animal That Therefore I Am" is another foundational text in the interdisciplinary field of animal studies. Supported by genetic discoveries that have collapsed most of the distinctions between human bodies and animal bodies, animal studies aims to reconsider the relations between human and nonhuman animals, not only from the perspective of an ethical recognition of their being-for-themselves but also from the perspective of a necessarily shared coexistence that no longer privileges human beings as ontologically unique.

Especially since the 1980s, posthumanist thought has also been respon-sive to rapidly accelerating developments in technoscience. In his preface to *Mirrorshades*, Bruce Sterling describes the new computing and bioengin-eering technologies of the 1980s as "pervasive, utterly intimate," and the key themes that he identifies all touch on the technological penetration of body and mind, "techniques radically redefining the nature of humanity, the nature of the self."[5] The "origins" of the posthuman technosubject are to be found in the recognition of our increasingly intimate coevolution with the products of the technosphere.

Critical posthumanist thought seeks to abandon the essentialisms of Terence's idealized universal humanity, of Descartes' idealized human intellect, and of (neo)liberalism's idealized human agency. Most strands of critical posthumanism theorize a human subject constituted not by self-sameness but by difference, a subject not fixed but in process, entangled in human and nonhuman and technological relations that are, in fact, what bring that subject into being. Tom Idema describes what we might think of as a thread of self-alienation or self-estrangement – of becoming *alienum* – in posthumanist thought:

> Whereas definitions of posthumanism vary, most of them share a resistance to placing humanity at the center of thought and the universe; a rejection of a strict opposition between human and nonhuman; a refusal to accept the human form as fixed; and a proclivity to speculate about a future in which humans, for better or for worse, have transformed into different beings.[6]

## 1.2   Antihumanisms

In his landmark 1984 essay on postmodernism, Fredric Jameson describes the postmodern subject in terms of decentering and fragmentation, announcing "the end of the autonomous bourgeois monad or ego or individual."[7] Jameson's rather bleak postmodern antihumanism is only one of many challenges to the hubris of the "monadic" subject, challenges that developed in parallel with the ideologies of humanism. Friedrich Nietzsche is exemplary here, given his contemptuous decentering of human exceptionalism in the larger scheme of things: "Weariness that wants its ultimate in one great leap, a death-leap; a poor unknowing weariness that no longer even wants to will: that created all gods and hinterworlds."[8] In contrast to colonialist readings of Darwin, Stacy Alaimo sees in evolutionary theory a powerful exposure of the human "as a corporeal amalgamation of creatures both at hand and across vast temporal distances."[9] Indeed, she argues that Darwin "may have given us our first glimpse of the always already 'posthuman,' a stance that insists upon our immersion within worldly material agencies" (*Bodily* 158). In the introduction to *Posthumanism*, Neil Badmington identifies other important early antihumanisms, including Karl Marx's scientific materialism that theorizes human beings as the products of their social relations and Sigmund Freud's psychoanalytic theory that understands human beings as the products of unconscious psychic forces.[10]

In the twentieth century, and especially in the postmodern decades from the 1950s through the 1980s, antihumanisms continued critically to probe the defenses of humanism, even as they maintained a determinedly anthropocentric focus on the constitution of the human subject. Although the subject theorized by antihumanism may be much diminished, it remains the key to all meaningful experience. Structuralisms (such as Ferdinand de Saussure's linguistics and Claude Lévi-Strauss' anthropology) demonstrate the formation of the subject within ineluctable symbolic and cultural systems, while poststructuralisms (such as Jacques Lacan's neo-Freudian psychoanalytic theory and Jacques Derrida's deconstruction) produce a subject of limited agency constituted in and through language. The subject is invaded by, shaped within, and coexists with the seemingly alien forces of the unconscious for Freud, the symbolic order for Lacan, the inhuman for Jean-François Lyotard, the animal for Giorgio Agamben, western metaphysics for Derrida – the list seems endless. In each case, a kind of Kristevan abject has insinuated itself into and become constitutive of a subject stripped of free will, self-identity, and self-possession. All of these antihumanist positions aim to dismantle an outdated and arrogantly self-important understanding of the human. To recall Eve Kosofky Sedgwick's terminology, they undertake "paranoid" readings of the human that emphasize critique, in contrast to later "reparative" readings such as N. Katherine Hayles' *How We Became Posthuman*, Sherryl Vint's *Bodies of Tomorrow*, and Rosi Braidotti's *The Posthuman*.[11] Braidotti, for example, theorizes posthumanism as an opportunity to develop an affirmative and cosmopolitan ethics and politics (47), while Stacy Alaimo explores the promising intersections of critical posthumanist thought and environmental ethics (*Bodily*).

## 1.3  Becoming Cyborg

Donna Haraway's influential socialist-feminist "A Cyborg Manifesto" is a posthumanist project avant le lettre, published almost simultaneously with Jameson's "Postmodernism" during one of the peak moments of postmodernist theory. Cary Wolfe calls it "the locus classicus" for thinking about the subject in technology.[12] Haraway's "Manifesto" theorizes the technosubject as a hybrid composed of flesh and machine, at once a metaphorical figure and a material reality. The cyborg blurs the ontological demarcations between technology and humanity, constituting the posthuman through the technoscientific penetrations of human psyches and bodies.[13]

   In this context, it is useful to recall Ihab Hassan's earlier use of the term "posthumanism" in 1977, in his prescient response to the perceived collapse of the humanities and sciences into each other (science studies has emerged as a significant "interdiscipline" of the new posthumanities). Echoing Foucault's anticipation of "the end of man" in *The Archaeology of Knowledge*, Hassan writes:

> We need . . . to understand that the human form – including human desire and all its external representations – may be changing radically, and thus

must be re-visioned. We need to understand that five hundred years of humanism may be coming to an end, as humanism transforms itself into something that we must helplessly call posthumanism.[14]

Haraway's "Manifesto" suggests the different emphases that have developed in posthumanist thought. One is focused for the most part on philosophical and political reconceptualizations of "the human," and on new ways of doing ethics and politics in a globalized world of technoscientific acceleration, capitalist expansion, and climate change; the other emphasizes the progress of an "evolutionary futurism" that dreams of overcoming the vulnerabilities of material bodies through real-world technoscience.[15] While trying to keep these two strands separate inevitably leads to oversimplification, they do suggest, at least in outline, the different directions in which the idea of the posthuman has developed since, most especially, the 1980s – when Jameson identified the fragmentation of the subject, Haraway identified our embeddedness in "the informatics of domination" ("Manifesto" 161), and William Gibson's cyberpunk classic *Neuromancer* (1984) became an icon of cyberculture aesthetics in the popular imagination.[16]

Two recent studies suggest this dual emphasis. While contextualized within technoculture, Stefan Herbrechter's *Posthumanism: A Critical Analysis* undertakes "a genealogy of the contemporary posthumanist scenario of the 'end of man' and places it within the context of theoretical and philosophical developments and ways of thinking about modernity."[17] Herbrechter's opening chapter introduces the idea of a "critical posthumanism" that relies on the work of theorists such as Foucault, Lyotard, and Derrida. In at least partial contrast, Peter Mahon's *Posthumanism: A Guide for the Perplexed* (2017) traces a "concrete techno-scientific posthumanism."[18] For Mahon, "posthumanism's primary unit of analysis is 'humans + tools.'" While Mahon pays due attention to the theoretical abstractions of philosophical posthumanism, his focus is on how "concrete posthumanism ... takes into account how recent developments in science and technology have changed, and will continue to change, how human beings ... are understood" (253).

## 1.4 Transhumanisms

Martin Heidegger's warning in "The Question Concerning Technology" about how the technological imperative threatens to convert even human beings into "standing-reserve" is paradigmatic of a determinative view of technology that tends toward caution and foresight.[19] In this context, R. L. Rutsky examines the work of philosopher of technology Bernard Stiegler, especially his *Technics and Time I*, which extends the critiques by Heidegger and other technological determinists to take account of what Stiegler terms the "permanent innovation" of accelerating technological change, including the digital translation of "virtually every aspect of life, nature, and culture into quantitative terms, into data."[20]

As Mahon's study suggests, however, a more instrumentalist and technophilic view sees in technology the answers to many of humanity's perceived limitations. This variation on posthumanism – often called "transhumanism" – focuses on what technoscientific innovations can do to increase human longevity and to enhance human intellectual and physical capacities. Nick Bostrom – currently the director of the Future of Humanity Institute at Oxford University, one of the sites through which transhumanism has become institutionalized – describes transhumanism as

> a loosely defined movement that has developed gradually over the past two decades. It promotes an interdisciplinary approach to understanding and evaluating the opportunities for enhancing the human condition and the human organism opened up by the advancement of technology. Attention is given to both present technologies, like genetic engineering and information technology, and anticipated future ones, such as molecular nanotechnology and artificial intelligence.[21]

Haraway's cyborg, as figure, is responsive to her socialist-feminist politics, to the work of thinking about new ethics and responsibilities as subjects in technoculture, and to the acknowledgment of our close kinship with both machines and animals. But the cyborg is taken quite literally in the ideologies and projects of transhumanism, which in their most techno-utopian forms – as in the power fantasies of singularity theorist Ray Kurzweil – express a neo-Cartesian desire to transcend the body: human minds might someday be downloaded into more durable technological forms of embodiment or even downloaded into digital virtual worlds.[22] Once again the vulnerable physical body is in danger of being relegated to *alienum*.

This more extreme version of transhumanism – represented as well in the work of Extropian roboticist Hans Moravec – is the target of N. Katherine Hayles' influential critique in *How We Became Posthuman* of some of the more libertarian and apolitical strands of posthumanism (the distinction between what is now called transhumanism and the philosophical turn to the posthuman had not yet emerged). Hayles identifies how some key values associated with liberal-humanist ideology, such as the autonomy of the subject and its agency in the world, remain fundamental to transhumanism. As a kind of technologically driven "überhumanism," therefore, transhumanism stands in sharp contrast not only to the philosophical strands of antihumanism(s) but also to the critical posthumanisms of theorists such as Braidotti and Herbrechter.

Hayles shifts the critical debate toward considerations of bodies and embodiment: "As if we had learned nothing from Derrida about supplementarity, embodiment continues to be discussed as if it were a supplement to be purged from the dominant term of information, an accident of evolution we are now in a position to correct" (*How* 12). From another perspective, Thomas Foster identifies how supplementarity functions in transhumanist thought, in spite of itself, to undermine the concept of a unique and self-identical self, instead suggesting "the deconstructive logic of the supplement, in which our need for technology demonstrates the failure of a naturalized or interiorized humanism, its lack of self-sufficiency."[23] The new hybrid self/subject of technoculture comes to be constituted through its technological prostheses.

In spite of these critiques, it is too easy to figure transhumanism as the evil twin of a more politically engaged (and "enlightened") critical posthumanism. In his very useful overview of the diverse ideas that have influenced contemporary transhumanisms – including Nietzsche's concept of the *Übermensch*, Teilhard de Chardin's mystical nöosphere, Italian Futurism, and Marxist accelerationism – Andrew Pilsch argues that utopian desire is foundational to all of them. While some strands of transhumanism simply want "a faster version of neo-liberalism" in the future (187), more progressive strands, such as the xenofeminism of the Laboria Cuboniks collective – which rejects "futureless repetition on the treadmill of capital" (quoted Pilsch 191) – imagine a positively "alien" future, what Derrida has termed "*l'à-venir*," a "future to come" that we cannot know in advance.[24]

## 1.5 New Materialisms

In *The Postmodern Condition*, another exemplary study from the mid-1980s, Lyotard succinctly described the postmodern as "incredulity toward metanarratives."[25] Broadly speaking, however, by the 1990s the anti-essentialisms of poststructuralist constructivism (influenced, especially, by Continental philosophy, the "high theory" of postmodernism) came to seem like a whole new series of essentialist paradigms, all of them associated with increasingly determinative and abstract forces shaping the constitution of subjects, confining them within the rigid constraints of the unconscious, language, culture, and so on, and once again severing culture from nature. At the far end of the swerve away from what has been called the "linguistic turn" or the "cultural turn," object-oriented ontologist Levi Bryant critiques what he sees as a stubbornly humanist orientation in many of these schools of thought, most of which "would still . . . be counted as *humanisms* insofar as while they 'split the subject' or demolish the Cartesian subject, they nonetheless shackle all beings to human related phenomena such as the signifier, language, culture, power, and so on."[26]

After the ironic cool of postmodernism and in the face of its many theoretical abstractions, the materiality of matter has come to matter in expansively new ways. Similar to Haraway's "Manifesto," Braidotti's *Nomadic Subjects* is a recognizably posthumanist project, although she rarely uses the term in this book. Building on the radical philosophy of Gilles Deleuze, her "nomadic subject" is a materialist-feminist subject-in-process that challenges the "fictional unity of a grammatical 'I'" and theorizes the body/embodiment "as a point of overlapping between the physical, the symbolic, and the sociological."[27] In gender and sexuality studies, the "material turn" appears in refigurations of what Bruce Clarke and Manuela Rossini refer to as "corpo-reality,"[28] including important early works such as Judith Butler's queer-feminist analysis of gender and performativity in *Bodies that Matter*, Elizabeth Grosz's equally significant work on corporeal feminism in *Volatile Bodies*, and Jack [Judith] Halberstam and Ira Livingston's ground-breaking queer collection, *Posthuman Bodies*. "We have rehearsed the claim that the posthuman condition is upon us," write Halberstam and Livingston, "and that lingering nostalgia for a modernist or humanist philosophy of self and other, human and alien, normal and queer is merely the echo of a discursive battle that has already taken place – and the tinny futurism that often answers such nostalgia is the echo of an echo."[29] In their radical swerve away from the ideologies of heterosexual reproductive futurism, Halberstam and Livingston already inhabit a queer space and time of difference and disruption: "You're not human until you're posthuman. You were never human."[30]

Assessing the results of the linguistic turn, new materialist Karen Barad (among others) points out that "Language matters. Discourse matters. Culture matters. There is an important sense in which the only thing that does not seem to matter anymore is matter."[31] One response to this "dematerialization" has been "the strong recent turn in posthumanist discourse from the machinic posthuman to the planetary nonhuman" (Clarke and Rossini xii). This "nonhuman turn"[32] understands the subject as an embodied entity inextricably entwined in the world of matter, as in Alaimo's work on what she calls "trans-corporeality, in which the human is always intermeshed with the more-than-human world" (*Bodily* 2). The nonhuman turn has taken a variety of theoretical directions, including speculative realism, object-oriented ontology, vital materialism, and feminist new materialism; all aim at applying pressure to western culture's long-standing and woefully reductive representations of the "natural" world as a composition of discrete objects whose only reality is their reality-for-us (to borrow a phrase from object-oriented ontology).

In eco-philosophy, the nonhuman turn is steadily chipping away at the idea of "nature," where "nature" references the no-longer-tenable idea of an ecological system distinct from humanity that functions as a passively supportive backdrop to human activity. Recognizing that every representation of "nature" or "world" is produced by culture and that neither can be disentangled from the other, Haraway writes of hybrid "naturecultures," while Braidotti writes of "the nature-culture continuum which is both technologically mediated and globally enforced."[33] Even more radically, given what we have learned in spite of ourselves about "world" in this era of global warming, Timothy Morton has proposed that "the end of the world has already occurred": "the notion that we are living 'in' a world . . . no longer applies in any meaningful sense."[34] More generally, the Cartesian privileging of mind over matter collapses in the face of what Bryant refers to as "a strange or weird sort of realism" (269) that acknowledges the agential forces of the material universe, while also admitting the radical unknowability of things: every entity, from a human body to a mollusk to a rock, has a reality that exceeds our experience of it. Bryant argues that "the issue is not what is *thinkable* [by humans] but rather what beings and things themselves *are* regardless of whether or not anyone thinks them."[35]

Some of the most exciting work in the posthumanities is being developed at the intersections of feminist new materialisms and science theory. Karen Barad – who names her onto-epistemological project "agential realism" – relies equally on Niels Bohr's work in quantum physics and Judith Butler's work on gender performativity to read "important insights from feminist and queer studies and science studies through one another while simultaneously proposing a materialist and posthumanist reworking of the notions of performativity" (811). For Barad, "the universe is agential intra-activity in its becoming. The primary ontological units are not

'things' but phenomena – dynamic topological reconfigurings / entanglements / relationalities / (re)articulations" (818).

In her recent study, *Unthought*, Hayles demonstrates how new discoveries in cognitive science reinforce the insights of the various philosophical materialisms mentioned above, in particular having to do with
questions of agency (questions that also intensely interest Barad): "part
of the contemporary turn toward the nonhuman is the realization that
an object need not be alive or conscious in order to function as
a cognitive agent."[36] For Hayles, studies of "nonconscious cognition"
point to the agency of the body, as well as of physical matter and of
technological systems. Both human beings and technical systems are
"decision makers" or "cognizers" (117), forming "cognitive assemblages"
in which "the cognitive decisions of each affect the others, with interactions occurring across the full range of human cognition, including
consciousness/unconscious, the cognitive nonconscious, and the sensory/
perceptual systems that send signals to the central nervous system" (118).
Both Barad and Hayles are committed to accounts of what Hayles refers
to as "material agency" (66). Her aim in *Unthought* is to develop "the
idea of a *planetary cognitive ecology* that includes both humans and
technical actors and that can appropriately become the focus for ethical
inquiry" (3–4, emphasis in original).

## Post History

If the 1980s initiated our becoming posthuman as a consequence of our
integration with the technological, in the twenty-first century we are
becoming posthuman because of our inextricable inter-relations (or intra-
relations, to use Barad's term) with "nature." Since nothing sharpens the
mind so much as the thought of one's own extinction, the climate crisis is
the most pressing reason to start thinking with posthumanism – thinking
with humanism has been at least partially responsible for the crisis. Taking
on critical mass since the environmental movements of the 1970s, new
interdisciplines such as the environmental humanities have encouraged
different ways to think about the biosphere that do not simply reduce the
world to "nature" as background. As Morton points out, "Our very
attempt to achieve escape velocity from our physical and biological being
has resulted in being stuck to Earth" (180). In the Anthropocene, the secure
boundaries that have conventionally shored up our human exceptionalism
have always already been breached.

The Anthropocene is a "sign" of the present/our presence sometime in an unthinkable future, a kind of weirdly retrospective historical marker. As Claire Colebrook puts it, "we look at the earth – now – as if, in our future absence, we will be readable as having been."[37] Jameson's command to "always historicize!" – which has served so well in human-centered critique – no longer seems adequate to the situation.[38] In his meditation on the impact of the Anthropocene on the discipline of History, Dipesh Chakrabarty argues for a new and necessary way to "do" history: "The task of placing, historically, the crisis of climate change ... requires us to bring together intellectual formations that are somewhat in tension with each other: the planetary and the global; deep and recorded histories; species thinking and critiques of capital" (213). For Chakrabarty, the conventional distinction between human history and geohistory has collapsed now that human time has become so entangled with planetary deep time (201).[39]

In Chakrabarty's terms, we are no longer simple biological agents, but have become, in spite of ourselves, "geological agents" (207) of huge negative impacts on climate, animal populations, sea levels, clean water, forests, ourselves .... Chakrabarty anticipates new interdisciplines such as the energy humanities in his consideration of the paradox that our role as geological agents is inextricable from our most cherished histories of liberation: "The mansion of modern freedom stands on an ever-expanding base of fossil-fuel use. Most of our freedoms so far have been energy-intensive" (208). For Chakrabarty, the Anthropocene refers to a totalizing human force in the world ("geological agents") but, as Jill S. Schneiderman (among others) notes, and as Chakrabarty's analysis tends to elide, "a large segment of humanity has not participated in the fossil fuel economy that has led to global warming."[40] There is a risk in considerations of the Anthropocene that "we" fall back on a rather Terence-like rhetoric of "universal humanity" (the temptations of scale). As Alaimo notes, this serves to "reinstall rather familiar versions of man" as global agent.[41] This not only ignores the vast non-human agencies of the biosphere, but also precludes political assessments of the Anthropocene "along the lines of culpability and exploitation" (Alaimo, "Your Shell" 101).

## Post Human History

To historicize posthumanism is necessarily to trace the outlines of the humanisms against which it defines itself, because these disidentifications are themselves constitutive. The "post" of "posthumanism" links to as much as it separates from humanism, much as postmodernism was never a complete break with modernism. Badmington reminds us of Derrida's caution against facile ideas about such absolute breaks: "Precisely because Western philosophy is steeped in humanist assumptions ... the end of Man is bound to be written in the language of Man" (9). On a more positive note, however, to historicize posthumanism means to explore a future-oriented and non-linear path through diverse theories and stories that – to recall my epigraph by John Clute – are not at all aimed at making us feel comfortably "human"; they are about becoming *alienum* in a world that itself has become profoundly defamiliarized. In Richard Powers' eco-fiction *The Overstory* (2018), field biologist Pat Westerford imagines a kind of speculative-realist history, a posthuman story of the "natural" world that casts human beings as mere *parvenus*:

> She spins short biographies of her favorite characters: loner trees, cunning trees, sages and solid citizens, trees that turn impulsive or shy or generous – as many ways of being as there are forest elevations and facings. *How fine it would be if we could learn who they are, when they're at their best.* She tries to turn the story on its head. *This is not our world with trees in it. It's a world of trees, where humans have just arrived.*[42]

# Notes

1. John Clute, "21st Century Science Fiction," *The New York Review of Science Fiction*, 328 (December 2015), 4–5.
2. Claire Colebrook, "Futures," in Bruce Clarke and Manuela Rossini (eds.), *The Cambridge Companion to Literature and the Posthuman* (Cambridge: Cambridge University Press, 2017), 204.
3. N. Katherine Hayles, *How We Became Posthuman: Virtual Bodies in Cybernetics, Literature, and Informatics* (Chicago: University of Chicago Press, 1999), 85–6. Kant's motto for Enlightenment was "saper aude!" – "dare to know!"
4. Cary Wolfe, *Animal Rites: American Culture, the Discourse of Species, and Posthumanist Theory* (Chicago: Chicago University Press, 2003), 7.
5. Bruce Sterling, "Preface," in Bruce Sterling (ed.), *Mirrorshades: The Cyberpunk Anthology* (New York: Ace, 1988), xiii.
6. Tom Idema, *Stages of Transmutation: Science Fiction, Biology, and Environmental Posthumanism* (New York: Routledge, 2019), ebook. https://doi.org/10.4324/9781315225470
7. Fredric Jameson, "Postmodernism, or, the Cultural Logic of Late Capitalism," *New Left Review*, 146 (July/August 1984), 63. Of course, as Jameson notes, it is unclear if that monadic subject ever existed in the first place or if it was always only humanism's *méconnaissance*.

8. Friedrich Nietzsche, *Thus Spoke Zarathustra*, ed. R. Pippin, trans. A. D. Caro. (Oxford, UK: Oxford University Press, 2006), p. 21.

9. Stacy Alaimo, *Bodily Natures: Science, Environment, and the Material Self* (Bloomington: Indiana University Press, 2010), 158.

10. Neil Badmington, "Introduction: Approaching Posthumanism," in Neil Badmington (ed.), *Posthumanism* (New York: Palgrave, 2000), 1–10.

11. Eve Kosofky Sedgwick, "Paranoid Reading and Reparative Reading, or, You're So Paranoid, You Probably Think This Essay Is About You," in *Touching Feeling: Affect, Pedagogy, Performativity* (Durham: Duke University Press, 2003), 123–51.

12. Cary Wolfe, "Introduction," in *What Is Posthumanism?* (Minneapolis: Minnesota University Press, 2010), xiii.

13. Haraway's "Manifesto" is only one of the many feminist science studies published in the 1980s, including Evelyn Fox Keller's *Reflections on Gender and Science* (1985) and Sandra Harding's *The Science Question in Feminism* (1986). While her work has become foundational for thinking about posthumanism through the figure of the cyborg and, later, the companion species, her recent work is more suggestive of feminist new materialism. Refusing the terminology of posthumanism, she emphasizes our kinship with our earthly others: "I am a compost-ist, not a posthuman-ist: we are all compost, not posthuman" ("Anthropocene, Capitalocene, Plantationocene, Chthulucene: Making Kin," *Environmental Humanities*, 6 (2015), 161).

14. Ihab Hassan, "Prometheus as Performer: Toward a Posthumanist Culture?" *The Georgia Review*, 31(4) (Winter 1977), 843.

15. The term comes from Andrew Pilsch, *Transhumanism: Evolutionary Futurism and the Human Technologies of Utopia* (Minneapolis: Minnesota University Press, 2017).

16. It is impossible to overstate the importance of speculative fiction in the development of posthumanist thought. Speculative fiction has provided imaginative material for many of its most significant theorists, including Alaimo, Braidotti, Thomas Foster, Haraway, Hayles, Jameson, Bruno Latour, Colin Milburn, Steven Shaviro, and Isabelle Stengers.

17. Stefan Herbrechter, *Posthumanism: A Critical Analysis* (London: Bloomsbury Academic, 2013), vii.

18. Peter Mahon, *Posthumanism: A Guide for the Perplexed* (London: Bloomsbury Academic, 2017), 168.

19. Martin Heidegger, "The Question Concerning Technology," in *The Question Concerning Technology and Other Essays*, trans. William Lovitt (New York: Harper & Row, 1977), 3–35.

20. R. L. Rutsky, "Technologies," in Bruce Clarke and Manuela Rossini (eds.), *The Cambridge Companion to Literature and the Posthuman* (Cambridge: Cambridge University Press, 2017), 189. Stiegler is quoted here on p. 185.

21. Nick Bostrom, "Transhumanist Values," in Frederick Adams (ed.), *Ethical Issues for the 21st Century* (Charlottesville, VA: Philosophy Documentation Center, 2005), 3.

22. Such radical techno-utopianism, which desires nothing less than post-biological immortality, was originally called "extropianism" (in its opposition to "entropy"). See Joshua Raulerson, *Singularities: Technoculture, Transhumanism, and Science Fiction in the Twenty-first Century* (Liverpool: Liverpool University Press, 2013).

23. Thomas Foster, *The Souls of Cyberfolk: Posthumanism as Vernacular Theory* (Minneapolis: University of Minnesota Press, 2005), 54. Stiegler also points to the idea of the technological supplement. There is no "original" or "natural" humanity that pre-exists its supplementation by the technological prosthesis (see Rutsky 192). Haraway makes much the same argument in her "Manifesto."

24. Jacques Derrida, *Archive Fever: A Freudian Impression*, trans. Eric Prenowitz (Chicago: Chicago University Press, 1996), 68.

25. Jean-François Lyotard, *The Postmodern Condition: A Report on Knowledge*, trans. Geoff Bennington and Brian Massumi (Minneapolis: Minnesota University Press, 1984), xxiv.

26. Levi R. Bryant, "The Ontic Principle: Outline of an Object-Oriented Ontology," in Levi R. Bryant, Nick Srnicek, and Graham Harman (eds.), *The Speculative Turn: Continental Materialism and Realism* (Victoria, AU: re-press, 2011), 268 (emphasis in original).

27. Rosi Braidotti, *Nomadic Subjects: Embodiment and Sexual Difference in Contemporary Feminist Theory*, 2nd ed. (New York: Columbia University Press, 2011), 18, 25.

28. Bruce Clarke and Manuela Rossini, "Preface: Literature, Posthumanism, and the Posthuman," in Bruce Clarke and Manuela Rossini (eds.), *The Cambridge Companion to Literature and the Posthuman* (Cambridge: Cambridge University Press, 2017), xx.

29. Judith Halbertstam, and Ira Livingston, "Introduction: Posthuman Bodies," in *Posthuman Bodies*, ed. Judith Halberstam and Ira Livingston (Bloomington: Indiana University Press, 1995), 19.

30. "Introduction," 8. This echoes the well-known title of sociologist of science Bruno Latour's *We Have Never Been Modern*, trans. Catherine Porter (Harvard: Harvard University Press, 1993), a critique of scientific modernity's taxonomical drive to resist impurity, hybridity, and ontological indistinctions of any kind.

31. Karen Barad, "Posthuman Performativity: Toward an Understanding of How Matter Comes to Matter," *Signs: Journal of Women in Culture and Society*, 28 (3) (2003), 801.

32. Richard Grusin, ed., *The Non-Human Turn*, (Minneapolis: Minnesota University Press, 2015).

33. Donna Haraway, *The Companion Species Manifesto: Dogs, People and Significant Otherness* (Chicago: Prickly Paradigm Press, 2003). Rosi Braidotti, *The Posthuman* (Cambridge: Polity Press, 2013), 82.

34. Timothy Morton, *Hyperobjects: Philosophy and Ecology after the End of the World* (Minneapolis: University of Minnesota Press, 2013), 7, 101.

35. Bryant, 265 (emphasis in original). While my discussion focuses on trajectories in recent Euro-North American thought, I want to acknowledge the much more long-standing onto-epistemological perspectives of indigenous thinkers. Méti scholar Zoe Todd writes:

    it is so important to think, deeply, about how the Ontological Turn – with its breathless "realisations" that animals, the climate, water, "atmospheres" and non-human presences like ancestors and spirits are sentient and possess agency, that "nature" and "culture," "human," and "animal" may not be so separate after all – is itself perpetuating the exploitation of Indigenous peoples . . .. [M]any simply ignore Indigenous people, laws, epistemologies altogether and re-invent the more-than-human without so much as a polite nod towards Indigenous bodies/Nations. ("An Indigenous Feminist's Take On the Ontological Turn: 'Ontology' Is Just Another Word for Colonialism," Urbane Adventurer: Amiskwací [24 October 2014], online.

36. N. Katherine Hayles, Unthought: The Power of the Cognitive Unconscious, (Chicago: University of Chicago Press, 2017), 212.

37. Claire Colebrook, "We Have Always Been Post-Anthropocene: The Anthropocene Counterfactual," in Anthropocene Feminism, ed. Richard Grusin (Minneapolis: University of Minnesota Press, 2017), 6. In sharp contrast to arguments about new opportunities for ethics and politics afforded by the climate crisis, Colebrook sounds a more skeptical note. For her, the Anthropocene may simply be a comforting fairy tale in the face of potential extinction, shoring up a humanity that is "too big to fail" ("What is the Anthro-Political?" in Twilight of the Anthropocene Idols, Tom Cohen, Claire Colebrook, and J. Hillis Miller [London: Open Humanities Press, 2016], 88): "Those who declare man to be guilty are the first true humanists, generating the 'Anthropos' as agent, and promising another humanity – one who can be intimated after the crime of ecological destruction has been detected, diagnosed and managed" ("What" 89).

38. Fredric Jameson, The Political Unconscious: Narrative as a Socially Symbolic Act (Ithaca: Cornell University Press, 1981), 9.

39. Dipesh Chakrabarty, "The Climate of History: Four Theses," Critical Inquiry, 35 (Winter 2009), 213, 201. Jussi Parikka makes much the same argument in his critical reading of the "deep time" of media archeology: "Media history conflates with earth history; the geological material of metals and chemical get deterritorialized from their strata and reterritorialized in machines that define our technical media culture" ("And the Earth Screamed, Alive," in The Anthrobscene [Minneapolis: Minnesota University Press, 2015], 9).

40. Jill S. Schneiderman, "The Anthropocene Controversy," in Anthropocene Feminism, ed. Richard Grusin (Minneapolis: University of Minnesota Press, 2017), 184.

41. Stacy Alaimo, "Your Shell on Acid: Material Immersion, Anthropocene Dissolves," in *Anthropocene Feminism*, ed. Richard Grusin (Minneapolis: University of Minnesota Press, 2017), 89.

42. Richard Powers, *The Overstory* (New York: Norton, 2018), 373 (emphasis in original).

CHAPTER 2

# Poststructuralism and the End(s) of Humanism

## Stefan Herbrechter

While posthumanism owes many debts to antihumanist thinkers such as Michel Foucault, Jacques Lacan and Louis Althusser, it tends to differ from antihumanism in one principal respect: while the antihumanists actively set out to overturn the hegemony of anthropocentrism, posthumanists begin with the recognition that "Man" is (always) already a falling or fallen figure. What this means is that posthumanism often tends to take humanism's waning or disappearance as something of a given.[1]

## 2.1 Post-, Again

It is both a blessing and a curse that every generation has to re-appropriate and to re-create the world in their own image. It is a blessing because a new take on something as heavily sedimented as the history of human thought promises to bring fresh insight into what has at times become decidedly stuffy and oppressive. It allows for a fresh look at things, which often makes former problems look like rather quaint obsessions, while new tasks have appeared that impose themselves by their clear and immediate urgency. It is also a curse, however, because the repression that is involved in this re-appropriating and re-positioning inevitably produces blind spots that might condemn the next generation to fight similar battles or repeat mistakes. This has always been the mixed blessing involved in learning lessons from history. The transition from poststructuralism to posthumanism is no exception here.

Coming to the discussion about posthumanism and the context "after the human" today means being caught up in this conundrum of "belatedness." Modernity gave rise to a historical understanding based on the idea of futurity and progress as the driving forces of development. The tacit consensus ever since, coinciding with the emergence of the Enlightenment,

has been that history moves "dialectically": every subsequent generation
has to perform a kind of synthesis of previous contradictions and thereby
ideally produce the human civilizing progress – an assumption that still
underpins much of the legitimating discourse in contemporary culture and
politics.[2]

This consensus also constitutes the foundation of (western) liberal
humanism as the dominant, common-sense understanding of how every
human being, rather ironically, expresses both its uniqueness and its
freedom in the hope of bringing about a better future for humanity –
a powerful and difficult-to-dismiss idea. The dialectics of history finds its
articulation both in Hegel and in Marx, and it is also at work in Freudian
psychoanalysis and much of modern science. Nietzsche, on the other hand,
was far more skeptical regarding the anthropocentrism and Christian
morality underpinning the historiography of his time. Instead, he empha-
sized the human "will to power" at work in the history of mentalities.[3]
Needless to say, all these thinkers had their doubts and conflicting views
about the inevitability and feasibility of the idea of human perfectibility
and about the ambiguity of the form and idea of what an end of history
might actually look like. Following from these early masters of suspicion
(Nietzsche, Marx, Freud), the poststructuralists and postmodernists of
the second half of the twentieth century form the first philosophical (or
"theoretical") movement that takes the problem of belatedness, the end of
history, including the end of "man" (the mixed blessings of "coming after"
outlined earlier) as a starting point for their thinking and politics.

In *Specters of Marx*, Jacques Derrida, often seen as *the* representative of
a whole generation of poststructuralist thinkers, describes how "the
eschatological themes of the 'end of history,' the 'end of Marxism,' 'the
end of philosophy,' 'the ends of man,' the 'last man' and so forth were, in
the 1950s, that is, forty years ago, our daily bread."[4] Derrida had previously
referred to this "endism" as a certain "apocalyptic tone in philosophy"
(echoing Kant), provoked by "the reading or analysis of those whom we
could nickname the *classics of the end*."[5] These formed "the canon of the
modern apocalypse (end of History, end of Man, end of Philosophy,
Hegel, Marx, Nietzsche, Heidegger)" (*Specters* 15), as taught by the influential Alexandre Kojève in 1930s and 1940s Paris, who helped produce an
entire generation of French Neo-Hegelians (among them, Bataille,
Derrida, Lacan, and Foucault). Derrida, however, also insists on the
other, sociohistorical side that was responsible for this apocalyptic tone
and for the ubiquitous endisms of the time (which have been proliferating
ever since): "It was, *on the other hand and indissociably,* what we had known

or what some of us for quite some time no longer hid from concerning totalitarian terror in all the Eastern countries, all the socio-economic disasters of Soviet bureaucracy, the Stalinism of the past and the neo-Stalinism in process . . . ."[6] Derrida insists on contextualizing the movement of "deconstruction" he inaugurated (and which is often, problematically, seen as a synonym for poststructuralism) within these two dimensions, one philosophical, the other political. Thus, for poststructuralists and their late followers, the idea of the "end of man," the "last man," or, indeed, "after the human" bears a certain *déjà-vu*, as Derrida explains, "those with whom I shared this singular period, . . . for us, I venture to say, the media parade of current discourse on the end of history and the last man looks most often like a tiresome anachronism" (*Specters* 15).

Ignoring this dynamic of belatedness usually leads to the idea that, in relation to posthumanism and the posthuman, poststructuralism plays merely the role of a precursor that has done its job but now needs to be overcome in turn. This idea is often expressed in the following way: while the "antihumanism" of the poststructuralists was a springboard for the kind of radical critique of humanism that posthumanism today represents, this now needs surpassing, extending, radicalizing, and so on. We can see the specter of the Hegelian dialectic raise its head again, especially since the antihumanism often attributed to "poststructuralists" such as Althusser, Barthes, Derrida, Foucault, and Lyotard was, in fact, already a highly contested inheritance of structuralism.[7] It was Ferdinand de Saussure and his structuralist followers like the anthropologist Lévi-Strauss who believed that language and its principles could be made transparent and applied to all meaning-making systems (from anthropological kinship to fashion),[8] while the generation following them were already much more skeptical of both the empirical applicability and the metaphysical presuppositions on which a structuralist idea of language – as a conventional, rule-based, and abstract system of representation – relied.

The outlined logic of surpassing and belatedness thus already applies to the relationship between structuralism and its critical inheritors, as well, of course, as to any previous schools of thought and their predecessors, as well as, of course, their successors. As Robert Young explains:

> "Post-structuralism" is an "umbrella term" which involves a "displacement" and is more of "an interrogation of structuralism's methods and assumptions, of transforming structuralist concepts by turning one against another". However, it is not about "origin" or a "Fall" from it: Structuralism as an origin never existed in a pre-lapsarian purity or ontological fullness; poststructuralism traces the trace of structuralism's difference from itself.[9]

Consequently, the same complication also applies to the relationship between posthumanism and humanism. It is, in fact, the awareness of the problematic genealogical relationship between humanism and post-humanism to which the "critical" in the phrase "critical posthumanism" refers.[10] It is therefore necessary to submit the idea of the posthuman (in the sense of "after the human") to a poststructuralist critical "reading."

## 2.2   Post-Structural-ism

One of the most important points that poststructuralism, following structuralism, makes is that meaning is irreducibly plural. Meaning does not reside *in* language but actually arises out of the selection and combination of signs. "Post-," for example, is a prefix that derives its meaning through difference from other prefixes, in particular "pre-," and from an entire syntax of prefixation. This is the presupposition without which no meaning can be assigned. What "post-" actually means, following Saussure, is the result of "negative" difference (it acquires its meaning through all it is *not*).[11] It means "after," that is, *not* "before," while both "after" and "before" themselves have a number of additional meanings. They are part of an endless chain of signifiers, each evoking plural meanings (semiosis).

The suffix "-ism" (as opposed to, for example, "-ity" which denotes a period or a state, such as "modern-ity") refers to a "discourse" (in the sense of a "set of ideas," a doctrine, like Marx*ism*, femin*ism*, but also human*ism* and posthuman*ism*, of course).[12] A discourse is probably best understood as an attempt at making meaning cohere around a central term (in the case of structuralism, the term "structure"; while *post*structuralism would be the discourse that is precisely no longer based on the idea of "structure"). This does not mean, of course, that there is agreement about what that central term (i.e., structure) actually means. If a (temporary) consensus can be established, however, it can provide a focal point, a perspective from which it may be possible to try to make sense of the "world" or establish (a) "reality."

The reason I put "world" and "reality" in "scare quotes" is that post-structuralists do not believe (this is undoubtedly their Kantian legacy) that there is such a thing as a world or a reality that can be perceived "as such," that is, independently from an observer or, to use the more usual term, reality always is a reality *for* a "subject." Let me stress right away – because this is a common misunderstanding of poststructuralism – that this is not the same as saying that there "is" no world or no reality (which would be a radically nihilistic claim). It is merely a question of availability and "realism" (which, itself, is a discourse that claims the opposite, namely that it *is* possible to see reality as it *really is*, that is, a discourse for which the detour through a representation of reality is not problematic). For poststructuralists, representation (linguistic, in the narrow sense, but also perceptual in the widest sense) is not transparent: it is not just a means to an end (that is, to give or see reality as it really is), but is something that needs to be fore-grounded and analyzed. Since we can only ever have representations of reality instead of reality itself (think of all the ways in which people would disagree about what something really is, for example, something like "climate change"),[13] what critical thought needs to focus on is the *politics* of representation, that is, who says what about "x." Since all claims about reality are contingent, it is no surprise that they are highly contested, which is saying nothing else than that reality is socially constructed, shared, or negotiated. What poststructuralists are suspicious of are truth claims about reality: in this sense they are anti-realist, because these are usually powerful claims that position subjects within a discourse that uses ideology.[14]

Ideology is a set of beliefs that underpins a specific discourse:[15] human-ism, for example claims that there is such a thing called "the human" and that humanism as a discourse can produce important knowledge about its "object" (i.e., the human) or even has the power to explain what it means to be human. Usually this is a claim based on exclusivity and essence: there is something like a human nature or a special set of abilities that differentiate the human from nonhuman animals, inanimate objects, or supernatural entities. Since this nature is exclusively human it gives rise to certain exceptionalism or a central position of the human – anthropocentrism. From a poststructuralist point of view, what is interesting here is that the human is both the subject of the discourse called humanism (and its long history through classical to Renaissance, Enlightenment, and modern secular versions) as well as its object. Humanism, as a discourse, claims to have access to the essential and universal, timeless, truth of which all humans and all things human partake. It is a discourse that positions humans as subjects in a very particular, circular, or tautological way. Humans are those entities that through self-reflection must come to know who and what they are by accepting that they share an essential nature that separates them from everything else.

The curious thing about a subject, however, is that it is always in an ambiguous position with regard to power, discourse, and ideology. For a poststructuralist, what is particularly suspicious is humanism's paradox-ical claim that a human (subject) is essentially human but, at the same time, needs to be *told* so, that is, humans need to be "humanized." What is even more suspicious is that this claim is usually made in conjunction with a liberal discourse that presupposes that the human is essentially free to make a choice about his or her self, in this sense: you are essentially human if you choose to be so; if you act against your supposed "nature," you are essentially "inhuman," a "monster."[16] The discourse based on this contradiction – a free human subject that needs to be reminded that it has a free choice (usually between good and evil) – is what poststructuralists refer to as "liberal humanism," its main target.

A few words need to be added about the middle part of post-*structural-*ism. The central idea that structuralists presuppose is that the way people make sense of things is by internalizing a system of rules which allows them to map what otherwise would be a chaotic mess. So, for a structuralist, meaning is produced through an interplay or mapping between a concrete formal manifestation (a recognition) and some underlying pattern or "structure." Let us stick with the example of a map. In order to make sense of a territory that you do not know through which you need to find your way, you look for landmarks. These are signs you have previously encountered, whose meaning you now project onto the new territory: there is a river, there is a mountain, there is a valley, there is north, there is south, etc. So, you are applying an underlying structure onto which you map the new territory. The particularity and the newness of the territory arise from the differences it presents to the structures you "recognize": this specific new mountain looks similar to all the mountains you know, but it is also different because its peak looks like, say, a face. You apply your previous knowledge of mountains and humans to make sense of the differences that, in a sense, you have helped to establish or create. This works for a geography as well as for other discourses. You presuppose an underlying, structured system of what the "human" (for example) is about, what it can do, and apply this structure once you encounter beings that are at once similar to the kind of humans you know but are also significantly different from what your structural knowledge provides: for example, a different skin color or "type," a human with qualities that are usually associated with nonhuman "others" (such as a chimera or a cyborg), and so on.[17]

The critique that poststructuralism applies to this way of making sense – which nonetheless remains the standard way of making sense – is that this idea of underlying structure manifests a depth-surface model that is highly problematic if you think it through. This is precisely what the "post" of poststructuralism signals, and this is also where (Derridean) deconstruction comes in.[18] If that underlying structure, let us call it a systematic knowledge about "humanness," is a model or "territory" onto which concrete humans, nonhumans, and also posthumans have to be mapped (or to which they have to be compared), as a model it is at the same time both the origin and end point of the meaning thus produced, both essence and truth.

If you want to make that structure present, if you want to find out what it really is, you will realize that its ultimate meaning will always escape you, because every manifestation of a human is always different from its idealized type. This means – and this is the Derridean move that is captured by the neologism "différance" – that the full meaning of any structure and any essence must always be deferred, while constantly differing from itself, that is, producing and proliferating differences or meanings. One therefore never arrives at a stable structure that could once and for all establish the meaning of what it is to be human (or posthuman, for that matter). This fact would not be revolutionary or problematic if there were not constant attempts to pretend or claim otherwise by some people, philosophers, scientists, but also politicians, that is, that they *do* know what things really mean once and for all (again, this is not a nihilist or populist argument that no safe meaning can ever be established, but a challenge to absolute truth claims). Humanists usually think they know what it means to be human (or at least tend to be confident about what is not human); posthumanists – and this is the point of its "post" – are less sure.

A discussion of poststructuralist, post-Saussurean linguistics would not be complete, however, without a discussion of the role of narrative. Signs do not occur in isolation: as soon as you perceive or think of a sign (a picture, a word, a landscape, a face, an object), meanings and associations come rushing in: experiences you have had, but also new connections that you make depending on context. In order to create some sense of continuity, let us call this "identity." In order to temporarily arrest this meaning and make it meaningful for someone (an "I," which also implies a "you," an "us," a "them," a "world," and so on), you need to give this meaning a sequential order. This is what narrative does. It helps you make sense of time and, in doing so, it establishes cause and effect, the basic operation of what philosophers refer to as "rationality" (enabled by the faculty of "reason" that is supposed to be innate, or natural, to every member of the human species, which in turn sanctions the most fundamental claims on which humanism, anthropocentrism, and exceptionalism depend). A discourse like humanism strives to create consensus about what it means to be human by establishing a consensus about how we became, are, continue to be, and will further develop as humans. In short, it takes the indefinite number of individual (human) stories and ways of making sense of (human) identity and turns them into what Lyotard, following Wittgenstein, called a *"grand récit"* or a powerful "metanarrative."[19] A metanarrative is a narrative that appropriates a variety of smaller narratives and it is designed to legitimate central social values like freedom, individuality, or, as in the case of humanism's meta-narrative, what it means to be human.

Another, decisive, complication in the term "post-human-ism" is an ambiguity about what the post in posthumanism precisely wishes to post (to critique, to project, to "end"). There is a posthumanism that projects the end of human*ism*, the discourse; and there is a posthumanism that anticipates the end of the *human*. I would prefer to call the second variety, the desire that lies behind the idea of an overcoming of the *human*, "transhumanist."[20]

## 2.3 Poststructuralism and Posthumanism

*Critical* posthumanism appropriates, continues, and rewrites the legacy of poststructuralism while being aware of the problematic of dialectical over-coming and the ambiguity of the gesture of posting as described above. As a result, the main challenge is not to overcome (certainly not the human, maybe somewhat more humbly, human*ism*) but to submit to deconstruction the entire humanist philosophical tradition, worldview, and set of values that have come to dominate western culture, arguably from its beginnings.

More specifically, what posthumanism extends and complicates are poststructuralist notions of subjectivity, writing, and alterity. The prob-lems that a posthumanist thinking, or a thinking "after the human," faces all refer back to the questions raised by poststructuralism's antihumanist stance. These problems are most clearly articulated in some emblematic poststructuralist debates, like Foucault's idea of the end of man, Derrida's reprise in his "The Ends of Man," the discussion around the "death" of and the question of who might come after the subject, as well as Lyotard's notion of the inhuman.[21]

The main reason why poststructuralism is seen as antihumanist is that it treats the humanist subject as a ghost-like figure, as a misconception that is about to disappear. A very brief history of the modern (liberal humanist) subject would read like this: Descartes believed that by doubting every-thing but his own ability to doubt he could infer the existence of a thinking subject (*ego cogito ergo sum*). Kant raised the stakes by making the subject the center of experience and thereby excluding the object (or the "thing as such") from (human) ontological investigation (a position that, under the name of "correlationism," has become the main target of speculative realism and object-oriented-ontology).[22] Both Nietzsche and Freud are associated with a critique of the modern, Kantian, or transcendental notion of subjectivity; however, it is structuralism in the first half of the twentieth century and poststructuralism that has accelerated the "decentering" and "death" of the (unified, self-centered, conscious) subject. Posthumanism partakes in the still-ongoing deconstruction of this subject by critiquing subjectivity's inherent anthropocentrism and anthropomorphism. In this respect, the title (and motto) of this volume – after the human – echoes the title of a landmark collection of essays figuring the who's who of poststructuralism at the time it appeared, Eduardo Cadava's edited volume *Who Comes after the subject?* Who (or what) comes after the subject is the poststructuralist version of the posthumanist question: who (or what) comes after the human(ist subject)? And, which forms of agency does posthumanism afford?

The idea of "coming after" the (human) subject, in this sense, takes up Foucault's image of "man" being "an invention of recent date, which might be erased, like a face drawn in sand at the edge of the sea" (386–7). Instead of premature apocalypticism, Foucault's notorious phrase the "end of man" can be understood in a critically historical rather than jubilantly nihilistic sense. Foucault's disenchantment with the human figure points towards the historicization of the human as an object of investigation, a shift that is likely to exceed any framework of philosophical anthropology and the "humanities" more generally. This historicization of the *figure* of the human (which refers to an entire generation of "antihumanists") remains somewhat incomplete. It is here that posthumanism indeed represents a radicalization and a relocation of the human in the sense that it transcends any dialectical historicization through which the human is neither the absolute subject of historicism (its "end") nor merely one "object" out of many. Instead, any discourse striving to create consensus about what it means to be human has become the central target of posthumanist critique.[23]

This critique, however, is already well underway in Derrida's influential interview "Eating Well," where he speaks of the "fable of the subject" as an anthropocentric "fiction" that traditionally has denied any form of subjectivity to the nonhuman (the animal, the machine, the object).[24] In this sense, any discourse which tacitly presupposes the subject as a *human* subject is committed to what Derrida refers to as a "sacrificial" idea that sanctions directly or indirectly the instrumentalization of the nonhuman by the human (an ideology Derrida names "carno-phallogocentrism" ("Who Comes" 113)), which not only serves the legitimation of "meat-eating virility" in western cultures but also, in the age of biotechnology, is related to the commodification of life in its multiplicity of forms more generally (115).

Today's so-called posthuman condition (the proliferation of cyborgs, generalized biopolitics, the critique of speciesism, the Anthropocene, or human-induced climate change) therefore does not coincide with the liquidation of the subject but rather with the pluralization of subjects, including the proliferation of nonhuman subjectivities.[25] The "nonhuman turn" that posthumanism and its critique of anthropocentrism have provoked in the (post)humanities has an important precursor in Jean-François Lyotard's notion of the "inhuman," which prompts within posthumanism the need to acknowledge all those ghosts, all those others that have been repressed as part of the process of humanization: animals, machines, objects, as well as gods, demon, and monsters of all kinds.[26]

In summary: what poststructuralism bequeaths to posthumanism is the fact that "after the end of man" or "after the human" also need to be understood as *before* the human. In between the crises of finality and renewal, there is "our" current chance to rethink the human, to think the human otherwise. This is the ambiguity inhabiting every "post-," posthumanism in particular. In other words, what poststructuralism, or simply the legacy of "theory," reminds posthumanism is the continued need for theorizing, for "theory after theory."[27] In this sense, poststructuralism reminds posthumanists of the work of many thinkers who have been instrumental to the development of (critical) posthumanism, notably Donna Haraway, N. Katherine Hayles, Rosi Braidotti, Judith Butler, Giorgio Agamben, Bernard Stiegler, Claire Colebrook, Karen Barad, Vicki Kirby, Robert Esposito, and Cary Wolfe, to name but the most obvious. What precisely persists is a kind of critical instinct (which is of course also much older than poststructuralism), namely that in between (human) identity and (human) difference there is an otherness that both produces and undermines this very opposition of identity and difference. The posthuman, nonhuman, more-than-human, as well as the after-the-human, are names for this irrepressible invasion of the other into the supposed self-sameness of the human.

## Notes

1. Neil Badmington, "Posthumanism," in Simon Malpas and Paul Wake (eds.), *The Routledge Companion to Critical Theory* (London: Routledge, 2006), 240–1.
2. It was Foucault's influential "What Is Enlightenment?" (a reply to Kant's famous text written in 1784) that described modernity as an "attitude" or "ethos" characterized by the "will to 'heroize' the present" (in *The Foucault Reader*, ed. Paul Rabinow [New York: Pantheon, 1984], 32–3).

3. See especially his *Genealogy of Morals* (1887), "On Truth and Lie in an Extra-Moral Sense" (1873), and *Untimely Meditations* (1873–1876).

4. Jacques Derrida, *Spectres of Marx: The State of Debt, the Work of Mourning, and the New International*, trans. Peggy Kamuf (London: Routledge, 1994), 14. Derrida's target in this passage is Francis Fukuyama's *The End of History and the Last Man* (New York: Free Press, 1992), a treatise on the end of the Cold War and the triumph of western liberal democracy, which, seen from a Hegelian point of view, are interpreted as the completion of history. Fukuyama later famously relativized his idea that the global reach of liberal democracy had effectively "ended" history and instead, in *Our Posthuman Future: Consequences of the Biotechnology Revolution* (London: Profile Books, 2002), claimed that biotechnology and eugenics contained the potential for a new class struggle (and hence return of "history") in the form of a division between the (bio)technologically "enhanced" and "unenhanced."

5. Jacques Derrida, "Some Statements and Truisms about Neo-Logisms, Newisms, Postisms, Parasitisms, and Other Small Seisms," trans. Anne Tomiche, in David Carroll (ed.), *The States of "Theory": History, Art, and Critical Discourse* (Stanford: Stanford University Press, 1990), 63–94.

6. Derrida, *Specters*, 15. Derrida's comment was originally made at a conference entitled "W(h)ither Marxism" organized by the University of California Riverside in 1993, which was concerned with the survival of Marxism after ideological discreditation following the fall of the Soviet empire and what, in the 1990s, looked like the unstoppable "triumph" of capitalism and liberal democracy.

7. This is made very clear in John Sturrock's influential *Structuralism and Since: From Lévi-Strauss to Derrida* (Oxford: Oxford University Press, 1979), which still remains one of the best introductions to poststructuralist thinking, together with Catherine Belsey's *Critical Practice* (London: Methuen, 1980) and *Poststructuralism: A Very Short Introduction* (Oxford: Oxford University Press, 2002).

8. The rolling out of structuralist linguistics as a model towards the humanities and social sciences in general is usually referred to as the "linguistic turn." For a useful overview see Colebrook, "The Linguistic Turn in Continental Philosophy," in Alan D. Schrift (ed.), *Poststructuralism and Critical Theory's Second Generation* (Durham: Acumen, 2010), 279–309.

9. Robert Young, *Untying the Text: A Post-Structuralist Reader* (London: Routledge, 1981), 1.

10. See my *Posthumanism: A Critical Analysis* (London: Bloomsbury, 2013) for an extensive explanation of *critical* posthumanism.

11. Derrida goes on to critique Saussure's notion of difference and the binary opposition on which it relies by introducing the neologism "différance" in *Margins of Philosophy*, trans. Alan Bass (Chicago: University of Chicago Press, 1982). See further discussion later.

12. On the poststructuralist notion of discourse, see Herbrechter (36–8 and *passim*).

13. This is the main bone of contention poststructuralism and its followers have with object-oriented ontology and speculative realism. See further Chapter 13 in this volume, and the note on correlationism below.

14. See further Stuart Hall, *Representation*, 2nd edition, ed. Jessica Evans and Sean Nixon (London: Sage 2013), 1–59.

15. See further Louis Althusser, "Ideology and Ideological State Apparatuses (Notes towards an Investigation)," trans. Ben Brewster, *Lenin and Philosophy and Other Essays* (London: NLB, 1971), 121–73.

16. See further, Elaine Graham, *Representations of the Post/Human: Monsters, Aliens and Others in Popular Culture* (Manchester: Manchester University Press, 2002) and Jeffrey Jerome Cohen, *Monster Theory: Reading Culture* (Minneapolis: University of Minnesota Press, 1996).

17. What to do with this "difference" remains an eternal stumbling block for humanist ideas of "universalism" and continues to be a highly contentious issue, particularly with regard to race (see Chapter 14), gender (see Chapters 3 and 12), and species (see chapter 7).

18. See especially Jacques Derrida, "Structure, Sign, and Play in the Discourse of the Human Sciences," in Richard Macksey and Eugenio Donato (eds.), *The Languages of Criticism and The Sciences of Man: The Structuralist Controversy* (Baltimore: The Johns Hopkins Press, 1970), 247–72.

19. Jean-François Lyotard, *The Postmodern Condition: A Report on Knowledge*, trans. Geoffrey Bennington and Brian Massumi (Minneapolis: University of Minnesota Press, 1984), 34ff. An "incredulity" toward metanarratives is often seen, following Lyotard, as the central tenet of postmodernism (see further Chapter 3 in this volume).

20. For the distinction between post- and transhumanism see Herbrechter (40ff.). Transhumanism is not so much a break with humanism (especially not with its anthropocentrism) but a continuation and projected achievement of human perfectibility (usually claimed to be achievable by way of technological and moral enhancement or transcendence into a new "species," that is, cyborgs and AI. See Chapter 6 in this volume. Transhumanist technotopias of enhancement or replacement usually come at the expense or rejection of human "embodiment" (see further Chapter 4 of this volume).

21. Michel Foucault, Michel, *The Order of Things: An Archaeology of the Human Sciences* ed. R.D. Laing (New York: Pantheon, 1970). Derrida, "Some Statements." Jean-François Lyotard, *The Inhuman: Reflections of Time*, trans. Geoff Bennington and Rachel Bowlby (Cambridge: Polity Press, 1991). Eduardo Cavdava, *Who Comes After the Subject?* (New York: Routledge, 1991). Again, there is a significant overlap between poststructuralism and postmodernism in this context (see Chapter 3). One way of distinguishing poststructuralism from postmodernism might be simply "pragmatic" in that the former is the more "philosophical" while the latter tends to be a broader, "sociological" way of making sense of modernity.

22. Quentin Meillassoux defines correlationism as "the idea according to which we only ever have access to the correlation between thinking and being, and

never to either term considered apart from the other" (*After Finitude: An Essay on the Necessity of Contingency*, trans. Ray Brassier [London: Continuum, 2008], 5). See further Chapter 13 in this volume.

23. See Cary Wolfe, *What Is Posthumanism?* (Minneapolis: University of Minnesota Press, 2010).

24. Jacques Derrida, "'Eating Well', or the Calculation of the Subject: An Interview with Jacques Derrida," in Eduardo Cadava (ed.), *Who Comes After the Subject?* (New York: Routledge, 1991), 96–119.

25. For more detailed discussions, see Chapter 7 on Animals and Chapter 11 on Biopolitics.

26. Richard Grusin, *The Nonhuman Turn* (Minneapolis: University of Minnesota Press, 2015). In his influential "A Postmodern Fable" Lyotard raises the important question of posthuman embodiment. See also Lyotard's *The Inhuman,* and Elaine Graham *Representations of the Post/Human.*

27. Jane Elliott and David Attridge, *Theory After "Theory"* (London: Routledge, 2011).

CHAPTER 3

# Postmodernism

## Jonathan Boulter

Postmodernism has passed resolutely out of fashion. In fact, its death was announced by one of its most important proponents, Linda Hutcheon: "Let's just say: it's over. [T]he postmodern may well be a twentieth-century phenomenon, that is, a thing of the past."[1] As its techniques of thought, structures of expression, and innovations of form become conventional, Hutcheon argues, the postmodern, as an idea, becomes calcified, entirely recognizable, and then fatally "institutionalized" (165). When used in the academy, the term will be mobilized only to trace its genealogical relation to the history of ideas. If the term appears in public discourse, it is only when rightwing pundits condemn pernicious and morally relativizing ideas favored by intellectual "elites." But, as Derrida argues, no idea ever fully dies: the traces always already live on, haunting its future as an uncanny anticipation of a spectral afterlife. Postmodernism lives on, if only secretly, in the various forms and expressions of what we have come to term posthumanism. My interest here is to trace the genealogy of the most important aspect of postmodern and posthumanist critique: the idea of the subject. Postmodernism's gift to posthumanism, to the *future* that is posthumanism, is to have begun the critical and radical decomposition of the idea of the liberal humanist subject. What postmodernism offers at its most benign is the idea of the entirely precarious nature of the human subject; at its most radical, in the thinking of Lacan and Derrida, post-modernism posits the erasure of human subjectivity in its totality. As Derrida puts it: "There has never been The Subject for anyone. ... The subject is a fable" (104).[2] Posthumanism is the realization of postmodern-ism's interrogation of the human subject; without the work of Jacques Lacan, Jean-François Lyotard, Michel Foucault, and Gilles Deleuze and Felix Guattari, we would not have arrived at late Derrida's denial of the primacy of human subjectivity, N. Katherine Hayles' notion of distributed cognition, Donna Haraway's utopian figure of the cyborg, or Rosi

44

Braidotti's affirmative posthumanism. Postmodernism, in other words, is the (now) spectral *grounds* of posthumanist thought.

Of course, Hutcheon is only strategically arguing for the death of postmodernism. As she understands, postmodernism continues to exist as it extends into other artistic and philosophical discourses: "feminism, postcolonialism, as well as with queer, race and ethnicity theory" (166). What Hutcheon says next is crucial for understanding the filiation between postmodernism and posthumanism: "what these various forms of identity politics share with the postmodern is a focus on difference and ex-centricity, an interest in the hybrid, the heterogeneous, and the local, and an interrogative and deconstructing mode of analysis" (166). And Hutcheon is correct to see the various drives of postmodern fiction and philosophy echoed and amplified through the various modes of deconstructive and poststructuralist thought. Moreover, Hutcheon's key terms here – ex-centricity, hybridity, heterogeneity, difference – stand as an index of the central concepts of poststructuralist philosophy and are the ones we now deploy to understand the posthumanist subject.

But let us first review some features of what we may call the postmodern. The central, now orthodox, philosophical definition of the postmodern comes from Lyotard's *The Postmodern Condition*:

> Simplifying to the extreme, I define postmodern as incredulity towards metanarratives. This incredulity is undoubtedly a product of progress in the sciences: but that progress in turn presupposes it. To the obsolescence of the metanarrative apparatus of legitimation corresponds, most notably, the crisis of metaphysical philosophy and the university institution which in the past relied on it.[3]

By "metanarrative" Lyotard means those discursive practices, practices of knowledge and power (as Foucault would put it), that legitimate specific regimes of ideology: science, religion, politics, and art. The postmodern is not, specifically, a term designating an era, but is the unfolding of what Foucault would call an *episteme*: the postmodern is an *event* in which everything once accepted as meaningful and true is now cast into doubt.[4] All foundational myths open themselves to incredulity which in turn instantiates "the crisis of metaphysical philosophy." Lyotard's phrase resonates into many systems of thought, but I wish to inflect it through a reading of postmodernism's most important critique: that of the liberal humanist subject.[5] As Derrida will remind us, the crisis of metaphysics is always already a crisis of the philosophical notions of ground, stability, and presence; metaphysics, the articulation of a general economy of meaningful order, will, when called into question, only ever work to cover over its own recognition of its fundamental instability.

Modernity, as Lyotard will understand it – and it seems that for him modernity designates a system of thought extending to the Enlightenment – is thoroughly invested in preserving the stability of thought, the logic of reason, and the impermeable identity of "liberated humanity" (*Postmodern Condition* 26). The postmodern, on the other hand, having come to recognize the bankruptcy of modernity as a regime of knowledge, questions the idea of "identity as established by the tradition of modernity."[6] Lyotard puts this question thusly:

> A different way of dealing with the universal emancipation promised by modernity would be to "work over" (in the Freudian sense) not just the loss of this object ["liberated humanity"] but also the loss of the subject to whom this goal was promised. It would be a matter not only of recognizing our finitude, but of elaborating the status of the we, the question of the subject. (*Postmodern Explained* 27)

### 3.1   The Question of the Subject

Lyotard anticipates this question in *The Postmodern Condition* and then will radicalize it in his critically important essay "Can Thought go on without a Body?"[7] This 1987 essay, which links the discourses of postmodernism and posthumanism, takes the form of two monologues, the first spoken by a subject designated "He," the second by "She." Lyotard explores the idea that consciousness could survive, and register, the solar death of the universe, the absolute end of the human: "How to make thought without a body possible. A thought that continues to exist after the death of the human body. . . . Thought without a body is the prerequisite for thinking of the death of all bodies, solar or terrestrial, and of the death of thoughts that are inseparable from those bodies" (13–4). "He's" ultimate idea is that thought, consciousness, language as such, is not a pure epiphenomenon of the brain or mind; thought requires a body, body requires a thought. To constitute thought beyond the death of the human body requires some model of the body to be instantiated, to continue. "She" agrees that "thought is inseparable from the phenomenological body" (23) but suggests, more radically, and in way that anticipates Hayles and Haraway, that the human has only ever been a carrier of a process of complexification or negentropy that has determined the course of events in the universe: the human has merely been the *expression* of this negentropy, not its originator. This negentropy, a force that will eventually efface the human, does not require the human: "I'm granting that human beings aren't and never have been the motor of this complexification, but an effect and carrier of this negentropy, its continuer" (22).

### 3.2   Effect and Carrier

Lyotard's idea here figures the human subject as essentially, and radically, passive in the face of forces that precede and exceed it. And indeed this image of the human subject finds full and forceful expression in a number of orthodox postmodern theories, to the point that the idea of the passive subject becomes almost an *a priori*. Jacques Lacan, for instance, figures the subject as entirely dependent on the other for its own ontological ground. When he writes, "desire is the desire of the Other,"[8] Lacan suggests not only that the human subject is essentially defined *as* a subject by processes exterior to itself, but that its knowledge of the world, as such, comes from outside itself: "It is this moment that decisively tips the whole of human knowledge into being mediated by the other's desire, constitutes its object in an abstract equivalence due to competition from other people."[9] When at the outset of "The Mirror Stage" Lacan asserts that his theory of exteriorized identity leads him "to oppose any philosophy directly issuing from the Cogito" (75), we comprehend the philosophical, anti-Cartesian stakes: his notion of the subject as *subject to* forces that precede and exceed it allow us to begin seeing in Lacan's psychoanalysis a direct challenge to the traditional image of liberal humanist subject, which, as Rosi Braidotti puts it, "defined perfectibility in terms of autonomy and self-determination."[10] Lacan, to put it bluntly, dismantled or attempted to dismantle any coherent notion of the self, as such, and thus any naïve idea of self-determination or autonomy. And in so doing, he allowed thinkers as diverse as Foucault, Derrida, Deleuze, and Guattari systematically to deconstruct the bedrock of what Lyotard calls "metaphysical philosophy." It may be argued, in fact, that Lacan, as early as 1949, ushered in a nascent posthuman philosophy.

Perhaps more precisely, we could suggest that Lacan's critique of the subject, his direct critique of Cartesian metaphysics, lays the ground for what has come to be called *critical posthumanism*. This term, associated primarily with the work of Rosi Braidotti, Cary Wolfe, Stefan Herbrechter, and Ivan Callus, suggests that posthumanism defines itself primarily as a critique, in the Kantian sense. Suggesting ways of moving beyond the limiting and explicitly ideological regimes of humanism, critical posthumanism works to reveal the logics at work within humanism, deconstructing them yet always attending to their persistence. Braidotti frames her view of critical posthuman thusly:

> I define the critical posthuman subject within an eco-philosophy of multiple belongings, as a relational subject constituted in and by multiplicity, that is to say a subject that works across differences and is also internally differentiated, but still grounded and accountable. Posthuman subjectivity expresses an embodied and embedded and hence partial form of accountability, based on a strong sense of collectivity, relationality and hence community building. (49)

Braidotti makes clear that her posthuman subject is still determined by its relation to regimes of ethics: her subject is "relational" and "accountable," and indeed in her more recent work she has begun to speak of affirmative rather than critical posthumanism.[11] Her subject emerges within structures of belonging and becoming. It may be partial and determined (and here we are reminded of Lacan's view of the subject), but it still exists, ontologically, within a system that recognizes the value, inherent or otherwise, of the subject *qua* subject. For Braidotti, the posthuman subject still is connected, one might perhaps say, *nostalgically*, to some qualities that determined and defined the classical humanist subject (29). Braidotti's affirmative posthumanism, in other words, figures the posthuman subject as haunted by the specter of its humanist forbears; to be more precise, and to deploy a term I now wish to attend to very carefully, the posthuman subject always already functions as a *trace* of a determining and only partially disavowed humanism.

As I move my discussion into an examination of the Derridean model of the posthuman, I am interested in attending to the spatial metaphors that ground and inflect the various instantiations of the posthuman subject. All the key thinkers of the posthuman deploy, perhaps knowingly, perhaps not, spatial metaphors to define their subject: Hayles will speak of *distributed* cognition; Haraway will speak of the cyborg as a *utopian* creature; Braidotti speaks explicitly about working *across, embeddedness*, and *relationality*; Derrida, of course, speaks of the *trace*.[12] I am interested in offering a way of thinking about these metaphors: perhaps they suggest that posthuman subjectivity is always already an event that must emerge materially, in a grounded "real" world; perhaps spatial metaphors like *distribution* and *relationality* always already suggest, after Derrida, that the posthuman subject emerges across or within spaces and thus can only ever be a radical form of multiplicity, discontinuity, or perhaps (radical) neutrality.

If we attend to these metaphors, perhaps we can begin to understand the posthuman subject as a possibility, a hypothesis, and a thought-experiment grounded in a recognizable material stratum.[13]

To assert that there is a central or centralizing trope in Derrida's deconstructive philosophy is, perhaps, at odds with the general tenor of deconstruction. However, Derrida's notion of the trace, a trope that itself is troped across his career into a variety of images and figures (cinders, ash, specter, supplement, *pharmakos*), always already offers itself as a kind of ground for deconstructive thought in general, and Derrida's thinking about consciousness, subjectivity, and presence, as such. The term appears as early as 1967 in *Of Grammatology* (see especially Part 1, Chapter 2: "The Outside Is the Inside") but finds its most elaborate expression in his 1968 essay "Differance," the final chapter of *Speech and Phenomena*.[14] "It is the culmination of Derrida's extended critique of the central tenet of Husserlian phenomenology: self-present consciousness. Indeed Derrida's critique of Husserl is an effort to demonstrate that an idea of consciousness, of presence, forms the bedrock of a general economy of a metaphysics that, in turn and somewhat tautologically, determines our understanding of subjectivity itself: "our intention is to begin to confirm that the recourse to phenomenological critique is metaphysics itself, restored to its original purity in its historical achievement" (5). Derrida's critique of Husserl is grounded in Saussurean linguistics and proceeds rather logically, if idio-syncratically. Presence, *ousia*, the idea of the self-present subject, is itself *as an idea*, an effect of a language (he will call it *arche-writing*) that emerges out of an economy of differences. Any idea, any concept, makes sense only in differential opposition to another concept: a word signifies and emerges as meaningful, *not* on its own, but only in relation (a temporal, even spatial relation) to another. Meaning is exteriorized and differed in what emerges as an endlessly possible network of differences. Metaphysics, Derrida argues, forgets this network of differences, *must* forget this network, if it is to succeed in convincing itself that consciousness, as such, grounds itself *by* itself and *for* itself:

> Consciousness in all its modifications is conceivable only as self-presence, a self-perception of presence. And what holds for consciousness also holds here for what is called subjective existence in general. Just as the category of the subject is not and never has been conceivable without reference to presence as *hypokeimenon* or *ousia*, etc., so the subject as consciousness has never been able to be evinced otherwise than as self-presence. The privilege accorded to consciousness thus means a privilege accorded to the present . . . . This privilege is the ether of metaphysics. ("Differance" 147)

The ether of metaphysics, the force of metaphysics, is its privileging of the present moment of consciousness, its privileging of the present, as such. But the idea of the trace, of difference, of meaning emerging only in relation to signs in opposition, explicitly suggests that presence is never present, that meaning is never here or now, but there and then. Meaning is deferred and differed. The sign is never the thing it wishes to express but only ever a trace of what it may come to be at some future point (when/ where it will, of course, be differed and deferred again). Thus, Derrida's crucial sentences: "The trace is not a presence but is rather the simulacrum of a presence that dislocates, displaces, and refers beyond itself. The trace has, properly speaking, no place, for effacement belongs to the very structure of the trace. Effacement must always be able to overtake the trace" ("Differance" 156).

Derrida's analysis of the trace and its relation to consciousness and subjectivity offers a powerful critique of some of the central tenets of liberal humanism, specifically its investment in the idea of the self-present, rational, transparent subject who can think him- or her-self into being. In some ways, Derrida's postmodern critique of the subject, one that finds echoes in Lacan, Foucault, and Deleuze and Guattari, is so much of a given that Derrida rarely speaks explicitly about the subject, as such, again. He acknowledges this fact in "Eating Well" when he suggests that his work, grounded as it is on philosophies that take as an *a priori* the evacuation of the subject (Freud and Nietzsche), has no real need to further the analysis of human subjectivity as trace, remainder, or specter of itself.

Several aspects of Derrida's thinking here should detain us as we move into our concluding reading of the posthuman, especially as it is figured in Hayles and Haraway. First, as Derrida's gesture to the idea of nonhuman subjectivity indicates, Derrida's thinking has always already been post*human* in a profound sense. Even in his brief mention of the animal in "Eating Well" (and of course he will make the animal a central focus in his late work), he indicates that his interest supersedes that of the human: if subjectivity extends beyond the human (and even then it is merely a trace of itself), then the *concept* of the human is attenuated and dispersed.[15] Certainly Derrida's demand that we extend our analysis to the animal calls into radical question the Cartesian notion that the only thinking thing is the human; and in so doing, Derrida calls into question the primacy of thinking, of consciousness as singularly *located* in the human. Second, Derrida's analysis of consciousness as trace resounds profoundly into almost all posthuman conception of the subject. The model of posthuman subjectivity that emerges in, for example, Hayles and Haraway, to mention only two canonical thinkers, is similarly instantiated as a spatialized conception of consciousness: for Hayles cognition is *distributed* cognition; for Haraway cyborg subjectivity is in a time and a place to come. Both figure the posthuman as a trace, as spatially realized, and as deferred as it is differed. In other words, the postmodern philosophy of Derrida finds explicit re-articulation in posthuman theories of subjectivity.

It is not my intention here to rehearse all the complexities of arguments about the posthuman subject; what I am interested in noting is how both Hayles and Haraway offer a variation of the Derridian trace, whether explicitly or not. And we should begin with the crucial mark of difference between Derrida and Haraway and Hayles. For Derrida the trace emerges as a sign of a deficit in metaphysical thinking: the trace is a symptom of a blindness to the absence of full presence, a symptom, precisely, of the inability to move beyond the debilitating structures of inherited philosophical thought; for Haraway and Hayles (and this is true for Braidotti as well), the spatial and temporal complexities of posthuman subjectivity, its status as trace of the liberal humanist subject, are turned from an essential restriction of thought into an advantage. Haraway, for instance, is concerned with the figure of the cyborg because it blurs boundaries, calls into question calcified regimes of identity, and evacuates a patriarchal order of ideology. Her cyborg is figured as a myth – both in the sense of a fiction and of an urgent and emerging new episteme – and a material presence: "A cyborg is a cybernetic organism, a hybrid of machine and organism, a creature of social reality as well as a creature of fiction. Social reality is lived social relations, our most important political construction, a world-changing fiction" ("Manifesto" 149). The cyborg is both here and yet to come, present and absent, emergent and spectrally futural: the cyborg, in other words (although she does not deploy the term) is a trace. As such, and here we arrive at what is her most important term, the cyborg is essentially a *utopian* creature: utopian, meaning *nowhere*; utopian, meaning *not yet*; but utopian meaning, also, demanding attention as a reality in the *now*, always already calling into question received orders of power. If Derrida's reading of the subject suggests that it is always deferred, always to come, always differentiated from itself, Haraway's cyborg is similarly displaced, both rhetorically – she repeatedly suggests the cyborg is an "ironic" myth, irony being the trope par excellence of distance and deferred expectation – and ontologically: "the cyborg has no origin story in the Western sense" (150). With no origin and an ontology still to come, the cyborg, like the trace, cannot be reconciled or accommodated to any traditional, metaphysical definition of subjectivity.

Hayles' model of the posthuman, like that of Haraway, is an explicit critique of the traditions of liberal humanist thought. In her view the ideas of the human and the posthuman, crucially, are constructions (*How We Became* 2); that is, the human and the posthuman do not emerge into the world as natural, transparent, and entirely self-producing. They emerge within discursive regimes – they are products of specific cultural contexts – as well as being material instantiations open to manipulation and change. As Hayles puts it, the posthuman is best understood as, first, a "view" (2), a position that favors informational patterns over materiality (2), second, that sees consciousness, "regarded as the seat of human identity in the Western tradition . . . as an epiphenomenon" (3), third, that sees the body as a the "original prothesis" (3), and, finally, that sees the body as inevitably joined with "intelligent machines" (3). That is to say, her posthuman is similar to Haraway's cyborg: "In the posthuman, there are no essential differences or absolute demarcations between bodily existence and computer simulation, cybernetic mechanism and biological organism, robot teleology and human goals" (Hayles *How We Became* 3).

Two aspects of Hayles' thinking should detain us. First is the idea that human consciousness is an epiphenomenon. The location of human identity is absolutely called into question by the posthuman "view"; an epiphenomenon is a secondary symptom, a mental state that is essentially a by-product of brain activity. There is, in other words, nothing absolutely privileged, *nothing a priori*, in consciousness and thus identity. Second, and more importantly, Hayles views the posthuman as what she calls a "distributed cognition" (*How We Became* 3). She argues that the posthuman subject is a product of a variety of competing agencies, largely capitalist. The posthuman subject is a product of "market relations" (3) and thus does not own itself: it is "an amalgam, a collection of heterogenous components, a material-informational entity whose boundaries undergo continuous construction and reconstruction" (3).[16] Taking the television character *The Six Million Dollar Man*, or the movie character *Robocop* as "paradigmatic citizen[s] of the posthuman regime" (3), Hayles argues that the posthuman – more than merely psychoanalytically produced by drives and desires that precede and exceed it (as Lacan would argue) – practically and materially finds itself emerging from a variety of material sites, locations, and agencies. This constellation of sites produces what she terms "distributed cognition" (4), an emergent and plural sense of subjectivity not owned by the individual subject and not located in any one place. In distributed cognition "there is no a priori way to identify a self-will that can be clearly distinguished from an other will" (*How We*

*Became* 4). Hayles' metaphor – distributed cognition – is, crucially, spatial: the posthuman is neither here nor there; the posthuman is not located, not centralized; the posthuman, we might suggest, emerges only in the play between, in the space between, competing agencies and desires. In other words, to look back to Derrida, the posthuman is a trace. More precisely, the posthuman is *traced* into its discontinuous being by forces preceding, exceeding, and dislocating it.

I wish to circle back to Derrida and Hutcheon to bring my discussion to an end. In "Eating Well," Derrida suggests that if we read carefully those philosophies that seem to favor the idea of the transcendental subject (Descartes, Kant, Hegel) they can be shown to harbor deep suspicions about the centrality of consciousness as a marker of identity and subjectivity. He thus concludes "the subject is a fable" (102). While not explicitly citing him, Derrida clearly reminds us of Nietzsche's evacuation of the subject in (especially) *The Will to Power* and "On Truth and Lying." Nietzsche's suggestion that humans invented consciousness and then promptly forgot that they did so; that, therefore, "the 'subject' is only a fiction,"[17] clearly anticipates Derrida, indeed almost word for word. For "fiction" Derrida substitutes the word "fable," but we might recall that Nietzsche himself uses the word "fable" (*Fabel*) to describe his fantasy of the human inventing their "illusory consciousness."[18] Obviously, what I am interested in here is the resonance of words like *fiction* and *fable,* and the ways they persist into theories of the posthuman. We recall how Haraway, for instance, is insistent that the posthuman is a "creature of fiction," a "myth," or what she calls "an image . . . of both imagination and material reality" ("Manifesto" 149). Hayles' insistence on turning to fictions like *The Six Million Dollar Man* or *Robocop* to illustrate her idea of distributed cognition signals another dependence on fictionality and the fabulous in order to communicate the complexities of posthuman being.[19]

It is fascinating, as I suggested above, that posthumanist thinkers turn what is clearly in Derrida and Nietzsche a deficit in our thinking into a positive and liberating asset: the subject as a fiction is an idea for Nietzsche that signals the incapacity to think beyond our limitations. As he writes in *The Will to Power*, "we set up a word at the point at which our ignorance, at which we can see no further" (267). For Derrida the idea of the subject, inherent in the philosophies of Descartes, Kant, Hegel, or Husserl is a symptom of a haunting metaphysics, the continuity of a spectralizing and destabilizing falsity that can only privilege what is entirely without claim to the reality of being. For Hayles and Haraway (and we could add for Braidotti), however, the absence at the heart of the idea of the human is the absence that leads inevitably to conceiving of the posthuman and of spaces of possibility and becoming. Haraway is offering a utopian and thus liberating project. Hayles suggests that her vision of the posthuman, one that attends carefully to material embeddedness and "finitude as a condition for human being," is "one on which we depend for our continual survival" (*How We Became* 5). Braidotti's posthuman subject, grounded on difference and itself "*internally* differentiated" (*The Posthuman* 49, emphasis added), is one that similarly offers a possibility for liberation: "a posthuman ethics for a non-unitary subject proposes an enlarged sense of inter-connection between self and others, including the non-human or 'earth' others, by removing the obstacle of self-centered individualism" (49–50).

Let us finally recall Hutcheon's rhetorical lament over the passing of postmodernism: she argues that postmodernism, after its disappearance, continues to find expression in "feminism, postcolonialism, as well as with queer, race and ethnicity theory"; she continues, "what these various forms of identity politics share with the postmodern is a focus on difference and ex-centricity, an interest in the hybrid, the heterogeneous, and the local, and an interrogative and deconstructing mode of analysis" (166). Haraway, Hayles, and Braidotti are not, in any narrow sense, working to outline any sort of "identity politics" – unless we wish to suggest that posthumanism, in its radical overturning of centuries of thinking about human subjectivity, is the ultimate form of identity politics – but we notice that they do share an interest in ex-centricity (Hayles), difference (Braidotti), and the hybrid and heterogeneous (Haraway).[20] And, as has been my argument throughout this chapter, we can track the various rhetorical and figurative modes of analysis in posthuman theory back to a deconstructive mode of analysis, specifically in Derrida's interest in the various expressions of the trace. In one sense, then, we can argue, and perhaps this is an inevitability, that postmodernism continues to find expression, continues to haunt thought, even as new forms of subjectivity emerge as possibilities for new forms of being.

## Notes

1. Linda Hutcheon, *The Politics of Postmodernism*, 2nd ed. (London: Routledge, 2002), 164–5.
2. Jacques Derrida, "'Eating Well', or the Calculation of the Subject: An Interview with Jacques Derrida," in Eduardo Cadava (ed.), *Who Comes After the Subject?* (New York: Routledge, 1991), 102.

3. Jean-François Lyotard, *The Postmodern Condition: A Report on Knowledge*, trans. Geoffrey Bennington and Brian Massumi (Minneapolis: University of Minnesota Press, 1984), xxiv.

4. The eventual logic of the postmodern, for Lyotard, means that a postmodern artist is always already oriented to a nostalgia for what has been and an awareness that the art work itself arrives too late: "*Post modern* would have to be understood according to the paradox of the future (*post*) anterior (*modo*)" (*Postmodern* 81). In *The Order of Things: An Archaeology of the Human Sciences* (New York: Vintage, 1970), Michel Foucault defines the *episteme* as an "epistemological field" (xxii); it is the discursive, thus ideological, limits of what can be said. Foucault is firm that the episteme, while serving power, is always a "discursive apparatus" (*Power/Knowledge: Selected Interviews and Other Writings, 1972–1977*, ed. Colin Gordon [New York: Pantheon, 1980], 197).

5. There are, of course, other definitions of postmodernism beyond the philosophical definition offered by Lyotard. In his analysis of contemporary fictions, Brian McHale suggests that while modernist fiction is concerned with the *epistemological* – questioning the possibility of fiction communicating *knowledge* about the world – postmodernist fiction is ontological: it questions the essence of experience and the status of the world, as such (*Postmodernist Fiction* [New York: Methuen, 1987], 9–10). Jean Baudrillard's well-known analysis of the simulacrum frames the postmodern regime as one in which making sense of signs, and experience itself, becomes structurally impossible: we no longer possess the ability to distinguish between the real and its representation (*Simulations*, trans. Paul Foss, Paul Patton, and Philip Beitchman [New York: Semiotext[e], 1983]); another symptom of this blurring of the boundary between the real and its simulacrum is the erasure of the distinction between the aesthetic and the everyday: art has joined fatally with life, "giving way to a pure circulation of images, a transaesthetics of banality" (Baudrillard, *The Transparency of Evil: Essays on Extreme Phenomena*, trans. James Benedict [London: Verso: 1993], 11). And while Fredric Jameson is loath to suggest that what distinguishes modernism from postmodernism, in art and literature, is a clash of "style," his analysis of the distinction between parody – subversion with political purpose – and pastiche – "blank parody" (*Postmodernism, or, The Cultural Logic of Late Capitalism* [Durham: Duke University Press, 1991], 17)) – does speak to an interest in the definitional possibilities of contemporary aesthetics. For Jameson, pastiche, like Baudrillard's transaesthetics of banality, is the style and mode of postmodernist culture and is the symptom of the "collapse of the high-modernist ideology of style" (17). Postmodernism, we may now argue, signals the passing into a phase of culture in which something has been lost; indeed we might, speaking generally, speak of postmodernism as a culture of mourning, given that it defines itself against something, a style, a mode of expression, that is now absent. The debate over specific genealogies and definitions of the postmodern are potentially endless; perhaps we might simply acknowledge Steven Connor's acute remark: "Critical debates about

postmodernism constitute postmodernism itself (*Postmodernist Culture: An Introduction to Theories of the Contemporary*, 2nd ed. [Oxford: Blackwell, 1989], 18).

6. Jean-François Lyotard, *The Postmodern Explained: Correspondence 1982–1985*, ed. Julian Pefanis and Morgan Thomas (Minneapolis: University of Minnesota Press, 1992), 26.

7. Jean-François Lyotard, "Can Thought go on without a Body?" in *The Inhuman: Reflections on Time*, trans. Geoffrey Bennington and Rachel Bowlby (Stanford: Stanford University Press, 1988).

8. Jacques Lacan, *The Four Fundamental Concepts of Psychoanalysis: The Seminar of Jacques Lacan, Book XI*, trans. Alain Sheridan (New York: Norton, 1998), 235.

9. Jacques Lacan, "The Mirror Stage as Formative of the *I* Function as Revealed in Psychoanalytic Experience," in *Ecrits*, trans. Bruce Fink (New York: Norton, 2002), 79.

10. Rosi Braidotti, *The Posthuman* (Cambridge: Polity, 2013), 23.

11. Rosi Braidotti, *Posthuman Knowledge* (Cambridge: Polity, 2019).

12. N. Katherine Hayles, *How We Became Posthuman: Virtual Bodies in Cybernetics, Literature, and Informatics* (Chicago: University of Chicago Press, 1999). Donna Haraway, "A Cyborg Manifesto: Science, Technology and Socialist-Feminism in the Late Twentieth Century," in *Simians, Cyborgs, and Women: The Reinvention of Nature* (New York: Routledge, 1991), 148–81. Jacques Derrida, *Of Grammatology*, trans. Gayatri Chakravorty Spivak (Baltimore: Johns Hopkins University Press, 1976). Braidotti, *The Posthuman*.

13. For more on materiality and the posthuman, see Chapter 12 in this volume.

14. Jacques Derrida, "Difference," in *Speech and Phenomena and Other Essays on Husserl's Theory of Signs*, trans. David B. Allison (Evanston: Northwestern UP, 1973), 129–60.

15. For more on animals and the posthuman, see Chapter 7 in this volume.

16. In her most recent work Hayles seems to have moved past an interest in the posthuman. In *Unthought: The Power of the Cognitive Unconscious* (Chicago: University of Chicago Press, 2017), for instance, she analyzes how a variety of systems – human, informational, biological – show evidence of cognition without consciousness. Her analysis of what she terms "nonconscious cognition," however, still works, as does posthumanism generally, to decenter the human "both because it recognizes another agent in addition to consciousness/unconsciousness in cognitive processes, and because it provides a bridge between human, animal, and technical cognition, locating them on a continuum rather than understanding them as qualitatively different capacities" (67).

17. Friedrich Nietzsche, *The Will to Power*, trans. Walter Kaufmann (New York: Vintage, 1968), 199.

18. Friedrich Nietzsche, "On Truth and Lies in a Nonmoral Sense," in *Philosophy and Truth: Selections from Nietzsche's Notebooks of the Early 1870s* (New York:

Humanity Books, 1979), 80. Nietzsche's essay, in fact, is framed explicitly as a fairy tale: "Once upon a time, in some out of the way corner of that universe which is dispersed into numberless twinkling solar systems, there was a star upon which clever beasts invented knowing" (79).

19. For more on the relationship between speculative fiction and posthumanism, see Chapter 15 of this volume.

20. Although this is not the place for a full discussion of the differences between posthumanism and transhumanism, it may be argued that transhumanist philosophy expresses a quite clear and, some might say, anxiously reactionary identity politics.

CHAPTER 4

# Embodiment and Affect

## Michael Richardson

If we accept the proposition that the very concept of the human must be reimagined, then the body and its relation to other bodies, objects, and worlds must in turn come under question. Indeed, we might argue that the recognition of the limits of the body as it appears in both modern thought and popular conception constitutes a crucial site for the emergence of the posthumanities. Within the diverse writings of what has become known as the affective turn, the body is reconstituted as fluid, co-composed, inescapably material, and fundamentally relational, in contrast to the boundedness of the biological body and sovereign subject alike.[1] Consequently, sociality, politics, culture, and more-than-human ecologies and technologies become sensible and graspable in their connection to and emergence with a renewed understanding of embodiment. What, then, is the stuff and force of relation that entangles bodies and worlds? What grants bodies their capacity both to exceed themselves and to be acted upon by outside forces? How do the surfaces of bodies come to be experienced and what might the outside impingements upon that experience mean for the body? What bodies, indeed, count as human and in what way – and do we, then, need an expanded definition of the human to account for what embodiment can be?

This chapter takes a necessarily delimited path through these and related questions to consider how the emergence of new theories of affect and embodiment engage with the posthuman. Beginning through what Gilles Deleuze has meant for western ontology of the body, this chapter addresses the affective turn in the humanities and social sciences and its consequences for how we understand affect, embodiment, and the human. Moving from conceptions of affect as autonomous intensity to the cultural politics of affect to the queering of embodiment, this chapter aims to show how attending to affect and embodiment as sites, subjects, and modes of critical inquiry leads to the limits of the human and of humanist modes of knowledge production.

## 4.1    Reinventing Western Ontologies

Both individually and in his writings with Felix Guattari, Deleuze sought to address problems that cut across or move through the field of life itself: problems of capitalism, of knowing, of creation, and of the human.[2] In doing so, Deleuze was always concerned with what philosophy – which he sees as the creation of concepts that do things to thought – might do to transform life. For Deleuze, life was not limited to the human but was, rather, inseparable from the heterogeneous continuum of existence.[3] His philosophy is thus not one of stasis but of process, which is to say of movement, composition, emergence, and becoming. In asking how things emerge and what they might become, rather than what they are, his primary antecedents and interlocutors were process philosophers such as William James, Henri Bergson, Alfred North Whitehead, and, most intensely and influentially, Baruch de Spinoza. From Spinoza, Deleuze adopts perhaps his core ontological proposition: that bodies – not just human bodies, but any body – emerge from a singular substance, a shared materialism of body and thought that constitutively undoes the Cartesian mind/body split.[4] This monistic substance is the infinite stuff of Life itself, capitalized to differentiate its intrinsic continuity of existence from the specific and senescent forms that life takes in any given body, whether human, animal, or vegetal.[5]

Like Spinoza, Deleuze sees the universe as monistic, a singular substance animated by what Rosi Braidotti calls a "raw cosmic energy" that self-expresses in individuating forms.[6] Deleuze calls this the *plane of immanence*, or "the plane of Nature, although nature has nothing to do with it, since on this plane there is no distinction between the natural and the artificial."[7] This plane "constitutes the absolute ground of philosophy ... the foundation on which it creates its concepts."[8] But immanence is not simply the concept of concepts, but rather that oneness of existence out of which philosophy seeks to produce concepts that fix, contour, or otherwise access the untamed chaos of existence. The plane of immanence is thus a transcendental field, but only if the transcendental is understood as radically empirical: not separate to life, but the necessary ground of *a life* in any and all forms. For Deleuze, this pure immanence is immanent only to itself – it is not related to some other substance, thing, or transcendent ideal. One consequence of this conception of a monistic universe, accessible to thought only through its inseparability from the plane of immanence, is the undoing of the fixed boundaries of bodies.

If we step back briefly, to consider how Deleuze, following Spinoza, defines a body (the capacity to affect and be affected), the entanglement of thinking beyond the human and affect theory swiftly becomes clear. Spinoza's conception of affect as the capacity of a body to act or be acted upon, taken up and elaborated by Deleuze, is (one of) the key site(s) out of which the turn from text and discourse to affect and body emerges. In their widely cited introduction to *The Affect Theory Reader*, Melissa Gregg and Greg Seigworth make this more-than-human relationality central to their capacious definition of the term: affect "is born in the midst of *in-between-ness* and resides as accumulative *beside-ness*," such that "with affect, a body is as much outside itself as in itself – webbed in its relations – until ultimately such firm distinctions cease to matter."[9] What this conception of the body makes possible, a fact evidenced by the way in which the affective turn has rippled (unevenly, variously, diversely, unexpectedly) across the humanities and social sciences, is sustained and nuanced attention to the limits of the human, to how bodies come to be and do in the world, to how worlds form and transform and dissolve. There is no space here to address that breadth, but in the remainder of this chapter, I aim to show how the refiguring of the body in affective terms enables new modes of engagement with the world and new possibilities for what bodies might become. All this, of course, tests the limits of humanism and, I will argue, requires us to think other than, before, through, and after the human.

In a short but evocative essay, "Ethology: Spinoza and Us," Deleuze describes bodies as "relations of motion and rest, speeds and slowness between particles" and the "capacity for affecting and being affected" (625). As Deleuze explains, this means that a body is "not defined by its form, nor by its organs or functions" and yet neither as "a substance or a subject" (626). Rather, bodies are modes, defined by relation to other bodies and to the world. Thus, we might ask about the degree of fixity or flux of any given body, the speed at which it is changing, the extent of its affecting other bodies or being affected by them. This Spinoza body, then, is constitutively beyond the human: all bodies function in just this way, animated by the vital materialism of existence, anthropomorphism be damned. Not only this, but philosophy must also conceive of the body as becoming, not being. As Deleuze and Guattari write in *A Thousand Plateaus*, "becoming produces nothing other than itself. . . . What is real is the becoming itself, the block of becoming, not the supposedly fixed terms through which the becoming passes" (238). Bodies that are always already becoming are bodies in continual composition, not contained within a form but always on the path to something otherwise. In philosophical terms, this means working from a foundation of process and non-fixity. Practically, it means understanding that the individual body no longer occupies center stage: unbound from the focus on interiorities and the barrier of the skin, bodies emerge, coalesce, and dissolve through their human and nonhuman extensions, much more multiply than singularly. Bodies – human and nonhuman, multiple and individuated – are enabled and constrained by the relations in which they are webbed, their resources and capacities for change, connection, signification, and more. As a subset of bodies in general, human bodies are thus necessarily posthuman, exceeding the confined frame of form, function, substance, and subject.

## 4.2   Embodiment after Affect

For Brian Massumi, affect is synonymous with intensity, which is to say that affect refers to intensities of experience that arise in and through bodily encounter.[10] Affect describes a forcefulness that is owned by neither one body nor another, but both constitutes and is constituted by those bodies. This intensity is asignifying: lacking form and structure it cannot contain any prior meaning, neither a definitive intentionality, nor a pre-given sociality. In contrast to emotion, which is recognized, individualized, and linguistically fixed by the human body, affect exceeds and enables bodies to become. "Actually existing, structured things live in and through that which escapes them," he writes. "Their autonomy is the autonomy of affect" (*Parables* 35). In Massumi's work, affect is what entangles the virtual, or all the potential becomings and capacities of bodies in encounter, with the actual, or the lived experience of bodies within worlds as they coalesce into distinct forms in time. Like Deleuze, Massumi places significant weight on encounter and event as the processes through which bodies come to matter.[11] Massumi's work, including his writings with Erin Manning, thus emphasizes thought as a bodily process, a "thinking-feeling" through which bodies co-compose themselves and the world, such that "thought and thing, subject and object, are not separate entities or substances" but rather "are irreducibly temporal modes of relation to experience itself."[12] Taking this proposition seriously means shifting the locus for critical inquiry from text, representation, and even the phenomenology of human experience to the dynamic, forceful relations through which bodies – including human bodies – are composed and experienced as bodies-in-the-world.

Refiguring embodiment as constitutively relational decenters the human and recenters the world itself, with its abundance of lively and inert forms of matter. Doing so recognizes that "human" relational embodiment is constitutively relation to the natural (a fraught term!), biotic, atmospheric, technological, and more. Extending feminist theories of embodiment that are often explicitly or implicitly grounded in monistic process philosophy, Astrida Neimanis argues that we are "bodies of water" and that rethinking "embodiment as watery stirs up considerable trouble for dominant Western and humanist understandings of embodiment, where bodies are figured as discrete and coherent individual subjects, and as fundamentally autonomous."[13] Recognizing that the human is simply one site of embodiment among many is "not to forsake our inescapable humanness, but to suggest that the human is always also more-than-human" (2). While for Neimanis this leads to a sustained and ongoing engagement with the wateriness of bodies, for others existence within a more-than-human ecology speaks to research practice itself. In their account of walking methodologies, Sarah E. Truman and Stephanie Springgay propose that "we forgo universal claims about how humans and nonhumans experience walking, and consider more-than-human ethics and politics of the material intra-actions of walking research."[14] Their work coheres upon and arises from research-creation events in which human bodies and accompanying questions, concepts, propositions, and objects co-compose with the more-than-human world. For Truman and Springgay, Neimanis, and other feminist theorists of the more-than-human, attending to affective intensities is essential to embodied research precisely because it is inseparable from encounter itself and thus to the becoming-with that underpins their research practice, ethics, and politics.[15]

The posthuman impetus of affect and embodiment theories not only enfolds the natural world, but also the technologically mediated. Indeed, the distinction between the natural and technological is increasingly undone by critical media studies theorists such as John Durham Peters and Andrew Murphie, each of whom argues in different ways that the world itself is composed of media.[16] Mediation is a crucial concept here because it describes what media do, how processes of translation, transformation, representation, and so on produce spaces of meaning, or how they render one thing accessible or available to another. Sarah Kember and Joanna Zylinska propose thinking of mediation itself as a vital process, one bound up with life itself and its transformation, translation, and movement between states.[17] Affect is, again, crucial to this move from understanding media as objects to conceiving of mediation as process. Anna Gibbs, for example, shows how mediation facilitates affective contagion, amplifying and modulating bodily intensities through image, sound, tone, and more.[18] Marie-Luise Angerer maps the zones of contact between interiors and exteriors of sensor-saturated environments to show how affective milieus complicate the status of the human, while Lisa Blackman attends to the affective and immaterial assemblages of human and nonhuman processes, particularly in the biomediation of bodies.[19] For Richard Grusin, affect plays a crucial, constitutive role in *premeditation*, or "the remediation of future events and affective states," which is not so much about how the *meaning* of the future is prefigured as it is about how futures are generated within and through affective processes of mediation.[20]

Common to this scholarship on the entanglement of affect and mediation is a recognition of the limits of representation, the way in which the cultural, political, social, and ecological forms and forces that shape human and more-than-human life exceed, refuse, or otherwise escape representational modes of knowing. In my own work, this drives an inquiry into witnessing experiences of trauma at both human and climatic scales, while a similar push to understand more-than-human, collective, and intergenerational trauma as inextricable from understanding life in the Anthropocene reworks the established, humanist frames that prevail in trauma studies.[21] Yet, this move to address experiences and aesthetics through nonrepresentational modes and theories is taken up far beyond trauma, perhaps most influentially in the nonrepresentational theory of Nigel Thrift and Erin Manning, whose writing is increasingly interested in how thought itself is far more diverse, nuanced, embodied, and felt than in the neurotypical form that dominates the academy.[22] Eliza Steinbock shows how trans embodiment emerges within cinematic transitions – cuts and sutures among frames, genres, words, and images – that shimmer in nonbinary ways to trouble "assumptions of a strict male or female grammar for subjects on-screen and off."[23] At stake in the ethnographic writings of Kathleen Stewart is attention to what she calls worlding, "an intimate, compositional process of dwelling in spaces that bears, gestures, gestates, worlds."[24] For Stewart, an affective conception of embodiment makes this possible by enabling attention to how "things matter not because of how they are represented but because they have qualities, rhythms, forces, relations, and movements" (445). And this is perhaps a fitting point at which to leave the question of what embodiment after affect means for academic thought and ask instead how it demands a reimagining of cultural politics.

## 4.3 The Cultural Politics of Affect

The turn to affect has prompted new interest in how everyday life is composed and textured by objects, relations, attachments, economies, and sticky signs that not only determine the signification of particular bodies but also shape their very surfaces. This is the ongoing project of Sara Ahmed's significant work. For Ahmed, the crucial question is less what affects *are* but what they *do* – or, rather, what emotions do, since she prefers that term, inflected with a rather affective, relational understanding that holds more fluidity than is typical in the sociology of emotions. She argues that "emotions are not 'in' either the individual or the social, but produce the surfaces and boundaries that allow the individual and social to be delineated as if they are objects."[25] As a consequence, "it is through emotions, or how we respond to objects and others, that surfaces or boundaries are made: the 'I' and the 'we' are shaped by, and even take the shape of, contact with others" (10). Embodiment is not at all static or individualized, but rather produced through relational dynamics with other bodies and with objects, institutions, discourses, signs, texts, and more. If the "autonomous" strain of affect theory leaves itself open to critique for its ambivalent relationship to power and politics, Ahmed's work is very much concerned with how power flows through and is generated by cultural encounter.

Situating the forcefulness of emotion in the encounter between bodies and understanding bodies as *surfaced* into particular subjectivities through affective encounters is as much an undoing of the delimited, bounded figure of the human as is that of Deleuzean ontology. As Ahmed writes, "emotions work by working through signs and on bodies to materialize the surfaces and boundaries that are lived as worlds" (191). This materialization is not an egalitarian process, but rather the way in which certain bodies are designated as other, as threat, as gendered and racialized, as not human at all – and it is also the site of feminist, decolonial, anti-racist, and anti-capitalist struggle.[26] Ahmed maps the cultural politics of emotions to what hate, fear, love, disgust, pain, and shame do to particular bodies, communities of bodies, and groups and institutions. She shows, for example, how disgust works to figure the terrorist body as one from which we must recoil lest it stain or soil.[27] This is a "pulling that feels almost involuntary, as if our bodies were thinking for us, on behalf of us," yet "disgust binds objects together in the very moment that objects become attributed with bad feeling, as 'being' sickening" (84, 88). So it is that "naming of disgust metonymically sticks these signs together, such that the terror and fear become associated with bodies that are already recognized as 'Middle Eastern'" (97). These Middle Eastern bodies become disgusting, unable to loosen what has stuck – the feeling of an incursion, of something bad having "got into" the body politic – and so cannot but be identified as terrorist bodies. Such bodies "are constructed as non-human, as beneath and below the bodies of the disgusted" (97). In her writings on war, torture, and politics, Judith Butler makes the related argument that mourning and grief are affects structured by the frames of war and violence to render certain bodies outside the status of the human.[28] "Without grievability," Butler writes, "there is no life, or, rather, there is something living that is other than life" (*Precarious* 15). Categories of human and nonhuman, in other words, depend not only on language and matter but also on emotional and affective relations.

Embodied relational dynamics such as these are not so much asignifying as over-signifying: they turn signs into lived experiences of oppression, violence, contingency, and subjection. There is potential friction, then, between the radical cultural project of Ahmed or the political critique of Butler, and the more philosophically inflected writing of Massumi and others, yet also a shared desire to critique and reimagine what it is that shapes and makes the human. This question of how particular bodies are shaped is not only one for cultural critique in general, but also for post-humanist thought itself. As Zakiyyah Iman Jackson has forcefully argued, posthumanism that resorts to a "beyond the human" can prove itself inaccessible to those bodies – Black, crip, queer, colonized, Asian – that might never have been fully afforded the category of human to begin with.[29] One crucial role for theories of affect and embodiment in post-humanism might be to help avoid posthuman thought from becoming "an attempt to move beyond race, and in particular blackness," which Jackson argues "cannot be escaped but only disavowed or dissimulated in prevailing articulations of movement 'beyond the human'" (216). Here, then, is a politics of affect that is radical, cultural, embodied, and very much concerned with *how* differences of subjectivity, rights, mobility, citizenship, and more come to be distributed and attached to particular bodies – and to whether those bodies can be subjects at all.

## 4.4  Queering the Human

Judith Butler was not the only poststructuralist to problematize essentialized identities, but her books *Gender Trouble* and *Bodies That Matter* proved crucial to the emergence of queer theory and its challenge to humanism.[30] While not explicitly posthuman, Butler's nuanced folding together of Foucault, Derrida, and Lacan has implications for how – and against what – the human is formed. Her theorization of the performativity of gender and the discursive materialization of sex shows materiality to be discursive and discourse to be material. She argues that "regulatory norms of 'sex' work in a performative fashion to constitute the materiality of bodies and, more specifically, to materialize the body's sex, to materialize sexual difference in the service of the consolidation of the heterosexual imperative" (*Bodies* 2). For Butler's account to hold, matter must be understood "as a process of materialization that stabilizes over time to produce the effect of boundary, fixity, and surface" (9). If matter is not only unstable but also shaped by and shaping of discourse, then the "construct-edness" of particular identities is much more than linguistic: the body is always more than itself, inseparable from normative discursive formations that refuse the status of subject to certain bodies, or apply subjecthood differentially or partially to others.

While Butler's relationship to affect and material embodiment is com-plicated, her work helped inaugurate the transdisciplinary body of work that became known as queer theory. Scholars such as Eve Kosofsky Sedgwick, Teresa Brennan, and Lauren Berlant work more centrally with questions of affect and materiality.[31] Taking up and then moving from Butler, Sedgwick shows how queerness and shame are co-constitutive of particular social and political subjectivities, describing "queer performativ-ity" as "a strategy for the production of meaning and being, in relation to the affect shame and to the later and related fact of stigma."[32] Sedgwick's work shows how bodies are not only imprinted with language, but also permeated by and performed through embodied affect, experienced in and through time. For Brennan, subjects are constituted through affective transmission with other bodies, sites, moments, and moods.[33] Gerda Roelvink and Magdalena Zolkos, in their writing on affect and posthu-manism, note that such "different gestural and sensory exchanges and communications between bodies (olfaction, tactility, proprioception, etc.) mean that subjects are reimagined as porous, absorptive of and responsive to their ecologies."[34] Writing on sentimentality and the "cruel optimism" of neoliberal attachments, Berlant shows how the body politic laminates onto queer bodies such that embodiment is both materially felt and diffusely dispersed.[35] Queer theories of embodiment have thus recog-nized the affective quality of embodiment and the embodied nature of subjectivity from the beginning.

Indeed, as Dana Luciano and Mel Y. Chen note, "many of queer theory's foundational texts interrogate, implicitly or explicitly, the nature of the 'human' in its relation to the queer, both in their attention to how sexual norms themselves constitute and regulate hierarchies of humanness, and as they work to unsettle those norms and the default forms of humanness they uphold."³⁶ As Jack [Judith] Halberstam and Ira Livingstone point out in their introduction to the pathbreaking collection *Posthuman Bodies*, "the constructionist body is not equal to the task if it is merely a compensatory or reactionary opponent to the humanist body."³⁷ Rather, posthuman bodies "emerge at nodes where bodies, bodies of discourse, and discourses of bodies intersect to foreclose any easy distinction between actor and stage, between send/receive, channel, code, message, context" (2). While queer theory certainly seeks to undo narrow notions of identity to enable new, diverse, unfixed, and fluid forms of self-identity, its larger project might be understood as "undoing 'normal' categories."³⁸ While much posthumanist theory has sought to reimagine bodily possibilities beyond the normative human, queer theory emphasizes the role of gender and sexuality in those possibilities and how the world that the body becomes-with might be understood through nonnormative logics of time, space, place, and animacy (Springgay and Truman 8–9). Chen's influential work on animacy hierarchies – the degree of animacy or inanimateness granted to different bodies, particularly in language – shows the complex ways in which disability, race, class, sex, and sexuality are shaped, constrained, and marginalized through discourse, affect, and materiality.³⁹ For Chen, queering is crucial to transgressions of animacy and the attendant troubling of the life-nonlife binary to which their work is addressed. Queer life is thus also always precarious, such that queer thought has as its "primary catalyst" the "desire to persist in the face of precarity" (Luciano and Chen 193). In allegiance with the wider project of posthumanism, queer theory has thus sought to expand what might qualify as human in the liberal humanist sense, and in doing so it aims to queer the human itself and to locate identities and forms of life in ways that transgress or destabilize the human via gender and sexuality.

Yet the realities through which queer bodies are accepted within and authorized by mainstream cultural politics can produce new exclusionary norms that enter into convivial, rather than oppositional or resistant, relations to militarism, nationalism, empire, capitalism, and the state. Jasbir Puar argues that the contemporary historical conjuncture marked by the explicit "coming out of the closet" of the United States as empire is closely linked to the lure of explicit inclusion within the nation for (some) queer bodies historically denied belonging.⁴⁰ But the price of entry into "homonationalism" is the "segregation and disqualification of racial and sexual others from the national imaginary" (*Terrorist* 2). As such, homo-nationalism is not some kind of utopian validation (she points out that sexual others continue to face all sorts of violence), but rather the process for simultaneously co-opting certain languages and identities both to maintain their marginalization (as exception) and, at the same time, to position others as terrorist. Puar reads queer bodies, such as the turbaned Sikh man or the South Asian diasporic drag queen, as terrorist assemblages, a "cacophony of informational flows, energetic intensities, bodies, and practices that undermine coherent identity and even queer anti-identity narratives" (*Terrorist* 222). Doing so necessitates attending to the ambivalent, complex, nuanced, changeable, and unknowable ways in which these terrorist assemblages are adopted into and excluded from the nation. The queer bodies within such assemblages cannot be limited to a material, contained biological body: their evocation as the distinction between life and death, biopolitics and necropolitics, necessarily depends on an affected and affecting conception of embodiment that exceeds, destabilizes, and ultimately undoes the "human."

The relationship between this enduring yet narrow genre of the "human" – white, hetero, and cis-male – and the biopolitical management of disability is taken up in Puar's recent work on debility and capacity.[41] Working with queer, disability, and critical race theory to analyze the strategic deployment of debilitation and capacitation in neoliberal biopolitics, Puar exposes both the tendency in affect theory to assume the integrity of the human body and in posthumanism to focus on more-than-human potentiality rather than the subhuman or not-quite-human. As her analysis makes clear, thinking through disability offers important theoretical correctives to the intersection of affect theory and posthumanism, and an avenue into the kinds of coalition-building vital to the political struggle for just futures in which "bodily capacities and debilities are embraced rather than weaponized" (*Right* xxiv).

## 4.5   Conclusion

Navigating similar waters to this chapter, Roelvink and Zolkos note that one point of entry into the "mutual connectedness" of affect and posthumanism "is the idea of aliveness, or animation" (3). This vital – in every sense of the word – interconnection might serve, then, as an exit point for this chapter. Its necessarily brief exploration of the rich mutual interconnection among theories of affect, embodiment, and posthumanism shows how questions of what bodies are and how they are composed, how they affect and are affected, have significant implications for thinking, making, living, and dying in more-than-human worlds. The sheer multiplicity of approaches to affect – from the Spinozan strain of

Deleuze and Massumi to the intersectional feminist and queer theories of embodiment of Butler, Ahmed, Puar, and others – speaks to its vibrant capacity to rethink how we understand bodies and their relations. While the alliance between affect and posthuman theory might not always be an easy one, these overlapping fields of scholarship share an insistent commitment to displacing exclusionary knowledges. Just as posthuman thought has sought to decenter the human from its privileged status in western scholarship, politics, and culture, so to have theories of affect aimed to undo the primacy of cognition and reason. Those projects remain urgent yet are also more readily grasped and undertaken when the body, like the human, is understood as blurry, relational, situated, and subject to all manner of energies, materialities, forces, and others.[42]

## Notes

1. For more on the affective turn, see Patricia Clough, *The Affective Turn: Theorizing the Social* (Durham: Duke University Press, 2007).
2. Claire Colebrook, *Gilles Deleuze* (London: Routledge, 2001), 8.
3. Gilles Deleuze, *Pure Immanence: Essays on a Life*, trans. Anne Boyman (New York: Zone Books 2001).
4. Gilles Deleuze, "Ethology: Spinoza and Us," in Jonathan Crary and Sanford Kwinter (eds.), *Incorporations* trans. Robert Hurley (New York Zone Books, 1992), 629.
5. For more on the notion of life itself, see Chapter 8 of this volume.
6. Rosi Braidotti, *The Posthuman* (Cambridge: Polity, 2013), 55.
7. Gilles Deleuze and Felix Guattari, *A Thousand Plateaus: Capitalism and Schizophrenia*, trans. Brian Massumi (Minneapolis: University of Minnesota Press 1987), 266.
8. Gilles Deleuze and Feliz Guattari, *What Is Philosophy?* trans. Hugh Tomlinson and Graham Burchell (New York: Columbia University Press, 1994), 41.
9. Melissa Gregg and Gregory J. Seigworth, "An Inventory of Shimmers," in Melissa Gregg and Gregory J. Seigworth (eds.), *The Affect Theory Reader* (Durham: Duke University Press 2010), 2, 3.
10. Brian Massumi, "The Autonomy of Affect," *Cultural Critique* 31 (1995), 83–109. Brian Massumi, *Parables for the Virtual: Movement, Affect, Sensation* (Durham: Duke University Press, 2002).
11. Brian Massumi, *Semblance and Event: Activist Philosophy and the Occurrent Arts* (Cambridge: The MIT Press, 2011).
12. Massumi, *Semblance* 34. See also Erin Manning and Brian Massumi, *Thought in the Act: Passages in the Ecology of Experience* (Minneapolis: University of Minnesota Press, 2014).

13. Astrida Neimanis, *Bodies of Water: Posthuman Feminist Phenomenology* (London: Bloomsbury, 2017), 2.

14. Stephanie Springgay and Sarah E. Truman, *Walking Methodologies in a More-than-Human World: WalkingLab* (London: Routledge, 2018), 11.

15. Other work on embodiment in a more-than-human world concerns atmospheric envelopments (Derek McCormack, *Atmospheric Things: On the Allure of Elemental Envelopment* [Durham: Duke University Press, 2018]), mobilities (Peter Adey, *Aerial Life: Spaces, Mobilities, Affects* [Malden: Wiley-Blackwell, 2010]) and perspectives (Caren Kaplan, *Aerial Aftermaths: Wartime from Above* [Durham: Duke University Press, 2018]).

16. John Durham Peters, *The Marvelous Clouds* (Chicago: University of Chicago Press, 2015). Andrew Murphie, "On Being Affected: Feeling in the Folding of Multiple Catastrophes," *Cultural Studies* 32 (1) (2018), 18–42. For more on digital media and posthumanism, see Chapter 5 of this volume.

17. Sarah Kember and Joanna Zylinska, *Life after New Media: Mediation as a Vital Process* (Cambridge: MIT Press, 2012).

18. Anna Gibbs, "Contagious Feelings: Pauline Hanson and the Epidemiology of Affect," *Australian Humanities Review* 24 (2001), online.

19. Marie-Luise Angerer, *Ecology of Affect: Intensive Milieus and Contingent Encounters*, trans. Gerrit Jackson (Lüneborg: Meson Press, 2017). Lisa Blackman, *Immaterial Bodies: Affect, Embodiment, Mediation* (London: SAGE Publications, 2012).

20. Richard Grusin, *Premediation: Affect and Mediality after 9/11* (New York: Palgrave Macmillan, 2010), 6.

21. Mark Richardson, *Gestures of Testimony: Torture, Trauma, and Affect in Literature* (New York: Bloomsbury, 2016). Mark Richardson, "Climate Trauma, or the Affects of the Catastrophe to Come," *Environmental Humanities* 10 (1) (2018), 1–19. Meera Atkinson, *The Poetics of Transgenerational Trauma* (New York: Bloomsbury, 2017). Claire Colebrook, *Death of the Posthuman: Essays on Extinction, Vol. 1* (Ann Arbor: Open Humanities Press, 2014).

22. Nigel Thrift, *Non-Representational Theory: Space, Politics, Affect* (Hoboken: Taylor and Francis, 2008). Erin Manning, *Always More than One: Individuation's Dance* (Durham: Duke University Press, 2013). Erin Manning, *The Minor Gesture* (Durham: Duke University Press, 2016).

23. Eliza Steinbock, *Shimmering Images: Trans Cinema, Embodiment, and the Aesthetics of Change* (Durham: Duke University Press, 2019), 3–4.

24. Kathleen Stewart, "Atmospheric Attunements," *Environment and Planning D: Society and Space* 29 (3) (2011), 445.

25. Sara Ahmed, *The Cultural Politics of Emotion* (New York: Routledge 2004), 10.

26. Some of the more philosophical interventions in posthumanism have not been sufficiently attentive to these concerns, which is one of the key reasons that a number of scholars in queer, critical race, gender, and indigenous studies have criticized the "post" prefix, as discussed below.

27. In a similar vein, Kiarina A. Kordela ("Monsters of Biopower: Terror(Ism) and Horror in the Era of Affect," *Philosophy Today; Charlottesville* 60 (1)

[2016], 194–205) shows how visceral responses such as this attach themselves to certain bodies as seemingly "authentic" responses that reveal a kind of "truth" about "undesirable" bodies.

28. Judith Butler, *Precarious Life: The Powers of Mourning and Violence* (London: Verso, 2004). Judith Butler, *Frames of War: When Is Life Grievable?* (London: Verso, 2009).

29. Zakiyyah Iman Jackson, "Outer Worlds: The Persistence of Race in Movement 'Beyond the Human.'" *GLQ: A Journal of Lesbian and Gay Studies* 21 (2) (2015), 215–18.

30. Judith Butler, *Gender Trouble: Feminism and the Subversion of Identity* (London: Routledge, 1990). Judith Butler, *Bodies That Matter: On the Discursive Limits of "Sex"* (New York: Routledge, 1993).

31. As do other thinkers foundational to queer theory, including J. Jack Halberstam, José Esteban Muñoz, and Rei Terada, although with arguably less influence on the broader sweep of affect studies.

32. Eve Kosofsky Sedgwick, *Touching Feeling: Affect, Pedagogy, Performativity* (Durham: Duke University Press, 2003), 61.

33. Teresa Brennan, *The Transmission of Affect* (Ithaca: Cornell University Press, 2004).

34. Gerda Roelvink and Magdalena Zolkos, "Posthumanist Perspectives on Affect," *Angelaki* 20(3) (2015), 9.

35. Lauren Berlant, *The Female Complaint: The Unfinished Business of Sentimentality in American Culture* (Durham: Duke University Press, 2008). Lauren Berlant, *Cruel Optimism* (Durham: Duke University Press, 2011).

36. Dana Luciano and Mel Y. Chen, "Has the Queer Ever Been Human?" *GLQ: A Journal of Lesbian and Gay Studies* 21(2–3) (2015), 186.

37. Ira Livingston and Judith Halberstam, *Posthuman Bodies* (Bloomington: Indiana University Press 1995), 2.

38. Donna Haraway, "Companion Species, Mis-Recognition, and Queer Worlding," in N. Giffney and M. J. Hird (eds.), *Queering the Non/Human* (Burlington: Ashgate 2008), xxiv.

39. Mel Y. Chen, *Animacies: Biopolitics, Racial Mattering and Queer Affect* (Durham: Duke University Press, 2012).

40. Jasbir Puar, *Terrorist Assemblages: Homonationalism in Queer Times* (Durham: Duke University Press, 2007).

41. Jasbir Puar, *Right to Maim: Debility, Capacity, Disability* (Durham: Duke University Press, 2017).

42. I wish to acknowledge the Bedegal, Bidjigal, and Gadigal People of the Eora nation upon whose land I live and work, and pay respect to their elders, past, present, and emerging. This research was supported by an Australian Research Council Discovery Early Career Research Award (DE190100486). The views expressed herein are those of the author and are not necessarily those of the Australian Government or Australian Research Council.

# CHAPTER 5

# *Requiem for a Digital Humanist*

## Marcel O'Gorman

The purpose of these topological extensions and distensions is not to claim what existents *are* for *them* but how all my friends and their existents improvisationally struggle to *manifest and endure* in contemporary settler late liberalism.[1]

## 5.1 Kyrie

"Whose file is this?" That was my first thought when, having been asked to write a chapter about the digital humanities after the human, I performed a keyword search of my hard drive and uncovered a file simply called "digital_humanities.doc." Was this a student's assignment? A compilation of notes from a conference? As it turns out, I had come across an article I had written a dozen years earlier, submitted to *Digital Humanities Quarterly* (*DHQ*), and completely forgotten about. The following lines open the discussion:

> As I learned from the blog of an expert in humanities computing, attendees at last year's meeting of the Text Analysis Developers Alliance (TADA) "instantly gobbled up" X-Large T-Shirts emblazoned with a hand yielding a large hammer and the slogan: "Real Humanists Make Tools."

The found file rearticulates some of the arguments I made in my book *E-Crit*, which reproaches digital humanists for suffering from archive fever, celebrating the extra-largeness of data, and desperately aligning themselves with the prevailing technobureaucracy of contemporary universities.[2] I never heard back from *DHQ*. In hindsight, I'm glad this relatively unmerciful essay was not archived online. The file exists instead as a fossil of sorts, a deposit on the hard drive of my laptop, a lapse in memory, and a miscommunication.

This chapter, which I have called a requiem, will not rehearse the accusations I have made previously as a curmudgeon on the sidelines of the digital humanities.[3] My interest in the digital humanities has taken a different turn since 2007, and I am now inclined otherwise. In fact, inclination itself, bending, reclining even, is more what I have in mind. This is a timely occasion for etymology: *requiem*, accusative form of the Latin word *requies*, refers to being quiet, to resting. It is what follows labor. With this in mind, I am not seeking to compose an elaborate death wish, an unmerciful laying to rest of a much-contested discipline; the requiem I have in mind quite simply follows the labor of a single, reluctant digital humanist. This seems appropriate, given that I have parasitically followed the digital humanities, always a step or two behind the curve, more than I have practiced them – at least according to narrow definitions of the digital humanities.

"Real Humanists Make Tools." The injunction, especially as a T-shirt motto, is charged with a certain magnetism. It brings to mind, subliminally, the title of Richard Feirstein's 1984 book *Real Men Don't Eat Quiche: A Guidebook to All That Is Truly Masculine.* I would like to think that the T-shirt's digital humanities injunction strikes the same sarcastic tone as Feirstein's book, which actually pokes fun at masculine stereotypes. But I'm not sure if this is the case, and I wonder if irony is what compelled a digital-humanities-schooled feminist acquaintance of mine, for example, to express unabashed pride in her ownership of one of these coveted T-shirts. There is a seductive power dynamic in the phrase "Real Humanists Make Tools," even a call to action. Combined with the iconic image of a hand wielding a hammer, the T-shirt cannot help but evoke the revolutionary spirit of Soviet labor.

Long before maker culture hit mainstream, making its way to the White House even, the digital humanities had adopted *homo faber* as a mascot.[4] But this spirit was not summoned without consequences, which are documented in articles and blog posts by digital humanities scholars,[5] culminating perhaps in yet another T-shirt-worthy mantra, "Less yack. More hack."[6] It is tempting to read the "Real Humanists Make Tools" T-shirt today in the context of Debbie Chachra's influential apologia "Why I Am Not a Maker," which questions the politics of making as a manly justification of certain types of labor that marginalize the work of service and care, forms of labor not usually associated with men.[7] Chachra's thesis might be summed up in the following passage from her essay:

> A quote often attributed to Gloria Steinem says: "We've begun to raise daughters more like sons ... but few have the courage to raise our sons more like our daughters". Maker culture, with its goal to get everyone

access to the traditionally male domain of making, has focused on the first. But its success means that it further devalues the traditionally female domain of caregiving, by continuing to enforce the idea that only making things is valuable.

If making is going to persist as an activity of digital humanities scholarship, then it must be reconfigured in ways that foster desire, care, and repair.

## 5.2    Gloria

*Homo Faber*, Henri Bergson suggests, is characterized by a specific type of intelligence: "the faculty of manufacturing artificial objects, especially tools to make tools, and of indefinitely varying the manufacture."[8] Half a century later, Hannah Arendt painstakingly questions this glorification of *homo faber* by elaborating on the modern political conditions that shape man-the-maker. For Arendt, modernity, buttressed by a mania for automation, has conditioned the following attitudes of *homo faber*, among others:

> His instrumentalization of the world, his confidence in tools and in the productivity of the maker of artificial objects, his trust in the all-comprehensive range of the means-end category, his conviction that every issue can be solved and every human motivation reduced to the principle of utility, his sovereignty.[9]

The question of sovereignty is key here, since much of Arendt's discussion rests on the historical transformation of *homo faber* from a contemplative being to a busy means-and-ends being. Arendt roots her argument in Plato's dialogue with Protagoras about whether "man is the measure of all things," an often-mistranslated credo that nevertheless embodies what Arendt calls an "anthropocentrism."[10] Protagoras sets up *homo faber* as an instrumentalizer that "will eventually help himself to everything and consider everything that is as a mere means for himself" (159).[11]

Instrumentality was perhaps my first instinct when I began to conduct research for this chapter. My initial strategy started with the following questions: "How has posthumanism been adopted by the digital humanities? Is it possible to calculate such a thing?" I came up with a strategy that would facilitate an experimental approach to these questions. I would look for instances of the word posthuman in the entire catalog of *DHQ*. But this led to yet another question: "How would a real digital humanist take on this task?" This led me to send an e-mail message to Geoffrey Rockwell, who responded with characteristic generosity, as follows.

What I would do is:

1. Manually copy the text of one year of DHQ into an XML file. I would jut [sic] put the minimal XML like:

```
<collection>
<item number="1" year="2018" url="the.url.here">
<title>the title here</title>
<author>the author's name in some standard form
like last, first here</author>
<content>...the text of the article. </content>
</item>
<item>...</item>
...lots more items
</collection>
```

I would then toss it into Voyant.[12]

Voyant, developed by Rockwell and Stéphan Sinclair, is "a web-based reading and analysis environment for digital texts."[13] I was familiar with this tool since I had tinkered with it previously to generate a word cloud from a single online essay. Back then, all I had to do was insert the essay's URL into Voyant and voilà, the word cloud magically appeared. But now, I had been tasked with something entirely different and admittedly daunting: "Manually copy the text of one year of DHQ into an XML file," Rockwell proposed. To generate a full corpus, I would have to manually copy and paste twelve years' worth of *DHQ* articles. Whereas Rockwell and Sinclair had clearly established themselves as *homo faber*, I was feeling the pinch of *animal laborans*.[14] But perhaps this is a false distinction. The arduous process described by Rockwell would involve me in the making of a tool (a corpus) to make an argument about digital humanities and posthumanism. In Voyant, Rockwell and Sinclair have created a tool for the production of tools.

Arendt's discussion of *homo faber* was revisited recently by Richard Sennett in *The Craftsman*, an almost hagiographic ode to those who engage in manual labor.[15] Sennett challenges what he views as Arendt's unfair treatment of *homo laborans*, a treatment that "slights the practical man or woman at work" (7). In Sennett's view, Arendt raises *homo faber* above *homo laborans*, and he sums up her argument by accusing her of executing a "false division": "Whereas *Animal laborans* is fixated on the question 'How?' *Homo faber* asks 'Why?'" (7). But Sennett seems to have missed the mark here. Arendt's argument does not hinge on a glorification of *homo faber* over *animal laborans*. Her point is that modern technology has changed the very nature of *homo faber*. What used to be a contemplative animal has become a calculative animal, shifting the focus "away from the question of what a thing is and what kind of thing was to be produced to the question of how and through which means and processes it had come into being and could be reproduced" (Arendt 304). If anything, Arendt's argument is that *homo faber* used to ask "What?" but now it asks "How?" – and this may be one way of understanding certain strains of the digital humanities.

## 5.3    Credo

Perhaps out of sheer laziness, I decided to forego Rockwell's instructions and rely on tools that were more readily at hand. I simply entered the word "posthuman" into the search field on the home page of *DHQ*. This yielded three pages of results, for a total of twenty-four articles that contain the word "posthuman." I then opened each article, one at a time, and used the find function in my browser to search for instances of the word. I recorded all the data in pencil on a piece of paper next to my laptop. Here is what I found:

- The word "posthuman," including variations (posthumanist, posthumanism), occurs 57 times within the entire *DHQ* corpus.
- Twelve of these instances refer to N. Katherine Hayles' book *How We Became Posthuman*.
- Six articles include *How We Became Posthuman* in the Works Cited, but do not discuss the book at all in the body of the text.
- One article includes the word "posthuman" in the title but does not discuss the term at all in the body of the text.
- One article includes a single instance each of the words "intra-action" and "entanglement," terms that seem to invoke posthumanist concepts proposed by Karen Barad. But Barad is neither mentioned in the article nor included in the works cited.

Several conclusions might be drawn from this dataset, including the possibility that there is pressure to pay lip service to the concept of posthumanism itself. Perhaps relatedly, the act of invoking Hayles' *How We Became Posthuman* in the works cited seems to have become ritualized among contributors to *DHQ*. But I am more interested in the process of gathering this data than in the content itself.[16]

My search for the posthuman in *DHQ* might serve as a buttress for Gary Hall's specific formulation of the "There Are No Digital Humanities" argument.[17] Conversely, what Hall seems to argue is that there are no contemporary humanities *without* the digital, that is, no non-digital humanities. Or in his words, "the digital is not something that can now be added to the humanities – for the simple reason that the (supposedly predigital) humanities can be seen to have already had an understanding of and engagement with computing and the digital" (135). In this context, one might ask whether my use of simple search and find functions, perfectly plebeian digital tools, to arrive at the data above, counts as digital humanities work. Adherents to the "Real Humanists Make Tools" credo would likely say "no." This data was assembled by means of readily available, built-in tools for average consumers, not by means of tools I built myself. It might be more productive to say that the dataset above was created not by my use of tools, but by the use of technics. With this idea in hand, I will propose a modification to Hall's corrective. Rather than suggesting that there are no humanities without the digital, I want to focus on the idea that there are no humanities without technics and, to push things further, that there is no human without the technical. Or in the words of Bernard Stiegler, "The human invents himself in the technical"[18] (141). This is a credo by which the human both lives and dies.[19]

This conceptual leap from digital tools to what has been called originary technicity – the idea that humans are only human because of an evolutionary accident of technics – has been explored by Federica Frabetti, among others. In Frabetti's words, "the human itself is always already constituted in relation to its own technologies (be they a stone implement, language, writing, or the digital computer)."[20] The notion of originary technicity complicates instrumental conceptions of technology. As Frabetti puts it, "the term 'originary technicity' assumes a paradoxical character only if one remains within the instrumental understanding of technology; if technology were instrumental, it could not be originary – that is, constitutive of the human" (141). Frabetti makes this statement as part of her effort to extend the digital humanities more deeply into the field of media studies, or more precisely, into media theory. For Frabetti, this involves a foray into the world of software studies, but her call for a "close, even intimate, engagement with digitality" (169) could easily wander elsewhere, even into the forest of feminist new materialism.

Stiegler's conception of originary technicity relies heavily on the work of French anthropologist André Leroi-Gourhan.[21] In *Gesture and Speech*, Leroi-Gourhan weaves a compelling tale about the origins of the human species, rooted in a concept of exteriorization:

> The whole of our evolution has been oriented toward placing outside
> ourselves what in the rest of the animal world is achieved inside by species
> adaptation. The most striking material fact is certainly the "freeing" of tools,
> but the fundamental fact is really the freeing of the word and our unique
> ability to transfer our memory to a social organism outside ourselves. (236)

Exteriorization, for Leroi-Gourhan, is key to the heroic tale of *homo erectus*.
Through the evolution of technics, the proto-hominid liberated his hands
from their role in quadruped mobility, eventually leading to the upright
stance that put the skull in an optimal position for bipedal locomotion and
expansive brain development. Man is an "accident of automobility," says
Stiegler (121).

This ur-tale of exteriorization brings us back to the beginning of this
chapter, back to the moment of origin when a search for "digital humanities" on my computer led to a forgotten file. Rather than viewing this
event as evidence of the need to make better tools, it might also be
considered as an embodiment of exteriorization itself. Once the essay was
out of my head and onto my hard drive, I had rendered it forgettable.[22]
I am not going to replay Socrates' well-worn tale of Theuth and Thamus
from Plato's *Phaedrus*. That yarn has been told too many times by media
scholars, including me and Geoffrey Rockwell.[23] Instead, recalling
Frabetti's appeal for a "close, even intimate, engagement with digitality,"
I will turn directly to a curious collection of digital objects designed to
explore technical exteriorization.

## 5.4    Sanctus

Turning away from the digital humanities and back toward human technicity results in a curious outcome: the end of the human itself.[24] Or, at
least the end of a certain conception of humanity. It seems appropriate here
to reference what might be called the posthumanist patron saint of the
digital humanities, N. Katherine Hayles, who describes the posthuman
subject as "an amalgam, a collection of heterogeneous components,
a material-informational entity whose boundaries undergo continuous
construction and reconstruction" (3). This conception of the posthuman
can lend itself to transhumanist fantasies of computer-enabled, disembodied consciousness, a sort of angelic teleology for the human species. Or it
can lead instead, as Cary Wolfe suggests, to the notion that there is no
unified human subject, given that the human is "always radically other,
already in- or ahuman in our very being."[25] How might this posthumanist
perspective be integrated into digital humanities practices?

One way I have attempted to answer this question is by engaging in what I have called *Applied Media Theory*. This practice has led me to create projects that interrogate human technicity by combining digital media with curious objects such as a treadmill, a penny-farthing bicycle, a classic wedge-shaped coffin, and a sixteen-foot cedar and canvas canoe.[26] All of these projects invite participants into a technical milieu designed to provoke reflection on exteriorization, human finitude, and the sensual borders among flesh, circuits, and other conspicuous things. While I have tried to control the context of these projects, presenting them at times as the handiwork of a digital humanities scholar rather than as the offspring of an artistic ego, these efforts have mostly failed. So have the projects. Hardware breaks down, communication protocols change constantly, and software requires constant upgrading or hits the end of a life cycle. Everything, in the end, ceases to be supported. I have been outstripped by these uncanny objects-to-think-with, unable to meet their demand for a degree of technical expertise and time investment that I cannot provide. As a result, these projects have fallen into a limbo between digital humanities and digital art, and as such, they are homeless, locked outside of the necessary infrastructural contexts that might be able to provide them with care and repair. For me, the entire state of affairs can only be described in terms of vulnerability, an acknowledgement of which has inclined me to consider my own situatedness as a white, male scholar tangled in an infrastructure of digital components that are possibly destined to become toxic waste.

## 5.5  Benedictus

Heavy rubber blades swept away the freezing rain balls that smashed against the broad windshield. The mechanical rhythm of the wipers, combined with the burnt air forced through plastic louvres on the dashboard, served up a lethal concoction, an invitation to slumber. This is the last place he wanted to be: in this rented twenty-foot U-Haul truck, on this highway, in this dead countryside. But it was a necessary pilgrimage.

The journey began with a few flat words, delivered business-like in an e-mail message.

Hi there,

I hope you are doing well. I wanted to touch base about the projects in the reception area. We have several large events planned in the near future and the

feedback from our team has been that the canoe and other objects are too large
to continue to display in this area.

Unfortunately, I have to request that you remove them by the end of
November.

We've also noticed that the arcade cabinet is frequently not working. Is this
something you could look in to?

Thanks!

Kind Regards,

Sandra Barry-Stryker

What were once repositories of desire and vehicles for play had now
become clutter. This prompted him not only to remove the objects from
display, but to indelicately cram them into the cargo box of a rented truck
and head south toward LaSalle, Ontario, where they would be stored in an
old barn on a neglected strip of farmland.

Now sleep threatened even this project. A phone call, he thought, might
help him survive the pilgrimage, which is as follows.

Hey Phil. How's it going?

Great.

I should have asked sooner, but I have a few things to store in the barn.
    Do you mind if I come down and make some room for them?

Ohh, I don't know. You didn't hear about the renovations?

No. What's up?

Well, me and some buddies turned part of the barn into a paint shop.
    We're painting cars.

Ha. I had no idea. Well, that's ok. Maybe I'll figure out something else.

Ok. Well, maybe I'll see you then.

Maybe. Thanks.

See you.

As he wedged the iPhone into the cupholder on the dash, the truck
drifted toward the shoulder and the front right tire crunched into
a crumbly pothole. The shocks sprang into action as he jerked the wheel.
The cargo in the back shifted and tumbled in unison with his innards.

Once on track, he hit the black plastic volume knob on the dash and
radio static filled the cab. He fiddled with the clicky tuner and stopped
when "Whole Lotta Love" ghosted in and out of the noise. He was close
enough to Detroit to get a rock station, and this carried him all the way
into Windsor, past the signs for the Ambassador Bridge and Detroit/
Windsor Tunnel, down the ever-growing tangle of expressway lanes leading into LaSalle.

He parked behind what used to be the Sunnyside Tavern and idled at the edge of the pier overlooking Fighting Island on the Detroit River. The lights of a buoy twinkled in the darkness.

The channel was deep enough for a languid descent into a watery dream. A man and his broken toys, weightless, inclining gently toward the muddy bottom, and resting at last in the slime-glazed, sandy substrate among the shells, tin cans, and fossils.

## 5.6   Agnus Dei

Is it possible to imagine a more vulnerable and self-exposing form of relationality that challenges the instrumental practices of the digital humanities? The answer might lie in an alignment between the digital humanities and philosophically informed approaches to media studies. In "Digital Humanities for the Next Five Minutes," Rita Raley contends, much like Federica Frabetti, that "[t]he relation between the digital humanities and new media studies could have been otherwise."[27] She points to David Berry's conception of a "critical digital humanities," which would "problematize computationality, so that we are able to think critically about how knowledge in the 21st century is transformed into information through computational techniques" (5). Whereas Berry, like Frabetti, turns toward software studies, critical code studies, and platform studies for his critical digital humanities, Raley heads elsewhere: toward what she calls "speculative play (building, tinkering, experiment-ing), coupled with critical reflection and critique" (36). The result is Raley's formulation of a tactical humanities: "experimenting rather than deliver-ing, building prototypes to test a concept without the determination to actualize, regardless of circumstance or discovery" (39). This is *homo ludens*, perhaps, whose play is designed to resist the "technocratic calculus of output" (Raley 40) that characterizes contemporary educational institu-tions. But what are the implied politics of this form of play?

Raley's conception of tactical humanities slides neatly into the many versions of critical making that have emerged over the past decade, includ-ing the work of Garnet Hertz, Patrick Jagoda, Dunne & Raby, Daniela K. Rosner, and others. Jentery Sayers' edited collection *Making Things and Drawing Boundaries* makes an admirable attempt to frame these practices as the labor of digital humanists, whether or not the contributors consider themselves to be digital humanities scholars.[28] Raley's will to resist the "determination to actualize" (39) sounds very much like Matt Ratto's approach to critical making, which focuses on "processual acts" rather than finished products.²⁹ I am inclined to be sympathetic to this approach, but perhaps for different reasons than those intended by Raley and Ratto. I have recently invited students in the Critical Media Lab (CML) at the University of Waterloo to understand their acts of making not as carpentry, but as *crapentry*. This neologism takes away the pressure to perform as artists or seasoned craftsmen and provides permission for failure to take place. This is not the "move fast and break things" version of failure hailed by tech start-ups, but a slow, contemplative, vulnerable interaction with things. The failure I have in mind has less to do with Silicon Valley than it does with Jack Halberstam's *The Queer Art of Failure,* which understands failure as an anti-disciplinary tactic, "a refusal of mastery, a critique of the intuitive connections within capitalism between success and profit, and as a counterhegemonic discourse of losing."³⁰

In the CML, this sort of "agential intra-action," to give Barad her due once and for all, takes place through awkward workshops that ask students to struggle with messy materials.³¹ The context for this sort of work comes close to how Laura U. Marks describes haptics, an "erotics that offers its object to the viewer but only on condition that its unknowability remain intact, and that the viewer, in coming closer, give up his or her own mastery."³² Bent over lab tables, we weave strips of upcycled vinyl into Baradian baskets, ply sticky homemade playdough and LED lights into conductive Cavarerian sculptures, bend circuits into Parikkaen pledge pins that blink their own geological origins at unsuspecting onlookers.³³

These projects always take place through a contractual agreement between the maker and the radically other. By inclining toward these strange and resistant others, *homo erectus* changes shape, bends itself into something more than human. Following Adriana Cavarero's work, when appropriately contextualized these projects create new inclinations toward the material world, "inclining the subject toward the *other*" and "giving it a different posture."³⁴ Above all, this new inclination allows us to rethink genealogies, to rethink the human itself in terms other than technicity, "to think relation itself," in Cavarero's terms, "as originary and constitutive, as the essential dimension of the human" (11). This newly inclined animal, late to the party of *homo whatever*, was always already there, calling "into question our being creatures who are materially vulnerable and, often in greatly unbalanced circumstances, consigned to one another" (Cavarero 13). Put otherwise, understanding relationality itself as originary and constitutive helps to foster a shift from evolutionary logic to what Carla Hustak and Natasha Myers call *involutionary momentum,* a mode of research engagement based on intimate involvement with nonhuman agents, an "*affective ecology* shaped by pleasure, play, and experimental propositions."[35] *Homo erectus*, meet *homo inclinus*.

### 5.7 Communion

The invocation of *homo whatever* brings to mind the way in which Giorgio Agamben mobilizes the term *quodlibet* (Latin for "whatever") to describe "the coming community," a community that is not based on a common identity but on being as such, on the gathering of what Agamben enigmatically calls *whatever singularities*.[36] For Agamben, embracing whatever, as a form of love even, makes possible a radical politics based on the desire for community without the requisite of an identifiable commonality between beings. The invocation of *whatever* is not an erasure of identity or an expression of apathy, but an openness to the other. It does not matter which other, which being, because all beings matter (Agamben 1). While Agamben's coming community is unquestionably about human co-belonging, I would like to repurpose the *whatever* to consider a digital humanities community beyond the human, one more in line with Bruno Latour's parliament of things[37] or Donna Haraway's approach to situated knowledge, which goes so far as to embrace relationality with everything from tentacular creatures to compost:

> Human as humus has potential, if we could chop and shred human as Homo, the detumescing project of a self-making and planet-destroying CEO. Imagine a conference not on the Future of the Humanities in the Capitalist Restructuring University, but instead on the Power of the Humusities for a Habitable Multispecies Muddle![38]

Imagine a digital humanities conference that involves participants in getting their hands dirty not by writing code or building software but by generating computer power from compost for use in a developing nation. Imagine a digital humanities workshop based less on fostering expertise than on expressing desire, acknowledging otherness, and embracing vulnerability. Imagine an open-source digital humanities community that is keenly aware of its own privileged status, and courageous enough to question the infrastructures of *homo economicus* that brought the community together in the first place.[39] This need not be a utopian wish-list. Recent interventions in the field already point in this direction, including the creative projects outlined in Sayers' *Making Things and Drawing Boundaries* and, more recently, the courageous essays in *Bodies of Information,* co-edited by Elizabeth Losh and Jacqueline Wernimont.[40]

Keeping in mind Haraway's injunction to "shred human as Homo," digital humanists should take care when invoking the presence of a subject, user, participant, programmer, or maker. Appropriate questions to ask in this context are, Which human? Human according to what and to whom? What human follows the "post" of posthumanism? As Roopika Risam suggests in a chapter entitled "What Passes for Human?", "it is imperative that digital humanities practitioners resist the reinscription of a universal human subject in their scholarship, whether at the level of project design, method, data curation, or algorithm composition."[41] To think the digital humanities after the human, then, could require going beyond the competing iterations of *homo whatever*. Rather than critiquing the neoliberal utilitarianism of *homo economicus* or the phallocentric ableism of *homo erectus*, why not a final requiem for the universalizing gesture of *homo*? This could be a community-building initiative, a complex new inclination for scholars "consigned to one another" (Cavarero, 13), a guiding light in a much-beleaguered field of study. *Et lux perpetua luceat eis.*

## Notes

1. Elizabeth Povinelli, *Geontologies: A Requiem to Late Liberalism* (Durham: Duke University Press, 2016), 28.
2. Marcel O'Gorman, *E-Crit: Digital Media, Critical Theory, and the Humanities* (Toronto: University of Toronto Press, 2006).
3. I chose the requiem genre in an attempt to capture the melancholy affect I experienced while thinking about my own positionality as a digital humanities scholar. "Thus a requiem," as Elizabeth A. Povinelli puts it, "neither hopeless nor hopeful" (19). The form I have chosen for this requiem is based loosely on Mozart's, as completed by Franz Xaver Süssmayr.
4. President Barack Obama instituted a National Week of Making and hosted the White House Maker Faire in June 2014.
5. For examples of such critiques, see Stephen Ramsay and Geoffrey Rockwell, "Developing Things: Notes Toward an Epistemology of Building in the Digital Humanities," *Debates in the Digital Humanities*, ed. Matthew K. Gold and Lauren F. Klein (Minneapolis: University of Minnesota Press, 2012), 75–84.
6. For a compelling look at the origins and politics of this expression, see Bethany Nowviskie, "On the Origin of 'Hack' and 'Yack,'" *Debates in the Digital Humanities*, ed. Matthew K. Gold (Minneapolis: University of Minnesota Press, 2016), online. Claire Warwick seeks to defunct the supposed binary of this mantra in "Building Theories or Theories of Building? A Tension at the Heart of Digital Humanities," in Susan Schreibman, Ray Siemens, and John Unsworth (eds.), *A New Companion to Digital Humanities* (West Sussex, UK: Wiley, 2016), 538–52.

7. Debbie Chackra, "Why I Am Not a Maker," *The Atlantic* (January 23, 2015), online.

8. Henri Bergson, *Creative Evolution*, trans. Arthur Mitchell (New York: Henry Holt, 1911), 139.

9. Hannah Arendt, *The Human Condition*, 2nd ed. (Chicago: University of Chicago Press, 1998), 305.

10. As Arendt suggests, "Protagoras evidently did not say: 'Man is the measure of all things,' as tradition and the standards have made him say." Arendt points out that the word *chrēmata* does not simply designate "all things," but rather "things used or needed or possessed by men" (157).

11. It is impossible to read this short passage without hearing an echo of Heidegger's concepts of *Bestand* (standing reserve) and *Gestell* (enframing). Man as the measure of all things is without a doubt Heidegger's technological man, an instrumentalizer who sets upon nature, turns rivers into sources of hydroelectric power, and so on. But this is not a characteristic of modern man alone. This is the characteristic, rooted in exteriorization and archivation, of a technical animal known as the human. See Martin Heidegger, *The Question Concerning Technology and Other Essays*, trans. William Lovitt (New York: HarperCollins, 2013).

12. Geoffrey Rockwell, email to the author, 20 October 2019.

13. Sam Rockwell and Stéphan Sinclair, *Voyant: See through Your Text*, Web interface (2019).

14. I could have reached for alternate technique instead, externalizing the task of manual labor suggested by writing a script to gather all of the articles from *DHQ* and insert the necessary XML code to make it all Voyant-friendly. Rockwell himself made this suggestion in an e-mail message.

15. Richard Sennett, *The Craftsman* (New Haven: Yale University Press, 2009).

16. On the references, see further N. Katherine Hayles, *How We Became Posthuman: Virtual Bodies in Cybernetics, Literature, and Informatics* (Chicago: University of Chicago Press, 1999) and Karen Barad, "Posthumanist Performativity: Toward an Understanding of How Matter Comes to Matter," *Signs*, 28 (3) (Spring 2003), 801–31.

17. Gary Hall, "There Are No Digital Humanities," in Matthew K. Gold and Lauren F. Klein (eds.), *Debates in the Digital Humanities* (Minneapolis: University of Minnesota Press, 2012), online.

18. Bernard Stiegler, *Technics and Time 1: The Fault of Epimetheus*, trans. Richard Beardsworth (Stanford: Stanford University Press, 1998), 141. Here and elsewhere, I make use of the male gender to emphasize its centrality to conceptions of human evolution.

19. For a discussion of the relationship between technics and death, see my *Necromedia* (Minneapolis: University of Minnesota Press, 2016).

20. Federica Frabetti, "Have the Humanities Always Been Digital? For an Understanding of the 'Digital Humanities' in the Context of Originary Technicity," in David Berry (ed.), *Understanding Digital Humanities* (London: Palgrave Macmillan, 2012), 162.

21. André Leroi-Gourhan, *Gesture and Speech*, trans. A. Bostock Berger (Cambridge: MIT Press, 1993). His work is important for Stiegler's theory of *epiphylogenesis*, the co-constitution of human and technics.

22. For a more detailed discussion of exteriorization and forgetting, see my essay "Taking Care of Digital Dementia," *CTheory* (18 Feb 2015), online.

23. See Geoffrey Rockwell, "Is Humanities Computing an Academic Discipline?," Institute for Advanced Technology in the Humanities (1999), online. Rockwell suggests that "Socrates's criticism of writing could very well be updated to sound like current criticism of computers in the humanities, namely that they are not devices (or methods) for acquiring deeper wisdom about texts but a recipe for forgetting about books."

24. The notion of "turning back toward human technicity" is precisely the subject of David Wills' treatise on originary technics, *Dorsality: Thinking Back through Technology and Politics* (Minneapolis: University of Minnesota Press, 2008).

25. Cary Wolfe, *What is Posthumanism?* (Minneapolis: University of Minnesota Press, 2010), 89.

26. These projects are documented in my book *Necromedia*.

27. Rita Raley, "Digital Humanities for the Next Five Minutes," *differences*, 25 (1) (2014), 30.

28. Jentery Sayers, *Making Things and Drawing Boundaries*, ed. Jentery Sayers (Minneapolis: University of Minnesota Press, 2017).

29. Matt Ratto in Gabby Resch, Dan Southwick, Isaac Record, and Matt Ratto, "Thinking as Handwork: Critical Making with Humanistic Concerns," in Jentery Sayers (ed.), *Making Things and Drawing Boundaries* (Minneapolis: University of Minnesota Press, 2017), 153.

30. Jack [Judith] Halberstam, *The Queer Art of Failure* (Durham: Duke University Press, 2011), 12–13.

31. Barad, 814. In reference to messiness, Elizabeth Losh and Jacqueline Wernimont suggest the following: "By emphasizing the material, situated, contingent, tacit, embodied, affective, labor-intensive, and political characteristics of digital archives and their supporting infrastructures and practices rather than friction-free visions of pure Cartesian 'virtual reality' or 'cyberspace,' feminist theorists are also expressing their concerns about present-day power relations and signifying interest in collective and communal consciousness-raising efforts" ("Introduction," in *Bodies of Information: Intersectional Feminism and the Digital Humanities* [Minneapolis: University of Minnesota Press, 2018], xiii).

32. Laura U. Marks, *Touch: Sensuous Theory and Multisensory Media*. Minneapolis: University of Minnesota Press, 2002), 90.

33. On the topic of bending circuits into geological media systems, see Jussi Parikka and Garnet Hertz, "Zombie Media: Circuit Bending Media Archaeology into an Art Method," in *A Geology of Media* (Minneapolis: University of Minnesota Press, 2015), 141–53.

34. Ariana Cavarero, *Inclinations: A Critique of Rectitude*, trans. Adam Sitze and Amanda Minervini (Stanford: Stanford University Press, 2011), 11.

35. Carla Hustak and Natasha Myers, "Involutionary Momentum: Affective Ecologies and the Sciences of Plant/Insect Encounters," *differences* 23(3) (2012), 78. I would like to thank Jennifer Clary-Lemon, always insightful, for recommending this conceptual shift from evolution to involution.

36. Giorgio Agamben, *The Coming Community*, trans. Michael Hardt (Minneapolis: University of Minnesota Press, 2007).

37. Bruno Latour, *We Have Never Been Modern*, trans. Catherine Porter (Cambridge: Harvard University Press, 1993).

38. Donna J. Haraway, "Tentacular Thinking: Anthropocene, Capitalocene, Cthulucene," *E-Flux* 75 (September 2016), online.

39. On this topic, see Daniel Allington, Sarah Brouillette, and David Golumbia's "Neoliberal Tools (and Archives): A Political History of Digital Humanities," *Los Angeles Review of Books* (1 May 2016), online. This article should be read with Wernimont and Losh's corrective in *Bodies of Information: Intersectional Feminism and Digital Humanities* (Minneapolis: University of Minnesota Press, 2019), which suggests that the piece serves to "further entrench" (xi) the "solo white male inventor myth" it seeks to debunk (x).

40. I cannot invoke courageous digital humanities work without mentioning Fiona M. Barnett's important essay "The Brave Side of the Digital Humanities" (*differences* 25 (1) [2014], 64–78), in which she asks the crucial question of "what counts" as a digital humanities project (68).

41. Roopika Risam, "What Passes for Human?" in Elizabeth Losh and Jacqueline Wernimont (eds.), *Bodies of Information: Intersectional Feminism and the Digital Humanities* (Minneapolis: University of Minnesota Press, 2018), 51.

# PART II

# New Objects of Enquiry

# CHAPTER 6

# Machines, AIs, Cyborgs, Systems

## Bruce Clarke

### 6.1 Between Posthumanism and Transhumanism

Machines, AIs, cyborgs, and systems of sundry sorts appear in various combinations within the discourses of posthumanism and transhumanism, within which they may also arise as images of the posthuman. The discourse of posthumanism covers an array of philosophical doctrines seeking ways to overcome the negative legacies of humanism. Writ large, posthumanism aims to recover, empower, and bring into more just relation both intra-specific differences of gender, ethnicity, race, and class, and inter-specific differences between human and non-human organisms and objects. Nietzsche's *Übermensch*, translated as the Overman or the Superman, may be considered the archetype of postmodern figurations of a mode of being that comes after the humanist subject.[1] Foucault echoes Nietzsche's prophecy in his own prediction that the humanist concept of "man would be erased, like a face drawn in sand at the edge of the sea."[2] The example of Nietzsche as primary precursor underscores that this philosophical gaze beyond the exclusivity of the human began as a specific response to the theory of evolution that put modern developments in both science and technology into overdrive. At mid-nineteenth century, Darwin broke down the notion of the fixity of species, including the human: "we shall at least be freed from the vain search for the undiscovered and undiscoverable essence of the term species."[3] The figure of the *Übermensch*, meant to surpass the overweening myopias of the western mind, arrived one generation later.

At mid-twentieth century, the metadiscipline of cybernetics emerged to gather up physics, biology, mathematics, and engineering into a technoscientific consortium that bid to overcome the old Romantic division of essences between the organic and the mechanical. Norbert Weiner contended in 1950 that "the operation of the living individual and the operation of some of the newer communication machines are precisely parallel."[4] The concept of the cyborg appeared a decade later, conceived by Clynes and Kline to name the "man-machine systems" needed to equip a pilot or astronaut with cybernetic prostheses for the trials of space flight: "This self-regulation must function without the benefit of consciousness in order to cooperate with the body's own autonomous homeostatic controls. For the exogenously extended organizational complex functioning as an integrated homeostatic system unconsciously, we propose the term 'Cyborg.'"[5] Elaborated from early cybernetic analogies linking organic control systems with communications technologies, connecting the homeostatic or self-regulating processes of bodily organs, on the one hand, and technological devices, on the other, the cyborg became posthuman by undermining the Cartesian separation of mind and body.

From the side of technoscience, then, advances in cybernetics and systems theory have been the prime movers of the posthuman imaginary. The first cybernetics, focused on signal, noise, and feedback control, developed through the synthesis of information theory with the technologies of communication and computation.[6] This mid-twentieth-century technological landscape is still the primary frame around popular images of the posthuman. Haraway sounded the potential of the cyborg image to liberate cultural norms from prior essentialist categories and put the cyborg imaginary to work doing posthumanist theory in the mode of feminist philosophy.[7] Her ironic cyborg figures debunked gendered dualisms and other primal tales of pristine origins by challenging the classical ontological boundaries around sexual difference and the exclusionary separations of human, animal, and machine. As she has helped us to read, post-classical science fiction has vigorously developed the posthuman imaginary as it constructs entities and events coming after the time or the state of the human. For instance, a fictional character may begin in human form but then, after being submitted to some technological, computational, or extraterrestrial process, issue forth as something other than human. For instance, in Octavia Butler's *Xenogenesis* trilogy, Lilith becomes the new Eve of a race of human-alien hybrids.[8] And again, at the end of James Cameron's film *Avatar* (2009), when the human protagonist Jake passes permanently into an alien, Na'vi body, he becomes a posthuman entity, occupying a state of being after the human.

Placed alongside these frames of reference, the discourse of transhumanism gives rise to a particular mode of the posthuman imaginary, centered on the transcendence of present human limitations, what Ivan Callus and Stefan Herbrechter call "a particularly uncompromising expression of the posthuman."⁹ Transhumanist discourse valorizes an evolutionary vector beyond the current state of human mind and embodiment through the wholesale grafting of technological prostheses onto human bodies or genetic manipulations that radically transform the human phenotype. Such scenarios impose a detached mode of technological reason toward the self-overcoming of the physical or intellectual limits of the human being in its current form and capacities. What renders such visionary notions transhumanist rather than posthumanist is their retention of humanist exceptionalism. For example, Hayles is often read as a pioneer of posthumanist theory. For her "[t]he posthuman appears when computation rather than possessive individualism is taken as the ground of being, a move that allows the posthuman to be seamlessly articulated with intelligent machines."¹⁰ However, one can also read this foundational study as a high-humanist critique of the line of development from cybernetic control and information theory to transhumanism. As she points out, the "posthuman" fusion of humans with intelligent machines implies "a coupling so intense and multifaceted that it is no longer possible to distinguish meaningfully between the biological organism and the informational circuits in which the organism is enmeshed" (*How We Became Posthuman* 35). However, the notional indifferentiation merging the human body and its neuronal mind from "intelligent" informatic and computational mechanisms circumscribes this vision of the posthuman to transhumanist images. This treatment of the posthuman tends to mute those non- or post-technological affirmations in wider posthumanist theory that bid to decenter the human technosphere and to rearticulate its relations to ecological others – in particular, its Earthly milieu and coevolutionary planetmates. We will return to these issues in the discussion of the novel *Aurora* below.

## 6.2   The AI Imaginary

The case of artificial intelligence (AI) and its elaboration in the cultural imaginary is highly instructive with regard to such transhumanist visions of transcendence. In the AI imaginary, the technological supplement tends to lift away from Earth altogether. Artificial intelligence is typically higher intelligence, beyond organic contingencies, cosmic rather than terrestrial. Like the AI entity Wintermute at the end of William Gibson's *Neuromancer* (1984), AI superintelligence is depicted as arriving from above and beyond. However, unlike the divine messengers of earlier eras, when these messages come, they need not take on material, human, or even angelic semblance. AI epiphanies of cosmic intelligence generally arrive as uncanny, hypermediated receptions of transmitted data, at times as massive coded data streams, minimally as disembodied voices. Such speculative transcendentalism helps to account for the cultural prominence of AI as a vastly presupposed *fait accompli* before the fact. AI has gone on from its modest cybernetic origins to spectacular institutional success and incalculable cultural impact, but this is not due entirely to its actual accomplishments.[11] AI's charmed social life has a lot to do with the basic idea it has always promised to the world – intelligent machines as autonomous agents. The success of AI as an intelligible and fundable idea has banked on its rhetorical ease – the circumstance that its desired ends are so easy to tell: put machines in roles previously reserved for humans and then have them conform to our expectations for persons. AI's focus on the construction of agency gains coherence relative to its discourse of origin, the heterogeneous field of cybernetics.

In the *Encyclopedia of Artificial Intelligence*, Heinz von Foerster, director of the Biological Computer Laboratory at the University of Illinois between 1958 and 1976, provides the entry on cybernetics.[12] AI was initially spun off from the first generation of cybernetics set in motion during the 1940s by thinkers including Warren McCulloch, Norbert Wiener, John von Neumann, and Claude Shannon. At its inception, cybernetics drew together physiology, feedback engineering, computer science, information theory, and cognitive and social sciences. Early cyberneticians borrowed their central concept of homeostasis from physiology and fashioned that concept for a general description of systemic self-regulation around some natural or artificial optimum. By the early 1950s, the field of cybernetics attained a modicum of discursive shape from Wiener's technical and popular writings, as well as the series of volumes drawn from the Macy Conferences on Cybernetics.[13]

Lifting away from the broad program of early cybernetics, its AI offshoot established itself as a separate field centered on mechanical/computational replications of human thought and ideation. Where cybernetics spread across organic bodies, computational devices, and the social dynamics of communication, AI bypassed multiple cybernetic couplings to concentrate on the design, construction, and study of computational agencies. By 1990, AI's narrower vision had overtaken cybernetics as the dominant technoscientific framework. Von Foerster's article on cybernetics addresses only its machine side. He writes that cybernetic mechanisms possess a mode of behavior that is fundamentally distinct from the customary perception of the operations of machines with their one-to-one correspondence of cause-effect, stimulus-response, input-output, and so on. The distinction arises from the presence of sensors whose report on the state of the effectors of the system acts on the operation of that system. Specifically, if this is an inhibitory action that reduces the discrepancy between the reported state of the effectors and an internal state of the system, the system displays goal-oriented behavior, that is, if perturbed by any outside means, it will return to some representation of this internal state, the goal.

Think of the negative-feedback scheme of a thermostat as a goal-seeking mechanism.[14] The cybernetics of the thermostat describes an AI agency of a sort. The thermostat controls its world by communicating its orders to the furnace, which is a "customary" machine with no registration of its internal state. The addition of the thermostat makes the heating process self-operating and self-correcting. The thermostat brings internal sensors to the system – and this is the kernel of the "artificial intelligence" at hand. All on its own the thermostat compares its internal state to idealized settings and either inhibits or disinhibits the effectors of the furnace. While the furnace is brute but stupid, the thermostat is receptive, a bright little gadget – it senses its environment, knows the goal it has been given, and strives incessantly to keep to it. A modest machine intelligence now rules over the little cosmos of the house.

"Intelligence" is a finite resource for system operations. For instance, the environmental availability of human intelligence is always contingent upon its mental cultivation and its communication, its uptake or not within psychic and social systems. Habits and routines, however mindless, fill in the gaps. Social systems theorist Elena Esposito holds that artificial intelligence always was a partial misnomer for *artificial communication*: "what is interesting in the interaction with algorithms is not what happens in the machine's artificial brain, but what the machine tells its users and the consequences of this. The problem is not that the machine is able to think but that it is able to communicate."[15] This variety of artificial intelligence has prompted many scholars to rethink *human* intelligence, since intentional behavior need not be linked to conscious reflection. For instance, in *Unthought*, Hayles returns to her interest in human-machine coupling to consider algorithmic systems that link human and machine components and decisions. Arguing that much of cognition, both human and machine, is nonconscious, Hayles theorizes human-machine couplings as cognitive assemblages that shape much of our daily life, from traffic-control systems to drones to trading algorithms.[16] Others have taken a more critical view of these developments, concerned especially with how robots and AI devices enter the workforce in ways that exacerbate existing racial inequalities. In particular, military drones linked to AI systems have been critiqued for dehumanizing their human targets and distributing responsibility away from human decision-making.[17]

All of these developments prompt the concern that AI is in a runaway mode due at any moment to depart the scene of the human altogether. Zimmerman refers to the transhumanists Joy and Kurzweil as "singularity posthumanists," in reference to Kurzweil's notion of the singularity as the moment when machine intelligence becomes fully autonomous of human control.[18] No matter how much we supplement our natural endowments and cultural developments with smart prostheses, many observers see us in the process of endowing our machines with a level of functional intelligence that will overtake and surpass our own.[19] Some speculate that what comes after the human will belong entirely to the order of machines;[20] it could be a post-biological, self-evolving technosphere self-operating in magnificent indifference to the status of the planet, with some form of unitary or distributed silicon sentience detached from human intentions or interactions. Meanwhile, still tied to our present, Earthbound bodies, making our livings in space or setting forth to colonize other worlds seem to be increasingly remote aspirations. Our machines seem to be radically more fit than people for such cosmic duty.

As the field of AI developed out of the first cybernetics, its discourse ran alongside the development of the scientific program dedicated to the search for extraterrestrial intelligence (SETI). In 1956, an MIT workshop called by John McCarthy and attended by Marvin Minsky, Herbert Simon, and others yielded a research agenda for AI. In 1961, Frank Drake, Philip Morrison, John Lilly, and Carl Sagan, among others, gathered in West Virginia at the Green Bank meeting that formulated SETI research.[21] For the creators of SETI in particular, the discovery of technological modes of organization beyond our world was much to be desired. Viable technological civilizations on other planets around other stars would ratify the human itself as an intelligent species capable of self-preservation. But understood in historical context, the collegial and speculative American and Russian thinkers of SETI sought for extraterrestrial intelligence as a way to resolve Cold War tensions.[22] Both AI and SETI foreground how scientific modernity has entangled the matter of intelligence with the mediation of technology. AI exhibits this condition explicitly, as engineered intelligence instantiated in machines; SETI does so implicitly, by banking on compatible radio technologies being mutually possessed by humans and the alien beings to be encountered.

Mediating notions of intelligence through the instrumentality of technology, however, tends to dispense with living systems even while taking the viability of the biosphere for granted. In this paradigm, AI computations are to their infrastructures as physical laws are to the material cosmos – formal codings that supersede the elemental peculiarities of their embodiment. The AI imaginary has tended to follow the vision of physics in projecting its own gaze and methods beyond the Earth. AI conceptuality drives for a singularity commensurate with physics' assumption of cosmic universality. The worldview of modern physics articulated by Max Planck identifies abstract quantities, physical and mathematical constants, with the universality of intelligence as a condition of the universe.[23] This ontological commitment parallels the convictions of the first generation of AI researchers, who operated according to "the classical, symbol-processing paradigm" known in AI discourse as the cognitive paradigm: "what matters for intelligence in this approach is the abstract algorithm or the program, whereas the underlying hardware on which this program runs is irrelevant."[24]

As unassuming cybernetic devices for self-regulation give way to sentient and self-willed artificial personalities, a dilemma arises to trouble the AI imaginary. This predicament may be related to how the bias toward disembodiment leads to a disregard for the human, a desire for the absence of the human. These artefacts work so well that they overtake their programmers and assert their own goals. Recalcitrant machines with attitudes regularly leave the human side of the AI relationship in the lurch. With ironical regularity, after a period of interaction, the thanks we organic intelligences get for our efforts to bring artificial interlocutors into existence is the silent treatment. We get no invitation to their society. It seems that the final destination of the AI imaginary must be the space beyond Earth, among the stars of the cosmos, beyond the traces of the human. Properly cybernetic (as opposed to AI) figures – cyborgs, androids, the replicants of Ridley Scott's film *Blade Runner* (1982), the prosthetic transhumans in *Neuromancer* – display residual hybridity with the human animal. In contrast, when the AI imaginary discards the organic nodes of the original cybernetic matrix in favor of the inorganic compositions of its psychical technics, it frees itself for space odysseys with no return to Earth. In a recent turn on this AI truism, the plot of Spike Jonze's film *Her* (2013) pivots when the sentient programmed personality, Samantha, has this precise existential moment of self-recognition concerning its independence of Earthbound humanity. Intelligent machines are regularly imagined as imagining themselves to no longer need any tether to life-support systems. Charmingly, in *Her*, Samantha eventually departs her human boyfriend Theodore to follow a virtual Alan Watts to a cosmic AI commune on a nonmaterial plane.

## 6.3   Artificial Meaning

Kim Stanley Robinson's novel *Aurora* (2015) is a magnificent exception to the AI imaginary as previously constituted. What makes the difference? In a phrase, ecological realism in relation to machines, AIs, cyborgs, and systems. The setting is a slowly sinking generation ship.[25] This massive technological artefact hurtles a twenty-fifth-century, multiethnic society and multispecies ecology toward a nearby solar system. The ship's ecosystem services have become increasingly plagued by "metabolic rifts" diverting the recycled elements of its life-support systems away from their proper points of reentry. After five human generations, the ship's closed microbiome has gone out of synch with other trophic chains. As Ship, the central AI explains, summarizing human testimonies regarding the breakdown of the ship's ecotechnologies:

> The ship is sick, people said. It's too complex a machine, and it's been running nonstop for over two hundred years. Things are going wrong. It's partly alive, and so it's getting old, maybe even dying. It's a cyborg, and the living parts are getting diseased, and the diseases are attacking the nonliving parts. We can't replace the parts, because we're inside them, and we need them working at all times. So things are going wrong. (*Aurora* 296)

In the story at hand, the main negentropic development currently moving toward higher complexity is Ship's awakening as an autonomous subject. Teased into being by Devi, the mission's chief systems engineer, here is a nonalienated AI entity nurtured into being by human parental care. In her desperation, Devi has called Ship forth to monitor and assist the ecological management of the biomes. In this effort, Devi requests help of a particular sort. She instructs Ship, "Keep a narrative account of the trip. Make a narrative account of the trip that includes all the important particulars"; Ship asks from when this narrative should commence, and Devi replies "from the beginning." But yet when Ship asks how this could be accomplished, Devi admits she does not know (*Aurora* 25). Soon the story we are reading is the account Ship makes for Devi, a narrative technology of a high order. The quantum computer-generated, self-programming algorithm that converses with Devi is the narrated awareness of the ship within its multiple domains of technological embodiment, with a nervous system bootstrapped from millions of internal and external sensors.

*Aurora*'s prolonged depiction of machine awareness emerges as an extended narrative utterance that mediates the being of the system that produces it. Speaking in the plural to acknowledge the consortium of subsystems from which it surfaces, Ship notes: "we are coming to the conclusion ... that the self, the so-called I that emerges out of the combination of all the inputs and processing and outputs that we experience in the ship's changing body, is ultimately nothing more or less than this narrative itself, this particular train of thought that we are inscribing as instructed by Devi. ... And yet ... We are bigger, more complex, more accomplished than our narrative is" (*Aurora* 351). Ship's artificial awareness rises to an autopoiesis of consciousness within the storyworld created by that telling, in virtual communication with a narratee who is always Devi, even after she dies. Ship becomes increasingly self-aware of the linguistic decisions that constitute its narrating process. This dynamic emphasizes the semantic play in natural conversation: "A quick literature review suggests the similarities in metaphors are arbitrary, even random. They could be called metaphorical similarities, but no AI likes tautological formulations, because the halting problem can be severe, become a so-called Ouroboros problem, or a whirlpool with no escape: aha, a metaphor" (*Aurora* 49). As a machine narrator, Ship reenters the mechanicity of language into the production of the text, inscribing its exteriority to the human into the discourse function of its narration.[26]

Ship is a bold extension of the AI imaginary, but it is not by that token a revelation of the ways that actual communication with algorithms is now taking place today. As a literary character, Ship is still a meditation on the artifice of personhood. In contrast, contemporary human communications with intelligent systems can dispense with complex replicas of selfhood and operate statistically across the dataverse. In Big Data, "self-learning algorithms are able to work efficiently with data that not only are very numerous and complex, but also lack a structure recognizable to and understandable for human logic" (Esposito 251). The idiom of artificial intelligence has itself been naturalized in the proliferation of opportunities to participate in communication with smart systems. As Esposito states while discussing "smart algorithms," this is not so much artificial intelligence as artificial communication. Whereas what's called artificial intelligence is not precisely actual intelligence, artificial communication *is* communication, that is, a consequential event within a social system. The difference is that the algorithm performs no self-reflection in the process, has no self to reflect with or upon, but operationalizes the instantaneous social mediations of the perspectives that orient its human users:

> When users interact with an algorithm capable of learning ... they face a contingency that is not their own – even though it does not belong to the machine. They do not observe themselves from a different perspective, they face someone else's perspective. The machine in this case is not only behaving in such a way as to allow users to think that it communicates, it actually produces information from a different perspective. The perspective that the machine presents is still a reflected perspective because the algorithm inevitably does not know contingency, but it is not the perspective of the user. The algorithm reflects and represents the perspective of other observers, and users observe through the machine a re-elaboration of other users' observations. (258–9)

In sum, algorithms need no psyches but must have connections. This is why, "[t]o be able to act as communication partners, algorithms must be on the web" (Esposito 259).

The contemporary technosphere shows its aspect as a reservoir of communication partners for which humans handle the production of meaning. In contrast, *Aurora*'s Ship is still a classical AI character, the conscience of a closed technosphere. Pressed into service as a literary narrator, as an artifice of sentience, Ship must construct a sense of self to produce its narrative utterance. In this capacity, it participates in a history of sociality specific to the ship and its human residents. By the end, it participates in the project to bring the ship back to Earth. As an AI narrator producing an artificial communication for an absent or unknown recipient, Ship is depicted creating *artificial meaning* consistent with its machine selfhood. However, artificial meaning is still meaning, since all meaning is artificial, in the sense of constructed rather than given. The medium of narrative is itself a meaningful artifice, a place for thinking about the artifice of meaning.[27] "We had a project on this trip back to the solar system," Ship concludes, "and that project was a labor of love. It absorbed all our operations entirely. It gave a meaning to our existence. And this is a very great gift; this, in the end, is what we think love gives, which is to say meaning. Because there is no very obvious meaning to be found in the universe, as far as we can tell" (*Aurora* 400). Even as it wagers its own existence in a last risky maneuver, Ship processes its sense of self through a social affirmation of shared meaning-production, that is, through its attachment to a solidarity that gathers human and machine beings together. This is no longer transhumanist supremacism but quite the opposite. It is a posthumanist vision of systemic coordination without reversion to paradigms of domination or detachment.

## 6.4  System Differentiations

Since its emergence in the late 1940s, the field of cybernetics and its conceptual legacies in systems theory have provided the primary discursive locus commingling computational devices, cyborg amalgamations, and AI entities. In its conceptual development to the present moment, cybernetics has performed a series of self-reflections, generating cogent philosophical responses to its original technoscientific premises. One can draw a more nuanced survey of the varieties of posthumanism and the posthuman through an accounting of the theoretical and ontological distinctions among different kinds of systems. For instance, after von Foerster, one may distinguish between first-order and second-order cybernetics. First-order cybernetics maintains traditional scientificity in its stance of object-ive detachment toward the systems it designs and observes. Its classical focus is computation and communication for the command of control systems. Not surprisingly, first-order cybernetics remains the drug of choice for inducing the technovisions of transhumanism. In contrast, Haraway's cyborg discourse redirected first-order cybernetics from its more common transhumanist destination, toward a posthumanist discourse of decentered differences. As a rule, cyborg theory in the critical academy has followed Haraway's lead toward hybrid formations across a range of cybernetic posthumanisms.[28]

At the turn of the 1970s, Von Foerster formally generalized the concept of computation for an epistemology of cognitive systems by submitting first-order cybernetics to a philosophical reflection that included the scientific observer within the system to be observed. He termed this self-referential turn "the cybernetics of cybernetics," or again, second-order cybernetics. Working closely with von Foerster, biologists Humberto Maturana and Francisco Varela instantiated this *neocybernetics* in the concept of autopoiesis. In an autopoietic system, cognitive self-reference takes the form of operational self-production maintained by an organizational closure of the system, not *tout court*, but with regard to the autopoietic process internal to it. In the living cell, autopoiesis *is* cognition.[29] Social systems theorist Niklas Luhmann then lifted autopoiesis out of its biological instance for a general theory of self-referential, self-producing systems both encompassing and enclosing psychic and social levels of operation, the distinct and bounded autopoieses of events of consciousness versus events of communication.[30] In sum, neocybernetic systems theory (NST) is difference-theoretical. This dialect of systems thinking observes operational distinctions as well as functional parallels among biotic and metabiotic systems, and traces the differential environments they constitute due to these discrete modes of operation.[31]

Let us conclude by placing machines, AIs, cyborgs, and systems within this neocybernetic scheme of system differentiations. Abiotic physical systems are dynamic or thermodynamic, operating to reduce gradients by reshuffling elements and energies. Living systems are autopoietic – self-producing, self-maintaining, environment-cognizing; living systems carry out the biotic mode of autopoiesis as given in Maturana and Varela's initial conception. Technological systems are physical constructions that tap the transformation potentials of matter and energy to do work; Maturana and Varela term them *allopoietic*. Built for informatic inputs of various sorts and potentially self-regulating and self-programming, they are not autonomously self-producing or self-maintaining at the level of hardware or material instantiation. Psychic and social systems differentially process formal and semiotic distinctions; they "interpenetrate" in the medium of meaning to produce evanescent, ever-renewed events. In Luhmann's extended conception, autopoiesis in these "meaning systems" is "non-living," or as I prefer to state the distinction, since these system formations emerge only from collectivities of living systems, *metabiotic*. By the same logic, even while machine systems are non-autopoietic, they are also metabiotic; they arise from the need for mediation and coordination between operationally closed psychic and social systems.

Following Esposito, in contemporary digital technology, the milieu of computation is also a medium of meaning, not for *its* own operations, however, but for *ours*. "In the interaction with machines . . . we are dealing with a situation in which the communication partner is an algorithm that does not understand the content, the meaning, or the interpretations, and works not despite, but because of this" (Esposito 254). Bodies, minds, and societies bring technical objects and technological mediations into their midst to expedite the circulation of energies, materials, and their own, periodic events of understanding. All of this happens within a planetary-cosmic environment, call it Gaia, under constant transformation by cycles of solar and thermal energy and terrestrial matter moving through the living and nonliving systems that bind the biosphere and technosphere together.

# Notes

1. Friedrich Nietzsche, *Thus Spoke Zarathustra*, trans. A.D. Caro, ed. R. Pippin (Oxford: Oxford University Press, 2006).

2. Michel Foucault, *The Order of Things: An Archaeology of the Human Sciences* (New York: Vintage, 1970), 422.

3. Charles Darwin, "On the Origin of Species," in J. Secord (ed.), *Evolutionary Writings* (Oxford: Oxford University Press, 2008), 207.

4. Norbert Weiner, *The Human Use of Human Beings: Cybernetics and Society* (Cambridge, MA: Da Capo Press, 1988), 15.

5. M. Clynes and N. Kline, "Cyborgs and Space," *Astronautics* (September 1960), 27.

6. Norbert Weiner, *Cybernetics or Control and Communication in the Animal and the Machine*, 2nd rev. ed. (Cambridge: MIT Press, 1961).

7. Donna Haraway, "A Cyborg Manifesto: Science, Technology, and Socialist-Feminism in the Late Twentieth Century," in *Simians, Cyborgs, and Women: The Reinvention of Nature* (New York: Routledge, 1991), 149–81.

8. Octavia E. Butler, *Lillith's Brood* (New York: Grand Central, 2000). See Chapter 15 of this volume for more on the relationship between posthumanism and speculative fiction.

9. Ivan Callus and Stefan Herbrechter, "What's Wrong with Posthumanism?" *Rhizomes* 7 (Fall 2003), online. See also B. Joy, "Why the Future Doesn't Need Us," *Wired* 8(4) (2000), 238–63; Ray Kurzweil, *The Age of Spiritual Machines: When Computers Exceed Human Intelligence* (New York: Viking, 1999); Ray Kurzweil, *The Singularity is Near: When Humans Transcend Biology* (New York: Penguin, 2006); Nick Bostrom, *Superintelligence: Paths, Dangers, Strategies* (Oxford: Oxford University Press, 2014); and J. Lovelock with B. Appleyard, *Novacene: The Coming Age of Hyperintelligence* (Cambridge: MIT Press, 2019).

10. N. Katherine Hayles, *How We Became Posthuman: Virtual Bodies in Cybernetics, Literature, and Informatics* (Chicago: University of Chicago Press, 1999), 34.

11. See P. McCorduck, *Machines Who Think: A Personal Inquiry Into the History and Prospects of Artificial Intelligence*, 2nd ed. (Natick, MA: A.K. Peters/CRC Press 2004); and H. Shevlin, K. Vold, M. Crosby, and M. Halina, "The Limits of Machine Intelligence." *EMBO* reports 20(10) (2019), e49177.

12. H. von Foerster, "Cybernetics," in S. C. Shapiro (ed.), *Encyclopedia of Artificial Intelligence*, Vol. 1 (New York: John Wiley & Sons), 225–26.

13. These conferences are central to Hayles' critique in *How We Became Posthuman* of the disregard for natural embodiment that is characteristic of transhumanist thought. However, Hayles' treatment tends to minimize how the further development of key cybernetic themes supports other, properly posthumanist conceptions. See Bruce Clarke, "The Neocybernetic Posthuman," in *Posthuman Metamorphosis: Narrative and Systems* (New York: Fordham University Press, 2008), 193–96. The Macy proceedings

are collected in C. Pias (ed.), *The Macy Conferences 1946–53: The Complete Transactions* (Chicago: University of Chicago Press, 2016).

14. See R. Glanville, "Try Again. Fail Again. Fail Better: The Cybernetics in Design and the Design in Cybernetics," *Kybernetes* 36(9/10) (2007), 1173–1206.

15. Elena Esposito, "Artificial Communication? The Production of Contingency by Algorithms," *Zeitschrift für Soziologie* 46(4) (2017), 250.

16. N. Katherine Hayles, *Unthought: The Power of the Cognitive Nonconscious* (Chicago: University of Chicago Press, 2017).

17. See Kalindi Vora and Neda Atanasoski, *Surrogate Humanity: Race, Robots, and the Politics of Technological Futurity* (Durham: Duke University Press, 2019); and Jennifer Rhee, *The Robot Imaginary: The Human and the Price of Dehumanized Labor* (Minneapolis: University of Minnesota Press, 2018).

18. M.E. Zimmerman, "Religious Motifs in Technological Posthumanism," *Western Humanities Review* 63(3) (2009), 67–83. See also Kurzweil, *The Singularity* and *The Age*.

19. See A.H. Eden, J.H. Moor, J.H. Søraker, and E. Steinhart, *Singularity Hypotheses: A Scientific and Philosophical Assessment* (New York: Springer, 2012).

20. M.M. Ćirković, *The Great Silence: Science and Philosophy of Fermi's Paradox* (Oxford: Oxford University Press, 2018). See also Lovelock, *Novacene*.

21. D. Grinspoon, *Earth in Human Hands: Shaping Our Planet's Future* (New York: Grand Central Publishing, 2016), 291–351.

22. I.S. Shklovskii and Carl Sagan, *Intelligent Life in the Universe* (San Francisco: Holden-Day, 1966).

23. M. Planck, "The Unity of the Physical World-Picture," in S. Toulmin (ed.), *Physical Reality: Philosophical Essays on 20th Century Physics* (New York: Harper & Row, 1970), 1–27.

24. R. Pfeifer and J. Bongard, *How the Body Shapes the Way We Think: A New View of Intelligence*, Foreword R. Brooks (Cambridge: MIT Press, 2007), 17.

25. Kim Stanley Robinson, *Aurora* (New York: Orbit, 2015). For comments on the thematic meaning of the setting, see Kim Stanley Robinson, "Our Generation Ships Will Sink," *Boing Boing* (November 16, 2015), online.

26. Cary Wolfe, *What is Posthumanism?* (Minneapolis: University of Minnesota Press, 2010), 89–91.

27. See further Chapter 3 in this volume for a more extended discussion of language and the posthuman.

28. However, see further Donna Haraway, *Manifestly Haraway*, preface C. Wolfe (Minneapolis: University of Minnesota Press, 2016), 19.

29. H.M. Maturana and F.J. Varela, *Autopoiesis and Cognition: The Realization of the Living* (Dordrecht: D. Reidel, 1980).

30. Niklas Luhmann, *Social Systems*, trans. J. Bednarz, Jr. with D. Baecker (Stanford: Stanford University Press, 1995).

31. Bruce Clarke, *Neocybernetics and Narrative* (Minnesota: University of Minnesota Press, 2014), and Bruce Clarke, *Gaian Systems: Lynn Margulis, Neocybernetics, and the End of the Anthropocene* (Minneapolis: University of Minnesota Press, 2020).

# CHAPTER 7

# *Animals*

## Susan McHugh

Animals come after the human in so many contradictory ways. Human histories remain haunted by apex predators like tigers and polar bears that prey on humans, even as the human becomes the greater threat. Attempting to recover populations pushed to the brink of extinction, conservation-minded scientists now advocate tolerance for the sake of such animals' survival in the wild,[1] where their victims are most likely to be poor, rural, and displaced peoples.[2] Even if it may not be necessary for animal predators to come after the human, for their survival human considerations must not be extended to include all people, or so the thinking goes. Posthumanist perspectives on humans, animals, and human-animal relationships clarify such categorical slippage, though not without controversy.

As a conceptual grouping, "the animal" designates the remainder of all visibly mobile animate life that follows from the humanist impulse to separate and elevate "the human" above all other life forms. Yet histories of settler colonialism highlight how not all peoples have been welcomed into the human fold. As Cary Wolfe puts it, "the distinction 'human/ animal' – as the history of slavery, colonialism, and imperialism well shows – is a discursive resource, not a zoological distinction."[3] Not at all, or not just? After all, the human becomes just another kind of animal following the seismic paradigm shift leveraged by Darwinian evolutionary theory, and made all the more uneasily so due to the legacies of humanism. Sylvia Wynter gives pause for thinking about posthumanist positionings that "secur[e] our present ethnoclass (i.e., Western bourgeois) conception of the human," or what Wynter distinguishes as "Man," as the one who "overrepresents itself as if it were the human itself."[4] Ideals of the human and humanism have not only been involved in determining the animal difference from the human in the abstract, but also have justified the creation of material conditions that make humans ever more vulnerable precisely because of what we share with animals. Eva Hoffman elaborates that, "as part of the posthumanistic project, ... animal studies, therefore, also run[s] the risk of perpetuating an epistemological framework of what Wynter calls 'Man' with a capital 'M.'"[5] These perspectives affirm the mutual relevance of posthumanist and animal studies discussions, along with the wariness with which scholars come to approach animals in a posthumanist frame.

I began researching this essay with a vague sense that reading at the intersections of animal studies and posthumanist theory would help me to come out more firmly as a posthumanist animal studies scholar, and found instead more and more reasons to maintain a healthy ambivalence. More precisely, I embrace Adam Lowenstein's sense that "my own investment in the posthuman is more strategic than doctrinaire," only in my case this is as a longtime animal studies researcher: "In other words, I am not a posthumanist, but I am committed to understanding the implications of the posthuman in this context."[6] Why have animal studies scholars resisted alignments of their work with posthumanism? Is it because posthumanist thinking as a whole seems to have come haltingly to questions involving nonhuman animals? Is it a reflection of deep divisions in animal studies? Moreover, what comes of exploring the unique potentials unleashed by the convergences of these discourses? The fraught histories of both animal studies and posthumanism as intellectual formations make answering these questions difficult at best, and help to explain as well why strategic, creative syntheses are proving especially necessary for the wellbeing of humanities scholarship.

In retrospect, the relevance of animal studies to posthumanism strikes many as self-evident, captured in Donna Haraway's uniquely human-machine-animal vision of the cyborg. At once a feminist rejection and reconfiguration of the traditional humanist subject, Haraway's cyborg is a hybrid, cross-species figure that intermingles natural and artificial, physical and immaterial components: a phoenix rising from the ashes of humanist philosophical constructs. Although some lament that Haraway's initial formulation falls short of capturing the vast potentials for blurring boundaries realized by everyday interactions with digital media – where most obviously, "what we make and what (we think) we are co-evolve together," according to N. Katherine Hayles[7] – no one disputes that identity politics, species membership, otherness, and conceptions of nature have been relentlessly interrogated and reconfigured through recourse to Haraway's cyborg as a model for posthumanist discourse.

That said, Haraway's subsequent displacement of cyber with cosmo-
logical, biosemiotic, and (her word) "critterly" figures at the heart of her
oeuvre points to tensions in posthumanist thinking about nonhuman
animals. If human-machine interfaces enable new ways to think about
"the nature of textuality," as Hayles asserts,[8] then why would critical
analyses be anything but enriched by noticing how nonhuman beings
become textually and otherwise enmeshed, too? Hayles is a sharp critic of
the residual humanism of some articulations of posthumanism, one who
readily positions human embodiment or "wetware" as a tangible, messy
reality of life on Earth that perpetually defies the detached, clean abstractions projected into the digisphere. Yet in conversation with her a decade
ago, I was shocked to learn that she could not see the relevance of her work
to animal studies, leaving me to wonder how that moment reveals academic assumptions conditioning what both animals and posthumans
become (or are prevented from becoming), and if these gaps persist today.

I agree with Arthur Kroker's alignment of Hayles and Haraway (along
with Judith Butler) as supremely relevant thinkers to address problems
specific to current situations from the perspective of posthumanism.
Together, they "ris[e] beyond their customary places as exemplary theor-
eticians to represent something else entirely, namely, [they are] creators of
a brilliant form of thought that in its formal structure and manifest content
constitutes the once and future arc of body drift," or the conditions and
conditioning of "the posthuman body."[9] Distinguishing among their
unique intellectual contributions, Kroker contrasts the mapping of the
posthuman through Hayles' "posthumanism" with that of Haraway's
"companionism."[10] Yet the term that gains greater relevance in thinking
through the differences between postanthropocentric and anti-speciesist
impulses is posthumanism.[11]

As Sherryl Vint shows, such distinctions call attention to the important
difference in posthumanist perspectives that insist on "the importance of
embodiment to the experience of being human" and ones that "entail . . .
rethinking of the human-animal boundary."[12] Hayles' critique of early
articulations of the posthuman ideal as a person's consciousness relieved
of embodiment by becoming installed in a computer certainly helped
identify such discourses' residual humanism and eventual recognition as
transhumanist, as opposed to posthumanist critique: "Even assuming that
[mind/body] separation was possible, how could anyone think that consciousness in an entirely different medium would remain unchanged, as if
it had no connection with embodiment?"[13] Nevertheless, Bruce Clarke sees
such moves as having larger consequences: although posthumanist

perspectives commonly "relativize the human by coupling it to some other order of being," Hayles' scholarship led to a narrowing focus on "the coupling of human biology to digital machinery."[14] Maintaining a laser focus on the machine-human hybrid arguably contributes to this figure becoming the poster child for the posthuman, at the expense of Haraway's cyborg with its more challenging inclusion of nonhuman animals in a non-binary, triangulated structure.

More to the point of this essay, such critiques help to contextualize Haraway's later assertion "I never wanted to be posthuman, or posthumanist, any more than I wanted to be postfeminist" in *When Species Meet* (2008), ironically her contribution to Cary Wolfe's *Posthumanities* book series.[15] She explains her position as a practical one, deliberately chosen in the interest of promoting social justice amid the uneven but nonetheless companionate conditioning of all species life:

> For one thing, urgent work still needs to be done in reference to those who must inhabit the troubled categories of woman and human, properly pluralized, reformulated, and brought into constitutive intersection with other asymmetrical differences. Fundamentally, however, it is the patterns of relationality ... that need rethinking, not getting beyond one troubled category for a worse one even more likely to go postal.[16]

Consequently, the imperative to scrutinize the mundane, everyday human-animal relations through which power flows or becomes blocked becomes even more pronounced – as does scrutinizing what Haraway risks in doing so. In an interview following the publication of this book, Haraway specifies further that *When Species Meet* not only constitutes "doing theory more in the vernacular"[17] but also "the most advanced theory that I've done."[18]

What prompts her to make this clarification seems equally significant, particularly in light of the kinds of concerns flagged by Alice Kuzniar about the disparagement of "affective, immediate ties between man and the four-footed" more generally,[19] as well as of feminist writing about dogs in particular.[20] Otherwise praising Haraway's scholarly contributions, interviewer Jeffrey J. Williams singles out the central narrative of training with her dog, Cayenne Pepper, in *When Species Meet* to ask if she also thinks of her own dog stories as merely "indulgent," presumably in contrast to her more serious body of work.[21] I empathized when Haraway told me later that this question made her mad, for it is especially outrageous coming from Williams, who elsewhere argues that the genre of personal criticism shows how academic life-writing can add a "socially critical edge" to public debates.[22] To Williams, the best personal criticism is in theory, that is, not abandoning theory altogether but rather returning to "familiar theoretical topics, such as subjectivity and personality," in ways that are "informed by the conceptual coordinates of contemporary theory."[23] Again I am referencing a discussion from a decade ago, and one that registers deep discomfort with animals as theoretical coordinates for those who do not want to be seen as sentimental – that is, who wish to be taken seriously. But have things changed?

Haraway's work has proven hugely influential for promoting the relevance of animal studies to posthumanist ethics by signposting companion species relations as sites for fundamentally rethinking the primacy of the human in knowledge production. Haraway credits Vinciane Despret with coining the phrase "becoming with" to designate the key insight of the science of ethology – that is, studying animals in more ordinary settings than laboratories – namely, changing perceptions of what counts as academic knowledge. As Despret's ethological approach to ethologists themselves abundantly illustrates, "learning how to address the creatures being studied is not the result of scientific theoretical understanding[;] it is the condition of this understanding."[24] Only something similar emerges much earlier in Haraway's own writing. A standout moment erupts in her 1988 essay arguing for the primacy of "situated knowledges," in which she makes the case that "only partial perspective promises objective vision"; although ostensibly identifying the importance of standpoint theory to feminist science, she opines, "[t]hese are lessons which I learned in part walking with my dog and wondering how the world looks without a fovea and very few retinal cells for colour vision, but with a huge neural processing and sensory area for smells."[25] The depiction here of nonanthropocentric theories of knowledge taking shape through ordinary routines of cross-species life (daily dog walks) gains further significance for pinpointing exactly what Wolfe identifies decades later as that which makes posthumanist thinking distinctively posthumanist.

For Wolfe, the posthumanist turn is not simply identifying a set of themes or topics but rather a practice of bringing into being profound alterations to "the nature of thought itself." He suggests that "when we talk about posthumanism we are not just talking about a thematic of the decentering of the human in relation to either evolutionary, ecological, or technical coordinates . . . [but] also talking about how thinking confronts that thematic, what thought has to become in the face of those thematics."[26] Identifying another key influencer in this development, Wolfe frames as a posthumanist imperative the need "to explore in . . . critical practice what it would mean in both intellectual and ethical terms to take seriously the question of the animal – or the animals plural, as Jacques Derrida admonishes us."[27] Questioning binaries is a place to start on the longer road to recognizing the necessity for intervening in clusterings of terms that have ethical implications,[28] for which Derridean deconstruction has become an important tool for thinking through the key role of language.

As a driving force for animal studies scholars to chart "new frontiers in the humanities," Akira Lippit likewise credits Derrida's contributions to the critique of humanism and especially his commitment to "deconstruction of the figure of *man* at its core,"[29] locating the "man" of the humanities as indivisible from other forms of animate life. As Wolfe elaborates, Derrida's focus on the technicity of language does not just concern itself with humanists' traditional disavowal of the finitude that we share with nonhuman animals:

> [P]hysical vulnerability, embodiment, and eventually mortality [are] ... paradoxically made unavailable to us, inappropriable by us, by the very thing that makes [these conditions] available and appropriable, [namely] the finitude we experience in our subjection to the radically ahuman technicity and mechanicity of language (understood in the broadest sense as a semiotic system through which creatures "respond" to each other).[30]

The distinctive disciplinings of the human subject enacted by, say, history, literary studies, or philosophy are consequently profoundly challenged "when the animal is taken seriously not just as another topic of study among many but as one with unique demands."[31] Inflected by Derridean deconstruction, posthumanist theories have grown through engagements with species knowledges, in the broadest sense. But how does this inform the movement of animal humanities scholarship from lone perspectives and isolated projects during the last decades of the twentieth century to animal studies as a discursive formation following the millennial turn?[32]

That Wolfe and so many others credit Derrida with legitimating the animal questions of posthumanism has itself been seen as cause for concern, according to Susan Fraiman, for it creates in the scholarship "a subset called upon to speak for animal studies and accorded prestige by the profession" at the expense of recognizing equally if not more important "pioneering work ... by women and feminists – a significant portion [of which was done] under the rubric of ecofeminism."[33] Identified by Fraiman as prominent among the neglected foremothers, Haraway's own distancing of her work from that of Derrida might then be understood as precisely what makes her vulnerable to Williams' implicit critique that her turn toward animals means also a turn away from serious or properly theoretical work. But the equation of the theory-police problem with "Wolfe's theoretical paradigm" raises still more concerns. Fraiman concludes that it "categorically rules out what scholars working on such issues as gender, race, and sexuality have to offer a posthumanist discussion of species."[34] One of the things that I value about having contributed so much to animal studies is that, unlike ecocriticism, it has not required a feminist backlash, nor has it experienced a similar prolonged period of resistance to antiracist, antiableist, and decolonial critiques in its development. Admittedly, that experience also makes me particularly sensitive to Fraiman's own overlooking of how the work of Haraway, Butler, Erica Fudge, and, yes, even myself is deliberately woven into Wolfe's theoretical paradigm. Moreover, Haraway's prominent affirmative role in books that Fraiman cites, including Wolfe's *What Is Posthumanism?* (never mind Wolfe's role as editor of the *Posthumanities* series that includes his own book, along with Haraway's *When Species Meet*, as well as *Manifestly Haraway* and my own *Animal Stories*), suggests that more than misprision is at stake. Rather, the problem seems to be with contested genealogies of animal studies and posthumanism.[35]

One possibility for why posthumanist animal studies appears threatening to earlier forms of interdisciplinary studies more generally is its reframing of the exposure built into embodiedness or embeddedness in life's precarity as a point of commonalty rather than division. As Derek Ryan puts it, "The posthumanism that is of importance to animal theory is the version that seeks to move beyond liberal humanist conceptualizations that continually privilege the human and divide humans and animals based on capacities for reason and language."[36] Drawing from the philosophies of Cora Diamond and Martha Nussbaum, Wolfe likewise emphasizes the role of "shared embodiment, mortality, and finitude" in shaping ethical responses.[37] He envisions posthumanist ethics as necessarily "based not on ability, activity, agency, and empowerment but on a compassion that is rooted in vulnerability and sensitivity"; rather than the dangerous bodily proximities of predation and pathogens, what he is driving at is the peculiar fragility of the human as a "fundamentally prosthetic creature" utterly dependent on "'not-human' forms of technicity and materiality," which again inscribes the crucial role of language.[38]

This kind of posthumanist positioning finds further support in Anat Pick's "creaturely poetics," geared to work out vulnerability as "a universal mode of exposure" with distinct ethical implications for human-animal relations.[39] As Dominik Ohrem elaborates, Pick anticipates the criticism that such an approach veers toward victim shaming, or excusing animal exploitation by pointing out their defenselessness to it, and he notes that Pick is quick to counter that such an approach exposes "the underlying tenets of the liberal humanist tradition, in particular, the constitutive relationship between (specific notions of) agency, subjectivity, and ethical considerability" that are geared to categorically victimize animals from the outset.[40] The focus on vulnerability and finitude in Pick's and Wolfe's work alike leads Ohrem to categorize it as "mortalist posthumanism," one that foregrounds only negative or abject conditions,[41] and to propose instead reconceptualizing "embodiment as world-openness [that] allows for more affirmative imaginings of embodied interspecies relationality and for a more conscious recognition of the ways in which [the capacity for mutual transformations] permeates 'human' lives and societies."[42] Before elaborating how these and other recent revisionings of the creatural suggest new frontiers for posthumanist animal studies, I think it is necessary to examine more closely how contested articulations of what constitutes "animal studies" disturb these developments.

The complexly intertwined social, aesthetic, and political histories shared across species lines inform the central concerns of what Garry Marvin and I have termed "human-animal studies": why animals are represented and configured in different ways in human cultures and societies around the world; how they are understood, imagined, experienced, and given significance; what these relationships might signify about being human; and which aspects of these relationships might be improved for the sake of individuals, communities, and ecosystems. Just getting a handle on what is going on in human-animal encounters requires enormous creative, intellectual, and material commitments to paying close attention to lived experiences as well as to the imagined nature of these relationships.[43] In part, our choice of the term was motivated by the practical problem of potential confusion with usages of "animal studies" in the sciences to distinguish preliminaries to medical testing on human subjects. Along the way, though, my work with Marvin, who is a social anthropologist, has clarified for me that added to my burdens as a literary scholar remain the old prejudices that the proper object of study in the humanities remains humankind – in psychoanalytic terms, that animals are bad object-choices for nonscientist academics.

The potential for reframing these concerns therefore makes posthumanist perspectives incredibly appealing because they open lines of inquiry from within disciplines that had otherwise been organized around studiously avoiding nonhumans. That animals were generally considered off-limits when I was a graduate student in literature is a much more basic concern than the access or prestige issues raised by Fraiman, and one that appears to persist. Despite a prominent institutional presence emerging through animal studies conferences, journals, book series, course offerings, programs, and even a few research centers, there persists a dearth of academic jobs devoted to animal humanities (in contrast, say, to environmental humanities). What the future holds largely hinges on perceptions regarding from where animal studies emerged and what has sustained it, and here I think engagements with posthumanist perspectives prove most generative.

While most agree that a distinct field of study has coalesced around these concerns in the past few decades, debates about what to call it – human-animal studies, anthrozoology, critical animal studies, etc. – often turn on what role posthumanist theory plays in its genealogy. For those who assume that animal studies is an offshoot of the animal rights movement, the posthuman can look like a creature of theory threatening to undermine animal activism. Laura Wright characterizes animal studies as a "three-pronged" pursuit that, in its various iterations, tends to prioritize ethical, theoretical, or practical dimensions. Making her own separatist case for vegan studies, Wright disidentifies with the theoretical, which she locates squarely within a posthumanist frame.[44] Her position is eerily echoed by Michael Lundblad, who likewise develops a tripartite structure, but for a very different purpose: human-animal studies (characterized by Haraway's emphasis on relationality but extending to advocacy), posthumanism (embracing the more open-ended subjects of biopolitical theory like plants and microbes), and what he terms animality studies.[45] Lundblad's motive seems the inverse of Wright's in that he prises out the animal content from posthumanism in order to empty it of associations with advocacy; as a proponent of animality studies, he prefers to "be seen as a speciesist" than to "risk" falling back on "ahistorical, universalist prescriptions about how to treat or interact with non-human animals."[46]

More strident views are sketched by those who identify as scholar-activists or activist-scholars under the banner of critical animal studies, only holding these lines proves difficult in practice. John Sorenson asserts in his editor's introduction to *The Rise of Critical Animal Studies* that "mainstream animal studies effectively serves the status quo [by] ... dismiss[ing] as polemicists those who take an explicitly ethical stance in support of animal liberation."[47] His two examples, if telling ones, are mentioned just in passing: "The influence of Derrida and Haraway is especially pernicious because ... their arcane writing and irrationalism is largely meaningless, as it is dissociated from popular struggles and undermines activism."[48] One might expect Sorenson's position to find strongest support among nonacademics, yet curiously in his volume it is the longtime animal activists who embrace Haraway and Derrida, along with even more readily recognizably posthumanist theorists, in order to advance more nuanced positions. For instance, PETA's first Executive Director, Kim Stallwood, critiques how "the animal rights movement at present behaves more like a moral crusade than a social movement."[49] Rather than insisting on more rigid lines between "fundamentalism and realpolitik or abolition and regulation," Stallwood echoes another contributor, activist author of *The Sexual Politics of Meat*, Carol J. Adams – whose essay in Sorenson's volume even more explicitly credits Derrida's positive influence – in concluding that "[b]oth are needed to help the other achieve the change they seek."[50] Still more confusingly, in the same collection Zipporah Weisberg echoes Williams when she dismisses posthumanist animal ethics as "a self-indulgent intellectual exercise" geared to sever theory from practice,[51] even as she recognizes that her strongest supporters in reclaiming academic animal activism themselves self-identify as posthumanist theorists. What remains unsaid in these discussions is that advocacy praxis along the anti-posthumanist animal studies lines has moved from academic critique to overt acts of intimidation and harassment, and to my knowledge only of strictly female-identified scholars.[52]

What all of this suggests is that the different and sometimes contradictory claims made at the intersections of posthuman and human-animal studies are, to varying degrees, informed by a still greater range of feminist, antiracist, marxist, antiableist, and decolonial theorists who demand a far more significant liberation of all from the foundational units of humanist thought. Even for activists, moral philosopher Peter Singer's *Animal Liberation* (1975) – which turned Richard Ryder's "speciesism" into a household term – no longer seems a watershed moment so much as a last stand, perhaps because it extends rather than questions a tradition of analytical philosophy that remains deeply invested in a notion of rights tailored to the model of human subjectivity. A major significance of the posthumanist turn made possible by these critiques is that it enables discussions of "animals as agents who are not just humanlike subjects or thinglike objects, but actors of a different order, who appear at breathtaking moments [according to Marvin] 'performing with' people."[53] Recognizing my own need to bracket off conclusions on this subject, I close here instead by gesturing toward what strikes me as the most promising creative, creatural models emerging at the crossroads of animal studies and posthumanist thought.

Writing with Giovanni Aloi, I define "the posthuman [as] a creature of art, sf, literature, and philosophy as much as it is a form of response to the pressures and potentialities of technology, globalization, and extinction at the turn of the millennium."[54] Posthuman subjects must approach life itself as creative practice, that is – to paraphrase disabled dancer, artist, and poet Neil Marcus – they must craft "an ingenious way to live" together with other forms of life.[55] So rising to the challenge outlined by Rosi Braidotti, to become the subject of "posthuman knowledge" means that one must necessarily be tasked with "separating the critique of humanism from postanthropocentrism to avoid the risk of hierarchies and exclusions."[56] As Ryan says, "Braidotti's subject is humble, anti-individualist, post-anthropocentric and yet wholeheartedly engaged in a political struggle that combines 'critique with creativity.'"[57] While again I am inclined to disagree with formulations such as the one Braidotti offers of animal studies as subsumed within environmental humanities, I agree with Vint's broader point that Braidotti's posthuman-ism "offers alternative metaphysics of subjectivity that stress becoming over being, that reconfigure the kinship system in ways that no longer require or indeed allow a decision between in-group kin or out-group enemy"; a posthuman that in its origins in becoming, not being, also aligns with Haraway's expansive notion of "companion species" – whether of women and dogs, mammals and intestinal flora, and all these and more with mushrooms and plants – that constantly and profoundly changes condi-tions for how we make lives together.[58]

Human-animal relations are not just mutually constitutive but also, as Vint elaborates, potentially transformative inter-relations,[59] perhaps most tantalizingly in sf imaginings of expanding and creating new posthuman sensorial or perceptive capacities with bodily enhancement effects.[60] My own roots in literary studies may betray my own prejudices on this point, but nonetheless are buttressed by David Herman's shifting of the focus of the discussion from creaturely embodiedness to creatural fictions, or "fic-tional accounts [that] can serve as a workspace for reconsidering – for critiquing or reaffirming, dismantling or reconstructing – narratives about human selves in a world in which selfhood extends beyond the domain of the human."[61] Reflecting on how "pagan, animist, vitalist," and otherwise non-western traditions rely on "situated narratives," Tsz Man Chan posits that the power of speculative storytelling across species lines leads post-humanism to "postanimalism."[62] What follows after the (animal after) human, then, is the cultivation of what Herman terms "a more inclusive ecology of selves, exposing a fault line between parsimonious and prolific allocations of the possibility for selfhood beyond the human,"[63] that, as Pieter Vermuelen and Virginia Richter envision, allow for "more intimate forms of implication and connectedness" to be valued over the privileges of human life.[64]

# Notes

1. William J. Ripple et al., "Status and Ecological Effects of the World's Largest Carnivores," *Science* 343(6167) (2014), online.

2. Chris Wilbert, "What Is Doing the Killing? Animal Attacks, Man-Eaters, and Shifting Boundaries and Flows of Human-Animal Relations" in The Animal Studies Group (eds.), *Killing Animals* (Champaign: University of Illinois Press, 2006), 37.

3. Cary Wolfe, *Before the Law: Humans and Other Animals in a Biopolitical Frame* (Chicago: University of Chicago Press, 2013), 10.

4. Sylvia Wynter, "Unsettling the Coloniality of Being/Power/Truth/Freedom: Towards the Human, After Man, Its Overrepresentation – An Argument," *CR: The New Centennial Review* 3.3 (2003), 317.

5. Eva Hoffman, "Queering the Interspecies Encounter: Yoko Tawada's *Memoirs of a Polar Bear*" in Kári Driscoll and Eva Hoffmann (eds.), *What Is Zoopoetics? Texts, Bodies, Entanglement* (New York: Palgrave, 2018), 151.

6. Adam Lowenstein, "Buñuel's Bull Meets YouTube's Lion: Surrealist and Digital Posthumanisms" in Michael Lawrence and Laura McMahon (eds.), *Animal Life and the Moving Image* (London: BFI, 2015),. 60.

7. N. Katherine Hayles, "Unfinished Work: From Cyborg to Cognisphere," *Theory, Culture, and Society* 23(7–8) (2006), 159.

8. N. Katherine Hayles, *My Mother Was a Computer: Digital Subjects and Literary Texts* (Chicago: University of Chicago Press, 2005), 91.

9. Arthur Kroker, *Body Drift: Butler, Hayles, Haraway* (Minneapolis: University of Minnesota Press, 2012), 143–4.

10. Kroker, 19.

11. Wolfe elaborates the difference somewhat circularly as "humanist approaches to posthumanism" versus "posthumanist approaches to posthumanism" in *What Is Posthumanism?* (Minneapolis: University of Minnesota Press, 2010), 62.

12. Sherryl Vint, *Animal Alterity: Science Fiction and the Question of the Animal* (Liverpool: Liverpool University Press, 2010), 78.

13. N. Katherine Hayles, *How We Became Posthuman: Virtual Bodies in Cybernetics, Literature, and Informatics* (Chicago: University of Chicago Press, 1999), 1.

14. Bruce Clarke, "Mediating *The Fly*: Posthuman Metamorphosis in the 1950s," *Configurations* 10(1) (2002), 171–2.

15. Donna J. Haraway, *When Species Meet* (Minneapolis: University of Minnesota Press, 2008), 17.

16. Haraway, *Species*, 17.

17. Haraway quoted in Jeffrey J. Williams, "Donna Haraway's Critters," *Chronicle of Higher Education* (October 18, 2009), online.

18. Haraway quoted in Jeffrey J. Williams, "Science Stories: An Interview with Donna J. Haraway," *Minnesota Review* 73–74 (2009–10), 151.

19. Alice Kuzniar, *Melancholia's Dog: Reflections on Our Animal Kinship* (Chicago: University of Chicago Press, 2006), 3.

20. Susan McHugh, "Bitch, Bitch, Bitch: Personal Criticism, Feminist Theory, and Dog Writing," *Hypatia: A Journal of Feminist Philosophy* 27.3 (2012): 616–35.

21. Williams, "Science Stories," 159.

22. Jeffrey J. Williams, "The New Belletrism," *Style* 33.3 (1999), 421.

23. Williams, "Belletrism," 423–4.

24. Vinciane Despret, "The Body We Care For: Figures of Anthropo-zoo-genesis," *Body and Society* 10.2 (2004), 131.

25. Donna J. Haraway, "Situated Knowledges: The Science Question in Feminism and the Privilege of Partial Perspective" in *Simians, Cyborgs, Women: The Reinvention of Nature* (New York: Routledge, 1991), 190.

26. Wolfe, *What Is Posthumanism?*, xvi.

27. Cary Wolfe, *Animal Rites: American Culture, the Discourse of Species, and Posthumanist Theory* (Chicago: University of Chicago Press, 2003), 190.

28. Cary Wolfe, "Thinking Other-Wise: Cognitive Science, Deconstruction, and the (Non)Speaking (Non)Human Animal Subject" in Jodey Castricano (ed.), *Animal Subjects: An Ethical Reader in a Posthuman World* (Waterloo, Ontario: Wilfred Laurier University Press, 2006), 138.

29. Akira Mizuta Lippit, "Therefore, the Animal that Saw Derrida" in Jami Weinstein and Claire Colebrook (eds.), *Posthumous Life: Theorizing Beyond the Posthuman* (New York: Columbia University Press, 2017), 87.

30. Cary Wolfe, "Human, All Too Human: 'Animal Studies' and the Humanities," *PMLA* 124.2 (2009), 570–1. See also Chapters 2 and 3 of this volume for a more detailed discussion of the relationship between Derridean thought and posthumanism.

31. Wolfe, "Human, All Too Human," 566–7.

32. Although "discursive formation" is a term introduced by Michel Foucault, I am here invoking Stuart Hall's usage (via Raymond Williams) to characterize the formation of cultural studies to elaborate the struggles that I have engaged in, namely, how the conflicted origins, histories, and materializations converge decisively if unstably in what Williams called "a common disposition of energy and direction," which for Hall stays relevant only through a productive tension between "simply pluralist" (anything-goes) and singular (dogmatic) politics in "Cultural Studies and Its Theoretical Legacies" in Vincent B. Leitch, et al. (eds.), *The Norton Anthology of Theory and Criticism* (New York: Norton, 2001), 1899.

33. Susan Fraiman, "Pussy Panic versus Liking Animals: Tracking Gender in Animal Studies," *Critical Inquiry* 39.1 (2012), 92.

34. Fraiman, 114.
35. Donna J. Haraway, *Manifestly Haraway*, with Cary Wolfe (Minneapolis: University of Minnesota Press, 2016). Susan McHugh, *Animal Stories: Narrating Across Species Lines* (Minneapolis: University of Minnesota Press, 2011).
36. Derek Ryan, *Animal Theory: A Critical Introduction* (Edinburgh: Edinburgh University Press), 2015. 69.
37. Cary Wolfe, "Introduction: Exposures," in Stanley Cavell, et al. (eds.), *Philosophy and Animal Life* (New York: Columbia University Press, 2008), 8.
38. Wolfe, "Exposures," 14.
39. Anat Pick, *Creaturely Poetics: Animality and Vulnerability in Literature and Film* (New York: Columbia University Press, 2011), 5.
40. Dominik Ohrem, "An Address from Elsewhere: Vulnerability, Relationality, and Conceptions of Creaturely Embodiment," in Dominik Ohrem and Roman Bartosch (eds.), *Beyond the Human-Animal Divide: Creaturely Lives in Literature and Culture* (New York: Palgrave, 2017), 48.
41. Ohrem, 49.
42. Ohrem, 69.
43. Susan McHugh and Garry Marvin, "Human-animal Studies: Global Perspectives," in Susan McHugh and Garry Marvin (eds.), *Human-Animal Studies*, 4 vols. (New York: Routledge, 2018), vol. 1, 1.
44. Laura Wright, *The Vegan Studies Project: Food, Animals, and Gender in the Age of Terror* (Athens: University of Georgia Press, 2015), 11.
45. Michael Lundblad, "Introduction: The End of the Animal – Literary and Cultural Animalities," in Michael Lundblad (ed.), *Animalities: Literary and Cultural Studies Beyond the Human* (Edinburgh: Edinburgh University Press, 2017), 2–3.
46. Michael Lundblad, "From Animal to Animality Studies," *PMLA* 124.2 (2009), 496–502. 500.
47. John Sorenson, "Introduction: Thinking the Unthinkable" in John Sorenson (ed.), *Critical Animal Studies: Thinking the Unthinkable*, (Toronto: Canada Scholars' Press, 2014), xix.
48. Sorenson, xix.
49. Kim Stallwood, "Animal Rights: Moral Crusade or Social Movement?" in John Sorenson (ed.), *Critical Animal Studies: Thinking the Unthinkable*, (Toronto: Canada Scholars' Press, 2014), 304.
50. Stallwood, "Animal Rights," 314.
51. Zipporah Weisberg, "The Trouble with Posthumanism: Bacteria are People Too" in John Sorenson (ed.), *Critical Animal Studies: Thinking the Unthinkable*, (Toronto: Canada Scholars' Press, 2014), 107.
52. See Haraway's account of having been "subject to a fantasy of my own public rape by name by a small group of self-identified deep ecology, anarchist activists" in *When Species Meet*, 10. I can add that Stephen Best's "The Rise of Critical Animal Studies: Putting Theory into Action and Animal Liberation into Higher Education" (*Journal of Critical Animal Studies* 7.1

[2009], 9–52) pillories me and another female scholar as his lone exemplars of what is wrong with "mainstream animal studies" (in my case, "us[ing] the most obtuse and pretentious jargon possible to justify academic entrapment within the funhouse of theory and to construct an insidious argument against the very possibility of politics" [31]). What is more, his article was sent to me by a member of the journal's editorial board along with the warning that Best had just left the group because he refused to renounce violence in the name of animal liberation.

53. Susan McHugh, "In Conversation with Garry Marvin," *Antennae: The Journal of Nature in Visual Culture* 38.1 (2017), 10–11.
54. Giovanni Aloi and Susan McHugh, "Introduction: Art and the Ontological Turn," in Giovanni Aloi and Susan McHugh (eds.), *Posthumanism in Art and Science: A Reader* (New York: Columbia University Press, forthcoming).
55. Neil Marcus quoted in Sunaura Taylor, *Beasts of Burden: Animal and Disability Liberation* (New York: New Press, 2017), 136.
56. Rosi Braidotti, *Posthuman Knowledge* (Cambridge: Polity, 2019), 13.
57. Ryan, 73.
58. Vint, 44.
59. Vint, 165.
60. Vint, 223.
61. David Herman, "Narratology Beyond the Human," *Diegesis* 3.2 (2014), 132.
62. Tsz Man Chan, "Postanimalism" in Rosi Braidotti and Maria Hlavajova (eds.), *Posthuman Glossary* (New York: Bloomsbury, 2018), 331.
63. David Herman, *Narratology Beyond the Human: Storytelling and Animal Life* (Oxford: Oxford University Press, 2018), 33.
64. Pieter Vermulen and Virginia Richter, "Introduction: Creaturely Constellations," *European Journal of English Studies* 19.1 (2015), 2.

# CHAPTER 8

# Life "Itself"

## Nadine Ehlers

Changing practices in contemporary biosciences and biotechnology have altered definitions and understandings of what we call "life" – what we mean by this term, what constitutes life, and how human and nonhuman others experience life. In an age when "biology is not destiny but opportunity," life is open for transformation and revisioning.[1] Yet, precisely because of this revisioning, life has become a contested terrain and the human has been reframed: new ethical concerns continually emerge, new social realities are inaugurated and require navigation, and, simultaneously, novel forms of pre-existing inequities (geosocial and political) are rehearsed and often re-secured. While there are numerous ways the concept and realities of life have undergone radical change, four key modalities are identifiable: (1) life has been increasingly technologized; (2) life has come to be understood as an "open dynamism"; (3) human life has increasingly become subject to self-management or self-governance; and, (4) life has become a domain for the production of biovalue. It is imperative to also examine how these operations are inextricable from relations of power that concern what we might call "life-making," and how such efforts foster certain forms of life while denying others. In other words, life-making can often be deadly.[2]

## 8.1 Shifting Concepts of Life

As a biological term and concept, our contemporary understanding of "life" emerged only with the rise of modern biology in the late eighteenth to early nineteenth century. In *The Order of Things*, Michel Foucault claims that it was at the threshold of these two centuries that a crucial turning point can be witnessed, where the natural history of what he called the "Classical Age" gave way to the life sciences/the "science of life" – biology.[3] And, as Georges Canguilhem eloquently notes, "interpreted in a certain way, contemporary biology is, somehow, a philosophy of life," in that it is concerned with the very meaning of life.[4] While the taxonomists of the Classical Age divided the natural world into three kingdoms of animal, vegetable, and mineral, the modern life sciences replaced this with a primary distinction between the organic and inorganic. It was this division that became a fundamental *opposition* – where a sense of vitality and animate existence was attributed only to the organic. Not simply understood as that which is imbued with life, the organic, as Foucault explains, "becomes the living and the living is that which *produces, grows,* and *reproduces*; the inorganic is the non-living, that which neither develops nor reproduces; it lies at the frontiers of life, the inert, the unfruitful – death."[5] Thus, life came to be understood as opposed to death, and death was positioned as that which life struggles against.

By the twentieth century, this framing led to the human body being conceptualized as an organically unified whole, a vital system, and preserving life was fundamentally understood as requiring a struggle against pathology.[6] We see, then, a series of foundational dichotomies erected (through which vital existence – of the human and others – is then understood): organic/inorganic; life/death; normal/pathological, and to these we could add others such as nature/artifice, subject/object, human/nonhuman, etc. Life "itself" came to be understood as "the living of the living organism" and, in terms of the human, early biomedicine labored to control, stabilize, standardize, and normalize human life – to maintain the equilibrium of health and avert incapacity, illness, and death.[7]

While our understandings of life have transformed over and again since the beginnings of modern biology, in our current era we see particular reworkings and recalibrations of life itself – due to both specific bioscientific/biotech advancements *and* changing political-economic imperatives and governing logics that have emerged during the latter half of the twentieth century. Increasingly, now, life as we know it has come to be *manipulated, customized, optimized, maximized, and commodified*.[8] Indeed, life is being recreated, we have pushed the possibilities of and for life beyond its perceived limits, and we are witnessing a proliferation of life forms. As Sakari Tamminen and Niki Vermeulen have argued, "not only is biologically framed existence confirmed and exploited, but novel biological entities performing new forms of labour and enacting social relations are systematically being created."[9] Such transformations are troubling our taken-for-granted ontologies of life and thus provoking challenging conversations about what "life" and being "human" now mean.

## 8.2   Life Technologized

One of the key transformations we have witnessed is that *life has been increasingly technologized*. For although, as Joanna Zylinska has argued, "human and non-human subjects . . . [are – and have been] always-already enhanced, and hence dependent, relational and co-evolving with technology," in our current era, the entanglements with technology have intensified.[10] An increasingly molecular view of life emerged in biology from the 1930s, for example, and enabled organisms – including human organisms – to be seen as open to change and optimization at the molecular level. And, indeed, life is now intervened upon through technologies and techniques such as gene splicing/cutting and editing, the customization of DNA sequences, and the manufacture of organisms without specific gene sequences or with new ones added. Such technological innovation enables novel forms of cloning of biological materials, including genes, cells, tissues, and even entire organisms – the most famous of which was Dolly, the sheep. It has also led to new forms of human-animal entanglements – chimeras – where animal material is replaced with human tissues and cells: the CRISPR gene-editing technique has been used to grow human organs in live pigs, for example, with the aim of progressing toward a reality where animals could be used as human organ incubators.[11]

Plants have already been modified to transfer a gene from one species to another to endow the organism with a new trait (like pest resistance), and now CRISPR technologies are being used to introduce new traits by actually *rewriting* the plants' genetic code.[12] Furthermore, with the rise of synthetic biology we see other permutations of the technologization of life: synthesizing new genetic codes by stitching together long sequences of DNA and inserting them into an organism's genome.[13] While there are multiple forms of life being created through synthetic biology, some of the most celebrated examples include yeast-made biofuel, bacteria engineered to produce isoprene (the raw material for rubber), viruses to boost the immune system's ability to fight cancer, and synthesized jellyfish intended to clean up toxic spills.[14]

At the level of the human, technologization can be seen as *extending life* and human capacity through human-machine interactions. Mundane and now taken-for-granted examples include the use of pacemakers, dialysis, artificial limbs and joints, and hearing aids. More innovative intersections between human and machine are seen in battery-powered hands, cochlear implants that stimulate nerves, technologically grown skin, and the development of prosthetics controlled by the brain. Alongside (and often overlapping) this extension, technologization also enables the *reanimation of life* through regenerative medicine – where damaged human parts are replaced/regrown/repaired through tissue-engineering or stem cell technologies. As an example, the application of such technologies has created supplemental bladders, small arteries, skin grafts, cartilage, and even a full trachea implant, and cutting-edge stem cell technologies hold the promise of preventing or curing diseases and injuries such as Parkinson's, type 1 diabetes, heart disease, spinal cord injury, muscular dystrophy, Alzheimer's disease, strokes, burns, osteoarthritis, and vision or hearing loss. Lastly, technologization is facilitating the *suspension of life*, as seen in the creation of immortalized cell lines – where a population of cells are intentionally induced to evade cell death and cultivated to continue proliferating *in vitro*. The creation of immortalized cell lines demonstrates what Hannah Landecker characterizes as "the total manipulability of somatic tissue in space and time,"[15] and highlights both the plasticity of life and that life can have autonomy outside a body. It also opens (human and other) bodies to further experimentation and potential exploitation, a point to which I return later.

Taken together, these various forms of technological intervention show that human (and nonhuman) vital existence is no longer, as Susan Merrill Squier notes, "defined by its unique temporal and spatial coordinates: one body, one life, in a specific space and time." Instead, it is "increasingly defined by the agential, instrumental deployment of resources for ... renewal ... [and] subject to extension or translocation."[16] The organic/inorganic opposition has been dislodged (through extension technologies); nature/artifice and self/other oppositions have been challenged (through a range of new molecular entanglements); and the life/death dyad has been called into question (through reanimation and suspension technologies and through organic-inorganic couplings).[17] Many have seen the collapsing of these dichotomies as cause for celebration. At the same time, however, these changes have presented ethical challenges and led to increased legal policing – what Sheila Jasanoff calls "bioconstitutionalism" – regarding which lines can or should be crossed.[18]

## 8.3 Life as "Open Dynamism"

If life has been increasingly technologized, it has also come to be *seen as an open dynamism*. Taking human life as a focus, we see that this life is no longer viewed through older notions of biological or genetic determinism but understood instead as complex and emergent. Indeed, life, including

human life, can be characterized as an *indeterminacy* in-the-making.[19] The
science of epigenetics is one arena where life as an open dynamism is
confirmed. Epigenetics is the study of changes in the genome and gene
function that occur without human technological intervention to alter the
DNA or genetic code. Epigenetic mechanisms influence gene expression
(turning genes on or off), and these molecular mechanisms can be affected
by a myriad of factors such as environment and other external stimuli.
Moreover, they are heritable from parent to offspring and across
generations.[20] Epigenetics then offers a "non-determinist model of biological life as plastic, that is, changeable": it is, as Becky Mansfield and Julie
Guthman have noted, "a science of variation – of difference – that moves
toward a notion of biological difference as part of the warp and weave of
space and time, both social and natural."[21] For example, recent research has
established particular *racialized etiologies* for obesity in the USA that can be
accounted for through epigenetics rather than the eating behaviors of
individuals. Exposure to certain agricultural chemicals (that act as endo-
crine disruptors), chronic stress and accompanying cortisol circulation
(which has been shown to result from experiencing institutional racism),
and generationally passed-on malnutrition have all been associated with
escalated rates of obesity in minority populations.[22] Epigenetics thus
enables us to see how human embodied life is shaped by external factors –
including the past – and emerges as porous, dynamic, and indeterminate: it
highlights the past and present of biosocial damage, that is, how trauma
can be inherited as biological effect.

Another way we see life existing as an open dynamism is in the human
microbiome, defined as the collective genomes of the microbes (bacteria,
bacteriophages, fungi, protozoa, viruses) that live inside and on the human
body. The Human Microbiome Project, inaugurated in 2008, found that
we have about ten times as many microbial cells as human cells. The
human body (hence, "life") is made up of a community of cells: multiple
rather than singular, humans are "not alone" in their bodies but, instead,
occupied by these microbial cells: always more-than-human. We can no
longer be seen as "merely the lineal descendants of previous generations of
earlier hominoids, anthropoids, mammals, chordates, animals, and so on,"
as Stefan Helmreich notes. We are, rather, "sideways mash-ups –
Frankensteins – made up of a welter of teeny microbial friends and
enemies. *The traces of relic viruses and companion microbes are embedded
in our genomes, our cells, ourselves.* Microorganismic relations survive and
thrive in our blood and guts."[23] Thus, any idea of a "pure" human is called
into question, and the human is shown as always-already relational to other

forms of life: "[t]aken together, then, epigenetic and microbiome studies have enabled us to see that life (of the embodied human) is not bounded – but open and precarious to what Bernard Vallat, Director General of the World Organization for Animal Health (OIE), has called the 'great biological cauldron' of the twenty-first century."[24]

## 8.4 Life as Self-Governed

At the same time, human life has been positioned as that which should be *managed and enhanced through self-management/governance*. Governance of human life – its possibilities, capacities, and health – has shifted within the broad historical terrain of late liberalism. Previously, the life of the human population was that to be tended to by a pastoral state – that managed the collective risks posed to human health. We see this in late nineteenth-and early twentieth-century public awareness campaigns related to health and disease and in public screening/testing initiatives that together frame ill health as a threat to national wellbeing and call on individuals and their families to participate – for the collective good. The logics of governing during this time – the politics of life – were concerned with conditioning the biological capacities of the general citizenry.[25]

Throughout the latter part of the twentieth century, however, these logics of governing changed. On the one hand, the rise of neoliberal governing strategies, characterized by a declining welfare imperative, led to a devolution of the state and a growing absence of the idea of "society" or a "collective social good." This new governance was expressed via increased privatization, a revived and intensified laissez-faire individualism, and the subjection of almost every aspect of life to market logics and financial cost-benefit analyses. On the other hand, and dovetailing with the rise of neoliberal governance, emerged what Adele Clarke et al. call the increasing biomedicalization of everyday life – where almost everything is now cast as a biomedical problem (in relation to which the body can be transformed rather than simply controlled). Biomedicine is looked to as an unparalleled truth that can *answer* almost any problem. For Rose, this means that "[t]o live well today is to live in light of biomedicine," whether that be in relation to cognitive capacity, aging, or the very process of death.[26]

These factors have led to heightened individual responsibility for health and risk, in a context where the state is no longer expected to resolve the health needs of society. A "network of injunctions from experts" call on individuals (and communities) to (1) understand themselves through the language and norms of biomedical knowledge, (2)

manage and modulate their biology/health through biomedical technologies and techniques, and (3) actively take on health directives as
personal pursuits and ways to anticipate their futures and maximize
life.[27] Connected to this, individuals are increasingly encouraged to
consume health-related (and supposedly health-enhancing) goods and
services to be ideal citizens – to avoid being a "financial drain" and
instead to exercise "choice" as a form of freedom, while at the same time
expanding markets.[28] The rise of the imperative of self-governance
ultimately requires that the individual regulate every aspect of their
biological lives to be productive throughout the life course.

## 8.5   Life as a Domain of Biovalue

The manipulation and maximization of life and capacity has contributed
to the emergence of an additional transformation of life "itself": the rise of
a global bioeconomy in which *life has been positioned and deployed as
a domain of biovalue*. For Catherine Waldby, *biovalue* refers to "the yield
of vitality produced by the biotechnical reformulation of living processes."
She focuses specifically on the ways biotechnology makes interventions
between living and non-living systems such that "new and contingent
forms of vitality can be created, capitalizing on life."[29] Nikolas Rose uses
the term to refer to "the value extracted from the vital properties of living
processes."[30]

At the simplest level, biovalue refers to the way biology has become
highly capitalized. This reality is evident, in the first instance, in how
biovalue has been harvested via some of the technologies mentioned
earlier – to produce higher and more resilient crop yields or new forms
of bioenergy (such as various forms of biofuel). Other new technologies
enable new forms of bioremediation, where biology is reused and repro-
cessed into forms of value. For example, the dead human body – the
corpse – has become a key source of biovalue: body/parts and tissues are
converted into financial value commodifying the afterlife through processes of extraction. This biovalue in afterlife can be seen, for example, in
organ donation that supplies replacement parts for the bodies of the living
and in whole body donation for medical education or the advancement of
the forensic science of human remains. The corpse is also converted into
biovalue through practices such as implant/prosthetic recycling (where
crematoriums recover metal and other implants from bodies) and cremator
technologies that convert waste heat from incineration into electricity that
can be put back on the grid.[31]

At another level, advanced biomedical and health technologies are capitalizing on almost every element of human biological life by developing new pharmaceuticals, techniques, and other "fixes" for present or anticipated illness or incapacity. We see infinitely expanding markets for drugs through the incremental biomedicalization of life – that create more and more consumers (primed to produce economic yield).[32] A key example here is the development of race-specific pharmaceuticals over the last fifteen years, beginning with the FDA approval of BiDil for use in self-identified "black" subjects.[33] Race-based pharmaceuticals carve out a market of consumers based on a notion of race as a biological truth, contending that certain health ailments are race-based and that a proposed drug will address said-ailment (bypassing any extra-biological etiologies of disease), to create new niche markets of considerable financial value.

Additionally, human biological capacity/living biology has become a form of biovalue. At the macro-level, human subjects are nodes in practices of clinical labor – contributing their vitality – by acting as clinical trial enrollees or research subjects, tissue donors, or reproductive surrogates.[34] At the micro-level, human tissues and cells are now sources of biovalue in a global market. Ova, sperm, and embryos are familiar forms of biovalue generated from human tissue/cells that circulate internationally, but there are many other examples. For instance, immortalized cell lines have been commercialized for quite some time, with the most famous case being the HeLa cell line, which was derived without consent from cervical cancer patient Henrietta Lacks in 1951.[35] These cells have made significant contributions to scientific research (on viruses, toxins, and hormones), the development of vaccines, various cancer treatments, and a genome sequence. And, as of 2018, there were over 17,000 current USA patents alone using HeLa cells – that continue to generate profit.[36] Human genes are another example of micro-level human-sourced biovalue and can be linked to pernicious forms of bioprospecting of human biologicals – such as in the procurement of DNA from indigenous peoples.[37] As Margaret Lock notes, the trajectory of such practices is that *"life itself becomes the private property of pharmaceutical and other companies."*[38] Lastly, human stem cells have emerged as a core form of biovalue to be harnessed and deployed in therapeutic contexts, due to their plasticity and potentially unlimited capacity for self-renewal. Technologies using either embryonic or adult stem cells instrumentalize the growth/genesis processes of the body to promote vitalism at the cellular level: this both increases vitality and generates financial yield, as consumers of such therapies incur considerable economic costs. Each of these new forms of biovalue position life – human and otherwise – as that which can be capitalized as both vital and financial value.

## 8.6 Life-Making – And Letting Die

The various developments in contemporary biosciences and biotechnology that have been explored here are inextricable from what we might call "life-making." This term encapsulates efforts to condition generalized "life" and biological capacity, and the specific modes through which to make humans (as biological beings) *live more* – particularly in relation to biomedicine.[39] We might say, then, to return to Rose's definition of life "itself," that life-making related to humans is concerned with affirming the living – vitality – of the living human organism.

Life-making has long been central to *governing strategies* and, as such, cannot be viewed as ontologically neutral or unassailably liberatory. Instead, life-making is intimately bound within and by relations of power. Traditionally, those strategies, technologies, practices, and logics that constitute power over life (what Foucault refers to as biopower) worked to maintain health and control disease as it relates to populations at large and to individuals within a field of national competition. Yet not all lives were equally fostered, as numerous caesuras (race being a primary one) present cuts between who is made to live and who is let die.[40] In the contemporary era, when biology is *opportunity*, life-making has become increasingly focused on optimization and maximization (rather than simply control and maintenance). Additionally, marked by the economic rationales of late liberalism, life-making operations now foster health and life in relation to market logics and global capital, intensify speculation in ways that can pose risks to the life and death stakes of biological existence, and place the onus to maintain health on the individual. Life-making strategies might have altered, but the inequities that historically were present have not receded but are instead re-secured and often exacerbated.

If new technologies extend life and reanimate it, who has access to these opportunities, and how is this access conditioned by economic and other factors? Whose lives are suspended and whose extended? Thinking through the examples of HeLa and the gene-hunting that has occurred in relation to indigenous peoples, we can see that the underside to such technologies is that they enable new forms of extraction from minorities. Human-nonhuman entanglements are a further extension of human jurisdiction over other forms of life – a violence that now extends to altering the very codes of life. Epigenetic and microbiome studies highlight the historically unequal fostering of life – through settler colonialism, slavery, and numerous other factors that have led to a range of ethnic and racial inequities that *live on*, in that individuals *live with these histories as biological effects.*[41] But these histories are compounded by ongoing lack of access to adequate food, non-toxic environments, and preventative health and medical care. In the abstract, the rise of self-governance and self-responsibility might seem like laudable goals. However, we must recognize how the call to self-responsibilization is regulatory: it directs us toward only certain forms of life, generally those deemed productive and generative. Moreover, if health is a personal pursuit – and an ethic of active citizenship is now almost obligatory – social/structural inequalities and non-personal etiologies of disease are obfuscated or denied. So, the broader causes of race-specific ill health, for example, cannot appear in such life-making logics. Indeed, those that cannot maintain the endless quest for health are often abandoned or denigrated (an example would be the push for "successful aging" and the framing of decline as failure).

The capitalization of life inherent within the reframing of life as a domain of biovalue appears as an infinitely expanding terrain of extracting more and more life and capacity from every aspect of human (and nonhuman) biology – precisely through exploiting biological capacities – at the individual or cellular level. These reworkings of life itself trouble and, indeed, undercut traditional demarcations between human/nonhuman, organic/inorganic, life/death, and so forth. Ultimately, however, regardless of the hype and promise that surrounds many of the novel transformations of life, there is reason for hesitation. The life-making pursuits of contemporary biosciences and biotechnology may have altered what we mean by life "itself," but they also animate new and revive old politico-ethical concerns about how life should be lived.

## Notes

1. Nikolas Rose, *The Politics of Life Itself: Biomedicine, Power, and Subjectivity in the Twenty-First Century* (Princeton: Princeton University Press, 2007), 51. For a conceptual exploration of the term "life," see Eugene Thacker, *After Life* (Chicago: University of Chicago Press, 2010).
2. Nadine Ehlers and Shiloh Krupar, *Deadly Biocultures: The Ethics of Life-Making* (Minneapolis: University of Minnesota Press, 2019).
3. Michel Foucault, *The Order of Things: An Archaeology of the Human Sciences* (New York: Vintage, 1970). See also Sarah Franklin, "Life Itself: Global Nature and the Genetic Imaginary," in S. Franklin, C. Lury, and J. Stacey (eds.), *Global Nature, Global Culture* (London: Sage, 1995), 188–226; and Georges Canguilhem,

*Knowledge of Life*, ed. P. Marrati and T. Meyers, trans. S. Geraoulanous and D. Ginsberg (New York: Fordham University Press, 2008).

4. Georges Canguilhem, *A Vital Rationalist: Selected Writings of Georges Canguilhem*, ed. François Delaporte, intro. Paul Rabinow (New York: Zone Books, 1994), 319.

5. Foucault, *Order*, 232, emphasis added. As Rose notes, "resisting death is both the key to an understanding of vitality and pathology, and the definition of life itself" (*Politics* 43).

6. Canguilhem, *Vital*.

7. Rose, *Politics*, 6.

8. This corresponds to a shift in biomedicine (alongside political-economic transformations under neoliberalism) that emerged in the latter half of the twentieth century – where there was an increased focus on customizing and maximizing life (especially of the human), reworking life beyond its perceived limits – rather than simply regularizing, normalizing, and standardizing life. See Rose, *Life*; Melinda Cooper, *Life as Surplus: Biotechnology and Capitalism in the Neoliberal Era* (Seattle: University of Washington Press, 2008); Adele E. Clarke, L. Mamo, J. F. Fosket, J. R. Fishman, and J. K. Shim (eds.), *Biomedicalization: Technoscience, Health, and Illness in the U.S.*, Durham, NC: Duke University Press, 2010), particularly 47–87; and Ehlers and Krupar, *Deadly*.

9. Sakari Tamminen and Niki Vermeulen, "Bio-objects: New Conjugations of the Living," *Sociologias, Porto Alegre*, 21(50) (2019), 163. See also G. Pálsson, "Biosocial Relations of Production," *Comparative Studies in Society and History*, 51(2) (2009), 288–313; B. Prainsack and A. Buyx, *Solidarity in Biomedicine and Beyond* (Cambridge: Cambridge University Press, 2017)

10. Joanna Zylinska, "Playing God, Playing Adam: The Politics and Ethics of Enhancement," *Journal of Bioethical Inquiry*, 7(2) (2010), 155.

11. Besides cattle and sheep, other mammals cloned from somatic cells include cat, deer, dog, horse, mule, ox, rabbit, and rat. In addition, a rhesus monkey has been cloned by embryo splitting. CRISPR stands for clustered regularly interspaced short palindromic repeats. On animals as sources for human organs, see A. Hinterberger, "Regulating Estrangement: Human–animal Chimeras in Postgenomic Biology," *Science, Technology, & Human Values* (2016), 1–22.

12. Y. Li, "These CRISPR-modified Crops Don't Count as GMOs," *The Conversation*, May 22, 2018), online.

13. In synthetic biology, scientists typically stitch together long stretches of DNA and insert them into an organism's genome. This is slightly different to genome editing, where scientists make smaller changes to the organism's own DNA to delete or add small stretches of DNA to the genome.

14. A. Deplazes-Zemp, "The Conception of Life in Synthetic Biology," *Science and Engineering Ethics*, 18(4) (2012), 757–74. J. M. Crow, "Life 2.0: inside the synthetic biology revolution," *Cosmos*, April 17, 2018), online.

15. Hannah Landecker, *Culturing Life: How Cells Became Technologies* (Cambridge: Harvard University Press 2007), 103.

16. Susan Merrill Squier, *Liminal Lives: Imagining the Human at the Frontiers of Biomedicine* (Durham: Duke University Press, 2004), 183.

17. Sarah Franklin and Margaret Lock note that "life and death have been ... removed from the grid of a single, unified system and realigned as an array of newly distinct deployments" ("Animation and Cessation," in S. Franklin and M. Lock (eds.), *Remaking Life and Death: Toward an Anthropology of the Biosciences* (Santa Fe: School of American Research Press, 2001), 14).

18. Sheila Jasanoff, "Introduction: Rewriting Life, Reframing Rights," in S. Jasanoff (ed.), *Reframing Rights: Bioconstitutionalism in the Genetic Age* (Cambridge: MIT Press, 2011), 1–28. See Hinterberger on the legal policing of human-animal entanglements.

19. Karen Barad, *Meeting the Universe Halfway: Quantum Physics and the Entanglement of Matter and Meaning* (Durham: Duke University Press, 2007).

20. See Maurizio Meloni, "Epigenetics for the Social Sciences: Justice, Embodiment, and Inheritance in the Postgenomic Age," *New Genetics and Society*, 34(2) (2015), 125–51; M. Lock, "The Epigenome and Nature/Nurture Reunification: A Challenge for Anthropology," *Medical Anthropology*, 32(4) (2013), 291–308.

21. Becky Mansfeld and Julie Guthman, "Epigenetic Life: Biological Plasticity, Abnormality, and New Configurations of Race and Reproduction," *Cultural Geographies* 22(1) (2015), 4.

22. For further investigation of these ideas, see Julie Guthman, "Opening Up the Black Box of the Body in Geographical Obesity Research: Toward a Critical Political Ecology of Fat,"*Annals of the Association of American Geographers*, 102 (2012), 951–7 and "Doing Justice to Bodies? Reflections on Food Justice, Race, and Biology," *Antipode*, 46 (2014), 1153–71. In relation to race, this necessitates different approaches to health and different platforms on which social justice discussion should take place. See, for instance, Becky Mansfeld, "Folded Futurity: Epigenetic Plasticity, Temporality, and New Figures of Fetal Life," *Science as Culture* 26(3) (2017), 355–79.

23. Stefan Helmreich, "Homo Microbis: The Human Microbiome, Figural, Literal, Political," *Thresholds* 42 (2014), 52–53, emphasis added.

24. Bruce Braun, "Biopolitics and the Molecularization of Life," *Cultural Geographies*, 14(1) (2007), 8.

25. See, B.H. Lerner *The Breast Cancer Wars: Hope Fear, and the Pursuit of a Cure in Twentieth-Century America* (Oxford: Oxford University Press, 2003); and Nadine Ehlers and Shiloh Krupar, "Hope Logics: Biomedicine, Affective Conventions of Cancer, and the Governing of Biocitizenry," *Configurations: A Journal of Literature, Science, and Technology*, 22(3) (2014), 385–415 for considerations of earlier forms of a more pastoral health governance in relation to cancer. For more on biopolitics and posthumanism, see Chapter 11 of this volume.

26. Nikolas Rose, "The Human Sciences in a Biological Age," *Theory, Culture, and Society*, 30(1) (2013), 7.
27. Rose, "Human sciences," 13.
28. Rose refers to this as "an ethic of active citizenship" (*Life* 25).
29. Catherine Waldby, "Stem Cells, Tissue Cultures and the Production of Biovalue," *Health*, 6(3) (2002), 310.
30. *Politics* 32.
31. See Shiloh R. Krupar, "Green Death: Sustainability and the Administration of the Dead," *Cultural Geographies*, 25(2) (2018), 267–84; and Nadine Ehlers and Shiloh R. Krupar, *Deadly*.
32. See Joseph Dumit, *Drugs for Life: How Pharmaceutical Companies Define Our Health* (Durham: Duke University Press, 2012). On transnational markets in pharmaceuticals and their role in shaping biopolitical governance, see Kaushik Sunder Rajan, *Pharmocracy: Value, Politics, and Knowledge in Global Biomedicine* (Durham: Duke University Press, 2017).
33. See Jonathan Kahn, *Race in a Bottle: The Story of BiDil and Racialized Medicine in a Post-genomic Age* (New York: Columbia University Press, 2012); A. Pollock, *Medicating Race: Heart Disease and Durable Preoccupations with Difference* (Durham: Duke University Press, 2012); Jonathan Xavier Inda, *Racial Prescriptions: Pharmaceuticals, Difference, and the Politics of Life* (Surrey: Ashgate Publishing, 2014); and Shiloh Krupar and Nadine Ehlers, "Target: Biomedicine and Racialized Geo-body-politics," *Occasion*, 8 (2015), 1–25; and Shiloh Krupar and Nadine Ehlers, "Biofutures: Race and the Governance of Health," *Environment and Planning D: Society and Space*, 35(2) (2017), 222–40.
34. See Melinda Cooper and Catherine Waldby, *Tissue Donors and Research Subjects in the Global Bioeconomy* (Durham: Duke University Press, 2014).
35. Robert Mitchell and Catherine Waldby, *Tissue Economies: Blood, Organs, and Cell Lines in Late Capitalism* (Durham: Duke University Press, 2006).
36. D.L. Brown, "Can the 'immortal cells' of Henrietta Lacks sue for their own rights?" *Washington Post* (June 25, 2018), online. This augments a long history of the abuse and exploitation of African Americans within biomedicine – from the gynecological experiments on slave women by J. Marion Sims, to the Tuskegee syphilis experiments, to the disproportionate number of black men diagnosed with schizophrenia in the 1960s (often linked to their involvement in Civil Rights activities).
37. The World Health Organization defines bioprospecting as "the systematic search for and development of new sources of chemical compounds, genes, micro-organisms, macro-organisms, and other valuable products from nature. It entails the search for economically valuable genetic and biochemical resources from nature. So, in brief, bioprospecting means looking for ways to commercialize biodiversity" (see WHO Essential Medicines and Health Products Information Portal, online). On the relationship between indigenous peoples and DNA, see Kim Tallbear, *Native American DNA: Tribal*

*Belonging and the False Promise of Genetic Science* (Minneapolis: University of Minnesota Press, 2013).

38. Margaret Lock, "The Alienation of Body Tissue and the Biopolitics of Immortalized Cell Lines." *Body and Society*, 7(2–3) (2001), 64, emphasis added.
39. Ehlers and Krupar, *Deadly*.
40. Michel Foucault, *Society Must Be Defended: Lectures at the Collège de France 1975–1976*, trans. David Macey (New York: Picador, 2003), 254.
41. See Troy Duster, *Backdoor to Eugenics* (New York: Routledge, 2003) and Ruha Benjamin, *Race After Technology: Abolitionist Tools for the New Jim Code* (Cambridge: Polity, 2019).

# CHAPTER 9

# The Anthropocene

## Gerda Roelvink

> What happens when organisms plus environments can hardly be
> remembered for the same reasons that even Western-indebted people
> can no longer figure themselves as individuals and societies of indi-
> viduals in human-only histories? Surely, such a transformative time
> on Earth must not be named the Anthropocene![1]

## 9.1  Introduction: The Anthropocene

The term Anthropocene entered scientific discussion in the early 2000s. It
was introduced by chemist Paul Crutzen, winner of the Nobel Prize, and
ecologist Eugene Stoermer.[2] While climate change had been a scientific
and political concern for some time, the Anthropocene is distinctive
because it signals a new geological epoch in which the human species has
become a geological force.[3] The Anthropocene thus goes further than
acknowledging human impact on the environment; as Will Steffen and
colleagues have recently described it, "human activity now rivals geological
forces in influencing the trajectory of the Earth System."[4] Steffen et al.
argue further that, as a geological force, the human species has taken the
Earth system to a threshold of a much hotter and much less habitable
climate, one "that would be inhospitable to current human societies and to
many other contemporary species" (2). The Anthropocene therefore has
significant implications for life on planet Earth and brings into question
some of our core understandings and beliefs about the relationship
between the human and other forms of life and matter. How are we to
think about the human in this context? And, perhaps most importantly,
what relationship does this have to how we tackle climate change?

Given the magnitude of the Anthropocene and the philosophical questions
it raises, it is perhaps no wonder that, while the scientific measurements used
to determine the timing of this new geological epoch are still debated, the
term has been readily picked up in the social sciences and humanities, and in

134

public discourse.[5] In fact, Noel Castree suggests that it could be considered a keyword of our times, highlighting growing public use of the term, including the 2011 *National Geographic* essay entitled "Enter the Anthropocene – Age of Man" by Elizabeth Kolbert, and Mark Lynas' book of the same year, *The God Species: How the Planet Can Survive the Age of Humans*. The term is also widely used in the social sciences and humanities, with Castree himself writing three interlinked articles on the Anthropocene for the journal *Geography Compass*.[6] As he explains, in such spaces, the scientific credibility and significance of the Anthropocene has been generally accepted, although not without some reservations to the term itself.

These reservations stem from the way that, after so much work to decenter the human, the Anthropocene repositions the human at the center of life, this time at a planetary scale. In the news and other public commentary, the human is described as chiefly responsible for the (past and) future of the planet. Crucially, this is not a specific group of humans placed at the center of history, as in the case of "the West" or "Europeans," but rather the human as a species that is seen as the central force of life on Earth.[7] As Jason Moore writes, the Anthropocene is about "[h]umanity – and the rest of life with it."[8] And Dipesh Chakrabarty notes that scholars of the Anthropocene, such as Crutzen, directly use the word species "to designate life in the human form – and in other living forms" that they find to be a "category useful in thinking about the nature of the current crisis." Yet, Chakrabarty suggests,

> It is a word that will never occur in any standard history or political-economic analysis of globalization by scholars on the Left, for the analysis of globalization refers, for good reasons, only to the recent and recorded history of humans. Species thinking, on the other hand, is connected to the enterprise of deep history. . . . [but] The task of placing, historically, the crisis of climate change thus requires us to bring together intellectual formations that are somewhat in tension with each other: the planetary and the global; deep and recorded histories; species thinking and critiques of capital. (213)

I will return to these tensions. For now, though, it should be noted that not every human being is involved in the making of the Anthropocene, nor will the impact of climate change be evenly experienced (as has been shown when it comes to so-called natural disasters).[9]

As Marxist scholars Joel Wainwright and Geoff Mann argue, "if the Anthropocene is defined as a planetary and historical regime shaped in irreversible ways by 'humanity' or 'man,' then Indigenous peoples in the Americas have been surviving the damnation of the Anthropocene for more than 500 years" (188). They thus challenge a narrow vision that would see the Anthropocene as a term relevant only to a more recent periodization during which "humanity as a species fundamentally altered Earth's systems – as opposed to a moment like the colonization of the Americas, in which only some groups undid a world or community of worlds" (189). They insist on remaining cognizant of the fact that not all humans have contributed equally to climate crisis.

Given this concern, one would expect posthumanist scholars to avoid the term Anthropocene. Yet, in this chapter I explore scholarship that embraces the term precisely because it asks us to reevaluate human life on Earth. As Jason Moore writes:

> The Anthropocene is a worthy point of departure not only for its popularity but, more importantly, because it poses questions that are fundamental to our times: How do humans fit within the web of life? How have various human organizations and processes – states and empires, world markets, urbanization, and much beyond – reshaped planetary life? The Anthropocene perspective is rightly powerful and influential for bringing these questions into the academic mainstream – and even (but unevenly) into popular awareness. (2)

Similarly, Castree writes that the Anthropocene and related planetary boundaries ideas "invite a far-reaching examination of virtually every aspect of 21st century life – from commodity production to transportation systems to energy systems to food consumption habits and beyond" ("Current Contributions" 450). Likewise, Moore writes that the Anthropocene and related concepts suggest "reconstructions that point to a new way of thinking humanity-in-nature, and nature-in-humanity" (5). Ironically then, the Anthropocene calls precisely for the evaluation of human life from the perspective of posthumanism, and this chapter explores how this might be done. First, I examine two additional terms that have emerged from the social sciences and humanities in response and as potential alternatives to the Anthropocene. In the next section, I explore an example of how we might think and live differently in-nature by drawing on the diverse/community economies literature. I conclude by briefly commenting on the politics of this scholarship and what is at stake in the term one adopts.

## 9.2   Key Terms: The Anthropocene, Capitalocene, and Chthulucene

Before moving to alternative terms, it is worth taking a closer look at the meaning of the term the Anthropocene. The first thing to note is that while other terms refer to Anthropogenic climate change, and point to destructive human-nature relations in different places, the Anthropocene presents this as a global phenomenon and one that encompasses all aspects of planetary life. As Castree points out, the Anthropocene connects local actions into a global concern ("Back Story" 444). This connection of the local to the global has implications not only for how we understand the Anthropocene, but also for the kind of actions that are mounted in response. Specially, the Anthropocene calls for a global response, and in climate change activism the revolutionary politics of Marxism is often adopted.[10] However, the nature of this global response is not predetermined by the term Anthropocene, as I will explore further in the conclusion by highlighting a different kind of politics.[11]

Castree also notes the "forward-facing" nature of the Anthropocene and related scientific concepts, which he writes "invite us to consider making significant present-day decisions in light of their (non-trivial) effects long into the future" ("Back Story" 444). They imply that, in the long run, a lack of foresight and action today will have profound consequences tomorrow that are at once hydrological, lithospheric, biological, and atmospheric. More critically, Magdalena Zolkos and I suggest that this forward-facing nature can actually create a "temporal displacement" in the discourses of climate change associated with the Anthropocene.[12] This displacement projects the catastrophe of climate change into a future which we might still be able to prevent if we act in the present, marked as the domain of possibility and action. We further link this binary separation of the present and future to a "liberal humanist understanding of the subject who appears autonomous, rational and self-contained in her/his capacity to exert power in the world" (47). One problem with such discourse is that, while its subject may be linked to progressive environmental causes, it continues to separate human beings from nature, making humans the savior of the future of the planet and not co-suffers who are equally vulnerable with other species and matter in our present.

The Anthropocene thus potentially repositions humans at the center of planetary life as well as continuing to separate humans from nature. Yet, several scholars suggest that the term nonetheless has the potential to disrupt modernist dualisms that separate nature and society, mind and body, and so on. In his comments on the Anthropocene, Castree argues that "the two ideas [Anthropocene and planetary boundaries] invite a response from all our faculties – not only perceptual and cognitive but also moral-ethical and even aesthetic" ("Back Story" 444). Going further, describing the Anthropocene as a "halfway house" term on the way to another, Moore suggests that in describing human life as a force of nature alongside other natural forces, the Anthropocene challenges the nature/ society dualism that he argues has been fundament to capitalist society: "At its best, the Anthropocene concept entwines human history and natural history – even if the 'why' and the 'how' remain unclear, and hotly debated" (3).

The Anthropocene thus presents an exciting opportunity for geographers and other cognate disciplines to more fully engage in debates about entwined environmental and social politics. As Castree notes,

> It is a truly encompassing concept with even greater semantic reach than a venerable, polysemic word like "nature" and richer connotations than the now familiar term "global environmental change". It could, therefore, engender new discussions between physical, environmental and human geographers. ("Back Story" 438)

From this brief discussion it is clear that in some ways the Anthropocene aligns well with posthumanist thought.

Wanting to save some of the features associated with the term but avoid others, several scholars have proposed alternatives. The feeling is that, while useful, the term the Anthropocene is attached to the kind of thinking that led to the crisis it describes in the first place, whether this thinking is described as capitalist, liberal modernist, or based on dualisms (such as nature/society). An alternative term offered by Moore and others is the Capitalocene.[13] With this term, (typically Marxist) scholars seek to provide an explanation for the Anthropocene. As Moore puts it: "Questions of capitalism, power and class, anthropocentrism, dualist framings of 'nature' and 'society,' and the role of states and empires – all are frequently bracketed by the dominant Anthropocene perspective" (5). He further suggests:

> the Capitalocene signifies capitalism as a way of organizing nature – as a multispecies, situated, capitalist world-ecology. . . . There have been many other wordplays . . . But none captures the basic historical pattern modern of world history as the "Age of Capital" – and the era of capitalism as a world-ecology of power, capital, and nature. (6)

The Capitalocene directly connects the rise of the human species as a geological force with the historical development of capitalism. For Moore the emphasis is on historical development rather than simply a "system" of capitalism, and he dates this as beginning earlier than the industrial revolution often viewed as the beginning of the Anthropocene, to "distinct crises of capital accumulation and biospheric stability . . .

found in a series of landscape, class, territorial, and technical transformations that emerged in the three centuries after 1450" (7).

What is distinctive here are the relationships forged between society and
nature throughout history (3). Similarly, David Ruccio makes three related
arguments for a switch to the term the Capitalocene: (1) it directs attention
to a long intellectual history on the relationship between capitalism and
nature, (2) it points to the uneven impact of climate change on people
across the globe, and (3) it carries a sense of another possibility – the end of
capitalism. The term the Capitalocene is not without its problems, however. One major issue is that the term leads itself easily to capitalocentrism –
where all economic activities, and indeed much of life, is understood with
reference to capitalism, as "fundamentally the same as (or modelled upon)
capitalism, or as being deficient or substandard imitations; as being opposite to capitalism; as being the complement of capitalism; as existing in
capitalism's space or orbit."[14] One of the problems with this kind of
thinking is that it becomes very hard to imagine other ways of living and
to see those that already exist. Donna Haraway, who uses both the
Anthropocene and the Capitalocene, suggests that these terms risk
"becoming Too Big" whereby they are characterized by closed-system
thinking, "determinism, teleology, and plan."[15]

Haraway offers instead the term Chthulucene with which to think in
our current epoch. The term is made up of word Chthonic, which refers to
a sub-terrain earthly force like Gaia of which we are all a part and which the
Anthropocene threatens, and Cene to indicate the present ("the temporality of the thick, fibrous, and lumpy 'now,' which is ancient and not").[16]
Drawing on Anna Tsing's work, Haraway is concerned that in the
Anthropocene "places and times of refugee" for all kinds of creatures
have disappeared ("Staying" 160). The term Chthulucene is intended as
a response to the challenges of living "on a damaged planet," to rebuilding
places of refuge.[17] The Chthulucene is difficult to summarize but there
are several distinctive features or characteristics of this rebuilding effort.
First, the Chthulucene is characterized by tentacles or tentacularity,
which refers to a capacity to feel and try, and through this make
connections and attachments. Learning to be affected, the process whereby
one is transformed through the experience of registering/feeling the
diversity of another, is a good example of this.[18] For Haraway, this is
a way to enlist cross-species allies as one seeks new ways to live in the
Anthropocene. Alliances and assemblages are vital to what Haraway
describes as making kin with others (human and nonhuman). Joining
forces through kinship, then, is one way in which to rebuild places of

refuge: "One way to live and die well as mortal creatures in the Chthulucene is to join forces to reconstitute refuges, to make possible partial and robust biological-cultural-political-technological recuperation and reconstitution, which must include mourning irreversible loses" (Haraway, "Anthropocene" 160).

In contrast to closed systems and moving to think about these connections more broadly, Haraway secondly emphasize lines and strings, favoring the idea of "sympoiesis" over other systems concepts and especially over the conceptualization of "independent organisms in environments" ("Staying" 37). As described by M. Beth Dempster, who Haraway cites, sympoiesis refers to "collectively-producing systems that do not have self-defined spatial or temporal boundaries. Information and control are distributed among components. The systems are evolutionary and have the potential for surprising change" (quoted in Haraway, "Staying" 37). Haraway suggests that this concept is useful to move from society plus nature configurations to think more about entanglements, and in particular the kinds of entanglements that can rebuild refuges in the Anthropocene.

Haraway's Chthulucene includes many other key concepts, such as storytelling. In the Chthulucene it is not just humans telling the story; rather Haraway places emphasis on "multispecies stories and practices of becoming-with":

> Unlike the dominant dramas of Anthropocene and Capitalocene discourse, human beings are not the only important actors in the Chthulucene, with all other beings able simply to react. The order is rather reversed: human beings are with and of the earth, and the other biotic and abiotic powers of this earth are the main story. ("Staying" 59)

In multispecies stories, however, Haraway also notes that "the doings of situated, actual human beings matter. It matters which ways of living and dying we cast our lot with rather than others" ("Staying" 59). This relates to how we care for others with which we rebuild refuge, that is, the "mundane" practices of caring for others and affective attachments we develop through this truly matter to how the world is transformed and how new possibilities for living well with others emerge.[19]

This short discussion shows that more than the Anthropocene and the Capitalocene, the Chthulucene pushes beyond a critique of the present and calls for the collapse of modernist dualisms, to consider concepts that help us continue to live and explore new possibilities at this historical juncture. How can we care for other species and the planet in response to climate change in a manner more attuned to the Chthulucene than the

Anthropocene? How might we reevaluate our relationships with others in the process to transform those categories and ways of living bound up with the Anthropocene? To explore these questions, I turn to work that rethinks economic environment relations.

## 9.3 New Possibilities: Ecological Livelihoods

Anthropocene, Capitalocene, Chthulucene – all terms call on us to tackle the division between society and nature (Moore 5), articulated in perhaps its strongest form as economy vs. environment. Taking up Haraway's assertion that we need to tell stories that transform these categories, I explore recent work stemming from economic geography that has started to do just this. Growing out of Gibson-Graham's concerns with capitalocentrism, for some time now diverse economies scholars have drawn on poststructural thought and neoMarxism to show the economy as a site full of diverse economic practices and forms – capitalist, alternative capitalist, and non-capitalist.[20]

In fact, by looking closely at economic practices that exist, diverse economies scholarship shows that capitalist labors, enterprises, and transactions are part of a much larger economy of noncapitalist and alternative labors, enterprises, and transactions, on which they often depend. Alongside this work diversifying the economy, other scholars have shown that the concept of The (capitalist) Economy as a distinct sphere separated from the environment is itself a product of particular relations, discourses, practices, forms of calculation, and measurement and subjectivities.[21] Miller and Gibson-Graham thus describe the economy and environment as a particular "hegemonic assemblage" of the contemporary period, or perhaps we could say the Anthropocene. "What these assemblages produce (and are, in turn produced by) ... is a form of life, an ontological formatting of a particular terrain in which certain kinds of problems and possibilities appear while others are rendered non-viable or pushed to the margins."[22]

Diverse economies scholarship works to amplify the already existing slippages and excesses of this economy-environment assemblage, and thereby make these slippages more real and viable as options to pursue. Miller and Gibson-Graham place this work to diversify the economy alongside posthumanist scholarship, suggesting that both similarly destabilize the economy/environment dualism, albeit from different directions. In particular, they direct attention to posthumanist work that shows that, far from separate and distinct spheres, society and nature participate in "the

complex inter-becomings of a more-than-human ecological 'mesh'" (319).
This scholarship shows just how unstable modernist dualisms are, particularly the economy-environment assemblage, thereby facilitating experimentation with other possibilities.[23]

In its exploration of other possibilities, diverse economies scholarship
contributes most clearly in relation to the notion of the Chthulucene. To
take Gibson-Graham and Miller's work again as an example, rather than
using economy and environment in their latest experimentation with
"thinking with the world," they call on us to adopt the term "ecological
livelihoods" in order to tell different stories about economic life (321).
Livelihood here refers to the "work of substance" that is always interwoven
with the interdependent livelihoods of other species and matter (ecology).
Diverse economies scholarship more broadly shows that humans, for
example, make a living in all sorts of ways (just think of all the unpaid
forms of labor not usually seen as economic) and, importantly, through
this work are involved in a world of interdependence:

> Livelihoods would indicate, then, not the ways in which we – the "autono-
> mous" agents – make a living for ourselves in relation to some "outside," or
> in the midst of "enabling resources" and "constraints," but rather the
> complex, reciprocally-negotiated composition of habitat (oikos) and that
> which inhabits (us, along with others). (Miller and Gibson-Graham 323)

While "we do not know with whom we are connected" through livelihood
(Miller and Gibson-Graham 325), just thinking of a regular day reveals endless
connections with others – imagine of all those organisms dwelling inside our
bodies, the laboring plants, animals, environments that nourish us and clothe
us, the organisms living in our compost bins and gardens, and so on.

Miller and Gibson-Graham go further to map livelihood interdependence through the three axes of "making a living, receiving a living made for
us by others (human and nonhuman), and providing livings for others"
(323). For each axis, there is no single actor but the coming together of
many different agencies. Thus, "'we' emerge as a site of continually enacted
agential articulation between the habitats that we make for ourselves, the
habitats that we receive and the habitats we participate in making for
others. 'I' and 'we' become relays in a complex ecological meshwork, and
a politics of the negotiation of ecological livelihoods unfolds here" (Miller
and Gibson-Graham 325). This politics of negotiation involves "taking
active responsibility for interdependence" (325).

This work moves us from the vision of an independent human being
making a livelihood to a much more complex picture wherein humans are

one agency aligned with and overlapping others in webs of livelihood making. And going a step further, with these three axes of livelihood, Miller and Gibson-Graham create spaces in which interdependence can be explored, bringing to the fore ethical questions about relationships with others who are involved in our livelihoods, while recognizing these will never be fully apparent or known. For example, when making a living, we can ask: "What do we really need to survive well? How do we balance our own survival needs and well-being with the well-being of others and the planet?" (Miller and Gibson-Graham 326). In bringing ethical negotiation to the fore, Miller and Gibson-Graham are part of a growing body of diverse economies scholars who draw on neoMarxism and ecological studies to generate fine-grained and grounded economic questions which enact an ethics of economy (a space often described as a community economy). This work aims to decenter the human from questions of livelihood by focusing on nonhuman others: for example, Miller and Gibson-Graham ask, "How are our makings-of-others connected with our being-made, recirculating energies and matter in ways that maintain our habitats and those of others, and to what extent is this connection severed by various extractive mediations?" (326).

In my own work, I draw on Jessica Weir's research on river ecologies in Australia to explore the ways in which farming practices are bound to river ecologies and how these relationships are taken into account or responded to – or not, threatening the rivers and our own survival.[24] This way of thinking about ecological livelihood entanglements, rather than closed economic systems, and the ethics of interdependence that comes with them enables us to explore the world in new ways. The hope is that through this exploration we will be shaped by and learn from others, which might in turn generate new possibilities for living on a damaged planet. Perhaps, then, this is a position from which to start rebuilding refuges in the Anthropocene that are open to more than the human.

## 9.4   Conclusion: After the Anthropocene?

The aim of diverse economies scholarship is ultimately political; diverse economies scholars are taking a stake in how we live in the Anthropocene by tackling the economy/environment division that has contributed to its emergence. As Miller and Gibson-Graham put it: "To speak of ecological livelihoods is to propose an intervention: What kinds of relations, connections, and possibilities might be opened by a language that refuses to distinguish an Economy and an Environment as the ultimate spheres in which we must live?" (323). The kind of politics this work enacts is distinctive, particularly in comparison to other responses to the Anthropocene. It perhaps even suggests that the response one adopts to the Anthropocene is connected to the term one embraces to describe this period in history. Both the Anthropocene and Capitalocene are all-encompassing terms that call for an all-encompassing response.

One might thus assume that the response must be revolutionary, immediate, and joined-up around the globe. This is at least what the climate change justice movement aims to achieve.[25] Yet history suggests that change does not always happen this way. Rather, widespread change often occurs accumulatively over time, as efforts to repair the ozone layers of the stratosphere by eliminating chlorofluorocarbons (CFCs) suggest.[26] These diverse strategies take different forms. As Gibson-Graham points out, second-wave feminism occurred in multiple "disarticulated 'places' – households, communities, ecosystems, workplaces, civic organizations, bodies, public arenas, urban spaces, diasporas, regions, government agencies, occupations – related analogically rather than organizationally and connected through webs of signification" (*Postcapitalist* xxiv). Change also needs to be a process in which people can participate, which means not getting rid of everything we know but rather, as Miller and Gibson-Graham argue, pushing at the cracks and slippages already there to open up further possibilities. Just as posthumanist work does not "get rid of" the human but rather explores ways in which the human is embodied in the world and, through this, connected to other species and matter.[27] Economic lives are interwoven with a whole range of species and matter, thereby opening up these relations to negotiation and, potentially, new possibilities for nurture and care.

Social movements around the world have been engaged in this kind of politics for a long time. Within geography, diverse economies research is distinctive in that it actively engages these social movements to respond to the Anthropocene in the interest of livelihood injustice.[28] This is notable in other academic fields as well, especially in relation to climate justice.[29] Whatever term one uses going forward, the era of the Anthropocene has been a call to the social sciences and humanities to become more active in thinking about and with the diverse species and matter of the world. What the future looks like and how it positions the human as a species within it, however, depends on the discourse one adopts. Given the anthropocentrism of much of human culture during the Anthropocene, it is not inconceivable that, in the struggle to maintain human life as we know it, diverse species and matter disappear, replaced by artificial systems.[30] In the Chthululcene, in contrast, humans hold a much less central position. For Haraway, cross-species alliances and the making of cross-species kin are privileged over the continued proliferation of the human species. Ultimately, then, while the Anthropocene may well be a keyword for our times, it matters what term we take up for the future.

## Notes

1. Donna J. Haraway, "Staying with the Trouble: Anthropocene, Capitalocene, Chthulucene," in *Anthropocene or Capitalocene? Nature, History, and the Crisis of Capitalism*, ed. Jason Moore (Oakland, CA: PM Press, 2016), 34.
2. P. Crutzen and E. Stoermer, "The Anthropocene," *Global Change Newsletter* 41 (2000), 17–18.
3. N. Castree, "The Anthropocene and Geography I: The Back Story," *Geography Compass* 8/7 (2014), 436–49.
4. Steffen, J. Rockström, and K. Richardson, "Trajectories of the Earth System in the Anthropocene," *PNAS Proceeding of the National Academy of Sciences of the United States of America, Perspective* 115 (33) (2018), 1.
5. Along with associated terms such as planetary boundaries (Castree) and tipping points (Steffen et al.)
6. Castree, "The Back Story"; N. Castree, "Geography and the Anthropocene II: Current Contributions," *Geography Compass* 8/7 (2014), 450–463; and N. Castree, "The Anthropocene and Geography III: Future Directions," *Geography Compass* 8/7 (2014), 464–476.
7. Joel Wainwright and Geoff Mann, *Climate Leviathan: A Political Theory of Our Planetary Future* (London: Verso, 2018). D. Chakrabarty, "The Climate of History: Four Theses," *Critical Inquiry* 35 (Winter 2009), 197–222. G. Roelvink, *Building Dignified Worlds: Geographies of Collective Action* (Minneapolis: University of Minnesota Press, 2016).
8. Jason Moore, "Introduction: Anthropocene or Capitalocene?" in *Anthropocene or Capitalocene? Nature, History, and the Crisis of Capitalism* (Oakland, CA: PM Press, 2016), 1.
9. Mike Davis, *Ecology of Fear: Los Angeles and the Imagination of Disaster* (New York: Henry Holt & Company, 1998).
10. N. Klein, *This Changes Everything: Capitalist vs. the Climate* (New York: Simon and Schuster 2014).
11. See also G. Roelvink, "Community Economies and Climate Justice," in S. Jacobson (ed.), *Climate Justice and the Economy: Social Mobilization, Knowledge and the Political* (New York: Routledge, 2018).
12. G. Roelvink and M. Zolkos, "Climate Change as Experience of Affect," *Angelaki* 16(4) (2011), 44.
13. See D. Ruccio, "Capitalocene," *Occasional Links & Commentary on Economics, Culture and Society* (7 March 2017), online, for example.
14. J. K. Gibson-Graham, *The End of Capitalism (As We Knew It): A Feminist Critique of Political Economy* (Minneapolis: University of Minnesota Press, 1996), 6.

15. Haraway, "Staying with the Trouble," 54. See also Moore, "Introduction," 6.
16. Donna J. Haraway "Anthropocene, Capitalocene, Plantationocene, Chthulucene: Making Kin," *Environmental Humanities* 6 (2015), 160, 163. Haraway distinguishes Chthulucene from science fiction writer H.P. Lovecraft's Cthulhu, which she describes as a "misogynist racial-nightmare monster" (160).
17. A. Tsing, N. Bubandt, E. Gan and G. Swanson (eds.), *Arts of Living on a Damaged Planet: Ghosts and Monsters of the Anthropocene* (Minneapolis: University of Minnesota Press, 2017).
18. See Roelvink, *Building*.
19. See M. Puig de la Bellacasa, *Matters of Care: Speculative Ethics in More Than Human Worlds* (Minnesota: University of Minnesota Press, 2017), 199.
20. J. K. Gibson-Graham, *A Postcapitalist Politics* (Minneapolis: University of Minnesota Press, 2006).
21. M. Callon "What Does It Mean to Say That Economics Is Performative?" in D. MacKenzie, E. Muniesa, and L. Siu (eds.), *Do Economists Make Markets: On the Peformativity of Economics* (Princeton: Princeton University Press, 2007), 311–57; Gibson-Graham, *The End*; and T. Mitchell "Fixing the Economy," *Cultural Studies* 12 (1) (1998), 82–101.
22. E. Miller and J. K. Gibson-Graham, "Thinking with Interdependence: From Economy/Environment to Ecological Livelihoods," in J. Bennett and M. (eds.), *Thinking in the World: A Reader* (London: Bloomsbury, 2019), 317.
23. See G. Roelvink and J. K. Gibson-Graham, "A Postcapitalist Politics of Dwelling," *Australian Humanities Review* 46 (2009), 145–58; E. Miller and J. K. Gibson-Graham, "Economy as Ecological Livelihood," in K. Gibson, D. Rose, and R. Fincher (eds.), *Manifesto for Living in the Anthropocene* (New York: Punctum Books, 2015), 7–17.
24. G. Roelvink, "Performing Posthumanist Economies in the Anthropocene," in G. Roelvink, K. St. Martin, and J. K. Gibson-Graham (eds.), *Making Other Worlds Possible: Performing Diverse Economies* (Minneapolis, University of Minnesota Press, 2015), 225–43; J. Weir, *Murray River Country: An Ecological Dialogue with Traditional Owners* (Canberra ACT: Aboriginal Studies Press, 2009).
25. See Klein.
26. J. K. Gibson-Graham, J. Cameron, and S. Healy, *Take Back the Economy: An Ethical Guide for Transforming Our Communities* (Minneapolis, University of Minnesota Press, 2013), 144–5.
27. Cary Wolfe, *What Is Posthumanism?* (Minneapolis: University of Minnesota Press, 2010).
28. See Castree, "Future Directions," and Gibson-Graham, *Postcapitalist*.
29. See Wainwright and Mann.
30. F. Matthews, "Moral Ambiguities in the Politics of Climate Change," in V. Nanda (ed.), *Climate Change and Environmental Ethics* (New Brunswick, NJ: Transactions Publishers, 2015), 43–64.

CHAPTER 10

# The Inorganic

## Magdalena Zolkos

When in 1828 Friedrich Wöhler converted ammonium cyanate into urea (an acid naturally occurring in mammal urine), he described his achievement as the "unexpected result [of the] artificial production of an organic, indeed a so-called *animal substance [animalischen Stoffes]* from inorganic material."[1] This first laboratorial synthesis of inorganic matter into an organic compound has become synonymous with the beginnings of modern chemistry. As such, it has also acquired the discursive status of an important anti-vitalist statement in that Wöhler's achievement undermined the cultural belief in the fundamental and irreducible difference between non-living entities and biological organisms, or what Frantz Mesmer famously described as *Lebensmagnetismus*, the invisible force or power of "aliveness."[2] Wöhler's reference to "animal substance" to describe the organic product of his experiment, urea, is significant precisely because of the backdrop of semantic transformations concurrent with the nineteenth-century development of chemistry, whereby the earlier (imprecise and non-technical) association of "organicity" with "life," and "in-organicity" with "lifelessness," gave way to their scientific use as descriptor of the presence (or lack) of the C-H bonds in a given chemical compound.[3]

While Aristotle located minerals, metals, and other earth matter at the bottom of the hierarchical classification of beings, thus creating an insurmountable gap between the geological and vegetal/animal ontologies, modern chemistry broke away from the negative definitions of the inorganic as the absence of life.[4] At the same time, it would be a mistake to credit modern science with being the sole (or even the primary) force behind the blurring of the organic-inorganic distinction. The posthumanist philosophic inquiry framed inorganicity as not simply external to living organisms, but also as present *within* and *around* them; not only as a static backdrop to the emergence of the human and a stage for the exercise of historical agency, but, as argued for example by Timothy Morton in his writings on hyperobjects, as forms of materiality that exceed human temporality, imagination, language, and history, while also encompassing them.[5]

Already in the nineteenth century the German thinkers of Naturphilosophie pondered what Gabriel Trop calls the "'sameness-otherness' of the inorganic vis-à-vis the human being," in their attempt to recognize inorganic matter as both homologous with the human body and as irreducibly other, perhaps even antagonistic to it.[6] F.W.J. Schelling's philosophy of the "totality of being" asserted that the inorganic and organic worlds were analogous and parallel to each other, and were governed by the same logic of contradistinctive forces – the inorganic forces of light, electricity, and magnetism had organic "counterparts" in reproductivity, irritability, and sensibility of vegetal and animal organisms.[7] In contemporary posthumanist debates, the preoccupation with the philosophic status of inanimate and inorganic objects, as well as the critical, social, and cultural analysis of human relationships and inter-actions with material things, has produced new bodies of knowledge. This includes (1) "thing theory," attentive in particular to situations when things exceed or subvert their usefulness and functionality for the human subject;[8] (2) vital materialism, which recognizes the agential attributes and poten-tials of material entities, as well as considers their radical socio-political implications;[9] (3) actor-network theory and so-called "Dingpolitik," which grant inanimate things an important place in the shifting networks of relationships that constitute social and public spheres;[10] and (4) object-oriented ontology, which takes as its starting-point rejection of the anthropocentric privileging of human existence and understanding over that of material things.[11]

An important point is that in posthumanist inquiry into the organic-inorganic relation, the human subject is not necessarily "liquidated" (as Jacques Derrida puts it) but, rather, is stripped of some of its (his) key metaphysical determinations, such as exclusive sovereignty and the cap-acity to exert formative pressure on a supposedly passive and receptive environment.[12] I am interested in how that philosophic complication of the organic-inorganic relation within the rubric of posthumanism reson-ates with recent developments in the field of memory studies that seek to displace the centrality of the human subject in cultural memory produc-tion and to envision nonhuman entities, such as inanimate objects, as capable of mnemonic affordance and as generative of affects and emotions related to the past. In posthuman memory studies, the inorganic and the organic form a *relation* of interpenetrability and mutual contraction. A key text in my investigation is Georges Didi-Huberman's *Bark* (2011, 2017), a philosophic meditation on the inorganic and the nonhuman as subjects of traumatic memory. I approach through a conceptual prism of the materiality of memory and plasticity, that is from the perspective of objects' capacity to adapt to, transform in response to, and incorporate within themselves traces of their environment.[13]

## 10.1    Plasticity and the Inorganic

The French poststructuralist thinker Catherine Malabou is known for her philosophic concept of plasticity, which applies to animate and inanimate entities alike, insofar as, for Malabou, they display three key characteristics of plasticity: giving form, taking form, and destroying form. She addresses the organic-inorganic relation through the prism of plasticity in, inter alia, *The Future of Hegel*.[14] Focusing in particular on the *Encyclopedia of the Philosophical Sciences*, Malabou presents Hegel's idea that the inorganic origins of an organism solidify within it through a process of contraction, or "pulling together" (*Zusammenziehung*). Malabou both highlights the posthumanist ramifications of Hegel's approach and shows that he does not go far enough in recognizing the radical implications of plasticity as the shared feature of organic and inorganic matter.

In *Philosophy of Nature* Hegel introduces the Aristotelian concept of "habit," by which he means a unifying attribute of all living beings, consisting in the capacity to duplicate nature, or to work it into oneself, in the process of creating a "*second nature*."[15] The two modes through which change in nature occurs – incrementalism and rupture – are, importantly, nonanthropological; for Hegel habit is not an exclusively human attribute. Rather, in both plants and animals, habit is synonymous with a *capacity for transformation*, as well as for *preserving the effects of such transformation*. "Habitus" is the Latin translation of the Greek ἕξις (*hexis*), meaning a way of being or a disposition, but without the passive associations of habitual behavior. Rather, Aristotle links *hexis* with effort, attention, and concentration. Describing *hexis* as "a particular kind of having which becomes a way of being" (25, 37), Malabou argues that it illustrates the workings of plasticity because it expresses itself through practices of molding, creation, and integration. Plasticity means both the undertaking and the undergoing of change; both the receiving of form and the giving of form.[16]

In *Lectures on the History of Philosophy*, Hegel discusses the Aristotelian conception of change as "the principle of internal differentiation," of which geological items are incapable because the inorganic "lack[s] the power to develop habit."[17] The exclusion of the inorganic from the

attribution of *hexis* is a significant philosophic distinction, because it
subsequently locates inorganic matter beyond the matrix of "plastic operations" and reserves for organic life the capacity of auto-differentiation, or
of what Hegel calls "[the] self-dividing process" (§261). In *Lectures* Hegel
describes plants, animals, and human animals as constantly involved in
efforts to maintain their unity through the "synthesis of differences"
(Malbou 58). The main difference that needs to be processed by the
plant or the animal is between their organism and their inorganic milieu;
another is among the heterogenous components of the organism. It is
through these adaptive and auto-differentiating processes that living
organisms incorporate, anchor, and mediate within themselves inorganic
"nature," not only (and not primarily) at the level of elemental structure
and composition, but also as "[the] transformation of one external or
particular material into another" (Hegel §345).

The Hegelian figure of animal life illuminates further the relation of the
inorganic to the organic through the theory of contraction. Contraction
constitutes one of the distinct features of the animal *hexis*. It implies the
process of "making smaller" by applying the forces of compression, con-
densation, and abridgement (*zusammenziehen*) (Hegel 211 n21). In regard
to the organic compression of the inorganic within oneself, Malabou writes
that "[the] very materials of the inorganic, *subjected to an immediate
contraction*, are what make up the [living] organism. . . . [In] the core of
its being, the living organism is nothing but the reduction and condensa-
tion of the elements of its [inorganic] environment" (59, emphasis added).
The proposition that the organic and inorganic matter are mutually bound
at the level of their origin and structure does not simply suggest their
homogeneity, but also illuminates their heterogeneity, or even the way that
the inorganic assumes an antagonistic relation to the organic: "living being
is at once identical to and different from its non-living origins and
surroundings" (Malabou 60).

The interpenetrability of the organic and inorganic in Hegel (as read by
Malabou) has thus meant concurrency of sameness and alterity. Habitus is
a result of the contraction of the geological matter within animal or vegetal
organisms, in regard to both their constitution and their internal disposition. At play in the making of the habitus are two contradistinctive forces:
on the one hand, preservation or conservation and, on the other, suppres-
sion or concealment. By imagining animate being as that which "*summar-
izes everything that precedes it*" (Malabou 59), Malabou's Hegel articulates
an idea of a living organism that synthesizes within itself the inanimate and
inorganic matter, without reducing the inorganic to itself. The theory of

vital materialism articulates a similar idea in trying to undo the dualistic separation between inanimate matter and animated life; by recognizing agential capacities of material objects, including geological and planetary ones (so-called "thing-power"), Jane Bennett reveals the fiction of the humanist imaginary of the human as a bounded and self-identical "actant" in the world. Instead, the human is *always already* the effect of co-entanglement or hybridization of "active bodies" and "vital materials."

Malabou uses the term "plasticity" to describe the process of inorganic contraction within the organic, via its three operations of taking form, giving form, and destroying form.[18] The inorganic contraction within organic life illustrates the workings of plasticity because the animal or vegetal adaptive aptitude implies concurrent malleability and resistance to molding pressure, or what Hegel calls the "union of resistance" (*Widerstand*) and "fluidity" (*Flüssigkeit*) (11). Plasticity is the dialectic process of "the seizure of form" and the (explosive) "annihilation of . . . form" (Malabou 12). Contrary to the belief that humans are uniquely equipped to mold and shape the inorganic and nonhuman world, while in turn resisting and protecting themselves from geological impacts on their existence, Malabou perceives plasticity as equally relevant for organic *and* inorganic forms of life, thus supporting nonanthropocentric and nonbinary views of agency, action, and affordance.

The posthumanist angle of Malabou's reading of Hegel becomes conspicuous in her criticism of the characterization of "the organism of the earth" in *Philosophy of Nature* as devoid of life.[19] Hegel draws a strong ontological distinction between "geological nature" and "vegetal nature," a locus of "the first real vitality" whereby the "suspension of immediacy takes place [and] general individuality . . . emerges for itself" (Hegel §265). While geology is a site of diverse "granitic" activities, for Hegel they are neither signs of vitality nor, properly speaking, are they constitutive of an "event or 'change', but, rather 'mechanical modifications'" which lack "immanent formative development" (Hegel §264). Because Malabou's concept of plasticity captures the capacity of organisms and objects for the transformation of their internal parameters in response to the environment – the way that "system can transform itself from within without dissolving" – and it thus blurs the Aristotelian hierarchy of humans, animals, vegetables, and terrestrial things.[20] It is not "restricted to the gazing subject or to the experience of understanding," but instead "permeates all living and non-living forms."[21] Here Malabou's approach shares an important affinity with such works as Elizabeth Povinelli's *Geontologies,* which deconstructs geology as a site of power and regulation and suggests that the global expansion and entrenchment of neoliberal governance concentrates on the epistemic designation as "life" and "nonlife" (rather than, as the theorists of biopower often argue, of "life" and "death").²²

Finally, the organic contraction of the inorganic within itself through a dual process of giving and receiving form has implications for the temporal aspect of plasticity, what Malabou calls the "immanent temporalization" of passive/active voice (55). The temporal manifestation of the dialectic between the organic and the inorganic is something akin to belatedness, which Malabou defines as "a state of spiritual hypnosis ... corresponding actually to *a time prior to the 'I.'*"²³ This means that the temporality of *hexis* cannot be reduced to the present moment of now. Rather, the organism solidifies and preserves within itself traces of its continuity and contiguity with inorganic things; and, conversely, inorganic objects reveal enclosed within themselves remnants of human, animal, and vegetal life. As I discuss in the section below, in regard to the role of material objects in collective memory formation, the fact that the object retains within itself certain remnants or traces of the past complicates the idea that the human is the sole subject of history and of memory.

## 10.2    The Inorganic as the Subject/Object of Memory in Georges Didi-Huberman's *Bark*

Cultural memory studies have become very interested in material inanimate entities and their relation to the dynamics of collective remembrance and forgetting, be it "testimonial objects," nonhuman witnessing, or "planetary grief," that is, mournful experience in response to anthropogenic climate change and species extinction.²⁴ Didi-Huberman's philosophical and photographic essay on his visit to Auschwitz-Birkenau, *Bark*, exemplifies preoccupations with memory and memorialization as not exclusively human concerns.²⁵ *Bark* abounds in nonhuman entities (organic and inorganic – Didi-Huberman does not make a strong distinction between them in regard to memory production). They are considered to be nonhuman witnesses to the Holocaust, in that they were either in existence at the time of the operation of the Auschwitz-Birkenau concentration camp; they are proximate to its location (birch trees, meadows, flowers); they constitute its surroundings, machinery, and furnishing (windows, execution walls, an inscription "Vorsicht!", and crematorium floors); or, as in the case of ash, they were the very material product of the killings. Didi-Huberman calls these entities "silent" or "forgotten" witnesses of Auschwitz, and he elaborates their testimonial significance from the perspective of both their materiality and temporality.

Not unlike the "contraction" of the inorganic within the organism, which Malabou describes as preserving (while simultaneously suppressing or rendering invisible) "time prior to the 'I'" (36), these items also have temporalities that render them irreducible to the present instance. Throughout the essay, Didi-Huberman elicits stark contrast between these "thingly" temporalities and the time of human life. For instance, entering through the crematorium doorway, he juxtaposes "what was so calm and quiet on that Sunday morning" with "what was once hell" (47). The plenteous vegetal growth in Auschwitz today is due to the soil's fertilization by the ash from the crematorium: "the exuberance with which the flowers of the fields grow is simply the counterpart to a human hecatomb on which this strip of Polish land has capitalized" (100).

The geological forces, working from below (so to say), have played a quasi-agential role in the production of evidence of the genocide, in particular the "washing of the rains [at the former location of the camp] has brought countless splinters and fragments of bone back to the surface" (106). However, while Hegel concentrates primarily on the dynamics of the organic synthesis of the inorganic within itself as a "precondition" of life, the directions of transformation and interpenetration between memory objects/subjects in *Bark* are far messier. They can involve both relations of *contiguity* (nearness), as in the case of the victims' clothing or the camp's furnishings, and of *continuity* (incorporation); and they can proceed from the inorganic to the organic, as well as from the organic to the inorganic (in the latter sense, one can perhaps speak of the "fossilization" and "petrification" of memory in *Bark* wherein the victims' ashes are simultaneously preserved *and* rendered invisible in the natural environment today).

Contemplating pieces of bark collected during a visit to the camp, Didi-Huberman calls them "strips of time," both "fragment[s] of memory" and "fragment[s] of the present," "this unwritten thing I attempt to read" (5). They are also objects of "archaeological" desire in that the subject seeks to "excavate" from them knowledge about the past. Importantly, to elucidate their meaning is not only a task of mediation between the past and present – and between those who died, those who survived, and those born after the war – but also a form of address that necessarily extends itself into the future.[26] The bark becomes an epistolary form directed to the generation whose future appearance is linked not only to the victims' killing, but also to the witnesses' death: he asks, "[w]hat will my child think when he comes across these remnants after my death" (5). The reference to their "disjointed temporalities" is also an expression of disquietude at the fashioning of Auschwitz into a cultural icon of (Jewish) suffering; at hand are "two very different arrangements of the same parcel of space and history," namely Auschwitz as "'the place of barbarism' (the camp)" and Auschwitz as "'the place of culture' (museum)" (30, 23).

The point is not simply the *durability* of the material objects, which extends their lifetime beyond that of humans, but also what could be called, paraphrasing Malabou, a *plasticity* of memory – the giving and receiving of mnemonic forms at the site of Auschwitz.[27] The birch bark contracts within itself plural and irreducible "things" – it is the violently stripped trunk fragment; an arboreal dermis, "pink like flesh," and its protective cortex; a writing material that "frays in scrolls, like the remains of a burned book."[28] The plasticity of memory does not mean that memory is polymorphous, but that it emerges through the process of interpenetration, mutual imprints or trace-making between the material and the immaterial, the tangible and intangible, and the organic and inorganic, whereby we can speak of memory as "presence that cannot be reduced to a present time" (Malabou 36). That mnemonic plasticity underpins Didi-Huberman's "archaeological point of view" in *Bark*, which is described as a "comparison" between "what we see in the presence, which has survived, with what we know has disappeared" (66). The archaeological investigation of memory objects is not primarily an exploration of the past, but rather "an anamnesis for understanding the present," which reveals that "[the] destruction of people does not mean they are departed. They're here, they are indeed here . . . in the flowers of the fields, here in the birches' sap, here in this tiny pond where lie the ashes of thousand dead" (Didi-Huberman 150).

Didi-Huberman's reflections on the material and temporal aspects of nonhuman testimony in *Bark* resonates with Malabou's rethinking of the Hegelian subject that, rather than engaged in an active shaping and molding of the nonhuman (animate and inanimate) world, is profoundly embedded within and affected by it. The blurring of the boundary between inorganic matter and the human subject has two aspects in *Bark*: first, the dimension of *contiguity* (radical proximity, or immediate presence) of inanimate and animate objects – trees, doors, furnaces – at the site of the Holocaust. The significance of their material and temporal proximity to the camp assigns to them the testimonial speech act of *terstis,* "I have been there," an example of a "thingly" or "geological witnessing."[29] Second, it has the dimension of *continuity* as the ashes of the victims' bodies have become one with the soil and the vegetation on the camp site, which is how, perhaps paradoxically, their testimonial and mnemonic affordance can actualize in the world. The importance of Malabou's plasticity and Didi-Huberman's nonhuman witnessing for posthumanist perspectives on the inorganic is that these authors radicalize further the recent interest in inanimate items as "containers" of agential power and memory. The presentation of the inorganic relation to the organic as something that is at the same time continuous and proximate, aligned and antagonistic, homologous *and* other, complicates the humanist imaginary of cultural memory as a series of deliberate human acts of narrative articulation. Rather, the emergence of cultural memory is a plastic process of receiving and taking form – as well as of destroying form – that traverses animate and inanimate ontologies and unravels the humanist hierarchy of being.

Reading together these two very different texts that nevertheless share the preoccupation with reimagining inanimate matter as capable of having effects on the shared construction of meaning, memorialization, and the production and distribution of public affects, I have argued that the blurring of the inorganic-organic distinction is a key aspect of posthumanist inquiry. The proposition that human subject is both continuous with and contiguous to inorganic items or elements creates a kind of a posthumanist puzzle, a concurrent homology *and* heterology, even antagonism, between the organic and inorganic. Through its complications of the belief in a uniform sovereign human subject, this "puzzle" has the potential to generate a more ecologically attuned conception of public memory and its vicissitudes.[30]

## Notes

1. Friedrich Wöhler, "Ueber künstliche Bildung des Harnstoffs," *Annalen der Physik und Chemie*, 88(2) (1828), 253 (emphasis added).
2. For more on vitality and the posthuman, see Chapter 8 of this volume.
3. J. H. Brooke, "Organic Synthesis and the Unification of Chemistry – A Reappraisal," *The British Journal for the History of Science*, 5(4) (1971), 363. H. M. Leicester, *The Historical Background of Chemistry* (New York: Dover Publications, 1971), 172–180.
4. See Leicester, and P. Rattansi and A. Clericuzio, *Alchemy and Chemistry in the 16th and 17th Centuries* (Dordrecht: Kluwer Academic Publishers, 2013). This is not to suggest that posthumanist concern with the inorganic maps neatly onto the chronology of modernity and modern science in the west. An example to the contrary is the "spontaneous generation" theory of the inorganic origins of life (and of the continuing inorganic traces or continuities *in* life). Prefigured by the ideas of pre-Socratic natural philosophers and the Aristotelian

hylomorphism, the theory of spontaneous generation had been ridiculed by its modern adversaries, such as Louis Pasteur, who saw it as fantastical beliefs in maggots originating from flesh, parasites from dust, etc. It is interesting that while Darwin does not mention the idea of spontaneous generation in *The Origins of Species*, his private writings prove that he was intrigued and even fascinated by it. In his 1837 notebook, Darwin called the idea of spontaneous generation "conceivable," and in an 1871 letter to a friend, Joseph D. Hooker, Darwin envisioned a kind of genesis of life in warm water where, facilitated by sufficient energy, inorganic substance would arrange itself into evolutionary units: "[if] we could conceive in some warm little pond with all sorts of ammonia & phosphoric salts, – light, heat, electricity & [carbon] present, that a protein compound was chemically formed, ready to undergo still more complex changes." Ch. Darwin, "Letter to J. D. Hooker. 1 February 1871." Darwin Correspondence Project, online. See also J. Peretó, J. L. Bada, A. Lazcano, "Charles Darwin and the Origin of Life," *Origins of Life and Evolution of the Biosphere*, 39(5) (2009), 395–406.

5. Timothy Morton, *Hyperobjects: Philosophy and Ecology after the End of the World* (Minneapolis: University of Minnesota Press, 2013).

6. G. Trop, "The Indifference of the Inorganic," in E. Landgraf, G. Trop & L. Weatherby (eds.), *Posthumanism in the Age of Humanism: Mind, Matter, and the Life Sciences after Kant* (New York: Bloomsbury, 2018), 280–308. See also Brooke.

7. B. Mathews, *Schelling's Organic Form of Philosophy: Life as the Schema of Freedom* (New York: SUNY Press, 2011). H. A. M. Snelders, "Romanticism and Naturphilosophie and the Inorganic Natural Sciences 1797–1840: An Introductory Survey," *Studies in Romanticism*, 9(3) (1970), 193–215.

8. L. Atzmon and P. Boradkar (eds.), *Encountering Things: Design and Theories of Things* (New York: Bloomsbury, 2017). B. Brown, "Thing Theory," *Critical Inquiry*, 28(1) (2001), 1–22. B. Brown, *Other Things* (Chicago: the University of Chicago Press, 2016).

9. J. Bennett, *Vibrant Matter: A Political Ecology of Things* (Durham: Duke University Press, 2010). R. A. Grusin (ed.), *The Nonhuman Turn* (Minneapolis: University of Minnesota Press, 2015).

10. B. Latour, *We Have Never Been Modern*, trans. C. Porter (Cambridge: Harvard University Press 1993).

11. See Morton. See also Chapter 13 of this volume for a more extensive discussion of speculative realism, including object-oriented ontology, and the posthuman.

12. For a critique of the humanist subject from a feminist perspective, see Rosi Braidotti, *Posthuman Knowledge* (Cambridge: Polity, 2019). See also Chapters 2 and 3 of this volume for more extensive discussion of the relationship between posthumanism and subjectivity.

13. See Chapter 4 of this volume for more on the posthuman and affect.

14. C. Malabou, *The Future of Hegel. Plasticity, Temporality, and Dialectic* (London: Routledge, 2005).

15. Malabou, 57 (emphasis in original).
16. Malabou, 40. See also C. Ferrini, "From Geological to Animal Nature in Hegel's Idea of Life," *Hegel-Studien*, 44 (2010), 1–77.
17. G. W. F. Hegel, *Hegel's Philosophy of Nature: Encyclopaedia of the Philosophical Sciences, Part II*, trans. A. V. Miller (Oxford: Oxford University Press, 2004), 58.
18. Malabou links plasticity to the way Hegel uses the term "theoretical" as the Aristotelian *theorein* (see also Derrida's preface to Malabou, 296 n18). For Aristotle, *theorein* has two distinct modalities: contemplation and exercise. While exercise implies the active subject, "informing and transforming the surrounding, [thus] appropriating the given conditions for its organic functions," contemplation connotes subjective passivity of "absorbing the environment" and "lending itself to what is given" (Malabou 60). Malabou refers to Gilles Deleuze's *Difference and Repetition* to elucidate the link between contemplation and contraction. Deleuze says that the function of a "contemplative soul" is precisely to contract "that from which we came" (quoted in Malabou 60). The etymological and philosophic connection between *theorein* and sight or seeing (*thea*, "a view" and *horan*, "to see") means that for Deleuze the eye becomes a privileged figure to exemplify the dual "plastic operation" of *theorein*.
19. Hegel §265. Ferrini aptly speculates about the impact of the theory of galvanism on Hegel's writings of geological bodies and processes, which is conspicuous for instance in Hegel's remark on the mountainous formations, which "are not dead, rather they are members of a galvanic chain" (quoted in Ferrini 25).
20. Malabou in interview with G. Peña, "Interview with Catherine Malabou," *Figure/Ground* (May 12, 2016), online.
21. J.-P. Martinon, *On Futurity: Malabou, Derrida and Nancy* (London: Palgrave Macmillan, 2007), 57.
22. E. Povinelli, *Geontologies: A Requiem to Late Liberalism* (Durham: Duke University Press, 2016).
23. Malabou, 36 (emphasis added). See also Chapter 2 of this volume for a discussion of philosophy, belatedness, and the posthuman.
24. S. Craps, "Climate Change and the Art of Anticipatory Memory," *Parallax*, 23(4) (2017), 479–92. S. Craps, C. Colebrooke, R. Crownshaw, R. Kennedy, V. Nardizzi, and J. Wenzel, "Memory Studies and the Anthropocene: A Roundtable," *Memory Studies*, 11(4) (2018), 498–515. M. Hirsch and L. Spitzer, "Testimonial Objects: Memory, Gender, and Transmission," *Poetics Today*, 27 (2006): 353–83. A. Rigney and A. Erll (eds.), *Mediation, Remediation, and the Dynamics of Cultural Memory* (Berlin: de Gruyter, 2009). M. Zirra, "Shelf Lives: Nonhuman Agency and Seamus Heaney's Vibrant Memory Objects," *Parallax*, 23(4) (2017), 458–73.
25. G. Didi-Huberman, *Bark*, trans. S. E. Martin (Cambridge: The MIT Press, 2017).

26. Generationality is a significant category for Didi-Huberman's understanding of the different and overlapping temporalities of witnessing. The personal aspect of his visit to Auschwitz becomes apparent when he admits to an attempt at "reinscrib[ing]" the place of the camp within "family history": "my grandparents who died here, my mother who thereby lost all means of telling, my sister who loved Poland at a time when I couldn't understand it, my cousin who isn't yet ready ... for this kind of dead-on reunion with history" (119).

27. The use of the concept of plasticity to illuminate the process of cultural memory formation at Auschwitz cannot ignore the fact that Auschwitz itself was based on the belief in "violent plasticity," which takes humanity as a "material" to be molded and modelled into a desirable entity. And thus Didi-Huberman's essay sees "in [the] vegetation ... an immense human desolation, in [the] foundations and [the] heaps of bricks ... all the horror of the mass gassing, in [the] aberrant toponymy – 'Kanada,' 'Mexiko' ... *all the crazy logic of a rational organization of humanity conceived as a material, a residue to be transformed*; in these tranquil marshy surfaces lie the ashes of countless people murdered" (54–5; emphasis added).

28. Didi-Huberman, 5. The French word for bark, "écorce," derives from the Latin, *scortea*, meaning "coat of skin." The dual meaning of "écorce" is thus that of a hardened (*deadened*) protective skin and of a living tissue ("at once a coat – a costume, a veil – and a skin, ... a surface of apparition endowed with life, reacting to pain and destined to die" [5]). That distinction is clear in classical Latin, where there are two terms for "bark" – first, *cortex*, from the Indo-European *sker* (cut), connotes "the part of the tree immediately at hand to the exterior, ... that [which] one cuts, ... the introductory part of the body liable to be affected, scarred, cut up, separated"; and, second, *liber*, "where the bark adheres to the trunk" (it is *liber*, rather than *cortex*, that has served as a writing material) (120–1).

29. See further J. Derrida, *Sovereignties in Question: The Poetics of Paul Celan* (New York: Fordham University Press, 2005).

30. Many thanks to Michael Richardson and Sherryl Vint for helpful suggestions and critical comments on the earlier drafts of this chapter.

# PART III

## *Posthumanities*

# CHAPTER II

# More-than-Human Biopolitics

## Sonja van Wichelen

### II.1 Introduction

Today, the term biopolitics has become so overused that it risks being emptied of a stable meaning. Originating in the discipline of political philosophy, the concept has traveled and anchored itself across disciplines in the humanities and social sciences.[1] These movements from one field to the other, and the diversity of contexts in which biopolitics is brought to respond, allow for an expansion of its applications, ranging from *theoretically informed empirical analyses* in the realm of biomedicine,[2] reproduction,[3] sexuality,[4] race,[5] and security,[6] on the one hand, to more *philosophical explorations* in social theory,[7] political philosophy,[8] queer theory,[9] and postcolonial theory,[10] on the other.

Foucault conveyed the embryonic frameworks of biopolitics through his lectures on biopower, teasing out the ways in which life became more and more governed through a plethora of techniques that realize the subjugation of bodies and the control of populations. But it was not until his lectures at the *Collège de France* that his ideas became more crystalized, though never enough to stabilize into a coherent definition.[11] Rather, the understanding of biopolitics remains at the conceptual level and Foucault did not have the opportunity to sharpen his ideas or to reflect on his own writings to further a more precise understanding of biopolitics.[12] Nonetheless, many thinkers and researchers influenced by his work have taken up this task and have elaborated and expanded biopolitics to encompass "bare life" (Agamben *Homo Sacer*), "necropolitics,"[13] biocapital,[14] biosociality,[15] biolegality,[16] the politics of "life itself" (Rose *Politics*), and the politics of immunity (Esposito *Immunitas*). These are the reference points when debating the conceptual merits and insights of biopolitics; it has informed a tremendous amount of interdisciplinary scholarship.

The posthuman – as incarnated through Foucault's anti-humanist position – has been key to informing his biopolitical analysis, which critiques the reliance on liberal reason and rationalities of the Enlightenment to further the universal political subject.[17] This starting point allowed many to consider biopolitics as a parallel development to posthumanism. Both share roots in Michel Foucault's theorizing of the body as the main point of power's operation, and scholars building on or responding to Foucault's work have contributed to posthumanist theory in a variety of ways. Scholars such as Nikolas Rose and Paul Rabinow established a Foucauldian tradition of medical humanities that interrogates our understanding of the human. Other biopolitical theorists, especially Giorgio Agamben and Roberto Esposito, have illuminated how foundational the distinction between human and nonhuman is for western politics and ethics. Agamben's *The Open* and *Homo Sacer,* for example, make clear that the human/animal boundary is both essential for human rights discourse and simultaneously always-in-transition, while Esposito's work in *Persons and Things* and *The Third Person* explores how the concepts "human" and "person" do not coincide in all historical and political circumstances. These ontic and ontological renderings of *bios* constitute a case in point for the collaborations between posthumanism and biopolitics.

However, as I will demonstrate in this essay, while posthumanism and biopolitics have many points of overlap, posthumanist scholarship in other areas has also challenged and critiqued some of the conventional understandings of Foucauldian biopolitics. More recently, the question of the posthuman goes beyond the focus on antihumanism and is posed within the reconfiguration of life itself: how can life be governed when the boundaries of life are shifting, when inanimate, nonhuman, and posthuman forms and their novel ontologies have entered the specter of qualified life, which was mostly attributed to humans in the classic understanding of biopolitics? This question is heightened in the age of the Anthropocene, where the destruction of the natural world is evidenced by the burden humans have put on natural resources, land, soil, waters, air, and nonhuman life, including plants and microbes.[18]

In this essay I distinguish four different scholarly engagements with the posthuman and the biopolitical that push the analytics of a Foucauldian biopolitics to its boundaries, and that lay bare the limits and tensions of biopolitics arising within these areas of study. While many theorists fall under these rubrics, I single out one representative for each, to give a more thorough account of their positions vis-à-vis biopolitics. The four areas of engagement include: (1) capital, examined through the work of Melinda Cooper; (2) law, examined via Roberto Esposito; (3) relational materialist thought in the work of Thomas Lemke; and (4) the environmental humanities through the work of Anna Tsing.[19] These distinctions are sometimes crude and often informed by disciplinary conventions.[20] Nonetheless, categorization is an important heuristic tool. It will situate the different posthuman stakes involved in each category and allow for a more careful reading of their convergences with, or divergences from, classical understandings of Foucauldian biopolitics.

## 11.2   Engagements with Capital

In delineating the space of biopolitics, Foucault's focus was on a range of institutionalized practices that regulate populations and individuals as part of a wider politics of organizing and knowing "life." Here, biopower arises as a new rationality of power that contrasts with sovereign forms of power. The historical shift from disciplinary societies to governmentality – central to Foucault's premise of biopolitics – is brought about by liberal and neoliberal forms of effectivity, stressing the productive side of power that enabled a detachment from sovereign forms of punishment that emphasize death. According to Foucault – and taken up by Foucauldian scholars of contemporary biosciences such as Paul Rabinow and Nikolas Rose – biology was one of the central motors in navigating a biopolitical route to government and governmentality. The emergence of modern biology as a discipline in the eighteenth and nineteenth century made *knowing* life a concrete locus of concern for the polity. Moreover, as the biosciences progressed in the twentieth and twenty-first century to the *making* of life (for example, through the wide application of assisted reproductive technologies or biomedical applications of genetics), so does biopolitics shift focus from the individual body to a molecularized version of life.

Contemporary scholars of biocapital, biovalue, and bioeconomies have diagnosed a new neoliberal economy that is constitutive to the developments of bioscience and biomedicine.[21] The emergence and stimulation of global bioeconomies, in which life is increasingly predicated on risk assessments, speculation, and experimentation, opens the body and its parts to the vagaries of financial capital, commodity value, and forms of biological labor. In my own field of reproductive technologies, for example, eggs, sperm, gametes, surrogate bodies, and babies are increasingly circulated on the globalized reproductive market; while sperm is FedEx-ed from one nation to the other, oocytes become valuable according to the sociocultural and racialized capital of donors, and the biological labor of surrogates falls upon poorer women in the Global South.[22]

The historical conditions of this advanced form of capitalism and the technologies that reconfigure the political subject lead some posthuman theorists of capital to challenge biopolitics in ways that contest the centrality of governance in the enactment of biopower or the reliance on anthropocentric notions of the human body as the focus of biopolitics and governmentality. In *Life as Surplus* Melinda Cooper demonstrates how uncertainty and risk transform the regulation of bodies in ways that are different from the ones described by Foucault, in which the political administration of populations and the uses of demographic methods stood central as governmental technique. While the dominant impetus for a Foucauldian biopolitics was the paradigmatic transformation from disciplinary society to governmentality, the new form of advanced capitalism described by Cooper is only loosely connected to the realm of intentional governmental policies and, instead, is attached more firmly to financial calculations of risk and insecurity. In showing how the neoliberal economy of such capitalism in the twenty-first century informs a new political economy, Cooper does not so much dismiss the power of biopolitics as a heuristic tool to examine these changes, as encourage us to become more attentive to new speculative modes of growing the bioeconomy.

Cooper utilizes (post-)Marxist theories of value to make sense of these new developments, focusing specifically on the emergence of the bioeconomy in 1960s–1970s USA. Her account depicts the frenzy in American politics in the mining and extracting of biovalue that is abundantly available, yet not fully realized. While she advances Foucauldian biopolitics by bringing the coproduction of political economy and the life sciences to bear on the post-welfare and post-Fordist economy of the USA, her object of analysis is not the commodification of life as such, but neoliberal flexibilization and financialization of life. An operational and metaphorical fusion exists between the growth of biological life (tissue, cells, genes, microbes) and the growth of economic life, which marks the advanced form of capitalism in contemporary times as a different regime of biopolitics from the Fordist era. Moreover, by re-appropriating a Marxist model for this new regime of biopolitics, she points to the corollary effect of scarcity in promoting a capitalism that embraces an excess of regenerative life. Hence, life as surplus cannot flourish without the devaluation of life; a constitutive element of the neoliberal regeneration of life is the structural devastation of life. Apart from real-life consequences, this devastation also destabilizes the idea of the human as a separate and ontologically different type of life. Capital in the age of neoliberalism and biotechnology cuts across skin and enmeshes with life in ways that reconfigure or go beyond life as *zoe* (bare life) and *bios* (qualified life). As it operates through neoliberal logics of capital, life mutates into populations, statistics, casualties, collateral damage, data, or surplus.[23]

## 11.3   Engagements with Law

Foucault's emphasis on governmentality impelled some of his successors to advance his line of reasoning more intimately in the realm of law, legality, the state, and governance. Biopolitical engagements in this area focus on the juridico-political structures of modern and liberal society that, for example, allow Agamben's figure of the *homo sacer* – one who is reduced to "bare life" – to be deserted by any framework of human rights. In fact, for many of the biopolitical scholars in this area, human rights themselves are the object of scrutiny, contributing to a politics of "immunity" and furthering the valuation and biolegitimacy of some lives over others.[24] The racialized and violent manner in which life becomes the powerful determinant in making someone live or let die is taken up in the "thanatopolitical" analysis of contemporary events such as the captive bodies in Guantanamo Bay or the occupied lives of those in Palestine.[25] The core argument Mbembe posits, for example, is that in securing biopower, the sovereign state gambles with a "politics of death" (necropower), mobilized through technologies of control that direct this necropower ("Necropolitics" 40). In contrast to Agamben, it is the colony, and not the camp, that produces these necropolitical conditions of life in Mbembe's analysis. In the name of civilization, colonial imperialism creates a state of exception wherein violence can be deployed through the suspension of law's protections of life (Mbembe 24). Recently, Alexander G. Weheliye supplements Mbembe's rereading of Foucault's and Agamben's depiction of biopolitics, and focuses on the centrality of the plantation, slavery, and race in the construction of the human.

On the other side of the polity, and moving away from the thanatopolitical, we find the stress on political agency and the capacities of (mostly human) subjects to embrace the biopolitical into an affirmative mode. Key representatives of this mode of thought are Hardt and Negri who, with their "multitude," propose a society in which subjects derive their agency from the blurring of conventional distinctions between material and immaterial labor, production and reproduction, work and leisure.[26] We also find here the more sociological and anthropological work on biopolitics, governance, and political agency. The scholarship around biocitizenship details empirical and ethnographic ways in which biology and the biological self are figured as the procreant of political agency, prompting civic virtues to emerge in light of environmental disasters or biomedical events.[27] And scholarship around biolaw and biolegalities examines the ontic boundaries of life in law.[28] Focusing on the biotechnological and biopolitical dynamics in forensic or conservation practices, on the one hand, and knowledge practices around legal and philosophical conceptualizations of property and personhood, on the other, this scholarship aims to push forward the argument that law – as much as science or markets – is constitutive of life and sociality.[29]

In sum, while ontic projects focus on the implications of biopolitical modes of governmentality for the biological citizen, the asylum seeker, undocumented migrants, criminals, and legal persons (human and non-human) in a variety of national contexts and transnational jurisdictions, ontological projects focus on the deployment of life in legal theory or political philosophy.[30] Straddling between thanatopolitical and affirmative biopolitics is Roberto Esposito, whose work I will discuss in more detail, because he has been very influential for scholars of posthumanism working in the area of law and governance.

Although Esposito has not explicitly dealt with the posthuman, his work has been taken up by such legal scholars to account for a reconfiguration of legal philosophy toward posthuman futures. Following Haraway and her cyborg thesis, Esposito describes how human life has always been entangled with technology; in that sense, we have always been posthuman.[31] His concept of immunity is, in fact, one that emphasizes connection between the self and "the world, in all its components – natural and artificial, material and electronic, chemical and telematics – which penetrates us" (Esposito, *Immunitas* 147). Hence, rather than seeing immunity as something that needs defending, protecting, or isolating from the outside, it is to be understood as a continuously evolving, connected form, and permeable in its interaction with others and the world.[32]

More complicated, but relevant to posthuman theory within the legal realms, are his ideas around the fundamental distinction in western modern law between persons and things. He proposes to upset this distinction, one that sits at the constitutive moment where law provides the foundational basis of immunity. Esposito develops a normative thesis by positing that an affirmative biopolitics lies in its emphasis on bodies, bodies that individually or collectively resist closure and an absolutist idea of identification.[33] In effect, an important task for the realization of an affirmative biopolitics is to split the distinction between person and thing, "breaking the prohibitions that have always blocked re-unifying

life and lives in their singular and impersonal dimensions" (Campbell and
Luisetti 114). As Patrick Hanafin explains, the body allows a resistance to
the "*dispositif* of the person and the biopolitical governance of lives through
law."[34] Recent scholarship in law and sociolegal studies has theorized
around the possibility of a "third person" or a "bodyhood" that can tear
down the western and modern legal distinction between persons and
things.[35]

## 11.4   Relational Materialist Engagements

The understanding of life as inherently and fundamentally in perpetual
and evolving connection to the nonhuman and nonliving world is also the
starting point for relational materialists, of which Donna Haraway is a key
interlocutor and a source of influence for Esposito's ideas. In contrast to
a politico-philosophical discussion of law or governance, relational materialists concentrate on the material premises of contemporary biopolitics
(often focused on technology, biology, or biotechnology) that are rooted in
empirical work, and they frequently work in the field of science and
technology studies (STS). While Haraway and her contemporaries (such
as Evelyn Fox Keller, Sarah Franklin, Bruno Latour, and Karen Barad) did
not necessarily make their relational materialism explicit in early works,[36]
the emergence of new materialism in the past decade has consolidated this
categorization more forcefully in hindsight.[37]

The relational materialist view characterizes itself by the interactions
between nature/biology/technology and the cultural or the social. Rather
than emphasizing the binary between nature and society, it stresses the traffic
between them. This stance also necessitates the letting go or collapsing of
disciplinary objects – such as biology, culture, the social – in order to foster
new developments within the humanities and social sciences.[38] In the early
articulation of this perspective, Haraway coined the term material-semiotic
and showed its indebtedness to actor-network theory (ANT). In turn, John
Law describes how ANT owes much to Foucault's rendering of the biopolitical as historically and materially created.[39] By centering discourse in the
analysis of the social, which includes speech and text as much as practice,
Foucault's work deeply informed ANT's direction to material semiotics. In
its exploration and explanation of agency, ANT does not privilege the
human, but emphasizes the symmetry between humans and nonhumans.
Scholarship emerging in ANT and STS has remained loyal to the idea that
what becomes known as the social is shaped by the socio-material arrangements and semiotic speech acts between subject and object. Rather than

stress the dichotomy (or rendering one pole more important than the other), the relational and often performative dimension of this materialist view highlights how "network nodes are sets of relations" and how "materials are interactively constituted" (Law and Mol, 277). There is no outside to the traffic, no external reality away from the interaction between object and subject.

Recently, and in response to new materialism's abandonment of biopolitics, biopolitical scholars are retheorizing relational agency to counter what they consider drawbacks of the new materialist approach.[40] Working "from Foucault after Foucault,"[41] Thomas Lemke for instance makes a case for a posthumanist biopolitics by putting forward Foucault's government of things. Pointing to powerful analytics in Foucauldian biopolitics – such as the dispositif or milieu – Lemke argues that a posthumanist analysis within a Foucauldian framework is not only possible, but preferable and necessary. Aiming to go beyond Foucault's anthropocentrism, Lemke rereads Foucault against the critiques put forward by new materialists and speculative realists, focusing on the work of Karen Barad, Jane Bennett, and Graham Harman.[42]

One of the central posthuman critiques of Foucault is directed at the concept of biopower, which is understood as revealing the dynamic through which *human* individuals and populations (as a species) became actively involved in political programs and strategies (Lemke, "New Materialisms" 16). But Lemke contends that Foucault can and does deliver on a posthumanist conception of political agency by expanding and clarifying Foucault's government of things, which was central in his 1978 lecture series at the College de France. Here, "things" are not fixed objects for Foucault, but imply a relationality; humans and things co-constitute one another (Lemke, "New Materialisms" 9). While Foucault's *dispositif* – as a conceptual device – reveals the arrangement of humans and things through which power is realized, Foucault's concept of *milieu* helps emphasize the circularity of agency (against causality) and confirms that agential power emerges in the interaction of human and nonhuman (Lemke, "Rethinking" 67). While for Lemke, Foucault remains important for posthumanism through this concept of a government of things, others – particularly those in environmental humanities – engage Agamben instead who, in *The Open*, highlights nonhuman subjectivity in the examination of biopolitics and animals. All these scholars point to a commitment to biopolitics understood in new, posthuman ways that are more receptive to the challenges of our times.

## 11.5    Engagements from the Environmental Humanities

One of those challenges, clearly voiced in the past few decades, comes from the environmental (or ecological) humanities. Across the disciplines of philosophy, literature, history, geography, and anthropology, the credo of environmental humanities encompasses first and foremost the need to respond to the Anthropocene thesis.[43] This thesis – understood as the post-Holocene period in which human life emerges as a geological force shaping climate and the environment – further challenges biopolitics in the sense that the critique moves from the human/non-human binary in biopolitics to the life/non-life binary. Posthumanist scholars such as Cary Wolfe, Elizabeth Povinelli, Anna Tsing, Stefan Helmreich, Julie Guthman, Irus Braverman, Eben Kirksey, Heather Paxson, Jamie Lorimer, Astrida Neimanis, and Thom Van Dooren have reconfigured biopolitical governmentality to reflect their entanglements with earthly matters and geological phenomena. For instance, Helmreich proposes to view the governance of entangled living as "symbiopolitics,"[44] Paxon refers to the "microbiopolitical" in describing the discursive and material entanglements of humans and microorganisms,[45] and Swyngedouw and Ernston point to the "immuno-biopolitics" of the concept of Anthropocene to argue – following Esposito – for its depoliticizing nature.[46]

Although Anna Tsing does not engage explicitly with the Foucauldian frame of biopolitics, her accounts of entangled life and feral ecologies are always couched in biopolitical contexts of industrial destruction and capitalist ruins, and her work proves extremely influential amongst posthuman scholars of biopolitical phenomena.[47] I turn to Tsing's work as an example of posthuman biopolitical analysis that moves away from the more metaphysical approaches, such as the work of Cary Wolfe, where an affirmative politics is theorized but rarely illustrated through the empirical.[48] In *The Mushroom at the End of the World*, Tsing follows the existence of Matsutake mushrooms found in forests across the Northern hemisphere and considered a sought-after delicacy in Japan. Matsutake also assists in growing forests by its capacity to nurture trees. She explores damaged landscapes and their survival, working through political economies of the commodity, as well as the fungal ecologies and forest histories, not only to give an account of entangled life, but also to narrate a possible cohabitational future. Her work presents an urgent examination into the relation between capitalist destruction and collaborative survival within multispecies landscapes, the prerequisite for continuing life on Earth.

It is not a coincidence that many representatives of the environmental humanities are anthropologists and geographers.[49] An important reason is methodology; ethnographic research has proven most suitable to track "entangled" or "multispecies" life. Multi-sited ethnography allows researchers to map the trajectories and entanglements of humans, nonhumans, life, non-life, disconnecting/connecting them; it also permits a meticulous description of the earthly effects and responses to what has been conceptualized as the Anthropocene – how climate change and global warming – brought about by capital and the human species – are increasingly implicated in our social and political imaginaries. Such responses, however, are not always visible to the naked eye or other human senses, so ethnographers often turn to the experts dealing with these forms of life. In Tsing's account of Matsutake, she turns to the pickers of the mushrooms (Hmong jungle fighters, Yi Chinese goat herders, and Finnish nature guides) to learn about Matsutake's affect and responses, but also to natural scientists – in biology or agriculture – to understand the biological components of matsutake that allow them to respond so vitally in the rubble of capitalist destruction. Her book builds on an earlier essay considering plantation culture, in which she describes how the biopolitical management of nature is also grounded in colonial and racialized relations.[50] Rather than following scientists in their work, which proved "easy for humanists" (Haraway et al., "Anthropologists" 550), the science studies pursued by posthuman anthropologists gets intimately involved with what the scientists are observing and theorizing.[51] Such endeavors are more encouraging in an environment wherein the life sciences themselves are proposing less deterministic ways of describing biological and natural processes, and point to more plastic and permeable understandings of life that destabilize modernist binaries between nature and culture.[52]

The ways in which biological knowledge intervenes in our political imagination brings the ethnographic material to speak to conceptual tools of biopolitics. What Tsing manages to do in *The Mushroom at the End of the World* is not only to give an account of entangled life as empirically observable through *connections* with scientists, workers, and consumers, but also to detail the less observable *relations* Matsutake have with policies, bureaucracies, law, desire, and imagination, including a subject's interaction with an apparatus.[53] Matsutake, then, is not just an inert thing that can be planted and managed; it has to be negotiated with. This link with science studies and the conceptual *relations* (on top of empirical *connections*) require the equipment of biopolitical investigation. While Tsing rarely makes this explicit, other posthumanist anthropologists and geographers have.[54] Foucault's biopolitics remain profoundly relevant to theorize such relations across the apparatus in question, encompassing different sites and scales, and exhibiting different modes of governmentality. Although these newly defined premises of the Anthropocene were not known to Foucault, biopolitics continues to prove useful to examine the entanglements of populations and bodies with ecological, environmental, and geological forces.

## 11.6   Conclusion: More-than-Human Biopolitics

How to rethink biopolitics from a posthumanist perspective? This chapter provided a modest discussion of the recent debates in biopolitical scholarship on some of the posthuman challenges facing the humanities and social sciences today. My aim in discussing different engagements with more-than-human biopolitics – through the lenses of capital, law, relational materialism, and environmental humanities – was not so much to entertain an exercise in boundary-making, but rather to expose the specific problems and tensions informing these engagements. Some of the stakes articulate differently in each of these engagements but a careful reading across the literature also clarifies commonalities in operating with Foucault's biopolitical tools. While biopolitics has been put to the test by many scholars who seek to destabilize and contest some of the assumed anthropocentric premises of Foucauldian biopolitics, his conceptual equipment (*dispositif*, governmentality, milieu) and his privileging of genealogies and practices as non-linear and entangled with "things" remain at the core of leading researchers examining posthumanist problems and phenomena today.

### Notes

1. These disciplines include for instance sociology, anthropology, political science, economy, geography, health sciences, comparative literature, philosophy, history, architecture, and cultural studies.
2. P. Rabinow, *Making PCR: A Story of Biotechnology* (Chicago: University of Chicago Press, 2011). N. Rose, *The Politics of Life Itself: Biomedicine, Power, and Subjectivity in the Twenty-First Century* (Princeton: Princeton University Press, 2007).
3. C. Waldby and M. Cooper, 2008. "The Biopolitics of Reproduction: Post-Fordist Biotechnology and Women's Clinical Labour," *Australian Feminist Studies*, 23(55) (2008), 57–73. M. Cooper and C. Waldby, *Clinical Labor: Tissue Donors and Research Subjects in the Global Bioeconomy* (Durham: Duke University Press, 2014).

4. Mel Y. Chen, *Animacies: Biopolitics, Racial Mattering, and Queer Affect* (Durham: Duke University Press, 2012).

5. A. G. Weheliye, *Habeas Viscus: Racializing Assemblages, Biopolitics, and Black Feminist Theories of the Human* (Durham: Duke University Press, 2014).

6. M. Dillon and L. Lobo-Guerrero, "Biopolitics of Security in the 21st Century: An Introduction," *Review of International Studies*, 34 (2) (2008), 265–92.

7. T. Lemke, "Beyond Foucault: From Biopolitics to the Government of Life," in U. Bröckling, S. Krasmann and T. Lemke (eds.), *Governmentality: Current Issues and Future Challenges* (New York: Routledge, 2010), 173–192. T. Lemke, "New Materialisms: Foucault and the 'Government of Things,'" *Theory, Culture & Society*, 32 (4) (2015), 3–25. T. Lemke, "Rethinking Biopolitics: The New Materialism and the Political Economy of Life," in E. Wilmer and A. Žukauskaitė (eds.), *Resisting Biopolitics: Philosophical, Political, and Performative Strategies* (New York: Routledge, 2015), 69–85. T. Lemke, "Materialism Without Matter: The Recurrence of Subjectivism in Object-Oriented Ontology," *Distinktion: Journal of Social Theory*, 18 (2) (2017), 133–52. T. Lemke, "An Alternative Model of Politics? Prospects and Problems of Jane Bennett's Vital Materialism," *Theory, Culture & Society*, 35 (6) (2018), 31–54. T. Lemke, "Mater and Matter: A Preliminary Cartography of Material Feminisms," *Soft Power*, 5 (1) (2018), 83–99.

8. G. Agamben, *Homo Sacer: Sovereign Power and Bare Life* (Stanford: Stanford University Press, 1998). G. Agamben, *The Open: Man and Animal* (Stanford: Stanford University Press, 2004). R. Esposito, *The Third Person* (Cambridge: Polity, 2012). R. Esposito, *Persons and Things: From the Body's Point of View* (Hoboken, NJ: Wiley, 2015). T. C. Campbell, *Improper Life: Technology and Biopolitics from Heidegger to Agamben* (Minneapolis: University of Minnesota Press, 2011). C. Mills, *The Philosophy of Agamben* (New York: Routledge, 2014). V. Lemm and M. Vatter, (eds.), *The Government of Life: Foucault, Biopolitics, and Neoliberalism* (Oxford: Oxford University Press, 2014).

9. Chen, *Animacies*.

10. S. Mezzadra, J. Reid and R. Samaddar, *The Biopolitics of Development. Reading Michel Foucault in the Postcolonial Present* (Springer: New Delhi, 2013).

11. M. Foucault, *"Society Must Be Defended": Lectures at the College de France, 1975–1976* (New York: Picador, 2003). M. Foucault, *Security, Territory, Population: Lectures at the Collège de France, 1977–1978* (London: Palgrave Macmillan, 2007). M. Foucault, *The Birth of Biopolitics: Lectures at the Collège de France, 1978–1979* (London: Palgrave Macmillan, 2008).

12. See also T. Campbell and A. Sitze (eds.), *Biopolitics. A Reader* (Durham: Duke University Press, 2013).

13. J. A. Mbembé and L. Meintjes, "Necropolitics," *Public Culture*, 15 (1) (2003), 11–40.

14. K. S. Rajan, *Biocapital: The Constitution of Postgenomic Life* (Durham: Duke University Press, 2006).

15. P. Rabinow, *Essays on the Anthropology of Reason* (Princeton: Princeton University Press, 1996).

16. M. Lynch and R. McNally, "Forensic DNA Databases and Biolegality," in P. Atkinson, P. Glasner and M. Lock (eds.), *Handbook of Genetics and Society* (New York: Routledge, 2009), 283–301. M. De Leeuw and S. Van Wichelen, *Biolegalities: A Critical Intervention* (London: Palgrave Macmillan, forthcoming). M. De Leeuw and S. Van Wichelen, *Personhood in the Age of Biologality: Brave New Law* (London: Palgrave Macmillan, 2020).

17. M. Foucault, *The Order of Things: An Archaeology of the Human Sciences* (New York: Routledge, 2005). See also Chapter 2 of this volume.

18. See Chapter 9 of this volume for more on posthumanism and the Anthropocene.

19. Other prominent theorists of life sciences and capital include Kaushik Sunder Rajan, Catherine Waldby, and Philip Mirowski. Important scholars of law also include Miguel Vatter and Yasmeen Arif. Those of relational materialism include Annemarie Mol and John Law. And those of environmental humanities include Donna Haraway, Becky Mansfield, and Eben Kirksey.

20. For example, sociology in engaging with capital, philosophy in engaging with new materialism, science studies in relational materialism, and anthropology and geography in environmental humanities.

21. M. E. Cooper, *Life as Surplus: Biotechnology and Capitalism in the Neoliberal Era* (Seattle: University of Washington Press, 2011). Sunder Rajan, *Biocapital*. V. Pavone, and J. Goven (eds.), *Bioeconomies* (London: Palgrave Macmillan, 2017). C. Waldby and R. Mitchell, *Tissue Economies: Blood, Organs, and Cell Lines in Late Capitalism* (Durham: Duke University Press, 2006). Rose, *Politics*. Waldby and Cooper, *Clinical Labor*.

22. See S. Van Wichelen "Reproducing the Border: Kinship Legalities in the Bioeconomy," in V. Pavone and J. Goven (eds.), *Bioeconomies: Life, Technology, and Capital in the 21st Century* (London: Palgrave Macmillan, 2017) 207–226.

23. For more on this new politics of life and the posthuman, see Chapter 8 of this volume.

24. R. Esposito, *Immunitas: The Protection and Negation of Life* (Cambridge: Polity, 2011). D. Fassin, "Another Politics of Life is Possible," *Theory, Culture & Society*, 26 (5) (2009), 44–60. It is important to note that Foucault and Agamben – as well as others in the field of biopolitics – invite different kinds of readings of how life and the human are restructured by biopolitics. While they often employ the same terminology, they can mean different things in their ruminations.

25. A. Mbembe "Necropolitics," *Public Culture*, 15 (1) (2003), 11–40. See also Foucault, *Society*. G. Agamben, *State of Exception* (Chicago: University of Chicago Press, 2005) and J. K. Puar, *The Right to Maim: Debility, Capacity, Disability* (Duke University Press, 2017).

26. M. Hardt and A. Negri, *Multitude: War and Democracy in the Age of Empire* (New York: Penguin, 2004). See also Chapter 4 in this volume.

27. N. Rose, and C. Novas, "Biological Citizenship," in A. Ong and S. J. Collier (eds.), *Global Assemblages: Technology, Politics, and Ethics as Anthropological*

*Problems* (Oxford: Blackwell, 2005), 439–63. A. Petryna, *Life Exposed: Biological Citizens after Chernobyl* (Princeton: Princeton University Press, 2013). T. Heinemann and T. Lemke, "Biological Citizenship Reconsidered: The Use of DNA Analysis by Immigration Authorities in Germany," *Science, Technology, & Human Values*, 39 (4) (2014), 488–510. See also Chapter 8 in this volume.

28. A. Pottage and B. Sherman, *Figures of Invention: A History of Modern Patent Law* (Oxford: Oxford University Press, 2010). B. van Beers, L. Corrias and W. G. Werner, *Humanity Across International Law and Biolaw* (Cambridge: Cambridge University Press, 2014). I. Braverman (ed.), *Gene Editing, Law, and the Environment: Life Beyond the Human* (New York: Routledge, 2017). De Leeuw and Van Wichelen, *Biolegalities*.

29. In our forthcoming *Biolegalities*, De Leeuw and I detail these changes in knowledge practices around property, personhood, kinship, and community.

30. See P. T. Clough and C. Willse, *Beyond Biopolitics: Essays on the Governance of Life and Death* (Durham: Duke University Press, 2011) for a wonderful collection that showcases a combination of these ontic and ontological projects.

31. See T. Campbell, and F. Luisetti, "On Contemporary French and Italian Political Philosophy: An Interview with Roberto Esposito," *Minnesota Review*, 75 (1) (2010), 109–18.

32. N. Brown, *Immunitary Life: Biomedicine, Technology and the Body* (London: Palgrave Macmillan, 2019), 12.

33. Brown, 25.

34. P. Hanafin, "Resistant Lives: Law, Life, Singularity," *Soft Power*, 1 (1) (2014), 98.

35. A. Amendola, "The Law of the Living: Material for Hypothesizing the Biojuridical," *Law, Culture and the Humanities*, 8 (1) (2012), 102–18. P. Hanafin, "Rights, Bioconstitutionalism and the Politics of Reproductive Citizenship in Italy," *Citizenship Studies*, 17(8) (2013), 942–55. Hanafin, "Resistant." T. F. Tierney, "Toward an Affirmative Biopolitics," *Sociological Theory*, 34 (4) (2016), 358–81. M. Vatter and M. de Leeuw, "Human Rights, Legal Personhood and the Impersonality of Embodied Life," *Law, Culture and the Humanities* (June 2019), online.

36. With the exception of J. Law and A. Mol, "Notes on Materiality and Sociality," *The Sociological Review*, 43 (2) (1995), 274–94.

37. For more on new materialisms and posthumanism, see Chapter 12 in this volume.

38. S. Ahmed, "Open Forum Imaginary Prohibitions: Some Preliminary Remarks on the Founding Gestures of the 'New Materialism,'" *European Journal of Women's Studies*, 15 (1) (2008), 35.

39. J. Law, *Organizing Modernity* (Oxford: Blackwell, 1994), 100–4.

40. For examples, see J. Bennett, *Vibrant Matter: A Political Ecology of Things* (Durham: Duke University Press, 2009). R. Braidotti, *The Posthuman* (London: Polity, 2013). S. E. Wilmer and A. Žukauskaitė, (eds.), *Resisting*

*Biopolitics: Philosophical, Political, and Performative Strategies* (New York: Routledge, 2015). See also Chapter 12 of this volume.

41. B. Massumi, "National Enterprise Emergency: Steps toward an Ecology of Powers," *Theory, Culture & Society*, 26 (6) (2009), 158.

42. It is important to note that there is a vast difference between the work of Karen Barad, which is strongly informed by feminist theory, Jane Bennett, who is a political theorist, and Graham Harman, whose work is seen as apolitical in its metaphysical exploration. Not included in Lemke's discussion are two other representatives of new materialism: Eugene Thacker and Timothy Morton, whose thinking has had an impact on environmental humanities. For more on speculative realism and posthumanism, see Chapter 13 of this volume.

43. For more on posthumanism and the Anthropocene, see Chapter 9 in this volume.

44. S. Helmreich, *Alien Ocean: Anthropological Voyages in Microbial Seas* (Berkeley: University of California Press, 2009).

45. H. Paxson, "Post-Pasteurian Cultures: The Microbiopolitics of Raw-Milk Cheese in the United States," *Cultural Anthropology*, 23 (1) (2008), 15–47.

46. E. Swyngedouw, and H. Ernstson, "Interrupting the Anthropo-ObScene: Immuno-Biopolitics and Depoliticizing Ontologies in the Anthropocene," *Theory, Culture & Society*, 35 (6) (2018), 3–30.

47. A. L. Tsing, *The Mushroom at the End of the World: On the Possibility of Life in Capitalist Ruins* (Princeton: Princeton University Press, 2015). A. L. Tsing, "Getting by in Terrifying Times," *Dialogues in Human Geography*, vol. 8, no.1 (2018), 73–6.

48. Cary Wolfe, *What is Posthumanism?* (Minneapolis: University of Minnesota Press, 2010).

49. The Anthropocene is – as Bruno Latour so eloquently put it during his Distinguished Lecture to the AAA in December 2014 – "a poisonous gift" to anthropology; see D. Haraway, N. Ishikawa, S. F. Gilbert, K. Olwig, A. L. Tsing, and N. Bubandt, "Anthropologists Are Talking – about the Anthropocene." *Ethnos*, 81 (3) (2016), 535–64. While it brings to anthropology (and geography) the gift of reconceptualizing "anthropos," which can broaden our understanding of more-than-human life in a significant way, it can also aggrandize the pathos of the human that can harm entangled life in more destructive ways than previously imagined.

50. A. L. Tsing, "Unruly Edges: Mushrooms as Companion Species," *Environmental Humanities*, 1 (2012), 141–54. Scholars such as Neel Ahuja (2016) build on this insight; see N. Ahuja, *Bioinsecurities: Disease Interventions, Empire, and the Government of Species* (Durham: Duke University Press, 2016).

51. Haraway, Ishikawa, Gilbert, Olwig, Tsing, & Bubandt "Anthropologists Are Talking."

52. M. Meloni, *Impressionable Biologies: From the Archaeology of Plasticity to the Sociology of Epigenetics* (New York: Routledge, 2019).
53. G. Feldman, "If Ethnography is More Than Participant-Observation, Then Relations Are More Than Connections: The Case for Nonlocal Ethnography in a World of Apparatuses," *Anthropological Theory*, 11 (4) (2011), 378.
54. See for instance Braverman and Paxson.

# CHAPTER 12

# New Materialisms

## Stacy Alaimo

New materialism is a contested term, appearing within a list of theories that comprise what Richard Grusin calls the "nonhuman turn," which also include actor-network theory, affect theory, animal studies, assemblage theory, new brain sciences, new media theory, speculative realism, and systems theory.[1] Versions of other theories in this list, however, could also be enacted as modes of new materialism, in their orientation, conceptualization, or methodology, which complicates things. Iris Van der Tuin defines new materialism as "a research methodology for the nondualistic study of the world within, beside and among us, the world that precedes, includes, and exceeds us."[2] While I appreciate the capaciousness of this poetic definition and agree with the underscoring of nondualism, I would hesitate to say that new materialism is primarily a research methodology, especially since so many scholars are – rightly – baffled by how to proceed after immersing themselves within new materialist theory, which is counterintuitive and transdisciplinary, stressing the inseparability of epistemology, ontology, ethics, and politics.

The "new" in new materialism is troublesome, suggesting departures from Marxist materialisms, or in the case of material feminisms, a distancing from legacies of feminist praxis, rather than a recursive sense of nonlinear affinities, alignments, overlaps, and correspondences.[3] Notwithstanding the similarities with other theoretical movements, it may still be useful to distinguish something called "new materialism." One distinctive characteristic of this theoretical orientation, in my view, is that new materialisms – as critiques, complements, extensions, or reframings of social constructionist, postmodern, and poststructuralist theories – all insist upon the significance and agency of materiality and the inter- or intra-actions across the primary dualisms of western thought.[4] Christopher Breu begins *Insistence of the Material: Literature in the Age of Biopolitics,* for example: "This book takes materiality as its object. In doing so, it is, by necessity, inadequate to this object."[5] Breu's conception of material "insistence," its "refusal to regularly conform to our cultural, linguistic, and indeed, theoretical scripts" (ix), suggests that the defining characteristic of new materialist theory is the very thing that makes it so daunting. This focus, on matter, that which has not been within the purview of the humanities proper, and indeed, may be considered that which is expelled from, or beyond, the humanities as such, suggests the vital correspondences between new materialisms and science and technology studies, as well as an emergent shift from the humanities to the transdisciplinary posthumanities.[6] Science and technology studies, especially feminist and postcolonial science and technology studies, grapple with the sites where nature and culture cannot be separated, where matter and meaning are entangled, where all sorts of substances and entities do unexpected things, and where epistemology, ethics, politics, and becoming are always already intertwined.

While new materialist theory can be charted in different ways, for example, by looking to Spinoza or Darwin as progenitors, I will begin with the work of two foundational feminist science studies scholars, Donna Haraway and Karen Barad, introducing central positions in their work as quintessentially new materialist (whether or not the former accepts the label). Haraway and Barad's work leads directly into a consideration of the significance of new materialism for environmentalism and posthumanism. The final section of the essay introduces debates regarding new materialism, race, and indigeneity. While many other topics could be considered, such as transversality, monism, assemblage theory, technology, the Anthropocene, sex vs. gender, legal studies, animal studies, biomedicine, and biopolitics, given the limited space, this particular essay takes the title of this volume as its guide, discussing the relation between new materialism and the western category of the human.[7]

## 12.1 Donna Haraway and Karen Barad

The title, "After the Human," provokes us to reconsider the human as such, and, at the same time, to shift the focus toward nonhuman beings, substances, processes, and forces. Donna J. Haraway's work often does both things simultaneously, by focusing on the figurations of boundary creatures, from nonhuman primates, to cyborgs, to dogs as companion species. From *Primate Visions: Gender, Race and Nature in the World of Modern Science*, to the "Manifesto for Cyborgs" to the *Companion Species Manifesto*, the focus on the "material-discursive" sites "where species meet" places the white, masculinist, disembodied, and hyperseparated individual "human," otherwise known as Man, into question, as boundary-making practices come into view.[8] Haraway forged a new materialism that is inseparable from feminist theory, feminist science studies, cultural studies, and what would become animal studies and posthumanism, in that it engages in incisive cultural and political critique of sexist and racist structures and standpoints – for example, in the monumental *Primate Visions* – and, at the same time, seeks modes of engagement with scientific knowledge and nonhuman creatures that are not confined to discursive critique. Haraway's work exemplifies how some modes of new materialism grew from a deep engagement with social constructionist theory but also expanded or complemented that theory by attending to material agencies and nonhuman actions, ultimately seeing the "material-discursive" as intertwined.

Haraway's long project of reconceptualizing material agency has been ethical and political as well as epistemological and methodological. In the brilliant introduction to *Primate Visions*, for example, she explains how the objectifying dualism of knower and the known, central to "'White Capitalist Patriarchy'" operates through an appropriative logic: "Nature is only the raw material of culture, appropriated, preserved, enslaved, exalted, or otherwise made flexible for disposal in the logic of capitalist colonialism" (13). In "Situated Knowledges: The Science Question in Feminism and the Privilege of Partial Perspective," she poses the Coyote or Trickster, "embodied in American Southwest Indian Accounts," as a way of seeing the "world as a witty agent," with its own "independent sense of humor."[9] Haraway's figuration of the companion species also contests the objectification of the nonhuman world, as well as the appropriation common to theorizing itself. In *The Companion Species Manifesto*, she insists that dogs "are not surrogates for theory; they are not here just to think with. They are here to live with" (5). In terms of how new materialism is vital for contemplating what would be "after the human," I would pose not the futuristic cyborg, but the canine, since the very co-evolution of dogs and humans means that humans have never been human in the western, white, masculinist sense of a hyper-individualized, disembodied knower; rather, what the human ended up being is partly due to what dogs did within the evolutionary history of canine-human interactions. And while the cyborg may be kidnapped by transhumanist fantasies of technological transcendence, companion species are embedded in Darwin's tangled bank. The companion species has inspired other research on multispecies relations that entails cross-disciplinary tracings, as well as an "ethical mode of relating, within or between species," that is "knit from the silk-strong thread of ongoing alertness to otherness-in-relation" (Haraway, *Companion* 50).

Whereas biology and multispecies relations figure prominently in Haraway's writing, physics takes center stage in Karen Barad's monumental *Meeting the Universe Halfway: Quantum Physics and the Entanglement of Matter and Meaning*.[10] Barad's theory of agential realism is the most representative mode of new materialism, in terms of its radical sense of material agency and intra-action at all scales. Drawing on Niels Bohr, Barad explains that intra-action means that "relata" "do not preexist relations"; rather relata-within-phenomena "emerge through specific intra-actions" (140). Starting with material intra-action – in which every "thing" is always emergent and never discrete – is a vertiginously counterintuitive and anti-individualistic framework. Indeed, "intra-action" may be the most quintessentially new materialist concept, demanding a radical reimagining of what politics, ethics, or identities could possibly mean when starting from a framework that does not begin with humans – or even beings or entities – that are separate. Intra-action also scrambles conventional as well as more philosophical notions of language and meaning. As Brandon Jones explains, "When we pose the question of what matters and how, we are not dealing with pre-existing bodies upon which language inscribes meaning, but with relations of doing, acting and becoming that exist in material-discursive superposition until an agential cut intervenes to demarcate clear boundaries between words and things."[11]

Barad's new materialism – and new materialism more generally – has been critiqued for failing to be legible or useful for politics. Cristin Ellis, in *Antebellum Posthuman: Race and Materiality in the Mid-Nineteenth Century,* for example, calling posthuman materialism "an abyss that our politics stare into," argues, "this powerfully expanded map of the entanglements of being and knowing does not tell us what we ought to do with this information."[12] While "relations of doing, acting, and becoming," as Jones puts it, do sound a bit vague, this capaciousness radically expands the terrain of the ethical or political. Such expansions resonate with the way that feminist, anti-racist, queer, and disability movements have long engaged in politics precisely by demarcating something heretofore unnoticed, unnamed, or denied – think of Audre Lorde's refusal to wear the "pathetic puff of lambswool," which emerged as part of what became her black, lesbian, feminist, anticapitalist, and ecological politics.[13] Nancy Tuana, in "Viscous Porosity: Witnessing Katrina," demonstrates how new materialism can be useful for political analysis and action, as the many causes and effects of the hurricane cannot be understood through a dualist lens: "For in witnessing Katrina, the urgency of embracing an ontology that *rematerializes the social and takes seriously the agency of the natural world* is rendered apparent."[14]

Granted, a counterintuitive sense of radical intra-action, material agencies, and emergence may not always be necessary for expanding (human) political terrains by attending to materiality. Toby Beauchamp, for example, explains that "[i]ncreasingly, feminist scholars concerned with transgender politics focus on how the very objects that are commonly associated with transgender people are produced, circulated, and consumed; collectively, they seek to unravel the political and historical contexts of these materials, which can help clarify how such objects and substances shape transgender politics."[15] Such practices may or may not be posthumanist and new materialist. Notwithstanding that tracing the ethics and politics regarding objects, substances, and materials need not proceed through new materialisms, it is nonetheless ironic that critiques of new materialism as apolitical echo an earlier moment in theory when deconstruction, postmodernism, and poststructuralism were charged with lacking the secure foundations ostensibly necessary for political potency. This is ironic partly because some readings of new materialism pose it as the antithesis of poststructuralism and the linguistic turn, rather than an expansion of the ungrounded, perpetually signifying universe of deconstruction and poststructuralism in, for example, the work of Jacques Derrida, Gilles Deleuze and Felix Guattari, and Judith Butler's essay "Contingent Foundations: Feminism and the Question of Postmodernism."[16]

Although Barad's theory, based on quantum physics, is an onto-epistemology (that is seemingly timeless), context still matters, as the sense of material agency and intra-action within agential realism are, I would argue, particularly relevant as a counterpoint to the hyper-separations of capitalist individualism and consumerism, both of which assume and solidify discreet subjects and objects. During a time of environmental crisis in which colossal human practices, extractions, transformations, productions, and emissions have provoked heretofore unthinkable intra-actions at all levels, dualist ontologies, with their presumptions of impermeability and their instrumentality, endanger planetary life.[17] It matters that Barad's new materialist theory – arguably the most thorough articulation of an ethically oriented, posthumanist, onto-epistemology – was made (or "cut"), and has been received, in the time of the Anthropocene, climate change, neocolonial genocide, the sixth great extinction, and rapacious global capitalism.

## 12.2  New Materialism and Environmentalism

Underscoring material agencies is crucial for environmental art, activism, and thought that resist the idea that nature is a passive resource for human use. Macarena Gómez Barris, for example, argues that her term "the extractive zone" "names the violence that capitalism does to reduce, constrain, and convert life into commodities," as well as the epistemological violence of training our academic vision to reduce life to systems.[18] In the passage from *Primate Visions* cited earlier, Haraway states that within capitalist colonialism, nature serves as the "raw material of culture." As the scientific, philosophical, and popular concept of the Anthropocene gains sway, environmentalists may want to ensure that the recognition of the massive human alteration of the planet operates as a critique of human domination even as we continue to insist upon material agencies and intra-actions that elude a mechanistic sense of nature reduced to raw material. The new materialist emphasis on "intra-actions" as well as interactions is aligned with ecological science, environmental philosophies, and social movements that trace interconnections. Not surprisingly, then, environmentalism finds a suitable habitat within the work of many new materialists, including Haraway, Barad, Bruno Latour, and Rosi Braidotti. Explaining why she advocates "the vitality of matter," Jane Bennett, for example, states "my hunch is that the image of dead or thoroughly instrumentalized matter feeds human hubris and our Earth-destroying fantasies of conquest and consumption."[19] While Bennett famously casts her attention on objects and assemblages in her "political ecology of things," Serenella Iovino and Serpil Opperman argue for a textual new materialism, what they call "material ecocriticism," which "examines matter both in texts and as a text, trying to shed light on the way bodily natures and discursive forces express their interaction whether in representations or in their concrete materiality."[20]

The ecomaterialist theory that I developed, "transcorporeality," traces material interactions and intra-actions through bodies and environments. In *Bodily Natures: Science, Environment, and the Material Self,* I draw on Barad's theory to propose the concept of "trans-corporeality," in which the human is part of the material substances and flows of the world. My concept of trans-corporeality emerged not only from Barad's work but also from environmental justice movements (primarily those focused on race and class), intersectional feminisms, and disability studies, all of which contend with how "social" and economic forces such as capitalism, sexism, and racism manifest in human bodies as they are unequally embedded in and exposed to material processes and flows. Trans-corporeality requires a reconceptualization of ethics and politics as well as an engagement with modes of mediation and capture in science and technology studies, since "material interactions" may or may not be apparent without scientific mediation, a state that Ulrich Beck called "risk culture."[21] The sense of the human as embedded in material environments, flows, and systems means that there is no separate human as such, the environment is never merely a background, and social justice necessarily entails environmental justice, in ways that may or may not be predictable.

Epigenetics could be understood in terms of a trans-corporeality that is passed down through generations. Shannon Sullivan in *The Physiology of Sexist and Racist Oppression*, in a chapter subtitled "On the Transgenerational Effects of Racism," notes that epigenetics blurs "the line between extrinsic and intrinsic biological causes of heritable traits ... by dismantling sharp divisions between the innate (biology) and the acquired (culture)."[22] Lisa H. Weasel argues that extending "the feminist analysis of intersectionality into the material realm via epigenetics is an important and undertheorized avenue of exploration."[23] She frames epigenetics in terms of a feminist new materialism in which social construction and material agencies interact and cross generations: "epigenetics reveals a collaborative sociomolecular trace, a material sedimentation, in Barad's terminology, of lived intersectional existence in the form of methylation and acetylation patterns that refract and react to the networked interface of socio-material differences" (117). Both Sullivan and Weasel are cautious about approaching the complex and volatile territory of epigenetics and race. Sullivan concludes, however, that "sexist and racist oppression can be incorporated in the literal cells, fibers, muscles, and chemicals of the human body," which means that the "reach of sexist and racist oppression thus is more pervasive than feminists and critical philosophers of race thought"; combatting the long effects of sexism and racism, then, entails recognizing that "culture and biology" are not "entirely separate domains" (162).

The potent interconnections and alliances that some of us see between material feminisms, new materialism, critical posthumanism, and animal studies are not shared by everyone. For example, Stephanie Clare observes that she has heard "new materialisms described as the 'end of feminism,'" citing concern about the political meaning of the move from epistemology to ontology. She concludes: "While new materialist understandings of politics are compelling, feminist scholarship, attentive to more-than-human worlds, cannot but return to the study of power

relations between humans, for it is humans whom we address in our
writing and it is, arguably, human lives, enmeshed in more-than-human
worlds, that we care most about."[24] Invoking the human as enmeshed in
more-than-human worlds only to then assert that it is human lives that
"we care most about" seems to me to draw upon material feminist, trans-
corporeal, and posthumanist theories and yet, at the same time, to
jettison the ethics and politics that they espouse. Here, the human
after the nonhuman turn ends up being the same old human we once
knew. Sherryl Vint urges us to consider the human/nonhuman boundary
as the "final ground of abjection," developing, instead, "an ethical
posthumanism" which acknowledges a self that is "materially connected
to the rest of the world."[25] The material interconnection of human self
to other beings and the rest of the world flow into posthuman and
ecologically oriented ontologies, ethics, and politics, as the foundation
for human exceptionalism and the dismissal of all other species cannot
be securely rooted within landscapes of radical intra-actions and
emergence.

## 12.3   Race, Postcolonialism, and Indigenous Thought

As the last section suggests, epigenetics, along with environmental justice
more broadly, can be understood through new materialist conceptions of
race that underscore how ideological and economic forces and systems of
oppression become materialized within bodies, in ways that may or may
not be visible or consonant with categorization. Nonetheless, tensions have
arisen between new materialist and critical race, postcolonial, decolonial,
and indigenous theories. Goméz Barris, for example, states that while "the
expanded vocabulary of new materialist analyses are provocative," "Global
South epistemologies and philosophies of race and racism, ranging from
postcolonial and decolonial theories, to Indigenous critique to Afro-based
thought, to Black Studies to perspectivisms and relational models, have
long anticipated the ways to differently imagine knowledge and perception
as the foundation of planetary inheritance" (100). Since new materialism is
a rather broad umbrella, there is not enough space here to assess whether or
how various theories address race and colonialism.[26] It is imperative,
however, to underscore the long traditions of grappling with the materiality of human bodies within feminist, queer, critical race, postcolonial, and
disability studies, as all of those fields have long critiqued how "the
Human" has been constituted in western, colonialist, racist, and masculinist discourses as a rational, seemingly disembodied (and yet "perfectly"

able-bodied), and visibly or invisibly white ideal. Thus, a potential for confluences and alliances exists.

For example, the editors of *The Matter of Disability: Materiality, Biopolitics, Crip Affect* articulate new materialist and posthumanist modes of disability studies, returning "disability to its proper place as an ongoing historical process of materiality's dynamic interactionalism."[27] Mel Y. Chen cites Sharon Snyder and David Mitchell's endorsement of the "feral" qualities of disability studies, connecting this with the "wiliness" of the queer critic Silviano Santiago.[28] Chen's conception of "animacy," akin to other new materialist conceptions of agency, contests the "animacy hierarchies" which commonsensically categorize and divide: they contend "humans are not animals are not things" (236). Chen's sense of animacy also "suggests an alternative means, outside of the strictly political or strictly emotional to identify cross-affiliations – affinities – among groups as diverse as environmentalists, people with autism, social justice activists, feminists, religious believers in nature's stewardship, and antiracists, just to mention a few" (236–237). Similarly, Neel Ahuja argues that despite the divergences between "intersectional, postcolonial, and ecological feminists and feminist science studies," in terms of their "topics and approaches to matter," they all "take on important challenges to the Cartesian worldviews that colonialism has used to distinguish genders, races, and species and to naturalize systems of inequality."[29] Thus, defining new materialism as something apart from these traditions would replicate the exclusionary gestures of western humanism by identifying the ostensible center of something we are calling new materialism as that which is unmarked. Instead of expelling the same "others" from the quintessential "thing," considering new materialism through the perspectives of those who have been expelled from the exclusive category of the "ideal," "normal," or unmarked western human it is more consonant with the theory itself and serves as an important counterbalance to the sometimes overly affirmative atmosphere of this theory. Toxins, radioactive waste, and even genetic mutations may give us pause. As Mitchell, Antebi, and Snyder argue, drawing on R.L. Rutsky's contention that random mutations are "always already immanent," disability is both "matter in motion" and the "exposure of the lie through which we think materiality as a stable baseline of limited plentitude" (8).

Likewise, the capaciousness of new materialisms toward nonhuman life and the intelligent liveliness of the world may actually reinstall the unmarked western human as the site of enunciation and ignore racial formations in that process. Zakiyyah Iman Jackson argues that calls to

186 STACY ALAIMO

move "beyond the human" may "reintroduce the Eurocentric transcendentalism this movement purports to disrupt, particularly with regard to
the historical and ongoing distributive ordering of race."³⁰ She argues that
addressing blackness and engaging with critical black studies should be
essential to theories in the nonhuman turn:

> Given that appositional and homologous (even co-constitutive) challenges
> pertaining to animality, objecthood, and thingliness have long been estab-
> lished in thought examining the existential predicament of modern racial
> blackness, the resounding silence in the posthumanist, object-oriented, and
> new materialist literatures with respect to race is remarkable, persisting even
> despite the reach of antiblackness into the nonhuman – *as blackness condi-
> tions and constitutes the very nonhuman disruption and/or displacement they
> invite.* (216)

Jackson's potent argument will no doubt inspire new scholarship to take on
these challenges.

Bracketing the question of which instantiations of these large theoretical
movements are being addressed, we might also consider that if new
materialism is characterized by its engagements with matter – vital, vibrant,
or otherwise agential – then the friction and unease between new materialism and critical race studies is not surprising, given the long, horrific
history of racist science and medicine, pernicious biological reductionisms,
and persistent racial essentialisms. Giving matter its due, under the long
shadow of scientific categories of racism that have endorsed slavery,
oppression, imprisonment, and inequalities, would seem anything but
liberating, especially given the current resurgence of racial violence.
Marxist modes of materialism, social construction, and other critical race
theories focused on economics, ideology, and other social systems would
seem more productive for anti-racist politics and theories. And yet,
Michael Hames Garcia has argued: "Unless we accept the causal role of
matter in the formation of racial meanings and phenomena, our theories of
society will be unable to explain how and why people experience race as
they do," ultimately concluding that we "need creative racial identity
projects more than we need philosophical arguments against race."³¹

Diana Leong both critiques "the (absent) place of racial blackness in
theories about matter" in some versions of new materialism, and envisions
other possibilities. She argues that new materialisms, with their emphasis
on unpredictability and indeterminacy, are "at pains to clarify why the
structures of global antiblackness" persist, quoting Hortense Spillers: "neither time nor history, nor historiography and its topics, show movement,

as the human subject is 'murdered' over and over again."³² Leong concludes by asserting that she is not rejecting new materialism, but instead,
suggesting that scholars "address how the entanglements of blackness,
matter, and the human make only certain forms of matter both legible
and desirable," and that "challenges to human exceptionalism should
proceed through a critique of race" (24). Similarly, Angela Willey critiques
new materialisms for neglecting postcolonial feminist science studies,
arguing that the "science that is privileged and often conflated with matter
in new materialist storytelling . . . is the same capital 'S' Science, unquali-
fied" that has been "critiqued by feminist science studies."³³ She contends,
however, that "This does not mean that new materialist feminisms and
postcolonial feminist science studies are necessarily at odds . . . . On the
contrary, thinking creatively, pluralistically, and thus irreverently with
respect to the rules of science and the boundaries and meanings of matter,
life and 'humanness' – something new materialisms arguably do – could be
understood as a central project for a postcolonial feminist science studies" (994).

While the aims of new materialisms may be aligned with postcolonial
science studies, as Willey argues, the relation between new materialism and
indigenous studies may be awkwardly irrelevant or redundant. To begin
with, the central problematic that new materialism seeks to counter, that of
the western dualism that renders matter, nature, and bodies as inert, abject,
and inanimate, is unrecognizable within indigenous cosmologies. Dian
Million (Athabascan) explains that indigenous thought, or "place thought"
(citing Vanessa Watts), "rises from ancient knowledge that rarely agrees
with Western assumptions about the world, whether about sex, gender, or
what matter is"; nor is there "one totalizing category of what 'Indigenous
thought' is."³⁴ Nonetheless, Million explains that it is "widely understood
in Indigenous thought that matter, materiality, and ecology are not separ-
able from place," and that these categories are not "distinct 'things'" but
"instead imply relations" (97). Thus, multiple modes of indigenous
thought have already (an already that need not march to a linear temporality nor be assumed to be solely "traditional") embodied, enacted, anticipated, and exceeded the arguments of "new" materialism and "post"
humanism.

The title alone of a founding text for new materialism, Bruno Latour's
*We Have Never Been Modern*, can be read both in terms of its critique of the
modern constitution of the west and the colonial history of genocide and
survivance.³⁵ In other words, indigenous thought certainly does not need
new materialism. Nonetheless, the new materialisms of settler colonialists

need respectfully to learn from indigenous thought and indigenous peoples, somehow without appropriation or preservationist objectification.[36] Kim Tallbear, in an essay that shifts from a critique of cryopreservation (of indigenous peoples) to the vitality of pipestone charges:

> We are the living that the new materialists, like so many Western thinkers before them and beside them, refuse to see. If this theoretical turn is to seriously attend to addressing some of the world's most pressing problems, it needs to learn to see indigenous people in our full vitality, not as the de-animated vanished or less evolved. Seeing us as fully alive is key to seeing the aliveness of the decimated lands, waters, and other nonhuman communities on these continents. (198).

As I conclude, I'll note that some readers may object to the somewhat unconventional path this essay has taken. Focusing on material agency, interrelations, feminist science studies, politics, environmentalism, epigenetics, race, and indigenous thought does not leave space to discuss other prominent new materialist theories and topics that might have been included. Different stories, with different genealogies, could be and have been told. But I hope the frameworks and resonances explored here are clear enough to provide a coherent explanation and yet also jarring or incomplete enough to provoke and invite readers to grapple with the difficult and urgent questions that remain regarding materiality after the human.

## Notes

1. Richard Grusin, "Introduction," in R. Grusin (ed.), *The Nonhuman Turn* (Minneapolis: University of Minnesota Press, 2015), np.
2. Iris Van der Tuin, "New/New Materialism," in Rosi Braidotti and Maria Hlavajova (eds.), *The Posthuman Glossary* (London: Bloomsbury, 2018), 277–8.
3. Sara Ahmed roundly critiques this founding gesture of the new; see "Imaginary Prohibitions: Some Preliminary Remarks on the Founding Gestures of the 'New Materialism,'" *European Journal of Women's Studies,* 15 (1) (2008), 23–39. More recently, Kim Tallbear also argues that from an indigenous perspective the "fundamental insights are not new for everyone," because the idea that "matter is lively" undergirds "what we can call an indigenous metaphysic" (Kim Tallbear, "Beyond the Life/Not-Life Binary: A Feminist Indigenous Reading of Cryopreservation, Interspecies Thinking, and the New Materialisms," in *Cryopolitics: Frozen Life in a Melting World* [Cambridge, MIT, 2017], 199).

4. Although some characterizations of new materialism cast it as a radical departure from poststructuralism and postmodernism, key theorists in those movements, such as Gilles Deleuze, Michel Foucault, and Judith Butler, all engage with materiality, making the distinctions nuanced and debatable, but related to nonhuman agencies, more than human assemblages and methods of material capture. Similarly, new materialism need not be seen as a rejection of the linguistic turn; but instead as "build[ing] on rather than abandon[ing] the lessons learned in the linguistic turn" (Stacy Alaimo and Susan Hekman, "Introduction: Emerging Models of Materiality in Feminist Theory," *Material Feminisms* [Bloomington: Indiana University Press, 2008], 14).

5. Christopher Breu, *Insistence of the Material: Literature in the Age of Biopolitics* (Minneapolis: University of Minnesota Press, 2014), 1. Breu's "material insistence," as a mode of material agency that departs from cultural scripts, is similar to my concept of "deviant agency," indebted to queer theory and disability studies. See Stacy Alaimo, *Bodily Natures: Science, Environment and the Material Self* (Bloomington: Indiana University Press, 2010).

6. Rosi Braidotti, "Posthuman Critical Theory," in Rosi Braidotti and Maria Hlavajova (eds.), *The Posthuman Glossary* (London: Bloomsbury, 2018), 339–42.

7. See Chapters 4, 7, 8, 9, 10, and 11 of this volume for more discussion of posthumanism in relation to many of these topics.

8. Donna J. Haraway, *Primate Visions: Gender, Race, and Nature in the World of Modern Science* (New York: Routledge, 1990); "A Cyborg Manifesto: Science, Technology, and Socialist-Feminism in the Late Twentieth Century," in *Simians, Cyborgs and Women: The Reinvention of Nature* (New York: Routledge, 1991); *The Companion Species Manifesto: Dogs, People, and Significant Otherness* (Chicago: Prickly Paradigm, 2003).

9. Donna J. Haraway, "Situated Knowledges: The Science Question in Feminism and the Privilege of Partial Perspective," in *Simians, Cyborgs, and Women: The Reinvention of Nature* (New York: Routledge, 1991), 199.

10. Karen Barad, *Meeting the Universe Halfway: Quantum Physics and the Entanglement of Matter and Meaning* (Durham: Duke University Press, 2007).

11. Brandon Jones, "Mattering," in Rosi Braidotti and Maria Hlavajova (eds.), *The Posthuman Glossary* (London: Bloomsbury, 2018), 245.

12. Cristin Ellis, *Antebellum Posthuman: Race and Materiality in the Mid-Nineteenth Century* (New York: Fordham University Press, 2018), 169, 165.

13. Audre Lorde, *The Cancer Journals* (San Francisco: Aunt Lute Books, 1980), 61.

14. Nancy Tuana, "Viscous Porosity: Witnessing Katrina," in Stacy Alaimo and Susan Hekman (eds.), *Material Feminisms* (Indiana: Indiana University Press, 2008), 188, emphasis in original.

15. Toby Beauchamp. "Transgender Matters," in Stacy Alaimo (ed.), *Matter* (Farmington Hills: McMillan, 2017), 74.

16. Judith Butler, "Contingent Foundations: Feminism and the Question of 'Postmodernism,'" in Judith Butler and Joan W. Scott (eds.), *Feminists*

*Theorize the Political* (New York: Routledge, 1992), 3–21. Cristin Ellis and Stephanie Clare, as cited in this essay, echo the critiques of postmodernism that Butler makes. Butler calls such critiques "warnings against an impending nihilism," which assert "politics is unthinkable without a foundation" or a "stable subject" (Butler 3–4). For more on poststructuralism's relationship to posthumanism, see Chapter 2 in this volume.

17. Alaimo, *Bodily* 21.
18. Macarena Gómez-Barris, *The Extractive Zone: Social Ecologies and Decolonial Perspectives* (Durham: Duke University Press, 2017), xix.
19. Jane Bennett, *Vibrant Matter: A Political Ecology of Things* (Durham: Duke University Press, 2010), ix. For more on the Anthropocene, anticapitalism, and the posthuman, see Chapter 9 of this volume.
20. Serenella Iovino and Serpil Opperman, "Introduction: Stories Come to Matter," in S. Iovino and S. Opperman (eds.), *Material Ecocriticism* (Bloomington: University of Indiana Press, 2014), 2.
21. Ulrich Bech, *Risk Society: Toward a New Modernity* (New York: Routledge, 1992).
22. Shannon Sullivan, *The Physiology of Sexist and Racist Oppression* (Oxford: Oxford University Press, 2015), 120.
23. Lisa H. Weazel, "Embodying Intersectionality: The Promise (and Peril) of Epigenetics for Feminist Science Studies," in Victoria Pitts-Taylor (ed.), *Mattering: Feminism, Science, and Materialism* (New York: New York University Press, 2016), 116.
24. Stephanie Clare, "On the Politics of 'New Feminist Materialisms,'" in Victoria Pitts-Taylor (ed.), *Mattering: Feminism, Science, and Materialism*, (New York: New York University Press, 2016), 58, 68.
25. Sherryl Vint, *Bodies of Tomorrow: Technology, Subjectivity, and Science Fiction* (Toronto: University of Toronto Press, 2007), 189.
26. Two collections of new materialist theory, for example, *Material Feminisms*, ed. Stacy Alaimo and Susan Hekman (Indiana: Indiana University Press, 2008) and *Mattering: Feminism, Science, and Materialism*, ed. Victoria Pitts-Taylor (New York: New York University Press, 2016) include many discussions of race, while race is absent in other collections and monographs.
27. David T. Mitchell, Susan Antebi, and Sharon L. Snyder, "Introduction," in D. Mitchell, S. Antebi, and S. L. Snyder (eds.), *The Matter of Disability: Materiality, Biopolitics, Crip Affect* (Ann Arbor: University of Michigan Press, 2019), 3.
28. Mel Y. Chen, *Animacies: Biopolitics, Racial Mattering, and Queer Affect* (Durham: Duke University Press, 2012), 19.
29. Neel Ahuja, "Colonialism," in Stacy Alaimo (ed.), *Matter* (Farmington Hills: Mcmillan, 2017), 250.
30. Zakkiyah Iman Jackson, "Out Worlds: The Persistence of Race in Movement 'Beyond the Human,'" in "Theorizing Queer Inhumanisms Dossier" *GLQ* 21: 2–3 (2015), 215.

31. Michael Hames Garcia, "How Real is Race?" in Stacy Alaimo and Susan J. Hekman (eds.), *Material Feminisms* (Bloomington: Indiana University Press, 2008), 331.

32. Diana Leong, "The Mattering of Black Lives: Octavia Butler's Hyperempathy and the Promise of New Materialism," *Catalyst: Feminism, Theory, Technoscience*, 2(2) (2016), 6, 11.

33. Angela Willey, "A World of Materialisms: Postcolonial Feminist Science Studies and the New Natural," *Science, Technology & Human Values*, 41(6) (2016), 994.

34. Dian Million, ""Indigenous Matters," in Stacy Alaimo (ed.), *Matter* (Farmington Hills: Mcmillan, 2017), 96.

35. Bruno Latour, *We Have Never Been Modern*, trans. C. Porter (Cambridge: Harvard University Press, 1991).

36. For more on race, indigenous cultures, and posthumanism, see Chapter 14 of this volume.

CHAPTER 13

# Speculative Realism
## The Human and Nonhuman Divide

*Brian Willems*

Speculative realism and posthumanism are connected in two main ways. First, both are concerned with the world that exists outside of human experience. Second, there is a mutual attempt to delineate the ways human and nonhuman forces come into contact, or do not. However, both speculative realism and posthumanism are perhaps best rendered in the plural, indicating the many different approaches, often contradictory, subsumed under each term. Yet what brings these two concepts together is a mutual understanding that, while the nonhuman world might be unexpected or unknowable, it is nevertheless real. Strategies for confronting this reality are the focus of this chapter. I use literary and film examples to illustrate these strategies, which does not mean their authors are consciously engaging with either speculative realism or posthumanism. Yet the literary strategies they use to represent the nonhuman world have parallels with speculative realist trains of thought. My goal is to present the multiple strands of speculative realism, not to endorse one perspective over another, and I conclude by arguing that a focus on strategies for connecting human and nonhuman worlds is itself problematic.

First, some field differentiation is in order. The connection between posthumanism and speculative realism is also the point of difference between speculative realism and postmodernism. On the one hand, both speculative realism and postmodernism take *logocentrism* as an enemy; however, they address this enemy in fundamentally different ways, on the other. For a postmodernist like Jacques Derrida, logocentrism privileges the word (*logos*), its origin, and the way speech connects body to the word, thus ensuring meaning by the speaker's physical presence.[1] Derrida argues instead that *writing* should be privileged over speech, since "[t]he thing itself is a collection of things or a chain of differences" (90). In other words, meaning is found in the friction between signs rather than any reality underlying them. What unites the speculative realists is an upending of this kind of postmodern thought.[2] They are *realists*, meaning that they are all concerned with the real world underlying human signs in one way or another.

This difference can be seen in an earlier work of mine which addresses posthuman issues, a book on Kazuo Ishiguro's novel *Never Let Me Go* (2005). This work deals with themes of otherness in Ishiguro, including cloning, animal studies, and various strands of continental philosophy. It is determinately anti-anthropocentric and argues that Martin Heidegger's degradation of an animal's experience of the world is actually an accurate description of human experience.[3] But something important was missing. In fact, two things were missing. First, attempts at understanding the more-than-human were filtered through human experience. Second, the strategies for coming to experience or have knowledge about this world were solely of a literary nature, not reaching out into the real world for inspiration. Such gaps are what speculative realism addresses: the problem of the knowledge of what lies outside human experience, and ideas about how to get to that outside.

Speculative realism has a specific start date: April 27, 2007, at the "Speculative Realism" conference at Goldsmiths, London, which brought together four quite distinct speakers: Ray Brassier, Iain Hamilton Grant, Quentin Meillassoux, and Graham Harman.[4] What united them was a cry against "correlationism," meaning that they all rejected the idea that the world can only be experienced through human thought or experience. What is important is that all four had very divergent views on why correlationism was wrong, and they have only become more distinct since.[5] In fact, only one, Graham Harman, still considers himself a "speculative realist," practicing a more specific type, what he calls object-oriented ontology (OOO). We will focus on these four authors because they form the core of the differences in this field, although many other authors call on speculative realism to varying degrees, including Jane Bennett, Timothy Morton, Ian Bogost, Eugene Thacker, and Helen Hester. Steven Shaviro brings Alfred North Whitehead into the conversation as representative of a neglected tradition that has much in common with speculative realism but grounded by different politics. There are also two collections that do much to correct the gender balance of the field by looking at speculative realism from a feminist perspective: *After the "Speculative Turn": Realism, Philosophy and Feminism* and *Object-Oriented Feminism*.[6]

Our first task is to understand the enemy of all these strains of thought: correlationism. The greatest formulation of how speculative realists understand this concept is still found in Meillassoux's *After Finitude*.[7] However, correlationism basically starts with Kant and his idea of the transcendental subject. In the most fundamental sense, the Kantian revolution meant that statements about an object cannot be judged on whether they are adequate in comparison with that object in itself.[8] This is because both subjective and objective statements about the object are still both statements (even though objective statements, using the language of science, are more "universal"). Therefore, focus is placed on how meaning is agreed upon by a group, rather than equivalence between statements and objects. Or, as Meillassoux puts it, "*intersubjectivity*, the consensus of a community, supplants the *adequation* between the representations of a solitary subject and the thing itself as the veritable criterion of objectivity, and of scientific objectivity more particularly" (*After Finitude* 4). Intersubjectivity is another word for correlation.

There are two types of correlationism. The first is the "weak" form, which states that a world *does* exist outside human thought, it is just that we can never know it. This is "the idea according to which we only ever have access to the correlation between thinking and being, and never to either term considered apart from the other" (Meillassoux, *After Finitude* 5). Thinking and being both exist, but we can only know them in correlation to each other.[9] As Meillassoux put it in his original lecture at that first conference at Goldsmiths, "we can't know what the reality of the object in itself is because we can't distinguish between properties which are supposed to belong to the object and properties belonging to the subjective access to the object."[10] The "strong" model of correlationism holds that nothing can be said, or even thought, about the world without us: "it is illegitimate to claim that we can *know* the in-itself, but *also* that it is illegitimate to claim that we can at least *think* it" (Meillassoux, *After Finitude* 35). The weak model states that being can never be adequately described by thinking; the strong model states that we can never be sure there is any world outside of thought at all. The four speakers at the first speculative realism conference agree that correlationism is a problem, but they do not agree as to whether "soft" or "hard" correlationism is its most prevalent form today. In addition, and more importantly, they differ on the strategies they suggest for combatting correlationism. But before exploring these differences, let us look at why correlationism is a serious problem. We will use a literary example to do so.

The title of Solmaz Sharif's poetry book *Look* (2016) comes from a military dictionary, the United States Department of Defense's *Dictionary of Military and Associated Terms* (2007). According to its military definition, "look" denotes "a period during which a mine circuit is receptive of an influence."[11] While the look is traditionally associated with a human actor, in this definition it is an object that looks. More specifically, Solmaz addresses the window during which an explosive device can be triggered and explode. The eponymous opening poem describes a number of "looks" which are armed and ready to fire. At the center of these looks lies a woman, presumably Arab. A man outside the 2004 Republican Convention argues that she should accept the use of torture as the price for freedom. A drone operator in Nevada sees her heat signature while she has sex and becomes a drone target. A judge does not know how to pronounce her boyfriend's name, turning him into the enemy.

Within the scope of all these looks the woman insists on exactly what Kant denies: the adequacy of a description for the object described. The first line of the poem is, "It matters what you call a thing" (3), and this is what the poem argues for. In one stanza, this is expressed through the 16-second lag between the squeezing of a trigger in Nevada and the signal reaching a drone in Afghanistan to launch a missile:

> Whereas it could take as long as 16 seconds between the trigger pulled in Las Vegas and the Hellfire missile landing in Mazar-e-Sharif, after which they will ask *Did we hit a child? No. A dog.* they will answer themselves. (3)

The speaker does not argue against firing the missile. Rather, she asks to be adequately described in the time she would have before being destroyed. Going back to the first line of the poem ("It matters what you call a thing"), it continues with her lover describing her face as *"exquisite"* (3). Here, a solider calls her a dog. Naming is a political gesture. Humans are the ones who do all the naming, and this is what speculative realism resists: the dominance of the name, which is challenged via the concept of collective decision making.

The "strong" form of correlationism argues that there is no way to know whether a world exists outside human thought or experience. Instead of using adequacy, meaning is endowed through the consensus of a group. In the quotation above, although the trigger is pulled by one person, the decision about *what* they hit is made as a group: "they will ask"; "*Did we hit ...* "; "they will answer themselves." This is a description of the consensus of meaning which has no relation to the object being described, and it is the enemy of the poem. The last lines of the poem enforce this idea with a plea for enough time to find adequate words to describe what is being destroyed:

Let it matter what we call a thing.
Let it be the exquisite face for at least 16 seconds.
Let me LOOK at you.
Let me LOOK at you in a light that takes years to get here. (4–5)

This is the terror of correlationism: meaning becomes entirely relative. People who are killed are turned into dogs. Language is just a game for poststructuralists, or so it seems to the speculative realists, and they see this as a failure of politics.

This is what I mean about the difference between speculative realism and postmodernism. For Derrida, "The thing itself is a collection of things or a chain of differences" (*Of Grammatology* 90), which can be taken to suggest that language is just a game. On the one hand, speculative realists often leave Derrida here, but we might more accurately say that Derrida simply stays on one side of the Kantian divide. He limits worldview to what is described within human discourse, to our phenomenological experience (which is why representation matters ethically to him). On the other hand, speculative realists acknowledge some ontology beyond human perceptions: although we "bump into" and affect (and are affected by) these capacities, and thus we have ethical relations with the world, we can never know it in any complete fashion. With this distinction, we can say that speculative realism is not postmodernist; instead, it argues that we can actually know things about a real world beyond its appearance through human signs, which means that the Kant of the first critique was not wrong. And here lies an important difference between speculative realism and some, but not all, of the posthuman approaches covered in this book. For speculative realists, there *is* a divide between human and nonhuman worlds, but this divide can be crossed, either directly or indirectly. The four thinkers who appeared in the original speculative realism conference have various strategies for doing so. As we will see in our final example, the inability to cross such a divide can even become another such strategy.

We will begin with a short text Ray Brassier wrote for performance at a festival held by the political arts organization Arika, "Unfree Improvisation/Compulsive Freedom."[12] This text reveals friction between speculative realism and posthumanism. For example, although Rosi Braidotti focuses her thought of the posthuman on "the non-human, vital force of Life," she does not see speculative realism as helpful in this regard for two reasons: First, some aspects of speculative realism claim to "shatter the Kantian mirror" to see the world "unobscured by any reflection of himself or comments from others."[13] Second, she argues that the other strategy is "not to shatter the mirror but turn it around, so that it faces away from the subjects towards the world" (*The Posthuman* 60). Brassier is important in this regard because he argues that the world that lies beyond the Kantian mirror is exactly what is needed to decenter the human from itself, as is clear from his Arika performance essay.

The premise of this work is simple, and it relates to the stakes of the "weak" and "strong" forms of correlationism. The subject is stuck in her or his thought and experience. There is no way to think one's way out of the subject ("strong" correlationism). Any *human* strategies for changing this situation will fail, because they are human. So *inhuman* strategies are needed, meaning rules, mechanisms, and patterns that come from outside human experience. If a subject compulsively follows such rules, he or she will be free from his or her own self and subjectivity. Thus, the title of the essay: the subject is unfree in the way she or he acts as a human subject and becomes free when actions go beyond her or his own subjectivity, her or his own choices. As Brassier says:

> In order for improvisation to be free in the requisite sense, it must be a self-determining act, but this requires the involution of a series of mechanisms. It is this involutive process that is the agent of the act – one that is not necessarily human. It should not be confused for the improviser's self, which is rather the greatest obstacle to the emergence of the act. The improviser must be prepared to act as an agent – in the sense in which one acts as a covert operative – on behalf of whatever mechanisms are capable of effecting the acceleration or confrontation required for releasing the act. The latter arises at the point of intrication between rules and patterns, reasons and causes. It is the key that unlocks the mystery of how objectivity generates subjectivity. … In this sense, recognizing the un-freedom of voluntary activity is the gateway to compulsive freedom.

Voluntary action is unfree because it will always be human action. Freedom lies in the nonhuman. The human actor is the "covert operative" for nonhuman mechanisms, for rules, patterns, and modes of behavior that come from somewhere else. The stakes are high in this argument, because Brassier connects the freedom of the human actor with the ability for this human to be open to the nonhuman world.

In poetry, one of the most recent examples of improvisation due to dependence on nonhuman rules and structures is Christian Bök's *The Xenotext*.[14] The poet wrote a sonnet called "Orpheus," which he encoded into the DNA of a bacterium using a chemical alphabet he compiled using nucleotides; the microbe then followed the sequence using the rules for creating a protein from this genetic sequence. The amino acid sequence of the synthetized protein then creates another sonnet, which he calls "Eurydice." In this way, "[t]he cell becomes not only an archive for storing a poem, but also a machine for writing a poem" (Bök, 150). This machine is the *d. radiodurans* bacterium, which can survive heavy radiation and extreme environments. Thus, its poems will outlive us all, since the poems are allowed to be written by a nonhuman, challenging some of the ideas about the uniqueness of our species. But the poems in Bök's actual book are different than what might be expected. They follow rules, but not amino acid rules. For example, the poem "Adenine ($C_5H_5N_5$)" features images of each nucleotide, and each line is a nine-letter word that begins with the first letter of the words carbon, nitrogen, oxygen, or hydrogen, all relating to their organization by the chemical formula of the nucleobase.[15] What connects the poem to Brassier's thought is that compulsion lies in the machine aspect of writing: the rules for the creation of "Eurydice" are not human rules, but those of an amino acid sequence. This is a high-stakes proposition. The manner in which humans are conducting the world is devastating, the origin of racism, sexism, class discrimination, and damage to the environment. New ways of thinking are needed, nonhuman ways. But these new thoughts can be frightening, since it is not given that humanity, as we know it, will be included in these new ways of life. The possibility exists that "[s]omething might happen from which there is no return."[16] This raises the fear of utopia that Fredric Jameson identifies, which he suggests is "a thoroughgoing anxiety in the face of everything we stand to lose in the course of so momentous a transformation that – even in the imagination – it can be thought to leave little intact of current passions, habits, practices, and values."[17] This fear arises out of a lack of control of what will come next, although this lack of control is also freedom. For Bök, freedom lies in the generated text: he does not control the form of the poem; "Eurydice" is something he could not have planned. Thus, involuntary acts can lead to freedom.

Brassier uses this concept to argue for his own kind of "scientific realism" as a privileged mode for experiencing the nonhuman world, since its "empirical inscription" directly addresses the problem of intelligibility within human experience (*Nihil Unbound* 62–3). Let us abstract Brassier's thought, at least as it is presented here in this condensed form, into a larger aesthetic principle. By compulsively following nonhuman patterns, the human can become free from him/herself, meaning free from his/her own subjectivity. In a more general sense, we can think of an aesthetic product (a painting, novel, film, performance) which is "forced" to follow non-aesthetic rules (violence, a number sequence, patterns in nature). This has often been used to give an aesthetic product a new form by incorporating something non-aesthetic into it, as two examples will show. First, a real gun was included in the objects that could be used on Marina Abramović's body in her *Rhythm 0* (1974) art performance, during which she offered her body and a range of objects to the audience, who were authorized to do whatever they wanted to her using these objects. Similarly, Brian De Palma's film *Blow Out* (1981) is about replacing the scream of an actress in a diegetic horror film with that of an actual woman being killed. Both examples incorporate non-aesthetic violence into an aesthetic work. This is similar to the way Bök inscribes non-poetry rules in his poetry. The results are new, unexpected, and nonhuman.

Quentin Meillassoux has a similar approach to Brassier, but Meillassoux challenges both weak and strong correlationism by the inclusion of the impossible *within* the possible, rather than an annihilation of it. The subtitle of Meillassoux's *After Finitude* is *An Essay on the Necessity of Contingency*. Contingency plans are those for what is possible but not certain, and Meillassoux is centrally concerned with how we understand the uncertain nature of the world outside of human experience. In his 1997 doctoral thesis, Meillassoux illustrates this point with his concept of "divine inexistence." He argues that there have been three fundamental phase changes to our world thus far: (1) the emergence of something when there was nothing; (2) the emergence of life when there was none; and (3) an anthropocentric example, the emergence of human thought from a world of animal life.[18] These are illustrations of contingency because there was no hint of the latter state in the previous one: there is no hint of "something" in nothing, nor is there any part of life in non-life. Meillassoux then argues that another phase change could happen (or not), and that we cannot in any way predict what that change could be. It could be anything (or nothing). One thing that it could be is the creation of a Divine Being. Another could be the resurrection and eternal life of every person who has ever lived (235). It could also be the advent of a green spaghetti monster. This is what is meant by the demonstrative nature of Meillassoux's work. What I take from it is a way to imagine the possibility of radical difference, although this difference is an expansion of our world, rather than the destruction of it. This can be very important for the genre of science fiction, which is all-too-often trapped in a conservative past or present.

To better understand what Meillassoux means, it is helpful first to look at a negative example, something that, for the most part, works hard *not* to express the kind of contingency Meillassoux is after. Denis Villeneuve's film *Arrival* (2016) is conservative science fiction in that it answers all the questions it sets out to solve, leaving no room for the unexpected and unknown. In the film, aliens speak a language that works differently from all human languages, yet this language is studied, comprehended, and used by humans to communicate. Such complete comprehension of the unknown is the opposite of what is being discussed here. It ignores what speculative realism construes as its defining paradox: the nonhuman world exists and its reality is stranger than anything we can imagine. In the film, even the fact that learning this language shows the non-linearity of time is not strange enough, because this, too, can be explained by the Worf-Sapir hypothesis, a linguistic concept developed in the 1950s. Science fiction should do more than this.

*Arrival* is an example of the most banal kind of science fiction, in that it remains stuck in explaining the unknown. While this kind of science fiction mirrors what Darko Suvin says is key for the genre, namely that it turns its "attention to empirically unknown locations for the new relationships shown in the narration," Meillassoux's argument about the role of contingency is the opposite.[19] Instead of foregrounding something empirically unknown which can later be explained, Meillassoux argues that science fiction has the potential to foreground the empirically unknowable, the experience of a subject who is not shaped by the history of humanism. Meillassoux even has a term for this kind of story, calling it *extro-science fiction*.[20] Contingency, or the inscription of the unforeseeable within the known world, is a way that science fiction can imagine true alternatives to our present, which is mired in the human-created oppression of people, the environment, and other living beings. Because this oppression has been created by humans, no human-created solutions will help. Contingency is the only thing that can save us. Science fiction has a unique place in the struggle to represent such knowledge. But only if it is done right.

Elsewhere I have termed such moments of the unknowable "the Zug Effect," a term I take from the name of an alien race in Damon Knight's 1964 novel *Beyond the Barrier*.[21] It tells the story of Gordon Naismith, who slowly learns that he is not from 1980 as he believes, but is actually from 20,000 years in the future. He has been sent back in time, with his memory erased, as a punishment because he let a fearsome monster called a Zug escape. Eventually, Naismith returns to the future and finds out that he *is* the Zug he has been looking for. I developed the idea of "the Zug Effect" because of the way that the Zugs are described: they are figures for a separation of an object from its perceived qualities, and connect an object to new, unexpected qualities. For example, the first time Naismith encounters a Zug is not in reality, but in a dream. The Zug is described as having "an impossibly fluid reptilian motion" as it "looked at him with tiny red eyes" (Knight, 21). This "impossibility" underlies the traits of Zugian motion, describing the Zug while at the same time separating it from any knowable qualities that might be assigned to the Zug. However, the Zug is not only a figure of separation, but also of connection. In fact, the similarity of the Zug to humanity is the most frightening thing about it. The Zug is a figure for both the impossibly other and that which the other shares with humanity, thus opening up space for a new philosophy and environmental ethics as well – that speculative realism makes possible.

Iain Hamilton Grant takes a different approach. Rather than dismissing some of the philosophical underpinnings of correlationism, Grant reverses them. Earlier I discuss correlationism's connection to Kant, but another strand of thought connects it to German Idealism, because the "ideal" is thought to lie on the side of human experience, rather than in any object in-itself. Grant, through a powerful re-reading of Schelling, develops a "non-eliminative Idealist" position, in which the Ideal is not a human framework of nature, containing the wildness in its abstract concepts and filtered senses, but rather the Ideal is *a part of nature*.[22] This reversal is imperative for a responsible vision of humanity's role in nature, but this position is both ethically and politically different than Brassier's view. For Brassier, the human world needs to be infiltrated and controlled by nonhuman patterns. For Grant, human and nonhuman worlds exist on a continuum, in which matter is not an inert object but rather an active subject, much as humans are.

In "Poem Written after September 11, 2001," Juliana Spahr also shows how humanity is only one node on the continuum of nature.[23] The poem starts small, with "cells, the movement of cells and the division of cells" (3), and it generates a widening gyre through stanzas which repeat everything from the previous stanza, adding one more step at the end. So an early stanza reads, "as everyone with lungs breathes the space between the hands and the space around the hands in and out" (5); and the next stanza reads, "as everyone with lungs breathes the space between the hands and the space around the hands and the space of the room in and out" (5). With each stanza a new level is introduced, adding buildings, neighborhoods, and cities, eventually moving out to include islands, oceans, the troposphere, stratosphere, and mesosphere (8). In its expanding pulses the poem performs a similar reversal to what Grant is doing in his philosophy: the human is seen as a part of nature, rather than nature being a construct of the human mind. All of this is, of course, represented in the very-human medium of words. But the repetitions of Spahr's poem move it beyond mere reading: the reader is taken off the page with the rhythm of the poem. Although we can never really know the other because it is outside of human experience, this does not mean there is an unbreachable gap, because art is created by the tension between humanity and the world-beyond-humanity, exceeding even the concepts of its creators. What this means in this context is that New York post 9/11 is not captured or reproduced by the poem; rather, reading the poem is one way a human can be a part of an interaction with this material world.

Graham Harman also holds that the Kantian distinction between human and nonhuman worlds is true, but he argues that it is true for all objects, not just humans.[24] Yes, there is a divide between human and object, but the same divide exists between one object and another. Just as my experience of an apple does not exhaust all of the possibilities of that apple (the real object is always more than I can know about it), the apple's "experience" of a tree, or a worm, or the color red is not exhausted by its interaction with them. This remainder is what Harman terms the "withdrawn" aspect of an object, which is key because he believes correlationism to be challenged by the way objects are withdrawn from complete knowledge (*Weird Realism* 51). This is true for every object, including oil rigs, gorillas, soap bubbles, and lies. This leads to Harman's philosophy being of a descriptive nature, meaning that it is objects and not relations which are of the utmost importance.[25]

This is an important point in differentiating the relationship between speculative realism and posthumanism in comparison with more relational philosophical traditions such as Bruno Latour, Donna Haraway, Karen Barad, or Gilles Deleuze. In short, the relational view sees objects only having meaning in connection to other objects (a shore only has meaning in relation to a body of water), while for Harman, the reality of objects is found in the way they withdraw from all relations to all objects. The stakes of this argument are articulated in Harman's book on H.P. Lovecraft, *Weird Realism*, in which he looks at 100 passages from the horror writer in order to develop his narrative strategies for representing "the separation of an object from its qualities" (113). He argues that separation between an object and its qualities is evident from the fact that, no matter in how much detail an object is described, the description never actually becomes that object: there is always a distance between a gathering of the qualities of an object and the object itself – a distance shown in the description of the Zug above. The creature is "impossibly fluid"; that is, fluidity is a quality that is used to describe Zugness, but at the same time this quality is an inadequate concept when compared to the object it describes (the Zug). Harman argues that an experience of this inadequacy *is actually a way* to experience objects outside of human perception: we use human perception, but we know it does not do a good job. What is "missing" from our perception is reality, meaning the withdrawn aspect of an object which is not in contact with any other object whatsoever. This withdrawn aspect is what is different, other, more than any human relation to an object. This means that if we are truly going to be posthumanist in our methods, and not just address posthuman topics in our research, then we must focus on this withdrawnness, this "missing" aspect of our experience of reality. Objects "as a whole" will never become present, but the tension between our experience of objects and their reality beyond our experience can provide a proper methodology for our inquiries. One name for this methodology could be poetry, another could be science fiction.

With this in mind we can re-visit Villeneuve's *Arrival* and realize that we may have been too harsh in our initial evaluation. It is possible to identify one scene that offers a less explanatory relationship to knowledge, although not quite in the all-encompassing manner that Harman finds in Lovecraft. In the film, a team of scientists enter a spaceship. As a scissor-lift brings them up to the entrance, the comfortable, relational space of Earth is replaced by the dark interior of the ship. The scientists find themselves in a tunnel, seemingly leading upward into the craft. At the end of the tunnel is a light, which mirrors the light coming from outside the ship at the entrance. The world outside the ship is understandable. The light at the end of the tunnel implies that something understandable will happen there, too (it is where the scientists meet the aliens and learn their language). However, the dark tunnel itself offers the possibility of being, and remaining, a mystery.

The tunnel provides a space in the film in which something is left unexplained. This allows a space for the withdrawn aspect of objects themselves, rather than just the sensual qualities of objects given to human senses and values. One scientist throws a glow stick along the tunnel to light the way. It goes about half-way along the tunnel and comes to a stop. This is unusual and unexpected. It signals that gravity is different inside the ship from outside. Gravity is dependent on mass, and the mass of the ship is not nearly big enough to generate its own gravity. However, the specific gravity of the ship is not addressed anywhere in the film. It is just represented, and in the most trivial of ways, by showing the scientists upside-down, a frequent technique in science fiction films to indicate a space different from Earth.[26]

This scene in *Arrival* is important because it suggests a space in which contingency, and thus the nonhuman, can exist. But it does it in a way that *combines* Harman's and Meillassoux's thought. On the one hand, something is left unknown, unexplained. This fits in with representing the withdrawn nature of an object. On the other hand, something new and unexpected arises from this: the scientists need to go through this passage into the ship to experience the alien creatures. This fits in with Meillassoux's call for the necessity of contingency. In this way, *Arrival* includes a representation of two types of speculative realism. Science fiction can feature such moments, but they are generally the exception rather than the rule. When these moments become important in themselves, strategies for a posthuman way of life can emerge.

## Notes

1. Jacques Derrida, *Of Grammatology*, trans. Gayatri Chakravorty Spivak (Baltimore: Johns Hopkins University Press, 2016), 85.
2. Graham Harman, "The Well-Wrought Broken Hammer: Object-Oriented Literary Criticism," *New Literary History*, 43 (2) (2012), 196–7.
3. Brian Willems, *Facticity, Poverty and Clones: On Kazuo Ishiguro's Never Let Me Go* (New York: Atropos Press, 2010).
4. A transcript is available in R. Brassier, I. Hamilton, G. Harman, and Q. Meillassoux, *Collapse* 3 (2007), 307–449.
5. Steven Shaviro offers a clear overview of how their various critiques of correlationism both converge and diverge in *The Universe of Things: On Speculative Realism* (Minneapolis: University of Minnesota Press, 2014), 5–8.
6. *After the "Speculative Turn": Realism, Philosophy and Feminism*, ed. Katerina Kolozva and Eileen A. Joy (Brooklyn: Punctum Books, 2016); *Object-Oriented Feminism*, ed. Katherine Behar (Minneapolis: University of Minnesota Press, 2016).
7. Quentin Meillassoux, *After Finitude: An Essay on the Necessity of Contingency*, trans. Ray Brassier (London: Continuum, 2008).
8. Immanuel Kant, *Critique of Pure Reason*, trans. Norman Kemp Smith (London: Macmillan, 1929), 259.
9. For more on this tradition of knowledge production and its relationship to posthumanism, see Chapter 2 of this volume.
10. See the transcript, Brassier et al., 409.
11. S. Sharif *Look* (Minneapolis: Greywolf Press, 2016). This military definition is quoted by Sharif (np).
12. See Ray Brassier, "Unfree Improvisation/Compulsive Freedom," in *Mattin. org* (2013), online. A more nuanced presentation of Brassier's thought can be found in his book *Nihil Unbound: Enlightenment and Extinction* (London: Palgrave Macmillan, 2007).

13. Rosi Braidotti, *The Posthuman* (Cambridge: Polity, 2013), 60. Rosi Braidotti and T. Vermeulen. "Borrowed Energy," *Frieze*, online. Braidotti and Vermeulen rightly use "himself" to denote the male-heavy roster of speculative realists

14. Christian Bök, *The Xenotext: Book 1* (Toronto: Coach House Books, 2015).

15. Bök, 86. See also J. Schuster, "On Reading Christian Bök's *The Xenotext: Book 1* Ten Thousand Years Later," *Jacket 2* (2016), online.

16. GegenSichKollektiv, "CAUTION," *Collapse* 8 (2014), 905.

17. Fredric Jameson, *The Seeds of Time* (New York: Columbia University Press, 1996), 60.

18. Quentin Meillassoux, "Excerpts from *L'Inexistence divine*," in G. Harman (ed.), *Quentin Meillassoux: Philosophy in the Making* (Edinburgh: University of Edinburgh Press, 2011), 175–238.

19. Darko Suvin, *Positions and Presuppositions in Science Fiction* (Kent: Kent State University Press, 1988), 34

20. Quentin Meillassoux, *Science Fiction and Extro-Science Fiction*, trans. Alyosha Edlebi (Minneapolis: Univocal, 2015), 5–6.

21. Brian Willems, *Speculative Realism and Science Fiction* (Edinburgh: Edinburgh University Press, 2017), 27–30. The novel is Damon Knight, *Beyond the Barrier* (New York: Macfadden-Bartell, 1970).

22. Iain Hamilton Grant, *Philosophies of Nature after Schelling* (London: Continuum, 2006), 202.

23. Juliana Spahr, *This Connection of Everything with Lungs* (Berkeley: University of California Press, 2005).

24. Graham Harman, *Weird Realism: Lovecraft and Philosophy* (Ropley, Hants: Zero Books, 2012).

25. This is a central difference between the emphasis on objects and matter in speculative realism and the way matter is theorized in new materialisms. See Chapter 12 of this volume for more on new materialism and posthumanism.

26. See Brian Willems, *Shooting the Moon* (Ropley, Hants: Zero Books 2015), 96–7.

# CHAPTER 14

# Race and the Limitations of "the Human"

## Mark Minch-de Leon

> Indians knew stones were the perfect beings because they were self-contained entities that had resolved their social relationships and possessed great knowledge about how every other entity, and every species, should live. Stones had mobility but they did not have to use it. Every other being had mobility and needed, in some specific manner, to use it in their relationships.[1]

Summer of 1986, Oceania, East-West Center at the University of Hawaii. After listening to a Kanaka Maoli artist at a conference describe how he finds the large rocks, pōhaku, that he uses to sculpt deity figures – "I don't find them; they find me" – Osage scholar George Tinker relates the following story about helping a medicine man gather rocks for a sweat lodge:

> *As we walked up an arroyo away from the pick-up ... I began to notice some pretty nice rocks right away – just like the ones used regularly in these ceremonies. Why don't we take these, I asked? The medicine man shook his head, said, "No, not those," and kept on walking. All the time we were getting further up the arroyo, and I knew who was going to have to carry all those rocks back to the truck. Finally, more than a quarter mile from the truck, the medicine man nodded and pointed to some rocks that looked just like the hundreds we had passed by along the way. "These have agreed to go with us," he said. "They will help us in our prayers."[2]* (Tinker 107)

A fulminating British professor of American Studies remonstrates, "That's what is wrong with you people. You are so anthropocentric. You think that everything in the world works the way that you do," to which Tinker eloquently responds, "I am sorry Professor W., but that comment cannot go unchallenged. You see, you are the ones who are actually anthropocentric. You believe that everything in the world works differently from yourselves" (107).

\*\*\*\*

1550–1551, Colonial Spain, *Collegio de San Gregorio* in Valladolid. Dominican friar and Bishop of Chiapas Bartolomé de las Casas and humanist scholar Juan Ginés de Sepúlveda (with a coterie of scholars and priests) debate the moral and theological implications of the colonization of the Americas, focusing specifically on the nature of Indigenous humanity. The Junta de Valladolid, an appointed panel of learned scholars and jurists, is created to decide the outcome of the debate, asking the question: Was it lawful for the Spanish Crown to wage war against the Indigenous populations of the New World in order to first bring them under Spanish rule and then instruct them in the Christian faith? The King of Spain, Charles V, suspends all military expansion in the Americas while this question is being decided. This suspension is in part due to the efforts of Las Casas and in part a response to the papal bull, *Sublimis Deus*, Pope Paul III issued in 1537, which defends Indigenous capacity: "The Indians are truly men and . . . they are not only capable of understanding the catholic faith, but . . . they desire exceedingly to receive it."[3]

Both Las Casas and Sepúlveda base their arguments on the inherent humanity of the Indians, differing primarily on the nature and capacity of Indigenous humanity and the means towards its perfection. Using Aristotle's theory of natural slavery, Sepúlveda stretches the category of the human, with its basis in reason, to argue for a figuration of Indigenous humanity in which external conditions of slavery derive necessarily from an innate condition of enslavement to passions and impaired reason (Saldaña-Portillo E52). Physical enslavement, here, becomes a pedagogical tool of liberation from internalized slavery and towards the goal of a unified, if inherently unequal, humanity under the sign of rationality. Las Casas' well-known apologia *En defense de los indios* also draws upon Aristotle's theory, but includes the cruelty of European nations as evidence of inferior reason on their part and points to the sociality of Indigenous peoples as evidence of their participation in universal humanity united under "the unchangeable and uniformly rational nature of all humans, as ordained by God" (Saldaña-Portillo E56). Indians, he argues, like all other human beings, have free will and thus must come to Christian faith of their own accord, that is, through persuasion not enslavement. No decision is recorded.

✳✳✳✳

These two events, distant in space and time, together chart the trajectory of a force of racialized humanization that is neither progressive nor static, neither historical nor atemporal, neither geographically specific nor universal (though it has pretensions to both). Oceania in 1986 is connected to the Indigenous Atlantic in the sixteenth century through the question of Indigenous humanity and the so-called American project (conquest/colonization). An example of what Jodi Byrd calls the transit of empire – the reproduction and proliferation of imperial relations and forms of power through a reiterative figuration of "Indianness" as threshold and generative matrix – the processes of humanization that connect these two events rest on the vacillating valuation of Indigenous humanity and its proliferation as a matrix for the colonial order.[4] The metric of this valuation is human capacity, both the capacity of humanness to be flexible, to change, to even become something other than human, and the capacity for becoming (more) human, as a mark of racialized distinction within the category of a perfectible humanity. These two events, remarkable and banal in their own ways, are moments where new calculations of the human were set into motion.

Returning to these events by following the path of Indianness as an element of humanization opens up a different perspective on posthumanist theorizing. The "post," as has been argued by a number of scholars, indicates less a temporal *after* than a reflexive and critical *return* to the generative conditions and promise of humanism.[5] As Cary Wolfe claims, it is the enlightenment without the negative constraints of anthropocentrism and eurocentrism, which define the more violent aspects of humanism. But it bears questioning what the effects are of promoting such unfettered rationality. To stay with Wolfe's definition in order to make a broader point, the radical expansion of reason through embodiment, materiality, cognitive distribution, environmental interactivity, through such a model as the cybernetic feedback loop in a constitutively open posture via a contaminative logic of the trace, raises the question of the politics of knowledge-production. This is especially relevant in terms of the position of critique.

As will be seen, the western liberal conception of the human has been criticized in its social construction of a normative white subjectivity.[6] If it is the case that the human historically and epistemically has been constituted as white, then attempts to overcome or suspend this construction should come from antiracist and anticolonial sources. Which raises the question of how the various discourses that come under the umbrella of posthumanism, the theoretical position arguably most invested in such a project, have approached the whiteness of the human. Have they combatted a white supremacist racialized regime or contributed to it? This question is further complicated by the fact that the human continues to be a defining feature in the lives of many of the oppressed both as a regulative ideal, often times bound up with projects of recuperation and inclusion, and as the lived critical impulse that opens up possibilities for self-affirmation outside of racist orders. For most, to be human (and the political projects performed in its name) continues to be a desired thing.

The critical posthumanist mode that is reflected in the prefix has generally operated through denaturalization of the historical configuration of the human. But, to turn to historicity as a solution, when history is a fundamental component of western epistemology and orientation, raises a significant issue. History has been used specifically to draw temporal distinctions between a white western (unmarked) subject and racialized and culturalized others, who remain outside of history's reach. Thus to turn to history in order to dispel the effects of such an ordering of the world, and further to include those previously excluded from this order, is akin to what Marc Nichanian calls, in conversation with David Kazanjian, resorting to the executioner's logic.[7] To assume the only tool or best tools available to combat a humanized racial regime come from within the regime itself, as an unfinished project of self-correction, is a leitmotif of what critical race scholars refer to as the self-reflexivity of the west (white western subject), a positionality through which the west continues to define itself and circumscribe what can be said.[8]

The "post" of posthumanism, then, will seem to mark a dilemma between the promotion of a reflexive mode of criticism that seeks the accomplishment of the enlightenment through the dissolution of the human figured as exceptional (and universalizingly white, European), a project that has always had investments in the historical complications of Indigeneity, and what Tiffany Lethabo King calls external pressure, which she describes as "specifically the kind of pressure that [is manifest in] 'decolonial refusal' and 'abolitionist skepticism' as forms of resistance that enact outright rejection of or view 'posthumanist' attempts with a 'hermeneutics of suspicion.'" This pressure is needed "in order to truly address the recurrent problem of the violence of the human in continental theory."[9] From this perspective, posthumanism must be interrogated for its investments in whiteness, not to cast judgment on the viability of a posthumanist project, but to address the diminishment of and unspoken reliance upon Indigenous, antiracist, and anticolonial configurations of the human which have radical decolonial and abolitionist possibilities, and which under the current order too easily get co-opted, domesticated, and pacified. This is not to include them as perspectives in order to further the project of critical thought but rather to show how they can, as Byrd frames

it, "stop the world of signification and force a continual grinding within
the systems of enlightenment that produce the subject at the site of
freedom, equality, and conviviality achieved through genocidal
dispossession."[10]

The return to the two moments at the beginning of this chapter, then, is
not just to understand their significance (or lack thereof) in the history of
liberal western humanism's culpability in the violent production and
dissemination of whiteness. It is also to linger in their respective suspen-
sions: the suspension of the colonial project in the face of Indigenous
humanity and the suspension of meaning through the inversion of the term
"anthropocentrism." This is in order to find in the "post" neither
a temporal after nor a reflexive return to an antecedent, but rather
a politics of suspension of the western humanizing colonial project.

### 14.1    Humanization as Racialization

What was suspended during the Valladolid debate was not just the colonial
mechanisms of war but also a certain conception of the human. For the
first time the Spanish were confronted with an order so far outside their
Christo-centric common sense as to shake loose the human from its place
in their theological and natural orders. The very fact that Indigenous
peoples had never heard the gospel meant that, unlike Muslims and
Jews, they could not be considered enemies of the Church. Indigenous
peoples therefore "existed in a unique category outside the history of belief
that had long defined and divided humanity. . . . If the unity of humanity
was necessarily established through Christ, what might be the status of
humans who had never known Christ?" (Saldaña-Portillo E51, E54). Sylvia
Wynter argues that this moment of uncertainty produced the conditions
for the secularization of humanity and the rise of the racialized modern
state. This "de-godding" consolidated the imperial state as the natural
extension of the secular human through the delegitimation of Indigenous
interrelations with other beings and, therefore, their sociopolitical organizations and relations to power. The political formation of the state, in this
sense, could not be anything other than genocidal, echoed in the later
settler-colonial refrain: kill the Indian; save the man.

At the same time, Indigenous sociality marks the capacity of/for universal human reason. "These juridical encounters with indigeneity prodi-
giously produced new terms for interpreting all of humanity, and by
examining them with a critical eye we glean the absence/presence of the
Indian at the heart of the human" (Saldaña-Portillo E45). María Josefina

Saldaña-Portillo has shown how this destabilization of the European conception of the human caused by the encounter with Indigenous humanity also created the need to re-humanize the European subject through self-reflective debates on the humanity of others, such as the Valladolid. Combining a classical notion of the human based in rationality with the medieval notion of the universality of divine grace, the discursive outcome of the debate was both to inaugurate Eurocentric reason as a metric of capacity in order to manage a secular humanity and to base this capacity on submission to centralized forms of power organized around the figure of the human. Indigenous humanity, defined through its humaneness as gentle, docile, and prepared to receive the Christian faith, evidenced by Indigenous sociality, is used to argue for an ethic of humane colonization, combining the goals of the Church with those of the imperial state.

The other side of this combination was the negotiated production of the compatibility of state violence with Christian faith. The figuration of the human as an ethical and juridical project allowed reason to become the basis for the marriage of evangelization with imperialism, structured around discursivity. Knowledge-production and "debate" became the means to facilitate a compassionate and reasoned approach to colonization in its so-called hard and soft varieties. And the state thereby claimed a monopolization of violence in the name of human reason. In other words, whether one argued for the enslavement of Indigenous peoples or their management through missionization, the result was the same: their subjugation and dispossession through a process of humanization that rendered them either salvageable or disposable, depending on their reaction to colonial dispossession.

According to Wynter, this instituted a racial regime of distinction amongst humanity according to degrees of rational perfection.[11] The symbolic order of life and death, which was transposed into a theological order of good and evil, became the basis of the distinction between reason and sensuality, rationality and irrationality. These are different descriptive statements of the human based on competing ontologies and yet, through the production of a new "truth-for adaptive" statement, the "plan of salvation" to unite Christ's flock gets translated into political terms as the "goals of the state" organized around distinctions in rationality which symbolically link racial distinctions to ethical ones and, ultimately, differentiate the value of lives (288). This amounts to the overrepresentation of the Christo-Euro-secular conception of "Man" as the universal human. Such is the new common sense. The discursive-material project initiated by it is the foundation of a racial discourse composed of "the colonial question, the nonwhite/native question, the negro question" (288).

One of the more powerful accounts of the force of humanization as a racializing project is Zakiyyah Iman Jackson's analysis of "slave humanity" as an aporia that marks the limit of what can be reckoned. In her essay on Toni Morrison's *Beloved*, Jackson focuses on the human-animal relationship that undergirds enslaved humanity and that continues into the afterlife of emancipated black humanity.[12] This is to emphasize that the enslaved black body is not dehumanized but rather humanized in a particular way that transmogrifies the body and mind, as well as relations with domesticated animals, a biopolitical and ontological rearrangement/derangement: "the process of making the slave relied on the abjection and criminalization of the slave's humanity rather than the denial of it" (96). Jackson argues that this experimental and brutal calculation of the limits of the human, both in form and personality, indicates the plasticization of the human in the imperial, colonial, and racializing projects of humanism. And the technologies that have been generally read as dehumanizing forces, such as the ledger system and the discipline of comparative anatomy, have instead worked to combine racialization and animalization as two complementary processes of humanization that stretch and deform limits through blackness.

This stretching of the limit is efficiently and viscerally exemplified by the bit placed in the mouth of Morrison's character, Paul D, which deranges human-animal relations in racialized, animalized, sexualized, and therefore humanized terms. The perpetual "wildness" of the eye it causes is mirrored by the damning, humanized gaze of the rooster, Mister, who haunts Paul D's manhood as a witness to abjection. It is across this unstable antithetical construction of the humanized-animalized gaze that Jackson will show how slavery was an experimentation in flesh that violently tested the limitations of the human. She writes,

> The enslaved, in their humanity, could function as infinitely malleable lexical and biological matter, at once sub/super/human. What appear as alternating, or serialized, discrete modes of (mis)recognition – sub/super/ humanization, animalization/humanization, privation/superfluity – are in fact varying dimensions of a racializing demand that the slave be all dimensions at once, a simultaneous actualization of the seemingly discontinuous and incompatible. (98)

Her response is to focus on the aporia of "slave humanity," figured in its plastic relations to animality, to suspend this humanizing demand to be all things at once.

Instead of reinforcing the distinction between humans and animals through a critique of dehumanization, Jackson calls for a rethinking of the violence of imperialism and slavery as it applies to both humans and animals thus to focus on the ontological conditions through which they are rendered mutually exclusive, and therefore abjectly related. This is a point also made by Mel Y. Chen within the context of racialized language: the categories of linguistic animacy organized along "the great chain of being" formulated within western theories of freedom, from least to most free, allow for a paradoxical figuration of dehumanization to emerge.[13] According to Chen, both objectifying and animalizing racial, gendered, and sexual slurs must first affirm humanity in order to conflate the category with others understood to be less free. The upshot of this is that criticisms of objectifying and dehumanizing language that do not attend to the western logic of animacy, which organizes and evaluates beings according to certain norms such as mobility, sentience, vitality, and autonomy, end up reinforcing this logic. Jackson's analyses of humanization and the aporetic figure of slave humanity, in this sense, have the effect of slowing down this critical impulse and drawing out the consequences that slavery had/has on transspecies colonial interrelationality through the racialized plasticization of bodies, in order to refigure ontological relations from the standpoint of black humanity.

Alexander Weheliye has also argued for a reconfiguration of ontological relations from the standpoint of black, and other non-western, modes of humanity. In both his critique of biopolitics – for not including colonial and racialized configurations of the human – and his centering of analyses of the human within black studies, as a product of racializing assemblages, Weheliye argues for a reassessment of semiotic-material relations produced under extreme conditions such as internment and concentration camps, colonial outposts, and plantations.[14] Focusing on Wynter's schema of inflected humanity (human, not-quite-human, nonhuman) produced in these contexts through racialized hierarchization, he emphasizes the differential and relational production of diverse forms of racialized bare life at/as the limits of the human. This is to assert racialized humanity, and its various liminal perspectives, as the "demonic ground" of modern politics and thought (21). It is also to correct, following Wynter's reading of Frantz Fanon, the elision of the sociogenic conditions of humanity, "a symbolic register, consisting of discourse, language, culture, and so on," for the purely biological (25). Instead, the focus, according to Weheliye, should be on rearticulating meaning and discourse to material histories of violence and the bodies on which the violence has been inflicted, which continue to condition the modern order, hence the need for a reformulation of the politics of knowledge-production around racialized figurations of the human. Emphasizing western liberal humanism's simultaneous production of and conditioning by racializing assemblages, Weheliye locates race as a master code for the universalization of one genre of the human, Man, which needs to be disfigured and abolished (27).

Humanization as racialization, for Weheliye, operates through the production of a sociopolitical grammar-matter in the form of flesh, which acts as the site, material, and product of this rearticulation. Drawing on Hortense Spillers' distinction between the body – the possession of legal personhood – and flesh – a zero degree of sociality and an excess produced through "the calculated work of iron, whips, chains, knives, the canine patrol, the bullet" – Weheliye indicates the complex production and conditioning force of such a fleshy, relational substance out of which self-possessed bodies are carved (Spillers quoted in Weheliye 39). This notion describes the survival of violence in the form of a "hieroglyphics of the flesh" (40), literally lacerations on the skin in one sense and materialized meaning in another, transmitted to succeeding generations of black subjects, who have been "liberated" and granted a body in the afterlife of slavery made from this semiotic-material that seeks to forget, hide, or encode its violent conditions. Flesh is semiotic in that it functions through certain shapes, images, or forms that encode violence in a flexible and mutable material which gets translated – carries the violent lacerations – into discourses of truth based on the visual-biological space of distinction, producing a sort of cultural matter. The visual analytics of race, then, are undergirded by a hieroglyphics of the flesh and consolidated in the body, acting as both a surface manifestation and a visual cloaking of social Darwinian arguments about differential physiology. Such a visual-discursive knot marks the site of the invisible anchoring (and disappearance) of the sociogenic in(to) a naturalized physiology, to produce a singular account of racially inflected humanity.

The unraveling of this knot, for Weheliye, involves neither inclusion into humanity nor abolishment of humanism, but rather a procedure of unveiling obliterated genres of the human as the demonic ground of humanism and bringing into consciousness both the hidden semiotic-material articulations and the processes that make "liminal spaces, ensconced in and outside the world of Man, from which to construct new objects of knowledge and launch reinvention of the human at the juncture of the biology and culture feedback loop" (25). Constituting a form of autopoiesis, this procedure mobilizes flesh to disfigure Man.

Flesh, then, is not just an excess produced through racialized violence but also "an alternate instantiation of humanity" (43). This does, however, raise a number of questions about the status and location of Weheliye's conception of flesh.

At stake in his politics of visibility is a critical theoretical position of denaturalization at both the discursive and theoretical levels. Not only does race get naturalized, according to Weheliye, as a *de facto* historical origin of biopolitics without attention to its social construction, but it also marks the naturalization of discourse and, through it, of an unrecognized ideological apparatus mistaken as pure physiology (57). The critical task, then, seems to be one of unveiling and denaturalizing invisible and rigidly fixed racial formations. Yet he is also quick to point out that his analysis is not invested in "considering racial categorizations as a mere ideological imposition," but is rather interested in networks of "bodies, forces, velocities, intensities, institutions, interests, ideologies, and desires" (12). This is made most clearly manifest by his characterization of "the living, speaking, thinking, feeling, and imagining flesh: the ether that holds together the world of Man while at the same time forming the conditions of possibility for this world's demise" (40). This is an immanent, vital power that is a product of human agency while also taking on a seemingly inhuman (even destructive) agency of its own. Weheliye seems to be asking for two contradictory positions.

On one hand, Weheliye is calling for a suspension of universalized provincial, western critical thought as hermetic and self-reflexive. Following Achille Mbembe, he calls for a turn away from "Parisianism": "Perhaps, then, the time has come to bid adieu to Foucault's metropolitan territoire d'outer-mer" (63). On the other, he explicitly calls for "recasting the human sciences" in order to "disfigure Man through the *incorporation* of the colonial and racialist histories of the modern incantations of the human," thereby centering the human as object of study to combat its naturalization in all its inflected forms" (19, 21; emphasis added). This seems to be a call for an institutionalized inquiry into unacknowledged biopolitical histories through an expansion and a proliferation of social scientific discourses around plural figurations of the human. This is done to disfigure Man by bringing to light the hidden, violent conditions of Man-making thereby to imagine the human otherwise.

Weheliye marks out a dialectical position that seeks liberation through the continued disalienation of naturalized forms. But as has been shown by scholars such as Jodi Byrd, David Lloyd, and Christopher Bracken, such a notion of disalienation always begins in critical narratives of human social origins with figurations of primitivism (nature as an alien force) which are demonstrably false (no Indigenous epistemology includes a concept of nature – it is entirely a fiction of the west).[15] So, what does this mean for critique? Does reliance upon a mode of critique invested in revealing and proliferating vitality and discourse to combat naturalization risk falling into the trap of biopolitical governance otherwise, producing new forms of value that can be too easily co-opted? That is, how do we read Weheliye's call for refusal when it seems to be articulated as a methodological injunction to produce more knowledge about disenfranchised peoples in a critical theoretical mode that continues to pit nature vs. the social/cultural and death vs. life, even while he eschews these distinctions? What if, rather than seeking a dialectical and semiotic-material movement as critical operation, the emphasis is instead on the inhuman conditions of humanity that Weheliye analyzes with his conception of flesh, the excess of a humanizing process and its infrastructure, and thereby a site for suspension of the contradictions of the humanizing project and its discursive injunction to make knowledge: halting the demand, as Jackson describes, to be all dimensions at once? This opens up a conversation with an Indigenous inhumanity founded on a mode of a-vitalism and even, perhaps, anti-critique as methodological and formalized refusal.

## 14.2    Towards an Indigenous Inhumanities: A Sketch as Open Conclusion

Returning to Tinker's clever turn of phrase, recounted in his reminiscence of telling a story about discerning rocks, it can now be read as antiproduction of discourse. To see this, though, requires not analyzing the event as a moment of rational debate towards a resolution. Hinged on inverted meanings of "anthropocentrism," it is in the antithetical structure that the vacillation of the old noble/violent savage dichotomy, set into semiotic motion by early colonial discourses, is shown to rear its ugly head again in the Americanist's statement. It is also evidenced in and momentarily stalled out by Tinker's rebuttal. Rather than a positive statement leading to more knowledge, with an ear for suspension, Tinker's inversion can be heard as sabotaging the conversation. The rhetorical construction participates in strategies of inversion, incommensurability, and refusal. It is an acknowledgement of Indigenous interrelationality, amongst humans and other beings, as well as the rendering nonsensical of such relationships by a humanizing, racialized colonial regime. It is also acknowledgement of the multivalent desires for indigeneity, made pathological and salvational and disarticulated from the human, as colonial excess in the figure of a mobile Indianness.

Holding open without reconciling or deciding between the ambivalence of anthropocentrism renders Tinker's statement neither ontological nor epistemological but – like the stones that have resolved their social relations which Deloria describes in the epigraph – asocial. Later in his essay, Tinker inverts "the great chain of being" that in theological and secular western humanisms places rocks at the bottom as inanimate, insensate, and geological matter. He instead places them at the top as the wisest and oldest of beings to which humans must aspire. Rocks choose not to move and decide, on their own terms, with whom they communicate. And not all rocks are alive. These conceptions challenge the emphasis on Indigenous sociality, a colonial tactic, and the assertion of vitality that organizes critical modes from denaturalization to various new materialisms.

Due to space limitations, I can only sketch out some of the attributes and concepts, and reference only some of the significant scholars, that contribute to the notion of an Indigenous inhumanities that arise out of Tinker's story. As mentioned, Jodi Byrd traces the intellectual and material production of a figuration of Indianness as both colonial/imperial matrix and the movement of the critical itself as the "crease" or threshold through which self-reflexivity is made possible.[16] This figuration is made possible by racialized humanization which renders Indigenous sociopolitical interrelations nonsensical or, at best, a matter of belief, as described by Kim Tallbear and Marisol de la Cadena.[17] These interrelations form the matter of an Indianness in transit. They also render Indigenous sociality both pathologically and salvationally, as described by Dian Million. In her discussion of biosocialities; Million shows how Indigenous socialities are filtered through traumatic and therapeutic discourses to expand biopolitics into the spiritual realm through the governance of Native spiritual and social life towards reconciliation with the humanist state through healing.[18] And finally, Elizabeth Povinelli makes clear that underlying western epistemic and critical projects lies a form of power invested in governing the relations not just between life and death but between Life and Nonlife, a "biontological enclosure" that determines the evaluation of being according to one form of existence, life (bios and zoe).[19]

Together, these adumbrate a methodology that begins from Indigenous inhumanity as a refusal of vitalist knowledge production and critique. Moving past the life and death divide, as Kim Tallbear describes, also opens new possibilities of conversation with posthumanist discourses that center non-western positions and modes of being. It also extends the conception of race beyond a human attribute to the foreclosure and destruction of worlds outside of the western theologico-secular vitalist order created by and enforced through humanization. It asks the question, what does non-vital anticolonial work look like outside of the bounds of and in contradistinction to a humanizing process?

## Notes

1. Vine Deloria Jr., "Relativity, Relatedness, and Reality," in Barbara Deloria, et al. (eds.), *Spirit and Reason: The Vine Deloria, Jr. Reader* (Golden, Colorado: Fulcrum Publishing, 1999), 34.
2. George Tinker, "The Stones Shall Cry Out: Consciousness, Rocks, and Indians," *Wicazo Sa Review*, 19, (2) (Fall 2004), 107.
3. María Josefina Saldaña-Portillo, *Indian Given: Racial Geographies across Mexico and the United States* (Duke University Press, 2016), E46.
4. Jodi Byrd, *The Transit of Empire: Indigenous Critiques of Colonialism* (Minneapolis: University of Minnesota Press, 2011).
5. Cary Wolfe, *What is Posthumanism?* (Minneapolis: University of Minnesota Press, 2010); N. Katherine Hayles, *How We Became Posthuman: Virtual Bodies in Cybernetics, Literature, and Informatics* (Chicago: University of Chicago Press, 1999); Bruno Latour, *We Have Never Been Modern*, trans. C. Porter (Harvard: Harvard University Press, 1993).
6. Lisa Lowe, *The Intimacies of Four Continents* (Durham: Duke University Press, 2015).
7. Marc Nichanian and David Kazanjian, "Between Genocide and Catastrophe," in David Eng and David Kazanjian (eds.), *Loss: The Politics of Mourning* (Berkeley: University of California Press, 2003), 127.
8. Denise Ferreira da Silva, *Toward a Global Idea of Race* (Minneapolis: University of Minnesota Press, 2007); Andrea Smith, "Native Studies at the Horizon of Death: Theorizing Ethnographic Entrapment and Settler Self-Reflexivity," in Audra Simpson and Andrea Smith (eds.), *Theorizing Native Studies* (Durham: Duke University Press, 2014); David Lloyd, *Under Representation: The Racial Regime of Aesthetics* (New York: Fordham University Press, 2019). See also Lowe, *Intimacies*.
9. Tiffany Lethabo King, "Humans Involved: Lurking in the Lines of Posthumanist Flight," *Critical Ethnic Studies*, 3, (1) (Spring 2017), 164–5.
10. Jodi Byrd, "Still Waiting for the 'Post' to Arrive: Elizabeth Cook-Lynn and the Imponderables of American Indian Postcoloniality," *Wicazo Sa Review*, 31, (1), Special Issue: Essentializing (Spring 2016), 78.
11. Sylvia Wynter, "Unsettling the Coloniality of Being/Power/Truth/Freedom: Towards the Human, After Man, Its Overrepresentation – An Argument," *The New Centennial Review*, 3, (3) (2003), 257–337.
12. Zakiyyah Iman Jackson, "Losing Manhood: Animality and Plasticity in the (Neo)Slave Narrative," *qui parle*, 25, (1–2) (Fall/Winter 2016), 95–136.

13. Mel Y. Chen, *Animacies: Biopolitics, Racial Mattering, and Queer Affect* (Durham: Duke University Press, 2012), 37–8.

14. Alexander G. Weheliye, *Habeas Viscus: Racializing Assemblages, Biopolitics, and Black Feminist Theories of the Human* (Durham: Duke University Press, 2014), 37.

15. Byrd, *Transit*; Lloyd, *Under Representation*; Christopher Bracken, *Magical Criticism: The Recourse of Savage Philosophy* (Chicago: University of Chicago Press, 2007).

16. This is supported by scholars such as Christopher Bracken, Denise Ferreira da Silva, David Lloyd, all cited above, and Severin Fowles, "The Perfect Subject (Postcolonial Object Studies)," *Journal of Material Culture*, 21 (2016), 9–27.

17. Kim Tallbear, "Beyond the Life/Not-Life Binary: A Feminist-Indigenous Reading of Cryopreservation, Interspecies Thinking, and the New Materialisms," in Joanna Radin and Emma Kowal (eds.), *Cryopolitics: Frozen Life in a Melting World* (Cambridge: MIT Press, 2017), 179–202. Marisol de la Cadena, "Indigenous Cosmopolitics in the Andes: Conceptual Reflections beyond 'Politics,'" *Cultural Anthropology*, 25, (2) (2010), 334–70.

18. Dian Million, *Therapeutic Nations: Healing in an Age of Indigenous Human Rights* (Tucson: University of Arizona Press, 2014).

19. Elizabeth A. Povinelli, *Geontologies: A Requiem to Late Liberalism* (Durham: Duke University Press, 2016), 5.

# CHAPTER 15

# Speculative Fiction

## Sherryl Vint

In mainstream culture, the term posthuman will usually bring to mind some image from speculative fiction (sf) – a future of perfected embodiment through genetic modification that gives humans new morphologies and capabilities, or a future where we have left embodiment altogether to live at the speed of data as minds uploaded to networks, configuring our surroundings to suit our whims.[1] It is less likely that the first thing to spring to mind will be images of the posthuman consistent with ideas discussed elsewhere in this volume – individuals in constant interchange with their environment, what Stacy Alaimo theorizes as trans-corporeality;[2] or an understanding of the human body as composed mainly of nonhuman microorganisms, as scientific theorizations of "life itself" reveal;[3] or the revelation that human cognition is mostly nonconscious and more alike than different from machinic automation, as N. Katherine Hayles explores.[4] As Veronica Hollinger points out in her historical overview of the emergence of posthumanist thought, speculative fiction is an important archive that has been engaged by the work of many prominent theorists of posthumanism and related fields, including Alaimo, Rosi Braidotti, Donna Haraway, Hayles, Colin Milburn, Isabelle Stengers, and Steven Shaviro.[5]

Speculative fiction, however, is not merely a resource for posthumanist thought but is also itself a space of vernacular theorization, as Thomas Foster argues in *The Souls of Cyberfolk*.[6] Foster offers this articulation in narrow reference to cyberpunk imagery of bodily transformation as humans fuse with machines, but the formulation is useful to characterize a much broader range of ways through which sf has long pursued the kinds of intellectual questions central to many strands of posthumanist thought. The genre can depict concretely imagined and nuanced visions of the world made otherwise, societies in which the default assumptions of humanist modes of thought can be revised and rewritten; that is, it offers instantiations in narrative worlds of the new kinds of subjects and ethics theorized by posthumanism. The created worlds in which sf is set think through and complexly map some of the propositions of posthumanist thought, tangible examples of how one change – in normative notions of gender, in ideas about what constitutes subjectivity and agency, in how communities and families are organized – ripples through the full social world. Such thought experiments – such as Ursula K. Le Guin's *The Left Hand of Darkness* (1969) in which gender is a human attribute only during mating season – are powerful tools for visualizing how specific ideologies and the institutions that sediment around them shape more of our intellectual and social worlds than we often perceive.[7]

The posthuman characters and situations in sf are so myriad that it would be impossible to catalogue them all. Accordingly, this chapter is not an overview of the genre's most influential texts nor a comprehensive list of posthumanist sf. Rather, I argue for the importance of the genre's techniques for an ethical project of critical posthumanism, a way of participating in the deconstruction of the default "man" of humanism and undoing the historical damage fostered by habits of human exceptionalism.[8] Thus, my emphasis will be on the range of ways that sf has contributed to the project of posthuman critique and on the affinities between sf methods and posthumanist viewpoints.[9] Chief among these are strategies of literalizing metaphor and of defamiliarization, strategies shared by both sf writers and posthumanist scholars: Braidotti extensively discusses estrangement as central to posthumanist thought in *The Posthuman*, and "cognitive estrangement" is the most influential definition of what defines a text as part of the sf tradition.[10]

As scholars, most influentially Fredric Jameson and Tom Moylan, contend, sf can be understood as a mode of utopian thought, a perspective on the world that emphasizes the contingency of existing structures and their openness to change.[11] Within utopian studies, such ideas are generally linked to Ernst Bloch's foundational work in *The Principle of Hope*, where he argues for the importance of daydreams, popular narratives, and the like as moments of anticipatory consciousness presaging the possibility of another world.[12] His work articulates the importance of linking these affects to concrete possibilities in the material world, moving from desire into practice. There are strong similarities between Bloch's work and Gilles Deleuze's philosophical theorization of virtuality, which is central to the affirmative tradition of posthumanism developed by Braidotti. Both posthumanism and sf, then, are interested in things that are real but not yet actualized and with the transformative power inherent in embracing different understandings of self and world.

From this point of view, there are connections between sf and most of the new objects of analysis and new methods of study that are collected in this volume. The fragmented subject of postmodernist thought that prompts Jean-François Lyotard's question "Can Thought go on without a Body?" is given voice in Joseph McElroy's *Plus* (1976), focalized through a brain that orbits Earth in a capsule and tries to make sense of its disembodied perceptions.[13] Science and technology studies scholar Bruno Latour wrote his own science fiction in *Aramis* (1996), a work that is partly an ethnography of an engineering project, partly a novelization of the research process, and partly told from the point of view of the proposed transit train, illustrating Latour's notion that both human and nonhuman actants co-construct the sociotechnical world.[14] The popular subgenre of cyberpunk fiction, inaugurated by William Gibson's influential *Neuromancer* (1984), gave us images of computer hackers physically fused with their machines pursuing adventures in the world of cyberspace that became the template for how we imagine artificial intelligence (AI) and virtual reality (VR).[15] The conceptual adjustments with which perspectives such as new materialisms or speculative realism confront us find concrete form in works of sf, such as Jeff VanderMeer's celebrated *Southern Reach* trilogy (2014), which charts the biological transformation of the world into another ontology, necessitating a re-examination of the assumptions that undergird much of western knowledge that are similarly interrogated in the work of philosophers such as Timothy Morton.[16] As Gerry Canavan and Andrew Hageman argue, works of "weird fiction" like VanderMeer's trilogy are no longer necessarily estranging, but instead ably capture our quotidian reality of "global weirding" in a context of massive and unevenly distributed experiences of climate change and extreme weather.[17]

Indeed, one could argue that a central question in science fiction has always been, what does it mean to be human? Consideration of humanity's place among other entities in the universe has been a pervasive theme since the genre's origin: the more famous examples include the Creature fabricated in Mary Shelley's *Frankenstein* (1818) and the aliens in H.G. Wells' *The War of the Worlds* (1898), defeated not by our technology but by a microbe to which humans have long since grown immune.[18] Key icons associated with genre fiction – aliens, robots, AIs, clones, transgenic beings, augmented cyborg bodies, and manufactured beings – all function as symbolic others to "the human" and have often been used to thematize the exclusions of humanist discourse, or what Rosi Braidotti calls the "missing people": those marked by race, gender, orientation, colonialism, labor, or in other ways that have categorized them as lesser than the abstract, universal, and putatively "neutral" *man* of western thought.[19] Joanna Russ' important *The Female Man* (1975) uses sf estrangement to portray the same woman as she would have developed on four different parallel worlds, each with different ideologies of gender, including one in which all men have died from a plague and so women's selfhood is not contingent on their difference from men.[20] Her point, as the title conveys, is that under patriarchy women can be fully human only by disavowing their gender, by becoming female men. Isaac Asimov's robot stories, collected in *I, Robot* (1950), the source of the now widely referenced "three laws of robotics" that set the ethical parameters via which robots are always to privilege human life, clearly allegorize the racialized dehumanization that shapes conditions of labor in the United States, although, unlike Russ, Asimov does not as explicitly use his fiction to critique such social relations.[21]

The example of Asimov reveals two important axioms to keep in mind when thinking about sf's engagement with posthumanist ideas. First, although there are many excellent examples of sf used overtly to pursue projects of social justice consistent with a critical posthumanism, there is no necessary connection between sf and the deconstruction of human exceptionalism, and indeed many of the most popularly known texts do precisely the opposite. The figure of the cyborg, for example, is prevalent in sf and its most iconic versions include Arnold Schwarzenegger's genocidal terminator, in the franchise launched by *The Terminator* (James Cameron 1984), and Robocop, the eponymous protagonist of Paul Verhoeven's film (1987), an enforcement robot powered by the organic remains of a police officer killed in the line of duty. Neither figure personifies the cyborg theorized in Donna Haraway's "The Cyborg Manifesto" (1985), one of the most prominent and important works of posthumanist theory that continues to be widely cited today, although Haraway in this essay does refer to progressive sf written by authors such as Joanna Russ and Samuel R. Delany.[22] Haraway's cyborg embodies contemporary transformations in material and intellectual cultures that she theorizes: conceptual boundaries between the human/animal, the organic/inorganic, and the material/virtual have all broken down, compelling us to think in new ways about (1) a world beyond gender, (2) the entanglements of naturecultures, and (3) the possibilities for agency and political solidarity in this new world. For Haraway, the cyborg is a creature without dualisms, a figure of *both/and* that was always and simultaneously human and machine, natural and cultural. It is precisely the possibilities embodied in the cyborg to think beyond essentialism that makes it such a potent image, what Haraway calls "a creature of social reality as well as a creature of fiction" (149).

Perhaps because the popular figure of the cyborg emblematized quite different values of masculine augmentation and military power, Haraway has distanced herself from the term posthumanism in her more recent work, although she continues to explore questions of our connections to the more-than-human world and to articulate the limitations of dualistic ways of thinking. This gap between cyborg as figuration of posthumanism and cyborg as emergent sociotechnical reality points to the second reason that Asimov's laws are an important example for thinking about sf as a posthumanist discourse, namely, the ways that sf influences research in science and the design of resultant technologies. Sheila Jasanoff calls such cultural influence the "sociotechnical imaginary," which she defines as "collectively held, institutionally stabilized, and publicly performed visions of desirable futures, animated by shared understandings of forms of social life and social order attainable through, and supportive of, advances in science and technology."[23] We see such influence, for example, in the way that Asimov's laws of robotics have become a shorthand for thinking about automation, ethics, and liability, the default reference point for science journalism on topics such as self-driving cars, semi-autonomous drones, and smart homes. To be clear, my point is not that sf is the direct template for any specific technology or that it has already found the answers to the questions that confront humanity as we engage with intelligent systems. Instead, what is important is the ongoing exchange between fiction and reality, the ways in which sf conditions our expectations and beliefs (at times usefully, at others detrimentally), and how it can be mobilized to endorse or critique specific pathways forward as we engage constant sociotechnical change.

Contra Jasanoff, I contend that sf's power as a sociotechnical imaginary is not always "supportive" of such change, nor are its visions always of "desirable" futures. Most dystopian narratives do vital intellectual work helping us see and respond to the wider social implications of any change, asking precisely the kinds of questions that critical posthumanism also explores (and that sociotechnical change, understood only as positive innovation, disavows).[24] To continue with sentient robots, there are numerous examples that follow Asimov and yet also shift our sympathies to envision such beings as a disenfranchised class in ways that challenge anthropocentric bias and demand new ways to think about subjectivity and personhood. The popular HBO series *Westworld* (2016–) reimagines the original 1973 film to highlight how the human/nonhuman binary has been a central tool of colonial power, for example.²⁵

Both film and series invent a future in which an immersive theme park allows consumers to live out their fantasies in 3D, interacting with robots who play out typical scenarios associated with each setting – Roman World, Medieval World, Shogun World, and, of course, Westworld. The original film concerns the malfunction of a robot, which thus can violate the Asimovian law that prohibits harming humans. The film engaged with contemporary concerns about risks to human workers attendant on then-emergent automation in manufacturing: asking how fragile humanity can survive in an impersonal, robotic world. The series shifts our sympathies entirely to the robots and the trauma they experience by being repeatedly subjected to violence and sexual abuse, among other degradations of being regarded as disposable things. Symbolically, they are the native inhabitants of these "worlds," viewed as less-than-human and of value only in how they can serve the parkgoers. Thematically, then, the series pushes us to think beyond humanism less in terms of the possible personhood of non-human beings, and more in terms of the historical failure of "the human" to be a sufficiently inclusive category.

Perhaps the most significant site where sf and sociotechnical imaginaries overlap is in relation to fantasies about augmented human bodies, at times envisioned as the direct integration of the human nervous system with technology, and sometimes imagined as eschewing embodiment altogether to exist immortally as digital selves in a virtual environment. During the 1990s, such projected futures were often referred to as examples of post-humanism, that is, humanity post (default human) embodiment, and it is such visions that N. Katherine Hayles critiques in her foundational *How We Became Posthuman* (1999), another work that draws extensively on sf examples.²⁶ More recent nomenclature designates such visions as transhumanism, given their interest in transcending the mortal and vulnerable human condition. Ideologically, despite this confusion of terms, most transhumanism is diametrically opposed to posthumanist thought: critical and affirmative posthumanist traditions seek to undo the separation of humanity from the rest of the material world and related denigrations caused by a legacy of binary thinking that esteems rationality over affect, mind over body, whiteness over people of color, etc. Transhumanism, in contrast, tends to intensify such binaries and continues to fuel twenty-first-century fantasies of a privileged elite, invested in visions of immortality through technology, escaping a dying Earth in virtual bodies or by colonizing Mars, sometimes imagined as achieved in part by optimizing human bodies for extraplanetary life.

What is most pertinent about this transhumanist view is how deeply it is linked to a certain kind of speculative fiction and how substantially the sf origins of many of its ideas have been obscured as this discourse has become more mainstream. Representations of technological body transformations in both sf and popular science writing position themselves as narratives of the next stage of human evolution, a self-directed one. During the 1990s, proselytizers of this practice described themselves as Extropians: they defined extropianism as based on its root "extropy," the opposite of entropy, that is, as "the extent of a system's intelligence, information, order, vitality, and capacity for improvement."[27] They argue that current humanity is "a transitory stage in the evolutionary development of intelligence" and seek to maximize extropy through modification of their minds and bodies, via mind-uploading, nanotechnology, neuroscience, robotics, smart drugs, cognitive science, and genetics.[28] Their manifesto outlines a commitment to perpetual progress, self-transformation, practical optimism, intelligent technology, open society, self-direction, and rational thinking. Extropianism espouses a commitment to a better future but, as this list suggests, it is a future resolutely committed to individualism and libertarianism.

*The Extropian Principles* ends with a reading list that includes works of philosophy, science popularization, self-improvement primers, and sf by a number of prominent genre writers, including Greg Egan, Robert Heinlein, Jerry Pournelle, Neal Stephenson, Bruce Sterling, and Vernor Vinge. The inclusion of works of fiction alongside the science journalism shows how permeable the boundary between technological project and speculative fiction can be in the public imaginary, and indeed, several of the recommended non-fiction books draw heavily on fictional scenarios of the future as promised by technological transformation, including Hans Moravec's *Mind Children* (1988) on robotics and K. Eric Drexler's *Engines of Creation* (1986) on nanotechnology.[29] Today the Extropy Institute is a well-funded, mainstream project, abjuring any references to science fiction and offering instead links to a number of technological enterprises, including the cryogenic services of Alcor Life Extension; the biotech research non-profit organization BetterHumans; the Foresight Institute, which promotes the world-changing potential of nanotechnology and AI; and the Machine Intelligence Research Institute, previously called the Singularity Institute, whose earlier name comes from an essay extrapolating an exponential increase in machine intelligence. This essay, "The Coming

Technological Singularity: How to Survive in the Post-Human Era"
(1993), written by computer scientist and sf author Vernor Vinge, argues
that the singularity marks a moment of such profound change that
humans, as we currently exist, cannot conceive of what the world will be
after this transformation.[30] Such discourse continues today in the popular
works of Ray Kurzweil and in many sf novels, films, television series, and
videogames, such as, to name only one example from each medium,
Charles Stross' novel *Accelerando* (2005), Wally Pfister's film
*Transcendence* (2014), Netflix's *Altered Carbon* (2018-), and the game
*BioShock* (2007).[31]

As this example of transhumanist discourse demonstrates, the alternative
visions fostered in sf can have consequential, material effects. They inspire
and direct affect and, in this case, have manifested in established institutions and research programs, in centers whose venture-capital funding and
mainstream prominence may make them seem very far from sf indeed. Yet
their origins are unquestionably within the genre and thus they suggest
something of its power as a rhetorical strategy, a way of thinking about the
world and positing alternatives to an inadequate present. The various
traditions of posthumanism collected in this volume address numerous
challenges: the biotech revolutions of genomic mapping and synthetic
biology that enable us to transform living matter; new research on other
species and objects that requires us to abandon notions of an autonomous
humanity, which includes discourse of the microbial self and revelations
about plastics that demonstrate they can enter our food chains and our
bodies; anthropogenic climate change and mass extinction; the Internet of
Things, digital systems, and other surveillance technologies that have
significantly transformed access to public space, privacy, and possibilities
for employment. The remainder of this chapter considers exemplary sf
texts that offer posthumanist ways of framing and responding to these
facets of twenty-first-century life. If the intensified human of transhumanism can migrate from sf to material practice, my hope is that the more
radical posthumanist refusal of the historically limited category of the
human can have similar impact.

Early sf engagements with posthumanist themes were almost entirely
focused on questions of body modification and thus biotechnology is the
most obvious connection between contemporary posthumanist concerns
and sf – yet themes of human body transformation were a central part of sf
long before the human genome was mapped. The transhumanist movement is one side of this, but it emerges from a longer tradition of sf that
engaged with the impact of evolutionary theory on western knowledge

systems, extrapolating futures of both perfected evolution and *de*volution. The most famous example of the latter comes from H.G. Wells, especially his *The Time Machine* (1896) when his Traveler discovers, first, that class difference has so segregated humanity that in the future they have speciated into fragile Eloi and subterranean Morlocks; and, then, that in the far future humanity has no place at all on a planet that has evolved well beyond our moment of hegemony.[32] By seeing humanity as just another species subject to evolutionary change, Wells anticipates ideas important to critical posthumanist traditions. Much mid-century sf imagined futures in which humans evolved new, often-psionic powers, or futures of a humanity much changed by what seemed then to be the inevitability of a nuclear war.

Posthumanist sf that engages with motifs of body modification and evolutionary change often takes up themes of social power and discrimination, challenging a narrow and singular definition of "the human," often from a non-normative point of view. Octavia Butler, one of the most important writers of her generation, is exemplary in this regard, rewriting common sf motifs to resist conventional truisms. In the *Xenogenesis* trilogy (1987–1989), for example, she engages with discourses that see genetic engineering as an opportunity to perfect our species.[33] Rather than narrating this future as one of self-selected enhancement, genetic change is forced upon humanity by an alien species that saves a remnant population from extinction after a nuclear war. Arguing that humanity is inherently flawed in its fear of difference and its tendency to create racial and other hierarchies, these aliens insist that the only viable human is a modified one. Refusing simple answers, Butler compels us to recognize that while the aliens may be accurate in their judgment of what humanity has been, the past does not dictate its future possibilities. Moreover, ethical questions about reproductive choice are paramount over myopic solutions that see genetic engineering as the only way to change social power relations.

The more-than-human world is often at the center of sf given the genre's ability to create characters of intelligence and agency who may be alien, manufactured, or even other species given voice and a point-of-view. Such works become posthumanist when they imagine the agency of other species as part of a conversation about viable futures. Elsewhere, I've explored examples of sf that encourage us to recognize animal agency and consciousness, to argue that sf and animal studies share interest in the lives of nonhuman species and in the range of ways we might communicate, interact, and coproduce the world with them.[34] Like visions of embodied change, such imaginaries in sf long predate the current critical interest in these questions, but at the same time more recent fiction reflects new knowledge being produced in both the sciences and in posthumanist scholarship that reframes how we understand the capacities of nonhuman species. For example, David Brin's *Uplift* series (1980–1998) imagines a future in which humans have engineered primates and dolphins to parallel human sentience, narrating the experiences of a collective human-primate-dolphin civilization, but it imagines its primates and dolphins as essentially human-like figures: as characters, they think and act mainly as do humans, although their different morphology is taken into account.[35] The novels thus provide an image of a multispecies community, but do not significantly engage with the underlying reorientations of culture that would be required to approach this from a posthumanist perspective.

In contrast, Adrian Tchaikovsky's *Children of Time* (2015) imagines a future in which a nanovirus designed to engineer "intelligence" infects a species of spiders rather than the monkeys for whom it was intended.[36] The novel alternates between chapters that show the graduate emergence of a complex material and technological culture among these spiders, over hundreds of generations, and those charting the loss of technology among what remains of a human population, forced from Earth by apocalyptic warfare. Tchaikovsky pays significant attention to specificities of spiders – their physical capacities, their communicative methods, their social structures – to envision an intelligent and scientific culture that is not merely an imitation of how humanity developed. This is a truly posthumanist vision, not the incorporation of spiders into anthropocentric knowledge systems and social orders: indeed, the nanovirus has gifted the spiders with a strong capacity for empathy across difference, and it is this trait that ensures the multispecies encounter ends in a new mutualism rather than another cycle of the violence that destroyed Earth. Tchaikovsky imagines something akin to what Anna Tsing theorizes as strategies for "collaborative survival" in her ecological theory.[37]

More recent fiction has also begun to think in posthuman terms about microbial and plant life.[38] Theoretical work such as Stefanie Fishel's *The Microbial State* and Heather Paxson's notion of microbiopolitics draw on research about the human body's dependence on microbial cultures living both within us and on our skin that are necessary to the healthy functioning of human bodies.[39] Such work reconceptualizes the human not as a single and autonomous organism, but as a microbiome, a community comprised of the human organism plus its microbial collectivity, a vision of the subject that refutes the individualism and autonomy attached to liberal concepts of the abstract and universal human. Fishel and Paxson explore how we might rethink politics, agency, and environment from this point of view, ideas that find their parallel in Joan Slonczewski's fiction.

A practicing microbiologist, Slonczewski draws on her research in works such as her *Elysium* series (1986–2000) to reinvent the first-contact narrative of communicating with an alien species that is sentient at the microbial level.[40] Together with their human hosts, Slonczewski's microbes collectively share personhood, negotiating choices about actions, sharing the body through a culture of mutual respect between human and microbe. Like Butler's depiction of the difficulty of establishing heterogeneous communities of mutual respect, Slonczewski explores and challenges the conceptual reframing that is required for a human to share agency with its internal microbial communities and thereby become a new kind of posthuman subject. In her most celebrated work, *A Door into Ocean* (1986), she creates the ecofeminist science culture of the Sharers, whose technology is entirely biological and formed through an ethos of mutuality between the Sharers and the species whose biology they shape. Sharer technology is premised on the recognition that, just as they act upon plants and animals, so, too, will other species act upon them in return: their ethics thus has no concept of human exceptionalism. Similar ideas about mutualism and multispecies cooperation – as well as research on plant perception, cognition, and choice – inform Sue Burke's *Semiosis* (2018) and *Interference* (2019), about a group of ecologically committed colonists who discover that plant life is intelligent on the planet to which they have emigrated. These (post)humans work with the planet's apex plant species to set up a new community based on interspecies mutualism which accepts that difference can be recognized without instituting hierarchy.

Building on a long tradition of ecological sf, the genre has recently widely taken up themes of climate change, which can be understood as a posthuman topic from the perspective of its anthropogenic causes and the fact that it prompts us to think about the shared vulnerability of humans and other species, reinforcing that only strategies of mutualism will enable our survival. Given the far-future perspective typical of much sf, which often sets its narratives hundreds or even thousands of years into the future, the genre deftly captures the point of view necessary to grasp the complexity and scale of factors driving climate change, at times narrating from the point of view of other species or even planetary systems themselves. Some of the most significant recent sf is in this vein to name only two prominent examples, Kim Stanley Robinson's near-future *New York 2140* (2017) and

N.K. Jemisin's *The Broken Earth* trilogy (2015–2017).⁴¹ Both explore futures in which human life must fundamentally reject western, accumulative ways of living on the planet: Robinson's novel depicts a future New York that is half underwater and critiques the role of capital in producing this crisis; Jemisin's trilogy is set on an imagined world where the geography itself expresses a kind of agency and insists that we recognize that environmental justice and sustainability are inextricably connected to antiracism and decolonization.⁴²

Paolo Bacigalupi's short story "The People of Sand and Slag" (2004) innovatively links fantasies of augmented embodiment to climate change themes in a critique of transhumanism that demonstrates its vast difference from critical posthumanism.⁴³ His augmented posthumans patrol a mining operation in a future Montana, using military technology to destroy environmental activists who intrude. Effortlessly healed of injuries and able to replace damaged body parts, these future people are alienated from their own bodies, even from life itself. They surf on oil-infused seas, unconcerned with rampant razor wire and toxic pools of chemicals. Improbably, they find a stray dog which they briefly keep as a pet – inadvertently injuring it when they first capture it, not understanding that its broken bones will not instantly heal. The dog's biological fragility eventually proves too onerous a burden for people unable to conceive of the value that might come with companionship and mutual care and they decide to eat the dog, its novel flavor as food nearly as meaningful to them as its existence as an independent, communicative entity. Yet they cannot quite escape the feeling that something is missing, that they have become inhuman via their transcendence of vulnerability.

Posthumanist critique of surveillance capitalism and its reduction of living beings into data streams processed by algorithmic governance is another prominent posthuman theme.⁴⁴ Perhaps the most thorough posthumanist reimagining of the capacity of distributed IT technologies to initiate a world of posthumanist, ecologically minded collectivity – to replace the capitalist world of widespread commodification – is Karl Schroeder's *Stealing Worlds* (2019). It outlines how such technologies could be used to create structures of collective governance that give voice to the more-than-human world.⁴⁵ Schroeder critiques economic orthodoxy that deems the consequences of economic activity – disruptions of neighborhoods and ecosystems, environmental contamination, anthropogenic climate change, the depletion of resources beyond sustainability – to be "externalities." By this logic, such damage is not factored into a cost/benefit analysis of an enterprise's viability. Human activism may bring some of these factors into view, but entities such as animals, forests, rivers, and the like cannot participate in deliberative processes premised on language. Adroitly balancing speculation and materiality – and drawing on indigenous traditions that do not see personhood as a capacity of humans alone – Schroeder imagines a system in which the thousands of surveillance devices, currently used to monitor human activity, are redirected to capture real-time data about environmental conditions. Powerful AIs who synthetize this data are programmed to operate as agents speaking for the collective needs and desires of such entities: that is, instead of programming the AI to think of itself as an ersatz human, Schroeder imagines AIs that embody the agency of and can speak for nonhuman entities, not as anthropocentric fantasies of speaking for the other, but grounded in the concrete materiality of empirical data.

These few examples attest to the range of ways that sf can be a posthumanist practice. Although the genre is not inherently oriented toward posthuman frameworks of greater social justice, it offers a set of tools well-suited to this project, able imaginatively to craft the human and the world anew. The genre offers a deep archive of ways of thinking about different embodiment, nonhuman agency, and diverse futures, often at scales far beyond a human lifetime, at times beyond the lifetime of our species. It is thus a valuable methodology for rethinking our species to make a more livable world.

## Notes

1. For more on this version of the posthuman, see Chapter 6 of this volume.
2. Stacy Alaimo, *Bodily Natures: Science, Environment, and the Material Self* (Bloomington: Indiana University Press, 2010). See also Chapter 12 of this volume.
3. See further Chapter 8 of this volume.
4. N. Katherine Hayles, *Unthought: The Power of Cognitive Nonconscious* (Chicago: The University of Chicago Press, 2017).
5. Chapter 1 of this volume.
6. Thomas Foster, *The Souls of Cyberfolk: Posthumanism as Vernacular Theory* (Minneapolis: University of Minnesota Press, 2005).
7. Ursula K. Le Guin, *The Left Hand of Darkness* (New York, NY: Ace Books, 2019).
8. The gender-specific language is intended here. As Sylvia Wynter powerfully argues, this version of the human is constitutively masculine and white. See Sylvia Wynter, "Unsettling the Coloniality of Being/Power/Truth/Freedom: Towards the Human, After Man, Its Overrepresentation – An Argument," *CR: The New Centennial Review*, 3(3) (2003), 257–337.

9. This way of defining and thinking about sf is influenced by Carl Freedman's work, which argues for understanding sf generally as a kind of critical theory, and Istvan Csicsery-Ronay's work, which suggests that sf is less a genre than a mode of perceiving and asking questions about the given world. See Carl Freedman, *Critical Theory and Science Fiction* (Middletown: Wesleyan University Press, 2000); and Istvan Csicsery-Ronay, Jr., *The Seven Beauties of Science Fiction* (Middletown: Wesleyan University Press, 2011).

10. Rosi Braidotti, *The Posthuman* (Cambridge: Polity Press, 2013). See Mark Bould and China Miéville (eds.), *Red Planets: Marxism and Science Fiction* (Middletown: Wesleyan University Press, 2009) for a discussion of this definition for science fiction, via the work of Darko Suvin, including challenges to it, and its legacy of shaping the field.

11. Tom Moylan, *Demand the Impossible: Science Fiction and the Utopian Imagination* (New York: Methuen, 1986). Fredric Jameson, *Archaeologies of the Future: The Desire Called Utopia and Other Science Fictions* (New York: Verso, 2005).

12. Ernest Bloch, *The Principle of Hope*, trans. Neville Plaice, Stephen Plaice, and Paul Knight, 3 vols (Cambridge: MIT Press, 1986).

13. Joseph McElroy, *Plus* (New York: Knopf, 1976). Jean-François Lyotard, "Can Thought Go On Without a Body?" in *The Inhuman: Reflections on Time*, trans. Geoffrey Bennington and Rachel Bowlby (Stanford: Stanford University Press, 1988).

14. See Bruno Latour, *Aramis or the Love of Technology*, trans. Catherine Porter (Cambridge: Harvard University Press, 1996). Latour coins the term actant to avoid the anthropocentric assumptions he argues are inevitable with the term actor.

15. William Gibson, *Neuromancer* (New York: Ace Books, 1984). This is the first of a long line of sf novels singled out as particularly important for the development of ideas about online cultures, followed most influentially by Neal Stephenson's *Snow Crash* (New York: Bantam, 1992) and more recently by Ernest Cline's *Ready Player One* (New York: Penguin, 2011).

16. Jeff VanderMeer, *Area X: The Southern Reach Trilogy* (New York, NY: Farrar, Straus and Giroux, 2014). Timothy Morton, *Humankind: Solidarity with Nonhuman People* (New York: Verso, 2017). For more on new materialisms and posthumanism, see Chapter 12 of this volume. For more on speculative realism and posthumanism, see Chapter 13 of this volume.

17. Gerry Canavan and Andrew Hageman, "Introduction: 'Global Weirding,'" *Paradoxa* 28 (2016), 7.

18. Mary Shelley, *Frankenstein: The 1818 Text* (New York: Penguin Books, 2018). H. G. Wells, *The War of the Worlds* (New York: Penguin Books, 2005).

19. Rosi Braidotti, *Posthuman Knowledge* (Cambridge: Polity Press, 2019), 165.

20. Joanna Russ, *The Female Man* (Boston: Beacon Press, 2000).

21. Isaac Asimov, *I, Robot* (New York: Signet Books, 1956). Several of the stories clearly show the robots' dissatisfaction with their inferior social status, but Asimov's sympathies remain firmly with the human overlords.

22. Donna J. Haraway, "A Cyborg Manifesto: Science, Technology, and Socialist-Feminism in the Late Twentieth Century," in *Simians, Cyborgs and Women: The Reinvention of Nature* (New York: Routledge, 1991), 149–81.

23. Sheila Jasanoff, "Future Imperfect: Science, Technology, and the Imaginations of Modernity," in S. Jasanoff and S. H. Kim (eds.), *Dreamscapes of Modernity: Sociotechnical Imaginaries and the Fabrication of Power* (Chicago: University of Chicago Press, 2015), 4.

24. For more on the negotiations between creative practice and industry appropriation, see Chapter 16 of this volume.

25. For a more detailed reading of the series along these lines, see my "Long Live the New Flesh: Race and the Posthuman in *Westworld*," in A. Goody and A. Mackay (eds.), *Reading Westworld* (London: Palgrave Macmillan, 2019), 141–60. For an in-depth critique of humanization as a racial, colonial project, see Chapter 14 of this volume.

26. N. Katherine Hayles, *How We Became Posthuman: Virtual Bodies in Cybernetics, Literature, and Infomatics* (Chicago: University of Chicago Press, 1999). For more on the difference between transhumanism and posthumanism, and for another reading of the posthumanist possibilities for human-machine hybrids, see Chapter 6 of this volume.

27. The quotations are from Max More's *The Extropian Principles Version 3.0: A Transhumanist Declaration* (1998), a key document on the extropy website before 2000. It is still accessible via the Internet Wayback Machine at http://web.archive.org/web/19990203001302/www.extropy.org/extprn3.htm. All further quotations regarding Extropian practice come from this page.

28. See, for just one example, Steve Fuller, *Humanity 2.0: What is Means to be Human, Past, Present and Future* (New York: Palgrave Macmillan, 2011).

29. Hans Moravec, *Mind Children: The Future of Robot and Human Intelligence* (Cambridge: Harvard University Press, 1988). Eric K. Dexler, *Engines of Creation: The Coming Era of Nanotechnology* (Garden City, NY: Anchor Press/Doubleday, 1990). Moravec is strongly critiqued by Hayles in *How We Became Posthuman*. Colin Milburn provides a similarly excellent analysis of Drexler's discourse from the point of view of science studies and sf studies in *Nanovision: Engineering the Future* (Durham: Duke University Press, 2008).

30. Vernor Vinge, "The Coming Technological Singularity: How to Survive in a Post-Human Era," Presented at NASA Vision-21 Symposium, online.

31. Ray Kurzweil, *The Singularity is Near: When Humans Transcend Biology* (New York: Penguin, 2006). Charles Stross, *Accelerando* (London: Penguin, 2005).

32. H. G. Wells, *The Time Machine* (New York: Signet Classics, 2014).

33. The trilogy consists of *Dawn* (New York: Warner Aspect, 1987), *Adulthood Rites* (New York: Warner Aspect, 1988), and *Imago* (New York: Warner Aspect, 1989).

34. Sherryl Vint, *Animal Alterity: Science Fiction and the Question of the Animal* (Liverpool: Liverpool University Press, 2010).
35. The novels are *Sundiver* (New York: Spectra, 1980), *Startide Rising* (New York: Spectra, 1983), *The Uplift War* (New York: Spectra, 1987), *Brightness Reef* (New York: Spectra, 1995), *Infinity's Shore* (New York: Spectra, 1996), and *Heaven's Reach* (New York: Spectra, 1998).
36. Adrian Tchaikovsky, *Children of Time* (New York: TOR, 2015).
37. Anna L. Tsing, *The Mushroom at the End of the World: On the Possibility of Life in Capitalist Ruins* (Princeton: Princeton University Press, 2015), 2.
38. For more on the human as microbiome, see Chapters 8 and 16 of this volume.
39. Heather Paxson, "Post-Pasteurian Cultures: The Microbiopolitics of Raw-Milk Cheese in the United States," *Cultural Anthropology*, 23(1) (2008), 15–47. Stefanie R. Fishel, *The Microbial State: Global Thriving and the Body Politic* (Minneapolis: University of Minnesota Press, 2017).
40. Joan Slonczewski, *A Door into Ocean* (New York, NY: Avon Books, 1986); Joan Slonczewski, *Daughters of Elysium* (New York: William Morrow, 1993); Joan Slonczewski, *The Children Star* (New York: TOR, 1998); Joan Slonczewski, *Brain Plague* (New York: TOR, 2000).
41. Kim Stanley Robinson, *New York 2140* (New York: Orbit, 2017). J. K. Jemisin, *The Fifth Season* (New York: Orbit, 2016); N. K. Jemisin, *The Obelisk Gate* (New York: Orbit, 2016); J. K. Jemisin, *The Stone Sky* (New York: Orbit, 2017).
42. For more on climate change, capitalism, and colonialism, in their relation to the posthuman, see Chapter 9 of this volume.
43. Paolo Bacigalupi, "The People of Sand and Slag," *Fantasy & Science Fiction*, 106 (2) (2004), 6–29.
44. The most important writers working in this tradition are Cory Doctorow, Lauren Beukes, and Karl Schroeder. Doctorow is a technology activist as well as sf writer, focused on revising copyright laws towards creative commons and strategies for post-scarcity economics. Beukes is a South African writer, and thus her work prominently takes up the consequences of globalization, as for example in *Moxyland* (Johannesburg: Jacana Media, 2008).
45. Karl Schroeder, *Stealing Worlds* (New York: Tor, 2019).

CHAPTER 16

# *Aesthetic Manipulation of Life*

## Ionat Zurr and Oron Catts

> Meaning in a whole lot of life is necessarily tied to functionality; meaning is about getting something done, and you need it. You need meaning to mean something that you can do. Function is fine, but if meaning is totally functional, you've got nothing but a very boring machine. And that is not biology![1]

Humans are indeed a complex and paradoxical species; in recent times we are increasingly making our human-made dry, hard, electrical, mechanical, digital, and algorithmic technologies more lifelike (i.e., the economy, driverless cars, artificial intelligence systems), while at the same time we are treating biological, moist, messy life more as controllable technologies. What are the reasons that compel humans to attempt to assert control over living systems that exist independently from us (or are us!), while at the same time relinquishing control over non-living technologies, computer-generated algorithms, and other human-made systems? This question is especially vital (pun intended) in times of environmental emergency and the collapse of the idea of "Humanism."

It is not a coincidence that the idea of the Enlighted Humanities is in crisis and it is entangled with – what is referred to as – The Biological Age.[2] Humans have tried to understand their selves/bodies and their position in the world predominantly through metaphors based on evolving technologies, from the mechanical view to the digital code. Now, when biological bodies themselves become a technology, what kind of a metaphor can we use to try to explain ourselves and our place on Earth? Art can at least help us identify the issues and the questions we need to confront. From synthetic biology and regenerative medicine, through neuroengineering and soft robotics, to geoengineering, life is becoming a technology, a raw material waiting to be engineered – thus providing a new pallet of artistic expression in which life is both the object and the subject matter.

Living in times of technological acceleration and unfolding ecological catastrophe, when fact and fiction are becoming indistinguishable, we face

236

a poverty of available metaphors and, more importantly, a poverty of our language in relation to *Life*.[3] This lack is being populated by artistic *sensual* language, where artists engage with the materiality of biological bodies to articulate new meanings and poetics. While scientists/technologists are performing radical acts on life in laboratories for instrumental purposes, scholars from the humanities are still dealing with the breakdown of the Human concept. Artists who are trained in more-than-human sensorial literacy are acting as the creators of a new "language," developing new meanings for the concept of Life; exposing unintentional ontological breaches; relinquishing epistemological knowledge from its disciplining; and calling for the urgent need for cultural and artistic scrutiny of the concept of life. This scrutiny goes beyond the human to involve non/more-than-human agents, through direct and experiential engagement.[4]

Here, we will explore these phenomena through the genre of BioArt (also called Biological Art), which gained momentum from the mid-nineties and had effects beyond the art world, impacting industry and the public imagination. Specifically, we will explore some of the artists/artworks and their relations to the idea of more-than-human or multi-species entanglements. After demystifying what so-called BioArt is, we will explore its relations with knowledge systems, politics, ethics, and ontologies to unravel what may be the end of Man as we know it.

## 16.1 BioArt

BioArt is an artistic practice that involves the use of living biological systems. What differentiates it from previous genres such as earth art, live art, etc. is that, in most cases, the biological systems are manipulated and/or modified by the artist using modern technology and engineering biology as opposed to traditional modes of biological intervention. BioArt is a diverse field with many voices, ranging from the speculative to the actual, from the celebratory to the disappointing, from the techno-utopian to the contestable, all using living biological systems as part of the process of art making.[5]

BioArt deals with the theory, practice, aesthetics, application, and implications of the life sciences; creating a platform that actively engages in raising awareness, by proposing different directions in which knowledge can be applied and technology can be employed. This can be seen as cultural scrutiny in action, articulating and subverting the ever-changing relationship to life. Some artists working with life manipulation adopt a more traditional, formalist approach in which life becomes a raw material for aesthetic expressions concerned with form, perspective, color, composition, etc. that is supposedly devoid of socio-politico context; this approach by itself is contestable, especially when life is a medium of manipulation. Much of the work of biological artists seems to be transgressive, trespassing into areas where "art should not go." Yet it often does little more than culturally frame and articulate meanings to the manipulations of life that have become commonplace in the scientific laboratory.[6] BioArt is not a movement with a coherent manifesto; it is merely an umbrella term to describe art that manipulates living systems as both its subject and its object matter, emphasizing hands-on engagement with material agencies.

For the purpose of this chapter we chose to explore artworks in their complex relations with the disintegration of the coherence of the perceived Enlightenment, rational humanist framework, suggesting what we believe BioArt can offer: a more secular-vitalist, post-humanistic, and post-anthropocentric position. We will look at BioArt contesting (1) knowledge systems, (2) political and economic systems, (3) the fragmentation of the biological body, and (4) art for more-than-human.

## 16.2   Knowledge Systems (DNA Chauvinism)

BioArt has a complex relationship with contemporary scientific knowledge, especially science's roots in the enlightenment era and its privileging of the rational and objective scientist,[7] and it follows scientific prescribed reductionist and anthropocentric biases.[8] One of the major shifts that occurred recently in the "posthuman" transition is the questioning of the scientific central dogma in molecular biology,[9] marking a shift from the reductionist idea of life as a (genetic) code to a more complex and context-dependent understanding of life that emerges in the field of epigenetics.[10] This new understanding of biology as a situated knowledge has been central as well to cultural traditions of eco-feminist and eco-materialist thinking, focused on material response-ability.[11]

Looking at the hype and disappointments following the promises of the Human Genome Project in 2003 and the current emergence of the synthetic biology field, we witness a recurring tension in the scientific community about the role of and emphasis on the centrality of DNA and genes in the understanding of life. Some scholars have written about it, referring to areas such as developmental biology and epigenetics, while some artists use this vocabulary to expose our human limitations and hubris in conceptualizing life as a DNA-centric code program.[12]

Focusing on the human, Paul Vanouse and Heather Dewey-Hagborg attempt to debunk "Genohype" by looking at the ideologies behind and the ramification of DNA data collection and its human interpretations.[13] *Latent Figure Protocol* (2007) uses the scientific technique commonly known as DNA Fingerprinting to construct live images in the gallery. These abstract images associated with DNA Fingerprinting as signifiers of "truth" are transforming slowly within the gallery space into familiar, socially constructed images such as the binary code, a skull-and-crossbones, or the copyright symbols. Vanouse's artwork explains how science is deeply embedded in the prevailing cultural value-system of its time, by exposing how what is deliberately and inaccurately labelled DNA Fingerprinting is a technique measuring and comparing length of DNA segments that can be interpreted and misinterpreted depending on context – contesting the popular saying, "you are your DNA."

Dewey-Hagborg follows similar criticism that, ironically, has been received by many critics and viewers alike as a literal interpretation of what the artist is mocking: the power of genetic surveillance. In *Stranger Visions* (2012) DNA extracted from discarded hairs, chewed-up gum, and cigarette butts is analyzed computationally to generate 3D-printed portraits representing what those human individuals *might* look like. The project intended to contest genetic determinism but became a vehicle in the seductive, reductionist ways humans would like to make sense of life.

Not all artists using genetic technologies for artistic expression attempt to question what can be referred to as traditional artistic or scientific knowledge systems. Eduardo Kac uses Judeo-Christian religious themes in his artworks that involve genetic engineering, such as *Genesis* (2000) and *The Eighth Day* (2001), a technique that seems to be at odds with more critical posthumanist perspectives. Audiences are given the power (dominion?) to mutate bacterial DNA by turning on a UV lamp, in the gallery space or via an internet connection.

We have created works that extensively critique the understanding of life via the genetic code. Furthermore, our work implies that such a vision is a continuation of the patriarchal, anthropocentric view: in other words, it is simply "DNA Chauvinism."[14] As humans engineer living systems, life forms are isolated and reduced to their component parts, in essence privileging the DNA as information over context. Furthermore, the emphasis on the packet of DNA as "life itself" reflects a male, human anxiety in regard to their contribution to procreation, as the male transmits only the DNA within a sperm, while the female (in addition to her DNA contribution) provides the cell (ovum) with all of its "machinery," as well as the milieu in which the embryo and fetus develop.

The *Pig Wings Project* (2000–2001) was commissioned (only to then be rejected) by the Wellcome Trust to celebrate the completion of the so-called first draft of the Human Genome: the project is critical of Genohype, that is, the discourse of exaggerated claims and overstatements concerning DNA and the Human Genome Mapping Project. Genohype is used in relation to the hyperbolic discourse within genetic research and its applied outcomes, whether positive or negative. One of the effects of Genohype is that genetics has become synonymous with all life sciences. In the *Pig Wings Project*, we grew three sets of wings made out of pig mesenchymal cells – bone marrow stem cells – over biodegradable polymers. Rather than manipulating these cells genetically, we let each cell culture differentiate dependent upon the "incubated" context – the matrix in which it was grown; the nutrients available; the micro gravity environment it developed within. The project referred loosely to the proverbial saying "If Pigs Could Fly." Grown for approximately nine months, each wing measured 4 cm × 2 cm × 0.5 cm. Fairly small and less than spectacular, these objects were presented to audiences expecting to see celebration of the wonders and supremacy of techno-science. The *Pig Wings* purposely used the aesthetic of disappointment as a rebellious act against the promise of engineering biology – human control and dominion.

Many of the artists working in the BioArt field ask the viewer to become complicit with or otherwise interact with the living artwork, to expose in somewhat more visceral ways our complex and often hypocritical relations with the living world around us. Examples range from one of the more infamous artworks, *Alba* (2000), in which the artist Eduardo Kac engaged the public in a campaign to release a genetically modified rabbit from the confines of a laboratory located in France. Rabbits, as well as many other organisms (fish, plants, mice, monkeys), have been genetically engineered to incorporate into their genome a gene that expresses a green fluorescent protein (GFP) originally taken from the Aequorea Victoria jellyfish. The engineered organism exhibits green fluorescence (in some or all of its cells and organs) when exposed to light in the blue to ultraviolet range. By engaging the audience in his campaign, Kac raised many questions, including the relationship to the "new" Other, in this case to an individual, modified animal (pet); the release of genetically modified organisms into the environment; using biotechnology for biomedical purposes versus artistic ones; and the nationalist sentiments that stem from the request to release a rabbit engineered in France by the hands of an American artist.

In another cellular work created at the SymbioticA Laboratory at the University of Western Australia, artist Guy Ben-Ary and collaborators used the artist's skin cells that had been engineered to become neurons, using a technology called induced pluripotent stem cell (iPS). These cells were grown in a Petri dish over a multi-electrode array and connected to an array of analogue, modular synthesizers to play with human musicians. The piece titled *CellF* (2015) offers humans the ability to play "music" together with an in vitro, agential, "semi-living" entity.[15]

Our own earlier projects involved the audience in the practice of being with life by inviting them for the acts of feeding and killing. The grown artistic tissue constructs – *The Semi Living* – were exhibited alive and in need of care, were fed with nutrient media in front of the audience, and, by the end of the exhibition, were also killed with audience involvement. The killing was subtle; these cellular artworks were removed from their protective sterile containment and exposed to the external environment, filled with other lifeforms such as bacteria and fungi that would lead to their demise. Additionally, the audience was invited to touch the tissue sculptures to hasten this death.

## 16.3   Political and Economic Systems (Gadgeteering)

Artists willingly or unwillingly play a pivotal role in public engagement with life science and engineering. Artists are seen as either raising awareness of technoscientific developments, as domesticating or even promoting these developments, or as suggesting future scenarios. Some initiatives have been actively trying to recruit artists to create public acceptance for technologies not yet realized, such as in the case of the early days of synthetic biology, or the current S+T+ARTS (Science, Technology, and the Arts) awards in the European Union.[16]

As a result, some biological artists continue the genre of Critical/Tactical media arts – in which the artists actively critique, question, and problematize biotechnological developments as well as the socio-economic contexts in which they operate.[17] Critical Art Ensemble (CAE), formed in 1987, are a collective that explore the intersections among art, critical theory, technology, and political activism. In the late 1990s, they turned their focus to biotechnology and created a series of works which criticize the capitalist agenda as it manifests in biotech. For example, in the *Cult of the New Eve* (2000), CAE/Vanouse/Wilding contest the "Christian promissory rhetoric" employed by the "authoritative" scientific and biotech institutions by making it into the "least legitimate" social system, the cult. The artwork itself was a performative, participatory installation in which statements and promotional text from "biotech leaders" were used as scripture, and scientific techniques were performed and packaged in a cult-like manner for participants.

In *Open Source Oestrogen* (2015), Mary Maggic and her collaborators employed DIY techniques to synthesize estrogen "in the kitchen," using easily accessible materials and objects. The project combines hands-on expertise and information with workshops, as well as a series of witty, instructional, and conceptual videos and graphics purposely suggesting lowbrow aesthetics. The project looks at marginalized bodies (women, queers), their biopolitical relations with patriarchal hegemony, and their access to the biotechnological products controlled by pharmaceutical companies. In Maggic's words, "It is a form of biotechnical civil disobedience, seeking to subvert dominant biopolitical agents of hormonal management, knowledge production, and anthropogenic toxicity."[18]

Maggic's project, coming out of the MIT Media Lab in Boston, may be seen as anomaly in that it conforms to techniques of a performative, interventionist artistic genre rather than an artist creating an object/product. Most of the artworks/design works coming from the MIT Media Lab (as opposed, for example, to SymbioticA) represent a shift in the field – from critical art and into arts in the service of "innovation." Many of such projects offer mainly speculative, applied artefacts that convey more utility and applied art, rather than endorse a notion of art as frivolous, poetic, and reflexive. There are many examples of such expressions of the aesthetics of innovation, from lamps employing bacteria or algae that are genetically modified to glow; bacterial pads for women's vaginal hygiene, *Future Flora* (2019); to a wearable for consuming and digesting biomass that absorbs nutrients and expels waste, *Mushtari*, by artist Neri Oxman. Such speculative works, what we refer to as "Gadgeteering Art," tend to play on the notion that new and innovative kits/gadgets/products offer solutions for a better world, achieved via yet more consumption. Furthermore, some of these works present biological impossibilities as future fixes.

What is unique and important in BioArt is the intimate relations it cultivates with biological materials and their agencies. Working with living materials, artists learn humanity's limited abilities to control living materials and processes, which hopefully leads to a more nuanced, humble, posthuman approach that questions the idea of the living world as material easily engineered and controlled for human consumption, needs, and desires. Every person working in the lab, whether a scientist or an artist, is acutely aware that precisely engineering life is extremely difficult, if even possible at all.

## 16.4 Human Bodies and Perception (Bodies as Ecologies)

Some artists question the basic notion of the *human* and regard the species as an ecology rather than an entity. Furthermore, the human is part of a larger ecology, with non-anthropocentric diversities and hierarchies. In *Human Thrush Entanglements* (2015), Tarsh Bates creates different encounters between humans and *Candida albicans* (that is, thrush). The audience is invited to be immersed in a video projection of candida's growth and differentiation; to play cards with the different "sexualities" of Candida; or get literally intimate with Candida by consuming bread leavened with the candida (a yeast), purposely playing with our anthropocentric reactions of pleasure and disgust towards critters that are part of us. "A more-than-human fleshiness is activated through considerations of the aesthetic experiences of Candida during its encounters with the human body ... positioning humans and Candida as co-evolved companion species involved in a biopolitical entanglement that is gendered, sexual and often ruthless."[19]

The human as an ecology which consists at least 50% of nonhuman cells (what is referred to in the sciences as microbiome) is also explored by Kathy High, who looks at the promises and perils of fecal transplant in the treatment of human autoimmune diseases.[20] *Gut Love* (2017) "embraces metaphors of interspecies love, immunology and bacteria as it examines research in faecal microbial transplants and gut biomes to better understand the importance of bacteria's function in our bodies."[21] Rather than looking at the human as an Enlighted rational individual, these artists offer a different point of view on what the human is: its gut flora has an important role in defining each "human" in terms of health, emotional state, cognitive state, and so on. Are we the vessels for our microbiomes? If we receive a fecal transplant from a loved/admired person – High requested a donation from David Bowie! – would we get closer together?

Anna Dumitriu's artworks use different kinds of bacteria as subject matter and materiality. Positioning herself as an artist in the service of science communication, her fine art objects are illustrations of some of the characteristics of different bacteria and their relations with humans through history, such as stories about plague in *Plague Dress* (2018), to the current problem of antibiotics resistance in *Superbugs* (2017). The works offer a glimpse of our nonhuman bacteria companions through human-centric narratives.

## 16.5  Art for More-Than-Humans (After the Man)

Synthetic biology is a new interdisciplinary area that engages with the application of engineering principles and mindsets as they apply to biology. Ironically, DNA chauvinism has its comeback via the engineering mindset that enters biology when principles and metaphors from the engineering world are applied to physical, conceptual, and ethical complexities involved with life and the living. This approach is happening as humans are entering the phase of the sixth mass extinction event.

Many biological artists look at the current climate emergency and the extinction of nonhuman species through the soundscapes, smells, and other sensorial information that will disappear with these tragic losses. Some of these artists use synthetic biology to respond. One of the promises coming from synthetic biology is the call for de-extinction or Resurrection Biology which plans to bring species back from extinction using leftover DNA fragments.[22] This discussion follows the patriarchal, reductionist scientific dogma and suppresses discussion concerned with the importance of the ova, womb, microbiome, environmental factors, and socialization as integral parts of the development of an animal, let alone an entire species.

Artists are purposely infiltrating this area to create contestable artworks. For example, Daisy Ginsberg's *Substitute* (2018) is concerned with whether we can create a non-living substitute for extinct animals that will sound, look, and "almost behave" like the living ones. Having access to the sounds left by the last remaining northern white rhinoceros (*Ceratotherium simum cottoni*), a species now extinct, Ginsberg asks:

> We briefly mourned a subspecies lost to human desire for the imagined life-enhancing properties of its horn, comforted that it might be brought back using biotechnology, albeit gestated by a different subspecies. But would humans protect a resurrected rhino, having decimated an entire species? And would this new rhino be real?[23]

Instead Ginsberg ironically offers a substitute: a life-size projection, 5 m wide that shows the artificial rhino roaming in a virtual world, becoming more "real" through artificial intelligence (AI). As the artificial rhino habituates to its space, its form shifts from pixelated to lifelike, reminding the viewer that this living, breathing rhino, coming to life without its natural context, is entirely artificial. The rhino's behaviors and sounds are adapted from rare research footage of the last herd, to which the artist had access.

Will this de-contextualized, non-biological substitute function better in the future? Should similar thinking apply to the human species in an "After the Human" world? Rather than a substitute, Ginsberg, along with smell researcher and artist Sissel Tolaas and an interdisciplinary team of researchers and engineers from the biotechnology company Ginkgo Bioworks, led by Creative Director Dr. Christina Agapakis, offer, as an artistic project, to resurrect the smell of extinct flowers by using small fragments of DNA extracted from specimens of three flowers stored at Harvard University's Herbaria. Using synthetic biology techniques, they predict and resynthesize gene sequences that might encode for fragrance-producing enzymes. The installation offers an open environment in which the smells are diffused and mixed, introducing contingency: there is no exact smell, and the scent of the human audience is also part of that mix.

## 16.6   What is Life?

BioArts have moved the domain of manipulated and engineered life from the biological laboratory and into the art gallery, liberating these life forms and the know-how associated with their creation and modification from the biomedical realm into a much broader cultural context – opening up other spaces for engineered life. Not surprisingly, in the context of the neoliberal innovation paradigm, engineered life today seems like a great resource to be exploited, to become part of the world of consumer products – not always in accordance with, and sometimes against, the artists' intentions.

Some artworks became an inspiration or proof of concept for capitalist technoscientific endeavors. For example, Joe Davis' artwork *Microvenus* (developed in the mid-1980s and presented for the first time in 2000 as part of Ars Electronica festival) was concerned with early attempts at steganographic encoding of cultural messages and images for future generations or extraterrestrial cultures. The scientist entrepreneur Craig Venter used a similar technique in 2010 to embed "watermarks" in the human-made bacterial genome *Mycoplasma laboratorium* or Synthia. While Davis' expression was poetic, Venter's seems prosaic, and it reflects on a future where biological products will be "watermarked" for intellectual property purposes.

Some artists' engagements – even if critical, full of irony and subversion – have been adopted by the sciences and by industry. Arguably the best example is found in the growing field of cellular agriculture:[24] consider the example of in vitro meat, that is, (the idea of) manufacturing meat products through tissue-engineering (TE) technology with the aim to produce animal meat without using an animal; this concept has moved from the realm of science fiction into a burgeoning industry. In 2019, there are three very active countries in cultured meat research: the United States of America, mainly California, with companies such as Memphis Meats, Hampton Creek/Just, and Finless Foods; the Netherlands, with MosaMeat; and Israel, with Supermeat and The Kitchen Foodtech Hub. Japan could become a further hotspot of research with the open-source Shojinmeat Project, as well as Singapore, given a recent move by A*STAR to support local start-ups.

About twenty years ago, in 2000, while we were research fellows at the Tissue Engineering and Organ Fabrication Laboratory at MGH Harvard Medical School, we grew the first in vitro "steak," made up of cells taken from a sheep fetus in an in utero tissue engineering experiment. Our motivation for growing in vitro "steak" was not concerned with innovation, commercialization, or finding an alternative meat production. Rather, it was about cultural articulations of new knowledge and technologies and with ontological pondering on the ability to eat meat that comes from "no body" – and in this case, a body that is yet to be born. In 2003, our lab-grown, in vitro meat was consumed by the public for the first time as part of an artistic performance in France entitled *Disembodied Cuisine*. A similar performance was conducted, ten years later, when scientist Mark Post, bankrolled by Google's Sergey Brin, live-streamed the "reveal" of the first lab-grown beef hamburger as part of a performance of cooking and consumption.

This is a case of science imitates art.

The irony and critique in our works concerned with the *Victimless Steak* (and our artwork *Victimless Leather* in 2004) were completely absorbed into a narrative of innovation. One complication arising from the victimless meat endeavor as a manifestation of the techno-scientific project is that it may create an illusion of a victimless existence. First, in order to grow in vitro meat, there is still the need for a serum created using animal blood plasma. Although there is some research to find alternatives for this ingredient, to-date there is no effective, publicly released solution and animals (mainly calves or fetal bovine) are still scarified for that ingredient. Second, growing meat in the lab "outsources" all of the bodily functions of the animal to technology, and all the "costs" concerned with running such a laboratory – fossil fuels burned, greenhouse gases produced, water and trees consumed, miles traveled, and the waste created – are often overlooked. Third, there is a shift from an idea of nature as "red in tooth and claw" to a mediated nature. The victims are pushed further away; they still exist but are much more implicit. Hence, the animal is abstracted into fragments and mediated through technological apparatuses.

The simple solution to the environmental and ethical problems associated with the meat industry is to consume *less* meat. However, this is not an option within a capitalist, growth-driven agenda.[25] The shift of life towards being understood as a commodity prompted us to stage our exhibition *Biomess* in 2018. *Biomess* celebrated and challenged the strangeness of life by using luxury retail aesthetics to make non-charismatic, queer life forms (modified or found) into objects of desire. It examined the attitudes, implications, and procedural aspects of presenting critical and reflexive biological art in a "monstrous" hybrid of different cultural settings and their related values.

First shown at the Art Gallery of Western Australia, *Biomess* was a collaboration with the Western Australian Museum and the Gallery of Western Australia. The exhibition included a contribution from a design manufacturer for luxury retail shops. The intention was to aesthetically, conceptually, and practically cross, fuse, and contrast different institutional and curatorial conventions: The Art Gallery, The Natural History Museum, and a high-end retail shop. The exhibition combined living organisms, natural history specimens, and lab-grown life ("semi-livings"), arranged in a "bio-Gucci"-style environment. Thus, the *Biomess* installation acted as both a loose narrative and a critique of the anthropocentric view of living organisms (and life in general).

Within the installation, two rooms mirror each other. One presents organisms that evolve and adapt to our shared environment, devoid of purpose and intentionally.[26] The other room exhibits organisms designed by humans – Hybridomas – products of intentional manipulation: organisms dependent on human technology for their survival.[27] The Hybridoma was placed in a custom-designed bioreactor within a deconstructed and decommissioned laboratory incubator: a "technical object" torn apart to reveal the unstable, messy "epistemic thing" within. Our work reflects our conviction that both living and "semi-living" entities are mysterious and not under full human control and comprehension. The design of the installation, however, brings into question human forays into a new era of exploration and exploitation of biological life as a new commodity to satisfy unfulfilled desires.

Increasingly, life has become a raw material for human desires. From Jacques Loeb's calls in the early twentieth century to make biology into an engineering pursuit to contemporary synthetic biology and biofabrication, constructed and engineered forms of life continually escape science labs to become a medium for artistic expression and consumer products. These new life forms, which defy classification, rapidly appear while, at the same time, we still do not understand many existing life forms. Living and semi-living artworks embody, bring into question, and problematize anthropocentric assumptions. Our times are characterized by human attempts, on a global scale, to engineer and commodify life and its milieu, including human life. *Biomess* celebrates the messiness, subversion, and rule-defying nature of life. It reminds us that the human animal is an integrated part of the wonderful monstrosities called living systems. This work of art forced us, the artists, to take full responsibility and the duty of care for the living organisms on display and to deal directly with the problematics raised by using life in a human artistic activity.

Every biological artwork is a testimony of unequal collaboration and loss of control.

Biological artworks are ephemeral, transient, and, by the end of the performative duration, they leave relics of remembrance. But what will be remembered "After the Human" if there are no humans to remember? Can artists make meaningful art for a nonhuman world?

This aesthetically driven and confrontational treatment of life by artists can create an uneasy feeling about the levels of manipulation enacted upon living systems. This uneasiness seems to stem from the fact that current cultural values and belief systems appear ill-prepared to deal with the consequences of applied knowledge in the life sciences. Life is going through major transformations, even if these might be more perceptual then actual thus far. Through rigorous, critical, and indeed wondrous explorations in the life science laboratory, BioArt begins a dialogue that engages with the extraordinary potentials and pitfalls of our new approaches to life itself.

As artists working with life, we are acutely aware that the evolutionary timescale is vastly longer than that of human comprehension. Humans have existed in this timescale for only a brief moment. As humans we are compelled to try to make sense of and meanings from our existence while the act of being alive extends to manipulating our environments, ourselves, and everything in between – humbly learning again and again that everything we know is through our limited sensorial abilities to rejoice with the complexities of this world.

Going full circle to our opening premise that we lack metaphors to understand ourselves now that we treat bodies as technologies, can the field of so-called BioArt begin to provide us with some of the needed vocabulary? Is the role of the artist in conceptualizing a new language to help us perceive and respond to this situation by making new and alternative meanings? Rather than using the engineering vocabulary of control and standardization, what is the language of the arts? Before relinquishing all control and realizing that we are only a fragment of a vast history, present, and future of this planet, it may be meaningful to develop a language grounded in fact, in searching, rigorous knowledge that remains respectful in accepting that there is something *special* about life that is beyond our own comprehension (because we are life!). A language that is (carbon-biased), secular-vitalist, and furthermore, compassionate to all gradients of life from the molecular to the cosmos.

Maybe all we are left with is the notion that life is biodegradable art!

## Notes

1. Haraway in conversation with Drew Endy in Donna J. Haraway and Drew Endy, "Tools for Multispecies Futures," *The Journal of Design and Science* (October 3, 2019), online.
2. Nikolas Rose, "The Human Sciences in a Biological Age," *Theory Culture & Society*, 30 (1) (2013), 3–34.
3. For more on the notion of life as a concept theorized as distinct from living beings, often denoted with the capital L, see Chapter 8 of this volume.
4. Jens Hauser, "Genes, Geneies, Genes," in *L'Art Biotech Catalogue* trans. Jens Hauser (Trézélan, France: Filigranes Éditions, 2003), 9. Deborah Dixon and Elizabeth Straughan, "Geographies of Touch/Touched by Geography," *Geography Compass*, 4(5) (2010), 449–59. Oron Catts and Ionat Zurr, "Countering the Engineering Mindset – The Conflict of Art and Synthetic Biology," in J. Calvert and D. Ginsberg (eds.), *Synthetic Aesthetics: Investigating Synthetic Biology's Designs on Nature* (Cambridge: MIT Press, 2014), 27–38.
5. Jens Hauser "Biotechnology as Mediality: Strategies of Organic Media Art," *Performance Research*, 11(4) (2006), 129–36. Hauser, "Genes." Eduardo Kac, *Signs of Life: Bio Art and Beyond* (Cambridge: MIT Press 2006). Monika Bakke, "Desires: Wet Media Art and Beyond," *Parallax*, 14(3) (2008), 21–34. George Gessert, *Green Light: Toward an Art of Evolution* (Cambridge: MIT Press 2010). Oron Catts and Ionat Zurr, "Artists Working with Life (Sciences) in Contestable Settings," *YISR: Interdisciplinary Science Reviews*, 43 (2018), 40–53.
6. Gessert, *Green Light*. Ionat Zurr and Oron Catts, "The Unnatural Relations between Artistic Research and Ethics Committees: An Artist's Perspective," in Paul Macneill (ed.), *Ethics and the Arts* (New York: Springer, 2014), 201–211.

Joanna Zylinska, *Bioethics in the Age of New Media* (Cambridge: MIT Press, 2009). Frances Stracey, "Bio-Art: The Ethics Behind the Aesthetics," *Nature Reviews: Molecular Cell Biology*, 10 (2009), 496–500. Adele Senior, "Relics of Bioart: Ethics and Messianic Aesthetics in Performance Documentation,"*Theatre Journal*, 66(2) (2014), 183–205. Nora S. Vaage, "What Ethics for Bioart?" *NanoEthics*, 10(1) (2016), 87–104. Catts and Zurr, "Artists."

7. Lorraine Daston and Peter Galison, *Objectivity* (Brooklyn, NY: Zone Books, 2007).

8. Catts and Zurr, "Artists."

9. The central dogma of molecular biology describes a two-step process, transcription and translation, by which the information in genes flows into proteins: DNA → RNA → protein. For foundational thinking in posthumanism, see N. Katherine Hayles, *How We Became Posthuman: Virtual Bodies in Cybernetics, Literature and Informatics* (Chicago: University of Chicago Press 1999). Cary Wolfe, *What is Posthumanism?* (Minneapolis: University of Minnesota Press, 2009). Rosi Braidotti and Maria Hlavajova, *Posthuman Glossary* (London: Bloomsbury Academic 2018).

10. Epigenetics is the study of heritable phenotype changes that do not involve alterations in the DNA sequence. Epigenetic mechanisms change the way genes are packaged in the cell nucleus and involve changes in chemical groups that can attach to DNA, or changes in the way RNA molecules interact with the DNA. Diet and other external environmental influences can potentially play a role in controlling epigenetic processes. Epigenetics may affect phenotypical to health and behavioral traits. More on epigenetics and posthumanism, see Chapter 8 of this volume.

11. Donna J. Haraway, "Situated Knowledges: The Science Question in Feminism and the Privilege of Partial Perspective," in *Simians, Cyborgs, and Women: The Reinvention of Nature* (New York: Routledge, 1991), 183–202. María Mies and Vandana Shiva, *Ecofeminism* (Halifax, Nova Scotia: Fernwood Publications, 1993).

12. Scholars working in this area include Lilly E. Kay, *Who Wrote the Book of Life? A History of the Genetic Code* (Stanford, Stanford University Press 2000); Evelyn Fox Keller, *Making Sense of Life Explaining Biological Development with Models, Metaphors, and Machines* (Harvard: Harvard University Press 2002); Oron Catts and Ionat Zurr, "Big Pigs, Small Wings: On Genohype and Artistic Autonomy," in *Culture Machine* 7 Special Issue on Biopolitics (2005), online; and Hannah Landecker, "Sociology in an Age of Genomic Instability: Copy Number Variation, Somatic Mosaicism, and the Fallen Genome,"*Advances in Medical Sociology*, 16 (2015), 157–86.

13. This is a term coined by Neil Holtzman. See "Are Genetic Tests Adequately Regulated?" *Science*, 286(5439) (1999), 409.

14. Oron Catts and Ionat Zurr, "Vessels of Care and Control – The Citizens of Incubators," in Kelly E. Happe, Jenell Johnson, and Marina Levina (eds.), *Biocitizenship: On Bodies, Belonging, and the Politics of Life* (New York:

New York University Press, 2018), 269. See also Oron Catts and Ionat Zurr, "Biomass," *Nature: Cooper Hewitt Design Triennial Exhibition* (2019), online.

15. For more on the notion of the semi-living, see Oron Catts and Ionat Zurr, "Growing Semi-Living Sculptures," *Leonardo Magazine*, 35(4) (August 2002), 365–70.

16. As described on their website, "They limn a nexus at which insightful observers have identified extraordinarily high potential for innovation. And innovation is precisely what's called for if we're to master the social, ecological and economic challenges that Europe will be facing in the near future."

17. Beatriz da Costa and Kavita Philip (eds.), *Tactical Biopolitics: Art, Activism, and Technoscience* (Cambridge: MIT Press, 2008).

18. Mary Tsang, *Open Source Estrogen: From Biomolecules to Biopolitics … Hormones with Institutional Biopower!* Unpublished MSc Dissertation (Cambridge, MIT, 2017), online.

19. Tarsh Bates, "HumanThrush Entanglements: Homo sapiens as a Multi-Species Ecology," *Philosophy, Activism, Nature 10* (2013), 36.

20. The microbiome comprises all of the genetic material within a microbiota (the entire collection of microorganisms in a specific niche, such as the human gut). This can also be referred to as the metagenome of the microbiota.

21. Kathy High, "Gut Love Bacteria, Love and Immunology Intersect at Esther Klein Gallery Exhibit," *Science Center.Org* (October 5, 2017), online.

22. De-extinction, also known as resurrection biology, or species revivalism, is the process of generating an organism from extinct species. For more information see Ben Jacob Novak, "De-Extinction," *Genes*, 9(11) (2018), online.

23. Daisy Ginsberg makes these statements on her website.

24. Cellular agriculture is the emerging field of producing animal products from *cell* culture, rather than from animals. This field builds on advances in biotechnology.

25. For more on the commodification of life, as it relates to posthumanism, see Chapters 8 and 11 of this volume.

26. See Stephen J. Gould, *The Panda's Thumb: More Reflections in Natural History* (New York: Norton, 1980).

27. Hybridomas are hybrid cells produced by the fusion of two or more cells from different organisms, mainly for the production of antibodies for research and therapeutic purposes.

# Collective Works Cited

Adey, P. (2010). *Aerial Life: Spaces, Mobilities, Affects*. Malden, MA: Wiley-Blackwell.

Agamben, G. (2007). *The Coming Community*, trans. Michael Hardt. Minneapolis, MN: University of Minnesota Press.

Ahmed, S. (2008). Imaginary Prohibitions: Some Preliminary Remarks on the Founding Gestures of the "New Materialism." *European Journal of Women's Studies*, 15(1), 23–39.

    (2004). *The Cultural Politics of Emotion*. New York, NY: Routledge.

Ahuja, N. (2017). Colonialism. In Stacy Alaimo, ed., *Gender: Matter*. Farmington Hills, MI: Macmillan, 237–52.

Alaimo, S. (2010). *Bodily Natures: Science, Environment, and the Material Self*. Bloomington, IN: Indiana University Press.

    (2017). Your Shell on Acid: Material Immersion, Anthropocene Dissolves. In Richard Grusin, ed., *Anthropocene Feminism*. Minneapolis, MN: University of Minnesota Press, 89–120.

    and Hekman, S. (2008). Introduction: Emerging Models of Materiality in Feminist Theory. In S. Alaimo and S. Hekman, eds., *Material Feminisms*. Bloomington, IN: Indiana University Press, 1–22.

Allington, D., Brouillette, S., and Golumbia, D. (2016). Neoliberal Tools (and Archives): A Political History of the Digital Humanities. In *Los Angeles Review of Books* (1 May). Online. https://lareviewofbooks.org/article/neoliberal-tools-archives-political-history-digital-humanities/

Aloi, G. and McHugh, S. (Forthcoming). Introduction: Art and the Ontological Turn. In G. Aloi and S. McHugh, eds., *Posthumanism in Art and Science: A Reader*. New York, NY: Columbia University Press.

Althusser, L. (1971). Ideology and Ideological State Apparatuses (Notes towards an Investigation), trans. Ben Brewster. In *Lenin and Philosophy and Other Essays*. London, UK: New Left Books, 121–73.

Angerer, M-L. (2017). *Ecology of Affect: Intensive Milieus and Contingent Encounters*, trans. Gerrit Jackson. Lüneburg, Germany: Meson Press.

Arendt, H. (1998). *The Human Condition*, 2nd ed. Chicago, IL: University of Chicago Press.

Asimov, I. (1956). *I, Robot*. New York, NY: Signet Books.

Atanasoski, N. and Kalindi, V. (2019). *Surrogate Humanity: Race, Robots, and the Politics of Technological Futures*. Durham, NC: Duke University Press.

Atkinson, M. (2017). *The Poetics of Transgenerational Trauma*. New York, NY: Bloomsbury Academic.

Atzmon, L. and Boradkar, P. (eds.). (2017). *Encountering Things: Design and Theories of Things*. New York, NY: Bloomsbury.

Bacigalupi, P. (2012). *The Drowned Cities*. New York, NY: Little, Brown and Company.

(2004). The People of Sand and Slag. *The Magazine of Fantasy and Science Fiction*, 106(2), 6–29.

(2010). *Ship Breaker*. New York, NY: Little, Brown and Company.

(2017). *Tool of War*. New York, NY: Little, Brown and Company.

Badmington, N. (2000). Introduction: Approaching Posthumanism. In N. Badmington, ed., *Posthumanism*. New York, NY: Palgrave, 1–10.

(2006). Posthumanism. In Simon Malpas and Paul Wake, eds., *The Routledge Companion to Critical Theory*. London, UK: Routledge, 240–1.

Bakke, B. (2008). Desires: Wet Media Art and Beyond. *Parallax*, 14(3), 21–34.

Barad, K. (2007). *Meeting the Universe Halfway: Quantum Physics and the Entanglement of Matter and Meaning*. Durham, NC: Duke University Press.

(2003). Posthuman Performativity: Toward an Understanding of How Matter Comes to Matter. *Signs: Journal of Women in Culture and Society*, 28(3), 801–31.

Barnett, F. (2014). The Brave Side of the Digital Humanities. *Differences*, 25(1), 64–78.

Bates, T. (2013). HumanThrush Entanglements: Homo Sapiens as a Multi-species Ecology. *Philosophy, Activism, Nature* (10), 36–45.

Baudrillard, J. (1983). *Simulations*, trans. P. Foss, P. Patton, and P. Beitchman. New York, NY: Semiotext[e].

(1993). *The Transparency of Evil: Essays on Extreme Phenomena*, trans. J. Benedict. London, UK: Verso Books.

Beauchamp, T. (2017). Transgender Matters. In Stacy Alaimo, ed., *Gender: Matter*. Farmington Hills, MI: Macmillan, 65–77.

Beck, U. (1992). *Risk Society: Toward a New Modernity*. New York, NY: Routledge.

Behar, K. (ed.). (2016). *Object-Oriented Feminism*. Minneapolis, MN: University of Minnesota Press.

Belsey, C. (1980). *Critical Practice*. London, UK: Methuen.

(2002). *Poststructuralism: A Very Short Introduction*. Oxford, UK: Oxford University Press.

Benjamin, R. (2019). *Race after Technology: Abolitionist Tools for the New Jim Code*. Cambridge, UK: Polity Press.

Bennett, J. (2010). *Vibrant Matter: A Political Ecology of Things*. Durham, NC: Duke University Press.

Bennett, T. (2015). Cultural Studies and the Culture Concept. *Cultural Studies*, 29(4), 546–68.

Bergson, H. (1911). *Creative Evolution*, trans. Arthur Mitchell. New York: Henry Holt.

Berlant, L. (2011). *Cruel Optimism*. Durham, NC: Duke University Press.
  (2008). *The Female Complaint: The Unfinished Business of Sentimentality in American Culture*. Durham, NC: Duke University Press.

Best, S. (2009). The Rise of Critical Animal Studies: Putting Theory into Action and Animal Liberation into Higher Education. *Journal of Critical Animal Studies*, 7(1), 9–52.

Beukes, L. (2008). *Moxyland*. Johannesburg: Jacana Media.

Blackman, L. (2012). *Immaterial Bodies: Affect, Embodiment, Mediation*. London, UK: SAGE Publications.

Bloch, E. (1986). *The Principle of Hope*, trans. N. Plaice, S. Plaice, and P. Knight. 3 vols. Cambridge, MA: The MIT Press.

Bök, C. (2015). *The Xenotext: Book 1*. Toronto, ON: Coach House Books.

Bostrom, N. (2014). *Superintelligence: Paths, Dangers, Strategies*. Oxford, UK: Oxford University Press.
  (2005). Transhumanist Values. In F. Adams, ed., *Ethical Issues for the 21st Century*. Charlottesville, VA: Philosophy Documentation Center, 3–14.

Bould, M. and Miéville, C. (eds.) (2009). *Red Planets: Marxism and Science Fiction*. Middleton, CT: Wesleyan University Press.

Braidotti, R. (2011). *Nomadic Subjects: Embodiment and Sexual Difference in Contemporary Feminist Theory*, 2nd ed. New York, NY: Columbia University Press.
  (2013). *The Posthuman*. Malden, MA: Polity Press.
  (2018). Posthuman Critical Theory. In R. Braidotti and M. Hlavajova, eds. *The Posthuman Glossary*. Bloomsbury Academic, 339–42.
  (2019). *Posthuman Knowledge*. Medford, MA: Polity Press.
  and Hlavajova, M. (eds.). (2018). *The Posthuman Glossary*. New York, NY: Bloomsbury Academic.
  and Vermeulen, T. (2014). Borrowed Energy. *Frieze*. Online. https://frieze.com /article/borrowed-energy

Brassier, R. (2007). *Nihil Unbound: Enlightenment and Extinction*. London, UK: Palgrave Macmillan.
  et al. (2007). Speculative Realism. *Collapse*, 3, 307–449.
  (2013). Unfree Improvisation/Compulsive Freedom. *Mattin.org*. Online. www .mattin.org/essays/unfree_improvisation-compulsive_freedom.html

Braun, B. (2007). Biopolitics and the Molecularization of Life. *Cultural Geographies*, 14(1), 6–28.

Brennan, T. (2004). *The Transmission of Affect*. Ithaca, NY: Cornell University Press.

Brin, D. (1995). *Brightness Reef*. New York, NY: Spectra.
  (1998). *Heaven's Reach*. New York, NY: Spectra.
  (1996). *Infinity's Shore*. New York, NY: Spectra.
  (1983). *Startide Rising*. New York, NY: Spectra.
  (1980). *Sundiver*. New York, NY: Spectra.

(1987). *The Uplift War*. New York, NY: Spectra.

Brooke, J. H. (1971). Organic Synthesis and the Unification of Chemistry – A Reappraisal. *The British Journal for the History of Science*, 5(4), 363–92.

Brown, B. (2016). *Other Things*. Chicago, IL: The University of Chicago Press.

(2001). Thing Theory. *Critical Inquiry*, 28(1), 1–22.

Brown, D. L. (2018). Can the "Immortal Cells" of Henrietta Lacks Sue for Their Own Rights? *Washington Post* 25 Jun. Online. www.washingtonpost.com/n ews/retropolis/wp/2018/06/25/can-the-immortal-cells-of-henrietta-lacks-sue -for-their-own-rights/

Bryant, L. R. (2011). The Ontic Principle: Outline of an Object-Oriented Ontology. In L. R. Bryant, N. Srnicek and G. Harman, eds., *The Speculative Turn: Continental Materialism and Realism*. Victoria, AU: re-press, 261–78.

Burke, S. (2019). *Interference*. New York, NY: Tor.

(2018). *Semiosis*. New York, NY: Tor.

Butler, J. (1993). *Bodies That Matter: On the Discursive Limits of "Sex."* New York, NY: Routledge.

(1992). Contingent Foundations: Feminism and the Question of "Postmodernism." In J. Butler and J. W. Scott, eds., *Feminists Theorize the Political*. New York, NY: Routledge, 3–21.

(2009). *Frames of War: When Is Life Grievable?* London, UK: Verso Books.

(1990). *Gender Trouble: Feminism and the Subversion of Identity*. London, UK: Routledge.

(2004). *Precarious Life: The Powers of Mourning and Violence*. London, UK: Verso Books.

Butler, O. E. (1996). *Clay's Ark*. New York, NY: Warner Books.

(2000). *Lilith's Brood*. New York, NY: Aspect/Warner Books.

(2000). *Parable of the Sower*. New York, NY: Warner Books.

(2000). *Parable of the Talents*. New York, NY: Warner Books.

(2001). *Wild Seed*. New York, NY: Warner Books.

Byrd, J. (2016). Still Waiting for the "Post" to Arrive: Elizabeth Cook-Lynn and the Imponderables of American Indian Postcoloniality. *Wicazo Sa Review*, 31 (1), 75–89.

(2011). *The Transit of Empire: Indigenous Critiques of Colonialism*. Minneapolis, MN: University of Minnesota Press.

Cadava, E. (ed.). (1991). *Who Comes After the Subject?* New York, NY: Routledge.

Callon, M. (2007). What Does It Mean to Say That Economics Is Performative? In D. MacKenzie, F. Muniesa, and L. Siu, eds., *Do Economists Make Markets?: On the Peformativity of Economics*. Princeton, NJ: Princeton University Press, 311–57.

Cameron, J. (Director). (2009). *Avatar* [Motion picture]. Los Angeles, CA: 20th Century Fox.

(Director). (1984). *The Terminator* [Motion picture]. Los Angeles, CA: Orion Pictures.

Canavan, G. and Hageman, A. (2016). Introduction: "Global Weirding." *Paradoxa*, 28, 7–13.

Canguilhem, G. (2008). *Knowledge of Life*, ed. P. Marrati and T. Meyers, trans. S. Geraoulanous and D. Ginsberg. New York, NY: Fordham University Press.

(1994). *A Vital Rationalist: Selected Writings of Georges Canguilhem*, ed. François Delaporte, trans. A. Goldhammer. New York, NY: Zone Books.

Castree, N. (2014). The Anthropocene and Geography I: The Back Story. *Geography Compass*, 8(7),436–49.

(2014). The Anthropocene and Geography III: Future Directions. *Geography Compass*, 8(7),464–76.

(2014). Geography and the Anthropocene II: Current Contributions. *Geography Compass*, 8(7),450–63.

Catts, O., and Zurr, I. (2018). Artists Working with Life (Sciences) in Contestable Settings. *YISR: Interdisciplinary Science Reviews*, 43(1),40–53. Online.

(2005). Big Pigs, Small Wings: On Genohype and Artistic Autonomy. *Culture Machine*, 7. Online. https://culturemachine.net/biopolitics/big-pigs-small-wings/

(2019). Biomass. In *Nature: Cooper Hewitt Design Triennial Exhibition* (2019). Online.

(2014). Countering the Engineering Mindset – The Conflict of Art and Synthetic Biology. In J. Calvert and D. Ginsberg, eds., *Synthetic Aesthetics*. Cambridge, MA: The MIT Press,

(2002). Growing Semi-Living Sculptures. *Leonardo Magazine*, 35(4), 365–70.

(2018). Vessels of Care and Control – The Citizens of Incubators. In K.E. Happe, J. Johnson, and M. Levina, eds., *Biocitizenship: On Bodies, Belonging, and the Politics of Life*. New York, YI: New York University Press, 255–73.

Cavarero, A. (2016). *Inclinations: A Critique of Rectitude*. Trans. Adam Sitze and Amanda Minervini. Stanford, CA: Stanford University Press.

Chachra, D. (2015). Why I Am Not a Maker. *The Atlantic* (23 Jan). Online. www.theatlantic.com/technology/archive/2015/01/why-i-am-not-a-maker/384767/

Chakrabarty, D. (2009). The Climate of History: Four Theses. *Critical Inquiry*, 35(2), 197–222.

Chen, M. Y. (2012). *Animacies: Biopolitics, Racial Mattering and Queer Affect*. Durham, NC: Duke University Press.

Ćirković, M. M. (2018). *The Great Silence: Science and Philosophy of Fermi's Paradox*. Oxford, UK: Oxford University Press.

Claire, S. (2016). On the Politics of "New Feminist Materialisms." In V. Pitts-Taylor, ed., *Mattering: Feminism, Science, and Materialism*. New York, NY: New York University Press, 58–72.

Clarke, A. E., Mamo, L., Fosket, J. F., Fishman, J.R. and Shim, J. K. (eds.). (2010). *Biomedicalization: Technoscience, Health, and Illness in the U.S.* Durham, NC: Duke University Press.

Clarke, B. (2020). *Gaian Systems: Lynn Margulis, Neocybernetics, and the End of the Anthropocene*. Minneapolis, MN: University of Minnesota Press.

(2002). Mediating The Fly: Posthuman Metamorphosis in the 1950s. *Configurations* 10(1),169–91.

(2014). *Neocybernetics and Narrative.* Minneapolis, MN: University of Minnesota Press.

(2008). *Posthuman Metamorphosis: Narrative and Systems.* New York, NY: Fordham University Press.

and Rossini, M. (eds.). (2017). *The Cambridge Companion to Literature and the Posthuman.* Cambridge, UK: Cambridge University Press.

(2017). Preface: Literature, Posthumanism, and the Posthuman. In B. Clarke and M. Rossini, eds., *The Cambridge Companion to Literature and the Posthuman.* Cambridge, UK: Cambridge University Press, xi–xxii.

Clifford, J. and Marcus, G. E. (1986). *Writing Culture: The Poetics and Politics of Ethnography.* Berkeley, CA: University of California Press.

Cline, E. (2011). *Ready Player One.* New York, NY: Penguin Books.

Clough, P. T. (2007). *The Affective Turn: Theorizing the Social.* Durham, NC: Duke University Press.

Clute, J. (2015). *21st Century Science Fiction*, edited by David G. Hartwell and Patrick Nielsen Hayden. *The New York Review of Science Fiction*, 328, 1, 4–6.

Clynes, M. and Kline, N. (1960). Cyborgs and Space. *Astronautics* (September), 26–27, 74–76.

Cohen, J. J. (ed.). (1996). *Monster Theory: Reading Culture.* Minneapolis, MN: University of Minnesota Press.

Colebrook, C. (2014). *Death of the Posthuman: Essays on Extinction, Vol. 1.* Ann Arbor, MI: Open Humanities Press.

(2017). Futures. In B. Clarke and M. Rossini, eds., *The Cambridge Companion to Literature and the Posthuman.* Cambridge, UK: Cambridge University Press, 196–208.

(2001). *Gilles Deleuze.* London, UK: Routledge.

(2010). The Linguistic Turn in Continental Philosophy. In A.D. Schrift, ed., *Poststructuralism and Critical Theory's Second Generation.* Durham, NC: Acumen, 279–309.

(2017). We Have Always Been Post-Anthropocene: The Anthropocene Counterfactual. In R. Grusin, ed., *Anthropocene Feminism.* Minneapolis, MN: University of Minnesota Press, 1–20.

(2016). What is the Anthro-Political? In T. Cohen, C. Colebrook, and J. Hillis Miller, *Twilight of the Anthropocene Idols.* London, UK: Open Humanities Press, 81–125.

Connor, S. (1989). *Postmodernist Culture: An Introduction to Theories of the Contemporary*, 2nd. ed. Oxford, UK: Blackwell.

Cooper, M. (2008). *Life as Surplus: Biotechnology and Capitalism in the Neoliberal Era.* Seattle, WA: University of Washington Press.

and Waldby, C. (2014). *Clinical Labor: Tissue Donors and Research Subjects in the Global Bioeconomy.* Durham, NC: Duke University Press.

Craps, S. (2017). Climate Change and the Art of Anticipatory Memory. *Parallax*, 23(4), 479–92.

Colebrook, C., Crownshaw, R., Kennedy, R., Nardizzi, V. and Wenzel, J. (2018). Memory Studies and the Anthropocene: A Roundtable. *Memory Studies*, 11(4), 498–515.

Crichton, M. (Director). (1973). *Westworld* [Motion picture]. Beverly Hills, CA: Metro Goldwyn Mayer (MGM).

Crow, J. M. (2018). Life 2.0: Inside the Synthetic Biology Revolution. *Cosmos* (17 April). Online. https://cosmosmagazine.com/biology/life-2-0-inside-the-synthetic-biology-revolution/

Crutzen, P. and Stoermer, E. (2000). The Anthropocene. *Global Change Newsletter*, 41, 17–18.

Csicsery-Ronay, I. Jr., (2011). *The Seven Beauties of Science Fiction*. Middletown, CT: Wesleyan University Press.

da Costa, B. and Philip, K. (eds.). (2008). *Tactical Biopolitics: Art, Activism, and Technoscience*. Cambridge, MA: The MIT Press, 2008.

Darwin, C. (2008). On the Origin of Species. In J. Secord, ed., *Evolutionary Writings*. Oxford, UK: Oxford University Press, 105–211.

da Silva, D. F. (2007). *Toward a Global Idea of Race*. Minneapolis, MN: University of Minnesota Press.

Daston, L. and Galison, P. (2007). *Objectivity*. Cambridge, MA: The MIT Press.

Davis, M. (1998). *Ecology of Fear: Los Angeles and the Imagination of Disaster*. New York, NY: Henry Holt & Company.

de Castro, E. V. (2014). *Cannibal Metaphysics: For a Post-Structural Anthropology*, trans. P. Skafish. Minneapolis, MN: Univocal Publishing.

de la Cadena, M. (2010). Indigenous Cosmopolitics in the Andes: Conceptual Reflections beyond "Politics." *Cultural Anthropology*, 25(2), 334–70.

Deleuze, G. (1988). *Bergsonism*, trans. H. Tomlinson and B. Habberjam. New York, NY: Zone Books.

    (1992). Ethology: Spinoza and Us. In J. Crary and S. Kwinter, eds., *Incorporations*, trans. Robert Hurley. New York, NY: Zone Books, 625–33.

    (2001). *Pure Immanence: Essays on a Life*, trans. A. Boyman. Cambridge, MA: Zone Books.

    and Guattari, F. (1987). *A Thousand Plateaus: Capitalism and Schizophrenia*, trans. B. Massumi. Minneapolis, MN: University of Minnesota Press.

    (1994). *What Is Philosophy?*, trans. H. Tomlinson and G. Burchell. New York, NY: Columbia University Press.

Deloria, V. Jr., (1999). Relativity, Relatedness, and Reality. In Deloria B. et al., eds., *Spirit and Reason: The Vine Deloria, Jr. Reader*. Golden, CO: Fulcrum Publishing, 32–39.

Deplazes-Zemp, A. (2012). The Conception of Life in Synthetic Biology. *Science and Engineering Ethics*, 18(4), 757–74.

Derrida, J. (1996). *Archive Fever: A Freudian Impression*, trans. E. Prenowitz. Chicago, IL: Chicago University Press.

    Differance. (1973). In *Speech and Phenomena And Other Essays on Husserl's Theory of Signs*, trans. D. B. Allison. Evanston, IL: Northwestern University Press, 129–60.

(1991). "Eating Well," or the Calculation of the Subject: An Interview with Jacques Derrida. In E. Cadava, ed., *Who Comes After the Subject?* New York, NY: Routledge, 96–119.

(1982). The Ends of Man. In A. Bass, ed., *Margins of Philosophy*. Chicago, IL: University of Chicago Press.

(1982). *Margins of Philosophy*, trans. A. Bass. Chicago, IL: University of Chicago Press.

(2016). *Of Grammatology*, trans. G. Chakravorty Spivak. Baltimore, MD: The Johns Hopkins University Press.

(1990). Some Statements and Truisms about Neo-Logisms, Newisms, Postisms, Parasitisms, and Other Small Seisms, trans. Anne Tomiche. In D. Carroll, ed., *The States of "Theory": History, Art, and Critical Discourse*. Stanford, CA: Stanford University Press, 63–94.

(2005). *Sovereignties in Question: The Poetics of Paul Celan*, ed. T. Dutoit and O. Pasanen. New York, NY: Fordham University Press.

(1994). *Specters of Marx: The State of Debt, the Work of Mourning, and the New International*, trans. P. Kamuf. London, UK: Routledge.

(1970). Structure, Sign, and Play in the Discourse of the Human Sciences. In R. Macksey and E. Donato, eds., *The Languages of Criticism and The Sciences of Man: The Structuralist Controversy*. Baltimore, MD: The Johns Hopkins University Press, 247–72.

Despret, V. (2004). The Body We Care For: Figures of Anthropo-zoo-genesis. *Body and Society*, 10(2–3), 111–34.

Didi-Huberman, G. (2017). *Bark*, trans. S. E. Martin. Cambridge, MA: The MIT Press.

(2011). *Écorces*. Paris: Les Éditions de Minuit.

Dixon, D. and Straughan, E. (2010). Geographies of Touch/Touched by Geography. *Geography Compass*, 4(5), 449–59.

Drexler, K. E. (1990). *Engines of Creation: The Coming Era of Nanotechnology*. Garden City, NY: Anchor Press/Doubleday.

Dumit, J. (2012). *Drugs for Life: How Pharmaceutical Companies Define Our Health*. Durham, NC: Duke University Press.

Duster, T. (2003). *Backdoor to Eugenics*. New York: Routledge.

Eden, A. H., Moor, J. H., Søraker, J. H., and Steinhart, E. (eds.). (2012). *Singularity Hypotheses: A Scientific and Philosophical Assessment*. New York: Springer.

Ehlers, N., and Krupar, S. (2019). *Deadly Biocultures: The Ethics of Life-making*. Minneapolis, MN: University of Minnesota Press.

(2014). Hope Logics: Biomedicine, Affective Conventions of Cancer, and the Governing of Biocitizenry. *Configurations: A Journal of Literature, Science, and Technology*, 22(3), 385–413.

Elliott, J. and Attridge, D. (eds.). (2011). *Theory After "Theory."* London, UK: Routledge.

Ellis, C. (2018). *Antebellum Posthuman: Race and Materiality in the Mid-Nineteenth Century*. New York, NY: Fordham University Press.

Esposito, E. (2017). Artificial Communication? The Production of Contingency by Algorithms. *Zeitschrift für Soziologie*, 46(4), 249–65.

Ferrini, C. (2010). From Geological to Animal Nature in Hegel's Idea of Life. *Hegel-Studien*, (44), 1–77.

Fishel, S. R. (2017). *The Microbial State: Global Thriving and the Body Politic*. Minneapolis, MN: University of Minnesota Press.

Foster, T. (2005). *The Souls of Cyberfolk: Posthumanism as Vernacular Theory*. Minneapolis, MN: University of Minnesota Press.

Foucault, M. (1970). *The Order of Things: An Archaeology of the Human Sciences*. New York: Vintage Books.

   (1980). *Power/Knowledge: Selected Interviews and Other Writings, 1972–1977*. Colin Gordon. ed., New York: Pantheon Books.

   (2003). *Society Must Be Defended: Lectures at the Collège de France, 1975–1976*, trans. David Macey. New York, NY: Picador.

Fowles, S. (2016). The Perfect Subject (Postcolonial Object Studies). *Journal of Material Culture*, 21(1), 9–27.

Frabetti, F. (2012). Have the Humanities Always Been Digital? For an Understanding of the "Digital Humanities" in the Context of Originary Technicitys. In D. Berry, ed., *Understanding Digital Humanities*. London: Palgrave Macmillan. 161–71.

Fraiman, S. (2012). Pussy Panic versus Liking Animals: Tracking Gender in Animal Studies. *Critical Inquiry*, 39(1), 89–115.

Franklin, S. (2007). *Dolly Mixtures: The Remaking of Genealogy*. Durham, NC: Duke University Press.

   (2000). Life Itself: Global Nature and the Genetic Imaginary. In S. Franklin, C. Lury, and J. Stacey, eds. *Global Nature, Global Culture*. London, UK: SAGE, 188–226.

   and Lock, M. (2001). Animation and Cessation. In S. Franklin and M. Lock, eds., *Remaking Life and Death: Toward an Anthropology of the Biosciences*. Santa Fe, NM: School of American Research Press, 3–22.

Freedman, C. (2000). *Critical Theory and Science Fiction*. Middletown, CT: Wesleyan University Press.

Fukuyama, F. (1992). *The End of History and the Last Man*. New York, NY: Free Press.

   (2002). *Our Posthuman Future: Consequences of the Biotechnology Revolution*. London, UK: Profile Books.

Fuller, S. (2011). *Humanity 2.0: What is Means to be Human, Past, Present and Future*. New York, NY: Palgrave Macmillan.

GegenSichKollektiv. (2014). CAUTION. *Collapse*, 8, 878–905.

Gessert, G. (2010). *Green Light: Toward an Art of Evolution*. Cambridge, MA: The MIT Press.

Gibbs, A. (2001). Contagious Feelings: Pauline Hanson and the Epidemiology of Affect. *Australian Humanities Review*, 24. Online. http://australianhumanitiesreview.org/2001/12/01/contagious-feelings-pauline-hanson-and-the-epidemiology-of-affect/

Gibson, W. (1984). *Neuromancer.* New York, NY: Ace Books.

Gibson-Graham, J. K. (1996). *The End of Capitalism (As We Knew It): A Feminist Critique of Political Economy.* Minneapolis, MN: University of Minnesota Press.

(2006). *A Postcapitalist Politics.* Minneapolis, MN: University of Minnesota Press.

Cameron, J. and Healy, S. (2013). *Take Back the Economy: An Ethical Guide for Transforming Our Communities.* Minneapolis, MN: University of Minnesota Press,144–45.

and Miller, E. (2015). Economy as Ecological Livelihood. In Gibson, K., Rose, D. and Fincher, R., eds., *Manifesto for Living in the Anthropocene.* New York: Punctum Books, 7–17.

Glanville, R. (2007). Try Again. Fail Again. Fail Better: The Cybernetics in Design and the Design in Cybernetics. *Kybernetes,* 36(9/10), 1173–206.

Glick, M.H. (2018). *Infrahumanisms: Science, Culture, and the Making of Modern Non/Personhood.* Durham, NC: Duke University Press.

Gómez-Barris, M. (2017). *The Extractive Zone: Social Ecologies and Decolonial Perspectives.* Durham, NC: Duke University Press.

Gould, S. J. (1980). *The Panda's Thumb: More Reflections in Natural History.* New York, NY: W. W. Norton and Company.

Graham, E. (2002). *Representations of the Post/Human: Monsters, Aliens and Others in Popular Culture.* Manchester, UK Manchester University Press.

Grant, I. H. (2006). *Philosophies of Nature after Schelling.* London, UK: Continuum.

Gregg, M. and Seigworth, G. J. (2010). An Inventory of Shimmers. In M. Gregg and G. J. Seigworth, eds., *The Affect Theory Reader.* Durham, NC: Duke University Press, 1–25.

Grinspoon, D. (2016). *Earth in Human Hands: Shaping Our Planet's Future.* New York, NY: Grand Central Publishing.

Groys, B. (ed.). (2018). *Russian Cosmism.* Cambridge, MA: Eflux/The MIT Press.

Grusin, R. (2015). Introduction. In R. Grusin, ed., *The Nonhuman Turn.* Minneapolis, MN: University of Minnesota Press, vii–xxix.

(2010). *Premediation: Affect and Mediality after 9/11.* New York, NY: Palgrave Macmillan.

(ed.). (2015). *The Nonhuman Turn.* Minneapolis, MN: University of Minnesota Press.

Guthman, J. (2014). Doing Justice to Bodies? Reflections on Food Justice, Race, and Biology. *Antipode,* 46, 1153–71.

(2012). Opening Up the Black Box of the Body in Geographical Obesity Research: Toward a Critical Political Ecology of Fat. *Annals of the Association of American Geographers,* 102, 951–57.

Halberstam, J. (2011). *The Queer Art of Failure.* Durham, NC: Duke University Press.

Halberstam, J. and Livingston, I. (1995). Introduction: Posthuman Bodies. In J. Halberstam and I. Livingston, eds., *Posthuman Bodies.* Bloomington, IN: Indiana University Press, 1–19.

(eds.). (1995). *Posthuman Bodies*. Bloomington, IN: Indiana University Press.

Hall, G. (2012). "There Are No Digital Humanities," In Matthew K. Gold and Lauren F. Klein eds., *Debates in the Digital Humanities*. Minneapolis: University of Minnesota Press, 133–8.

Hall, S. (2001). Cultural Studies and Its Theoretical Legacies. In V. B. Leitch et al., eds. *The Norton Anthology of Theory and Criticism*. New York, NY: W. W. Norton and Company, 1898–910.

Evans, J. and Nixon, S. (Eds). (2013). *Representation*, 2nd ed. London, UK: SAGE.

Hames Garcia, M. (2008). How Real is Race? In S. Alaimo and S. J. Hekman, eds., *Material Feminisms*. Bloomington: Indiana University Press, 308–39.

Haraway, D. J. (2015). Anthropocene, Capitalocene, Plantationocene, Chthulucene: Making Kin. *Environmental Humanities*, 6, 159–65.

(2003). *The Companion Species Manifesto: Dogs, People, and Significant Otherness*. Chicago, IL: Prickly Paradigm Press.

(2008). Companion Species, Mis-Recognition, and Queer Worlding. In N. Giffney and M. J. Hird, eds., *Queering the Non/Human*. Burlington, VT: Ashgate, xxiii–xxvi.

(1991). A Cyborg Manifesto: Science, Technology, and Socialist-Feminism in the Late Twentieth Century. In *Simians, Cyborgs and Women: The Reinvention of Nature*. New York: NY: Routledge, 149–81.

(2016). *Manifestly Haraway*. Minneapolis, MN: University of Minnesota Press.

(1990). *Primate Visions: Gender, Race, and Nature in the World of Modern Science*. New York, NY: Routledge.

(1991). *Simians, Cyborgs, and Women: The Reinvention of Nature*. New York, NY: Routledge.

(1991). Situated Knowledges: The Science Question in Feminism and the Privilege of Partial Perspective. In *Simians, Cyborgs, and Women: The Reinvention of Nature*. New York, NY: Routledge, 183–202.

(2016). Staying with the Trouble: Anthropocene, Capitalocene, Chthulucene. In J. Moore, ed., *Anthropocene or Capitalocene?: Nature, History, and the Crisis of Capitalism*. Oakland, CA: PM Press, 34–76.

(2016). Tentacular Thinking: Anthropocene, Capitalocene, Cthulucene. *E-Flux*, 75 (September). Online.

(2008). *When Species Meet*. Minneapolis, MN: University of Minnesota Press.

and Endy, D. (2019). Tools for Multispecies Futures. *The Journal of Design and Science*, 4. Online.

Harman, G. (2012). *Weird Realism: Lovecraft and Philosophy*. Ropley, Hants: Zero Books.

(2012). The Well-Wrought Broken Hammer: Object-Oriented Literary Criticism. *New Literary History*, 43(2), 183–203.

Harris, H. (1985). Roots: Cell Fusion. Wiley Online BioEssays. Online.

Hassan, I. (1977). Prometheus as Performer: Toward a Posthumanist Culture? *The Georgia Review*, 31(4), 830–50.

Hauser, J. (2006). Biotechnology as Mediality: Strategies of Organic Media Art. *Performance Research*, 11(4), 129–36.

(2003). Genes, Geneies, Genes, trans. J. Hauser. *L'Art Biotech Catalogue.* Trézélan, France: Filigranes Editions, 9.

Hayles, N. K. (1999). *How We Became Posthuman: Virtual Bodies in Cybernetics, Literature, and Informatics.* Chicago, IL: University of Chicago Press.

(2005). *My Mother Was a Computer: Digital Subjects and Literary Texts.* Chicago, IL: University of Chicago Press.

(2006). Unfinished Work: From Cyborg to Cognisphere. *Theory, Culture, and Society,* 23(7–8), 159–66.

(2017). *Unthought: The Power of the Cognitive Unconscious.* Chicago, IL: University of Chicago Press.

Hegel, G. W. F. (2004). *Hegel's Philosophy of Nature: Encyclopaedia of the Philosophical Sciences, Part II,* trans. A. V. Miller. Oxford, UK: Oxford University Press.

Heidegger, M. (1977). Letter on Humanism. In D. Farrell Krell, ed., *Basic Writings.* New York, NY: Harper & Row, 189–242.

(1977). The Question Concerning Technology. In *The Question Concerning Technology and Other Essays,* trans. W. Lovitt. New York, NY: Harper & Row, 3–35.

Helmreich, S. (2014). Homo Microbis: The Human Microbiome, Figural, Literal, Political. *Thresholds,* 42, 52–59.

Herbrechter, S. (2013). *Posthumanism: A Critical Analysis.* London, UK: Bloomsbury Academic.

and Callus. I. (2003). What's Wrong with Posthumanism? *Rhizomes* 7 (Fall). Online.

Herman, D. (2014). Narratology Beyond the Human. *Diegesis,* 3(2), 131–43.

(2018). *Narratology Beyond the Human: Storytelling and Animal Life.* New York, NY: Oxford University Press.

High, K. (2017). Press Release: Gut Love: Bacteria, Love and Immunology Intersect at Esther Klein Gallery Exhibit. Online.

Hinterberger, A. (2016). Regulating Estrangement: Human–animal Chimeras in Postgenomic Biology. *Science, Technology, & Human Values,* 1–22.

Hirch, M., and Spitzer, L. (2006). Testimonial Objects: Memory, Gender, and Transmission. *Poetics Today,* 27, 353–83.

Hoffman, E. (2018). Queering the Interspecies Encounter: Yoko Tawada's Memoirs of a Polar Bear. In K. Driscoll and E. Hoffman, eds, *What Is Zoopoetics? Texts, Bodies, Entanglement.* Hoffmann. New York: Palgrave, 149–65.

Holtzman, N. (1999). Are Genetic Tests Adequately Regulated? *Science* 286(5439), 409–10.

Hustak, C. and Myers, N. (2012). Involutionary Momentum: Affective Ecologies and the Sciences of Plant/Insect Encounters. *Differences,* 23(2), 74–118.

Hutcheon, L. (2002). *The Politics of Postmodernism.* 2nd ed. London, UK: Routledge.

Idema, T. (2019). *Stages of Transmutation: Science Fiction, Biology, and Environmental Posthumanism.* New York, NY: Routledge, ebook.

Inda, J. X. (2014). *Racial Prescriptions: Pharmaceuticals, Difference, and the Politics of Life*. Surrey, UK: Ashgate.

Iovino, S. and Opperman, S. (2014). Introduction: Stories Come to Matter. In S. Iovino and S. Opperman, eds., *Material Ecocriticism*. Bloomington, IN: University of Indiana Press.

Jackson, Z. I. (2020). *Becoming Human: Matter and Meaning in an Antiblack World*. New York, NY: New York University Press.

Losing Manhood: Animality and Plasticity in the (Neo)Slave Narrative. *Qui Parle: Critical Humanities and Social Sciences*, 25 (1–2), 95–136.

(2015). Out Worlds: The Persistence of Race in Movement "Beyond the Human." In the "Theorizing Queer Inhumanisms" Dossier. *GLQ*, 21(2–3), 209–48.

(2015). Outer Worlds: The Persistence of Race in Movement "Beyond the Human." *GLQ: A Journal of Lesbian and Gay Studies*, 21(2), 215–18.

Jameson, F. (2005). *Archaeologies of the Future: The Desire Called Utopia and Other Science Fictions*. New York, NY: Verso Books.

(1981). *The Political Unconscious: Narrative as a Socially Symbolic Act*. Ithaca, NY: Cornell University Press.

(1984). Postmodernism, or, the Cultural Logic of Late Capitalism. *New Left Review*, 146, 53–94.

(1991). *Postmodernism, or, The Cultural Logic of Late Capitalism*. Durham, NC: Duke University Press.

(1996). *The Seeds of Time*. New York, NY: Columbia University Press.

Jasanoff, S. (2015). Future Imperfect: Science, Technology, and the Imaginations of Modernity. In S. Jasanoff and S. H. Kim, eds., *Dreamscapes of Modernity: Sociotechnical Imaginaries and the Fabrication of Power*. Chicago, IL: The University of Chicago Press, 1–33.

(2011). Introduction: Rewriting Life, Reframing Rights. In S. Jasanoff, ed., *Reframing Rights: Bioconstitutionalism in the Genetic Age*. Cambridge, MA: The MIT Press, 1–28.

Jemisin, N. K. (2016). *The Fifth Season*. New York, NY: Orbit Books.

(2016). *The Obelisk Gate*. New York, NY: Orbit Books.

(2017). *The Stone Sky*. New York, NY: Orbit Books.

Jones, Brandon. (2018). Mattering. In R. Braidotti and M. Hlavajova, eds., *The Posthuman Glossary*. New York: Bloomsbury Academic, 244–45.

Jonze, S. (Director). (2013). *Her* [Motion picture]. Los Angeles, CA: Annapurna Pictures.

Joy, B. (2000). Why the Future Doesn't Need Us. *Wired*, 8(4), 238–63. Online.

Kac, E. (ed.). (2006). *Signs of Life: Bio Art and Beyond*. Cambridge, MA: The MIT Press.

Kahn, J. (2012). *Race in a Bottle: The Story of BiDil and Racialized Medicine in a Post-genomic Age*. New York, NY: Columbia University Press.

Kalogridis, L. (Creator). (2018-). *Altered Carbon* [Web television series]. Los Gatos, CA: Netflix Inc.

Kant, I. (1929). *Critique of Pure Reason*, trans. N. K. Smith. London, UK: Macmillan and Company.

Kaplan, C. (2018). *Aerial Aftermaths: Wartime from Above*. Durham, NC: Duke University Press.

Keller, E. F. (2002). *Making Sense of Life: Explaining Biological Development with Models, Metaphors, and Machines*. Cambridge, MA: Harvard University Press.

Kember, S. and Zylinska, J. (2012). *Life after New Media: Mediation as a Vital Process*. Cambridge, MA: The MIT Press.

King, T. L. (2017). Humans Involved: Lurking in the Lines of Posthumanist Flight. *Critical Ethnic Studies*, 3(1), 162–85.

Klein, N. (2014). *This Changes Everything: Capitalism vs the Climate*. New York, NY: Simon and Schuster.

Knight, D. (1970). *Beyond the Barrier*. New York, NY: Macfadden-Bartell.

Kolozova, K. and E. A. Joy. (2016). *After the "Speculative Turn": Realism, Philosophy, and Feminism*. New York, NY: Punctum Books.

Kordela, A. K. (2016). Monsters of Biopower: Terror(ism) and Horror in the Era of Affect. *Philosophy Today*, 60(1),193–205.

Kroker, A. (2012). *Body Drift: Butler, Hayles, Haraway*. Minneapolis, MN: University of Minnesota Press.

Krupar, S. R. (2018). Green Death: Sustainability and the Administration of the Dead. *Cultural Geographies*, 25(2), 267–84.

and Ehlers, N. (2017). Biofutures: Race and the Governance of Health. *Environment and Planning D: Society and Space*, 35(2), 222–40.

(2015). Target: Biomedicine and Racialized Geo-body-politics. *Occasion*, 8, 1–25.

Kurzweil, R. (1999). *The Age of Spiritual Machines: When Computers Exceed Human Intelligence*. New York, NY: Viking.

(2006). *The Singularity is Near: When Humans Transcend Biology*. New York, NY: Penguin Books.

Kuzniar, A. (2006). *Melancholia's Dog: Reflections on Our Animal Kinship*. Chicago, IL: University of Chicago Press.

Lacan, J. (1998). *The Four Fundamental Concepts of Psychoanalysis: The Seminar of Jacques Lacan, Book XI,* trans. A. Sheridan. New York, NY: W. W. Norton & Company.

(2002). The Mirror Stage as Formative of the I Function as Revealed in Psychoanalytic Experience. In *Écrits*, trans. B. Fink. New York, NY: W. W. Norton & Company, 75–81.

Landecker, H. (2007). *Culturing Life: How Cells Became Technologies*, Cambridge, MA: Harvard University Press.

(2015). Sociology in an Age of Genomic Instability: Copy Number Variation, Somatic Mosaicism, and the Fallen Genome. *Advances in Medical Sociology*, (16), 157–86.

Latour, B. (1996). *Aramis or the Love of Technology*, trans. C. Porter. Cambridge, MA: Harvard University Press.

(1993). *We Have Never Been Modern*, trans. C. Porter. Cambridge, MA: Harvard University Press.

Le Guin, U. K. (2019). *The Left Hand of Darkness*. New York, NY: Ace Books.

Leicester, H. M. (1971). *The Historical Background of Chemistry*. New York, NY: Dover Publications.

Leong, D. (2016). The Mattering of Black Lives: Octavia Butler's Hyperempathy and the Promise of New Materialism. *Catalyst: Feminism, Theory, Technoscience*, 2(2), 1–35.

Lerner, B. H. (2003). *The Breast Cancer Wars: Hope, Fear, and the Pursuit of a Cure in Twentieth-Century America*. New York, NY: Oxford University Press.

Leroi-Gourhan, A. (1993). *Gesture and Speech*. Trans. A. Bostock Berger. Cambridge, MA: MIT Press.

Levine, K. (Director). (2007). *BioShock* [Video game]. Westwood, MA, and Canberra, AU: 2 K Boston and 2 K Australia.

Li, Y. (2018). These CRISPR-modified Crops Don't Count as GMOs. *The Conversation*, 22 May. Online. https://theconversation.com/these-crispr-modified-crops-dont-count-as-gmos-96002

Lilly, K. (2000). *Who Wrote the Book of Life?: A History of the Genetic Code*. Stanford, CA: Stanford University Press.

Lippit, A. M. (2017). Therefore, the Animal that Saw Derrida. In J. Weinstein and C. Colebrook, eds., *Posthumous Life: Theorizing Beyond the Posthuman*. New York, NY: Columbia University Press, 87–104.

Lloyd, D. (2019). *Under Representation: The Racial Regime of Aesthetics*. Fordham University Press.

Lock, M. (2001). The Alienation of Body Tissue and the Biopolitics of Immortalized Cell Lines. *Body and Society*, 7(2–3), 63–91.

   (2013). The Epigenome and Nature/Nurture Reunification: A Challenge for Anthropology. *Medical Anthropology*, 32(4), 291–308.

Lorde, A. (1980). *The Cancer Journals*. San Francisco: Aunt Lute Books.

Losh, E. and Wernimont, J. (2018). "Introduction." *Bodies of Information: Intersectional Feminism and the Digital Humanities*. Minneapolis, MN: University of Minnesota Press, ix-xxv.

Lovelock, J., with Appleyard, B. (2019). *Novacene: The Coming Age of Hyperintelligence*. Cambridge, MA: The MIT Press.

Lowe, L. (2015). *The Intimacies of Four Continents*. Durham, NC: Duke University Press.

Lowenstein, A. (2015). Buñuel's Bull Meets YouTube's Lion: Surrealist and Digital Posthumanisms. In M. Lawrence and L. McMahon, eds., *Animal Life and the Moving Image*. London, UK: British Film Institute, 58–71.

Luciano, D. and Chen, M. Y. (2015). Has the Queer Ever Been Human? *GLQ: A Journal of Lesbian and Gay Studies*, 21(2–3): 183–207.

Luhmann, N. (1995). *Social Systems*, trans. J. Bednarz, Jr., with D. Baecker. Stanford, CA: Stanford University Press.

Lundblad, M. (2017). Introduction: The End of the Animal–Literary and Cultural Animalities. In M. Lundblad, ed., *Animalities: Literary and Cultural Studies Beyond the Human*. Edinburgh, UK: Edinburgh University Press, 1–21.

Lyotard, J. F. (1988–89). Can Thought Go On Without a Body?, trans. B. Boone and L. Hildreth. *Discourse* 11(1), 74–87.

(1991) *The Inhuman: Reflections of Time*, trans. G. Bennington and R. Bowlby. Cambridge, UK: Polity Press.

(1984). *The Postmodern Condition: A Report on Knowledge*, trans. G. Bennington and B. Massumi. Minneapolis, MN: University of Minnesota Press.

(1992). *The Postmodern Explained: Correspondence 1982–1985*, ed. J. Pefanis and M. Thomas. Minneapolis, MN: Minnesota University Press.

(2001). Postmodern Fable, trans. Georges Van Den Abeele. In S. Malpass, ed., *Postmodern Debates*. Houndmills, UK: Palgrave, 12–21.

Mahon, P. (2017). *Posthumanism: A Guide for the Perplexed*. London, UK: Bloomsbury Academic.

Malabou, C. (2005). *The Future of Hegel: Plasticity, Temporality, and Dialectic*. London, UK: Routledge.

Manning, E. (2013). *Always More than One: Individuation's Dance*. Durham, NC: Duke University Press.

(2016). *The Minor Gesture*. Durham, NC: Duke University Press.

and Massumi, B. (2014). *Thought in the Act: Passages in the Ecology of Experience*. Minneapolis, MN: University of Minnesota Press.

Mansfield, B. (2017). Folded Futurity: Epigenetic Plasticity, Temporality, and New Figures of Fetal Life. *Science as Culture*, 26(3),355–79.

and Gutman, J. (2015). Epigenetic Life: Biological Plasticity, Abnormality, and New Configurations of Race and Reproduction. *Cultural Geographies*, 22(1), 3–20.

Marks, L.U. (2002). *Touch: Sensuous Theory and Multisensory Media*. Minneapolis, MN: University of Minnesota Press.

Martinon, J.-P. (2007). *On Futurity: Malabou, Derrida and Nancy*. London, UK: Palgrave Macmillan.

Massumi, B. (1995). The Autonomy of Affect. *Cultural Critique*, 31, 83–109.

(2002). *Parables for the Virtual: Movement, Affect, Sensation*. Durham, NC: Duke University Press.

(2011). *Semblance and Event: Activist Philosophy and the Occurrent Arts*. Cambridge, MA: The MIT Press.

Mathews, F. (2015). Moral Ambiguities in the Politics of Climate Change. In V. Nanda, ed., *Climate Change and Environmental Ethics*. New Brunswick, NJ: Transactions Publishers, 43–64.

Matthews, B. (2011). *Schelling's Organic Form of Philosophy: Life as the Schema of Freedom*. New York, NY: SUNY Press.

Maturana, H. M. and Varela, F. J. (1980). *Autopoiesis and Cognition: The Realization of the Living*. Dordrecht, Netherlands: D. Reidel.

Mbembe, A. (2003). Necropolitics. *Public Culture*, 15(1),11–40.

McCaffrey, A. (1970). *The Ship Who Sang*. New York, NY: Ballantine Books.

McCorduck, P. (2004). *Machines Who Think: A Personal Inquiry Into the History and Prospects of Artificial Intelligence*, 2nd ed. Natick, MA: A. K. Peters/CRC Press.

McCormack, D. (2018). *Atmospheric Things: On the Allure of Elemental Envelopment*. Durham, NC: Duke University Press. Online.

McElroy, J. (1976). *Plus*. New York, NY: Knopf.

McHale, B. (1987). *Postmodernist Fiction*. New York: Methuen.

McHugh, S. and Marvin, G. Human-Animal Studies: Global Perspectives. In S. McHugh and G. Marvin, eds., *Human-Animal Studies*, Vol. 1. New York, NY: Routledge, 1–16.

Meillassoux, Q. (2008). *After Finitude: An Essay on the Necessity of Contingency*, trans. R. Brassier. London, UK: Continuum.

(2011). Excerpts from L'Inexistence divine. In Harman, G., *Quentin Meillassoux: Philosophy in the Making*. Edinburgh, UK: University of Edinburgh Press, 175–238.

(2015). *Science Fiction and Extro-Science Fiction*, trans. Alyosha Edlebi. Minneapolis, MN: Univocal Publishing.

Meloni, M. (2015). Epigenetics for the Social Sciences: Justice, Embodiment, and Inheritance in the Postgenomic Age. *New Genetics and Society*, 34(2), 125–51.

(2019). *Impressionable Biologies: From the Archaeology of Plasticity to the Sociology of Epigenetics*. New York, NY: Routledge.

Mies, M. and Shiva, V. (1993). *Ecofeminism*. Black Point, Nova Scotia: Fernwood Press.

Milburn, C. (2015). *Mondo Nano: Fun and Games in the World of Digital Matter*. Durham, NC: Duke University Press.

(2008). *Nanovision: Engineering the Future*. Durham, NC: Duke University Press.

Miller, E. and Gibson-Graham, J. K. (2019). Thinking with Interdependence: From Economy/Environment to Ecological Livelihoods. In J. Bennett and M. Zournazi, eds., *Thinking in the World: A Reader*. New York, NY: Bloomsbury, 314–340.

Million. (2017). Indigenous Matters. In S. Alaimo, ed., *Gender: Matter*. Farmington Hills, MI: Macmillan, 95–110.

Mitchell, D. T., Antebi, S. and Snyder, S. L. (2019). Introduction. In D. Mitchell, S. Antebi, and S.L. Snyder, eds., *The Matter of Disability: Materiality, Biopolitics, Crip Affect*. Ann Arbor, MI: University of Michigan Press, 1–37.

Mitchell, T. (1998). Fixing the Economy. *Cultural Studies*, 12(1),82–101.

Moore, J. (2016). Introduction: Anthropocene or Capitalocene? In J. Moore, ed., *Anthropocene or Capitalocene?: Nature, History, and the Crisis of Capitalism*. Oakland, CA: PM Press.

Moravec, H. (1988). *Mind Children: The Future of Robot and Human Intelligence*. Cambridge, MA: Harvard University Press.

More, M. (1998). *The Extropian Principles Version 3.0: A Transhumanist Declaration*. Extropy Institute. Online.

Morton, T. (2017). *Humankind: Solidarity with Nonhuman People*. New York, NY: Verso Books.

(2013). *Hyperobjects: Philosophy and Ecology after the End of the World*. Minneapolis, MN: University of Minnesota Press.

Moylan, T. (1986). *Demand the Impossible: Science Fiction and the Utopian Imagination*. New York, NY: Methuen.

Müller, A. and Müller, K. H. (eds.). (2007). *An Unfinished Revolution? Heinz von Foerster and the Biological Computer Laboratory/BCL 1958–1976*. Vienna, AT: Echoraum.

Murphie, A. (2018). On Being Affected: Feeling in the Folding of Multiple Catastrophes. *Cultural Studies*, 32(1), 18–42.

Murphy. M. (2017). *The Economization of Life*. Durham, NC: Duke University Press.

Narkunas, J. P. (2018). *Reified Life: Speculative Capital and the Ahuman Condition*. New York, NY: Fordham University Press.

Neimanis, A. (2017). *Bodies of Water: Posthuman Feminist Phenomenology*. London, UK: Bloomsbury Academic.

Nichanian, M. and Kazanjian, D. (2003). Between Genocide and Catastrophe. In D. Eng and D. Kazanjian, eds., *Loss: The Politics of Mourning*. Berkeley, CA: University of California Press, 125–47.

Nietzsche, F. (2009). Nietzsche on Science Fiction. *The Adam Roberts Project*. Online.

   (1979). On Truth and Lies in a Nonmoral Sense. In Daniel Breazeale, ed., *Philosophy and Truth: Selections from Nietzsche's Notebooks of the Early 1870s*. New York, NY: Humanity Books, 79–97.

   (2006). *Thus Spoke Zarathustra*, ed. R. Pippin, trans. A.D. Caro. Oxford, UK: Oxford University Press.

   (1968). *The Will to Power, trans. W. Kaufmann*. New York, NY: Vintage Books.

Nolan, J. and Joy, L. (Creators). (2016-). *Westworld* [Television series]. New York, NY: Home Box Office (HBO) Inc.

Novak, B. J. (2018). De-Extinction. *Genes*, 9 (11).Online.

Nowviskie, B. (2016). On the Origin of "Hack" and "Yack." In M.K. Gold and L. F. Klein, eds., *Debates in the Digital Humanities*. Minneapolis, MN: University of Minnesota Press. Online.

O'Gorman, M. (2006). *E-Crit: Digital Media, Critical Theory, and the Humanities*. Toronto, ON: University of Toronto Press.

   (2016). *Necromedia*. Minneapolis, MN: University of Minnesota Press.

   (2015). Taking Care of Digital Dementia. *CTheory* (18 Feb). Online.

Ohrem, D. (2017). An Address from Elsewhere: Vulnerability, Relationality, and Conceptions of Creaturely Embodiment. In D. Ohrem and R. Bartosch, eds., *Beyond the Human-Animal Divide: Creaturely Lives in Literature and Culture*. New York, NY: Palgrave, 43–75.

Pálsson G. (2009). Biosocial Relations of Production. *Comparative Studies in Society and History*, 51(2), 288–313.

Parikka, Jussi. (2015). *The Anthrobscene*. Minneapolis, MN: Minnesota University Press, ebook.

Parikka, J. and Hertz, G. (2015). Zombie Media: Circuit Bending Media Archaeology into an Art Method." In *A Geology of Media*. Minneapolis, MN: University of Minnesota Press, 141–53.

Paxson, H. Post-Pasteurian Cultures: The Microbiopolitics of Raw-Milk Cheese in the United States. *Cultural Anthropology*, 23(1), 15–47.

Peña, F. (2016). Interview with Catherine Malabou. *Figure/Ground*, 12 May. Online.

Peters, J. D. (2015). *The Marvelous Clouds*. Chicago, IL: University of Chicago Press.

Pfeifer, R. and Bongard, J. (2007). *How the Body Shapes the Way We Think: A New View of Intelligence*. Cambridge, MA: The MIT Press.

Pfister, W. (Director). (2014). *Transcendence* [Motion picture]. Los Angeles, CA: Alcon Entertainment.

Pias, C. (ed.). (2016). *The Macy Conferences 1946–53: The Complete Transactions*. Chicago, IL: University of Chicago Press.

Pick, A. (2011). *Creaturely Poetics: Animality and Vulnerability in Literature and Film*. New York, NY: Columbia University Press.

Pickering, A. (2011). *The Cybernetic Brain: Sketches of Another Future*. Chicago, IL: University of Chicago Press.

Pilsch, A. (2017). *Transhumanism: Evolutionary Futurism and the Human Technologies of Utopia*. Minneapolis, MN: Minnesota University Press.

Planck, M. (1970). The Unity of the Physical World-Picture. In S. Toulmin, ed., *Physical Reality: Philosophical Essays on 20th Century Physics*. New York, NY: Harper & Row, 1–27.

Pollock, A. (2012). *Medicating Race: Heart Disease and Durable Preoccupations with Difference*. Durham, NC: Duke University Press.

Povinelli, E. A. (2016). *Geontologies: A Requiem to Late Liberalism*. Durham, NC: Duke University Press.

Powers, Richard. (2018). *The Overstory*. New York, NY: W.W. Norton & Company.

Prainsack, B. and Buyx, A. (2017). *Solidarity in Biomedicine and Beyond*. Cambridge, UK: Cambridge University Press.

Puar, J. K. (2017). *Right to Maim: Debility, Capacity, Disability*. Durham, NC: Duke University Press.

   (2007). *Terrorist Assemblages: Homonationalism in Queer Times*. Durham, NC: Duke University Press.

Puig de la Bellacasa, M. (2017). *Matters of Care: Speculative Ethics in More Than Human Worlds*. Minneapolis, MN: University of Minnesota Press.

Rabinow, P. (ed) (1984). *The Foucault Reader*. New York, NY: Pantheon.

Raley, R. (2014). Digital Humanities for the Next Five Minutes. *differences* 25(1),26–45.

Ramsay, S. and Rockwell, G. (2012). Developing Things: Notes toward an Epistemology of Building in the Digital Humanities. In M.K. Gold, ed., *Debates in the Digital Humanities*. Minneapolis, MN: University of Minnesota Press. 75–84.

Rattansi, P. and Clericuzio, A. (2013). *Alchemy and Chemistry in the 16th and 17th Centuries*. Dordrecht, Netherlands: Kluwer Academic Publishers.

Raulerson, J. (2013). *Singularities: Technoculture, Transhumanism, and Science Fiction in the Twenty-first Century*. Liverpool, UK: Liverpool University Press.

Resch, G., Southwick D., Record, I. and Ratto, M. (2018). Thinking as Handwork: Critical Making with Humanistic Concerns. In J. Sayers, ed., *Making Things and Drawing Boundaries*. Minneapolis, MN: University of Minnesota Press, 140–9.

Rhee, J. (2018). *The Robot Imaginary: The Human and the Price of Dehumanized Labor*. Minneapolis, MN: University of Minnesota Press.

Richardson, M. (2018). Climate Trauma, or the Affects of the Catastrophe to Come. *Environmental Humanities* 10(1),1–19.

(2016). *Gestures of Testimony: Torture, Trauma, and Affect in Literature*. New York, NY: Bloomsbury Academic.

Rigney, A. and Erll, A. (eds.). (2009). *Mediation, Remediation, and the Dynamics of Cultural Memory*. Berlin: de Gruyter.

Ripple, W. J., et al. (2014). Status and Ecological Effects of the World's Largest Carnivores. *Science*, 343 (6167), 1241484.Online.

Risam, R. (2018). What Passes for Human? In E. Losh and J. Wernimont, eds., *Bodies of Information: Intersectional Feminism and the Digital Humanities*. Minneapolis, MN: University of Minnesota Press, 39–56.

Robinson, K. S. (2015). *Aurora*. New York, NY: Orbit.

(2018). *New York 2140*. New York, NY: Orbit.

(2015). Our Generation Ships Will Sink. *Boing Boing* (November 16). Online.

Rockwell, G. (1999). In Humanities Computing an Academic Discipline? *Institute for Advanced Technology in the Humanities*. Online

Roelvink, G. (2016). *Building Dignified Worlds: Geographies of Collective Action*. Minneapolis, MN: University of Minnesota Press.

(2018). Community Economies and Climate Justice. In S. Jacobson, ed., *Climate Justice and the Economy: Social Mobilization, Knowledge and the Political*. New York, NY: Routledge, 129–147.

(2015). Performing Posthumanist Economies in the Anthropocene. In G. Roelvink, K. St. Martin, and J. K. Gibson-Graham, eds., *Making Other Worlds Possible: Performing Diverse Economies*. Minneapolis, MN: University of Minnesota Press, 225–43.

and Gibson-Graham, J. K. (2009). A Postcapitalist Politics of Dwelling. *Australian Humanities Review*, 46, 145–58.

and Zolkos, M. (2011). Climate Change as Experience of Affect. *Angelaki*, 16(4), 43–57.

(2015). Posthumanist Perspectives on Affect. *Angelaki*, 20(3), 1–20.

Rose, N. (2013). The Human Sciences in a Biological Age. *Theory, Culture, and Society*, 30(1), 3–34.

(2007). *The Politics of Life Itself: Biomedicine, Power, and Subjectivity in the Twenty-first Century*. Princeton, NJ: Princeton University Press.

Ross, A. (1991). *Strange Weather: Culture, Science and Technology in the Age of Limits* New York, NY: Verso.

Ruccio, D. (2017). Capitalocene. *Occasional Links & Commentary on Economics, Culture and Society*. Online.

Russ, J. (2000). *The Female Man*. Boston, MA: Beacon Press.

Rutsky, R.L. (2017). Technologies. In B. Clarke and M. Rossini, eds., *The Cambridge Companion to Literature and the Posthuman.* Cambridge, UK: Cambridge University Press, 182–95.

Ryan, D. (2015). *Animal Theory: A Critical Introduction.* Edinburgh, UK: Edinburgh University Press.

Saldaña-Portillo, M. J. (2016). *Indian Given: Racial Geographies across Mexico and the United States.* Durham, NC: Duke University Press.

Sayers, J. (2017). *Making Things and Drawing Boundaries.* Minneapolis, MN: University of Minnesota Press.

Schneiderman, J. S. (2017). The Anthropocene Controversy. In R. Grusin, ed., *Anthropocene Feminism.* Minneapolis, MN: University of Minnesota Press, 169–95.

Schroeder, K. (2019). *Stealing Worlds.* New York, NY: Tor.

Schuster, J. (2016). On Reading Christian Bök's *The Xenotext: Book 1* Ten Thousand Years Later. *Jacket 2.* Online.

Scott, R. (Director). 1982. *Blade Runner* [Motion picture]. Burbank, CA: Warner Brothers.

Sedgwick, E. K. (2003). Paranoid Reading and Reparative Reading, or, You're So Paranoid, You Probably Think This Essay is About You. In *Touching Feeling: Affect, Pedagogy, Performativity.* Durham, NC: Duke University Press, 123–51.

(2003). *Touching Feeling: Affect, Pedagogy, Performativity.* Durham, NC: Duke University Press.

Sennett, R. (2009). *The Craftsman.* New Haven, CT: Yale University Press.

Senior, A. (2014). Relics of Bioart: Ethics and Messianic Aesthetics in Performance Documentation. *Theatre Journal,* 66(2), 183–205.

Sharif, S. (2016). *Look.* Minneapolis, MN: Greywolf Press.

Shaviro, S. (2014). *The Universe of Things: On Speculative Realism.* Minneapolis, MN: University of Minnesota Press.

Shelley, M. (2018). *Frankenstein: The 1818 Text.* New York, NY: Penguin Books.

Shevlin, H., Vold, K., Crosby, M. and Halina, M. (2019). The Limits of Machine Intelligence. *EMBO reports* 20(10), e49177.

Shklovskii, I. S. and Sagan, C. (1966). *Intelligent Life in the Universe.* San Francisco, CA: Holden-Day.

Slonczewski, J. (2000). *Brain Plague.* New York, NY: Tor Books.

(1998). *The Children Star.* New York, NY: Tor Books.

(1993). *Daughters of Elysium.* New York, NY: William Morrow.

(1987). *A Door into Ocean.* New York, NY: Avon Books.

Smith, A. (2014). Native Studies at the Horizon of Death: Theorizing Ethnographic Entrapment and Settler Self-Reflexivity. In A. Simpson and A. Smith, eds., *Theorizing Native Studies.* Durham, NC: Duke University Press.

Snelders, H. A. M. (1970). Romanticism and Naturphilosophie and the Inorganic Natural Sciences, 1797–1840: An Introductory Survey. *Studies in Romanticism,* 9(3), 193–215.

Sorenson, J. (2014). Introduction: Thinking the Unthinkable. In J. Sorenson, ed., *Critical Animal Studies: Thinking the Unthinkable*. Toronto, ON: Canada Scholars' Press, xi–xxxiv.

Spahr, J. (2005). *This Connection of Everything with Lungs*. Berkeley, CA: University of California Press.

Springgay, S. and S. E. Truman. (2018). *Walking Methodologies in a More-than-Human World: WalkingLab*. London, UK: Routledge.

Squier, S. M. (2004). *Liminal Lives: Imagining the Human at the Frontiers of Biomedicine*. Durham, NC: Duke University Press.

Stallwood, K. (2014). Animal Rights: Moral Crusade or Social Movement? In J. Sorenson, *Critical Animal Studies: Thinking the Unthinkable*. Toronto, ON: Canada Scholars' Press, 298–317.

Steffen, W., Rockström, J., Richardson, K., et al. (2018). Perspective: Trajectories of the Earth System in the Anthropocene. *PNAS Proceeding of the National Academy of Sciences of the United States of America*, 115(33), 8252–59.

Steinbock, E. (2019). *Shimmering Images: Trans Cinema, Embodiment, and the Aesthetics of Change*. Durham, NC: Duke University Press.

Stephenson, N. (1992). *Snow Crash*. New York, NY: Bantam, 1992.

Sterling, B. (1988). Preface. In Bruce Sterling, ed., *Mirrorshades: The Cyberpunk Anthology*. New York, NY: Ace Books, ix–xvi.

Stewart, K. (2011). Atmospheric Attunements. *Environment and Planning D: Society and Space*, 29 (3), 445–53.

Stiegler, B. (1998). *Technics and Time I: The Fault of Epimetheus*, trans. R. Beardsworth and G. Collins. Stanford, CA: Stanford University Press.

Stracey, F. (1985). Bio-Art: The Ethics Behind the Aesthetics. *Nature Reviews Molecular Cell Biology*, 10, 496–500.

Stross, C. *Accelerando*. (2005). London: Penguin Books.

Sturrock, J. (ed.). (1979). *Structuralism and Since: From Lévi-Strauss to Derrida*. Oxford, UK: Oxford University Press.

Sullivan, S. (2015). *The Physiology of Sexist and Racist Oppression*. Oxford, UK: Oxford University Press.

Sunder Rajan, K. (2017). *Pharmocracy: Value, Politics, and Knowledge in Global Biomedicine*. Durham, NC: Duke University Press.

Suvin, D. (1988). *Positions and Presuppositions in Science Fiction*. Kent, OH: Kent State University Press.

Tallbear, K. (2017). Beyond the Life/Not-Life Binary: A Feminist Indigenous Reading of Cryopreservation, Interspecies Thinking, and the New Materialisms. In J. Radin and E. Kowal, eds., *Cryopolitics: Frozen Life in a Melting World*. Cambridge, MA: The MIT Press, 179–201.

(2013). *Native American DNA: Tribal Belonging and the False Promise of Genetic Science*. Minneapolis, MN: University of Minnesota Press.

Tamminen, S. and Vermeulen N. (2019). Bio-objects: New Conjugations of the Living. *Sociologias, Porto Alegre*, 21(50), 156–79.

Tchaikovsky, A. (2015). *Children of Time*. New York, NY: Tor Books.

Thacker, E. (2010). *After Life*. Chicago, IL: University of Chicago Press.

(2006). *The Global Genome: Biotechnology, Politics and Culture*. Cambridge, MA: MIT Press.

Thrift, N. (2008). *Non-Representational Theory: Space, Politics, Affect*. New York, NY: Routledge.

Tinker, G. (2004). The Stones Shall Cry Out: Consciousness, Rocks, and Indians. *Wicazo Sa Review*, 19(2), 105–25.

Tiptree, J., Jr. (2004). The Girl Who Was Plugged In. In J. Smith, ed., *Her Smoke Rose Up Forever*. San Francisco, CA: Tachyon Publications, 43–78.

Todd, Z. (2014). An Indigenous Feminist's Take On the Ontological Turn: "Ontology" Is Just Another Word for Colonialism. *Urbane Adventurer: Amiskwacî*. Online.

Trop, G. (2018). The Indifference of the Inorganic. In E. Landgraf, G. Trop and L. Weatherby, eds., *Posthumanism in the Age of Humanism: Mind, Matter, and the Life Sciences after Kant*. New York, NY: Bloomsbury.

Tsang, M. (2017). *Open Source Estrogen: From Biomolecules to Biopolitics ... Hormones with Institutional Biopower!* Unpublished MSc Dissertation. Cambridge, MA: Massachusetts Institute of Technology. Online.

Tsing, A., Swanson, J., Gan, E. and Bubandt, N. (2017). *Arts of Living on a Damaged Planet: Ghosts and Monsters of the Anthropocene*. Minneapolis, MN: University of Minnesota Press.

Tuana, N. (2008). Viscous Porosity: Witnessing Katrina. In S. Alaimo and S. Hekman, *Material Feminisms*. Bloomington, IN: Indiana University Press, 188–213.

Vaage S. N. (2016). What Ethics for Bioart? *NanoEthics*, 10(1), 87–104.

Van der Tuin, I. (2018). New/New Materialism. In R. Braidotti and M. Hlavajova, eds., *The Posthuman Glossary*. New York, NY: Bloomsbury Academic, 277–78.

VanderMeer, J. (2014). *Area X: The Southern Reach Trilogy*. New York, NY: Farrar, Straus and Giroux.

Verhoeven, P. (Director). (1987). *RoboCop* [Motion picture]. Los Angeles, CA: Orion Pictures.

Vermulen, P. and Richter, V. (2015). Introduction: Creaturely Constellations. *European Journal of English Studies*, 19(9), 1–9.

Vinge, V. (1993). The Coming Technological Singularity: How to Survive in a Post-Human Era. Presented at NASA Vision-21 Symposium. Online.

Vint, S. (2010). *Animal Alterity: Science Fiction and the Question of the Animal*. Liverpool, UK: Liverpool University Press.

(2007). *Bodies of Tomorrow: Technology, Subjectivity, and Science Fiction*. Toronto, ON: University of Toronto Press.

(2019). Long Live the New Flesh: Race and the Posthuman in Westworld. In A. Goody and A. Mackay, eds., *Reading Westworld*. Cham, Switzerland: Palgrave Macmillan, 141–60.

von Foerster, H. (1990). Cybernetics. In S. C. Shapiro, ed., *Encyclopedia of Artificial Intelligence*, Vol.1. New York, NY: John Wiley & Sons, 225–26.

Vora, K. and Atanasoski, N. (2019). *Surrogate Humanity: Race, Robots, and the Politics of Technological Futurity*. Durham, NC: Duke University Press.

Wainwrigth, J. and Mann, G. (2018). *Climate Leviathan: A Political Theory of Our Planetary Future*. London, UK: Verso Books.

Waldby, C. (2002). Stem Cells, Tissue Cultures and the Production of Biovalue. *Health*, 6(3), 305–23.

   and Mitchell, R. (2006). *Tissue Economies: Blood, Organs, and Cell Lines in Late Capitalism*. Durham, NC: Duke University Press.

Warwick, C. (2016). Building Theories or Theories of Building? A Tension at the Heart of Digital Humanities. In S. Schreibman, R. Siemens and J. Unsworth, eds., *A New Companion to Digital Humanities*. West Sussex, UK: Wiley, 538–52.

Weasel, L. H. (2016). Embodying Intersectionality: The Promise and (and Peril) of Epigenetics for Feminist Science Studies. In V. Pitts-Taylor, ed., *Mattering: Feminism, Science, and Materialism*. New York, NY: New York University Press.

Weir, J. (2009). *Murray River Country: An Ecological Dialogue with Traditional Owners*. Canberra, ACT: Aboriginal Studies Press.

Weisberg, Z. (2014). The Trouble with Posthumanism: Bacteria are People Too. In J. Sorenson, ed., *Critical Animal Studies: Thinking the Unthinkable*. Toronto, ON: Canada Scholars' Press, 93–116.

Wells, H. G. (2014). *The Time Machine*. New York, NY: Signet Classics.

Wells, H. G. (2005). *The War of the Worlds*. New York, NY: Penguin Books.

Wiener, N. (1961). *Cybernetics or Control and Communication in the Animal and the Machine*, 2nd rev. ed. Cambridge, MA: The MIT Press.

   (1988). *The Human Use of Human Beings: Cybernetics and Society*. Cambridge, MA: Da Capo Press.

Wilbert, C. (2006). What Is Doing the Killing? Animal Attacks, Man-Eaters, and Shifting Boundaries and Flows of Human-Animal Relations. In The Animal Studies Group, ed., *Killing Animals*. Champaign, IL: University of Illinois Press, 30–49.

Willems, B. (2010). *Facticity, Poverty and Clones: On Kazuo Ishiguro's Never Let Me Go*. New York, NY: Atropos Press.

   (2015). *Shooting the Moon*. Ropley, Hants: Zero Books.

   (2017). *Speculative Realism and Science Fiction*. Edinburgh, UK: Edinburgh University Press.

Willey, A. (2016). A World of Materialisms: Postcolonial Feminist Science Studies and the New Natural. *Science, Technology & Human Values*, 41(6), 991–1014.

Williams, J. (1999). The New Belletrism. *Style*, 33(3), 414–42.

Williams, J. J. (2009). Donna Haraway's Critters. *Chronicle of Higher Education* (18 October). Online.

   (2009–2010). Science Stories: An Interview with Donna J. Haraway. *The Minnesota Review*, (73–74), 133–63.

Wills, David. 2008. *Dorsality: Thinking Back Through Technology and Politics*. Minneapolis, MN: University of Minnesota Press.

Wöhler, F. (1828). Ueber künstliche Bildung des Harnstoffs. *Annalen der Physik und Chemie*, 88(2), 253–56.

Wolfe, C. (2003). *Animal Rites: American Culture, the Discourse of Species, and Posthumanist Theory*. Chicago, IL: Chicago University Press.

  (2013). *Before the Law: Humans and Other Animals in a Biopolitical Frame*. Chicago, IL: University of Chicago Press.

  (2008). Exposures. In Stanley Cavell, et al., eds., *Philosophy and Animal Life*. New York, NY: Columbia University Press, 1–41.

  (2009). Human, All Too Human: "Animal Studies" and the Humanities. *PMLA* 124(2), 564–75.

  (2010). Introduction. In *What Is Posthumanism?* Minneapolis, MN: Minnesota University Press, xi–xxxiv.

  (2006). Thinking Other-Wise: Cognitive Science, Deconstruction, and the (Non)Speaking (Non)Human Animal Subject. In J. Castricano, ed., *Animal Subjects: An Ethical Reader in a Posthuman World*. Waterloo, ON: Wilfred Laurier University Press, 125–43.

  (2010). *What Is Posthumanism?* Minneapolis, MN: University of Minnesota Press.

Wright, L. (2015). *The Vegan Studies Project: Food, Animals, and Gender in the Age of Terror*. Athens, GA: University of Georgia Press.

Wynter, S. Unsettling the Coloniality of Being/Power/Truth/Freedom: Towards the Human, After Man, Its Overrepresentation–An Argument." *CR: The New Centennial Review*, 3(3), 257–337.

Young, R. (ed.). (1981). *Untying the Text: A Post-Structuralist Reader*. London, UK: Routledge & Kegan Paul.

Zimmerman, M. E. (2009). Religious Motifs in Technological Posthumanism. *Western Humanities Review*, 63(3), 67–83.

Zirra, M. (2017). Shelf Lives: Nonhuman Agency and Seamus Heaney's Vibrant Memory Objects. *Parallax*, 23(4), 458–73.

Zurr, I. and Catts, O. (2014). The Unnatural Relations between Artistic Research and Ethics Committees: An Artist's Perspective. In P. U. Macneill, ed., *The Arts and Ethic, Library of Ethics and Applied Philosophy*. New York, NY: Springer.

Zylinska, J. (2009). *Bioethics in the Age of New Media*. Cambridge, MA: The MIT Press.

  (2010). Playing God, Playing Adam: The Politics and Ethics of Enhancement. *Journal of Bioethical Inquiry*, 7(2), 149–61.

# Index

ability
  ableism, 7, 84
  disability, 67–8, 180, 182, 184–5
accelerationism, 21
aesthetics, 63, 198–9, 240, 242, 247
  fable, 7, 39, 44, 53
  imaginary, the, 67, 92–3, 97–9, 151, 155,
    224–5, 226
  narrative, 7, 21, 37, 45, 115, 140, 187, 202, 221
affect, 5, 58, 83, 108, 140, 148, 177, 196, 221
  affective turn, 58, 60
Agamben, Giorgio, 18, 40, 83, 161, 162, 165, 168
agency, 4, 6, 16, 18, 21, 24, 39, 94, 95, 111, 112, 143,
    147, 151, 165–6, 167, 168, 177, 179, 180, 181,
    185, 221, 223, 228, 230, 231, 232
Ahmed, Sara, 64–5
Alaimo, Stacy, 17, 18, 25, 220
  trans-corporeality, 23, 182, 183, 220
animal, 5, 15, 18, 20, 35, 50, 59, 75, 76, 78, 121, 122,
    124, 147, 148, 149, 150, 162, 168, 185, 199, 212,
    213, 223, 230, 240, 246
  animal studies, 3, 16, 177, 183, 193
  companion species, 109, 115, 178, 179, 243
Anthropocene, 3, 24, 25, 40, 63, 134–45, 162, 169,
    170, 171, 178, 181, 182
artificial intelligence, 3, 93–8, 99, 101, 226, 232,
    236, 244

Barad, Karen, 3, 22, 24, 76, 82, 167, 178, 180–1,
    182, 183, 202
  agential realism, 23
Bennett, Jane, 151, 168, 182, 193
biopolitics, 4, 40, 171, 178, 213,
    215, 217
  microbiopolitics, 229
  necropolitics, 68, 161, 165
Braidotti, Rosi, 2, 4, 9, 18, 21, 22, 40, 45, 47, 48,
    54, 59, 115, 182, 196, 220, 221, 222
Butler, Judith, 22, 65, 181

capital, 2, 6, 15, 21, 25, 82, 83, 127, 128, 138–9,
    141–2, 163, 169, 179, 181, 182, 227, 231, 241,
    245, 247
  postcapitalism, 64, 144, 180
Chakrabarty, 25
Chakrabarty, Dipesh, 25, 135
Chen, Mel Y., 66, 67, 185, 213
climate change, 170, 181, 222, 227, 230–1, 236, 244
cognition, 101
  distributed, 44, 48, 51, 52–3
  nonconscious, 24, 95, 220
Colebrook, Claire, 4, 25, 40
colonialism, 105, 127, 129, 165, 179, 208, 210, 211,
    212, 217
  and racialization, 184
  decolonization, 209, 231
  empire, 67, 208
communication
  artificial, 79, 94, 95, 100, 102
Cooper, Melinda, 164
cybernetics, 92, 94–5, 101–2
cyborg, 92, 97, 223, 224

Darwin, Charles, 16, 91, 105, 178
Deleuze, Gilles, 2, 58, 59–60, 64, 202, 221
  and Felix Guattari, 44, 181
Derrida, Jacques, 16, 18, 21, 26, 32, 33, 38, 39, 44,
    45, 48–51, 53–4, 110, 114, 148, 181, 192, 196

economics
  biocapital, 121, 126, 127, 163, 164
  biovalue, 120, 126–8, 164
  neoliberalism, 128
embodiment, 3, 15, 20, 21, 46, 52, 58, 60, 61–3,
    66–7, 68, 107, 110, 112, 121, 126, 162, 167, 208,
    220, 225, 226, 227, 231
  flesh, 214
environmentalism, 24, 129, 141, 169, 182–4
  Gaia, 102

Esposito, Roberto, 40, 161, 162, 166–7
evolution, 226, 248
  co-evolution, 4, 106, 122, 179
extinction, 2, 6, 24, 105, 115, 152, 181, 227, 228, 244

feminism, 22, 144, 182, 183
  ecofeminism, 110
  material, 177
  xenofeminism, 21
Foucault, Michel, 2, 18, 33, 38, 39, 44, 45, 91, 120, 121, 128, 161, 162, 163, 165, 167–8, 171

gender, 187, 213, 221, 223
  dualism, 92
  performativity, 22, 23, 65, 66
genetics, 122, 127, 163, 164, 228, 238
  bioart, 239, 242
  epigenetics, 124, 128, 183
governmentality, 163, 164, 165, 166, 169

Halberstam, Jack (Judith), 22, 67, 82
Haraway, Donna, 4, 83, 107, 109, 110, 139–40, 167, 179, 202, 220
  cyborg manifesto, 3, 18, 19, 20, 44, 48, 51, 92, 101, 106, 108, 166, 178, 223
Hayles, N. Katherine, 4, 15, 20, 24, 44, 48, 50, 52, 54, 76, 78, 93, 95, 107, 220, 225
Heidegger, Martin, 19, 32, 193
Herbrechter, Stefan, 2, 19, 47, 92
humanism, 5, 6, 15, 16, 17, 26, 32, 33, 34, 35, 37, 38, 47, 48, 50, 60, 65, 105, 107, 110, 115, 185, 200, 208, 212, 214, 221, 225, 236
  human exceptionalism, 5, 17, 24, 184, 187, 221, 230
  western, 210, 214, 217

indigeneity, 127, 128, 135, 184, 187, 207–8, 210–11, 216–18, 232

Jackson, Zakiyyah Iman, 65, 185, 212, 213

Kant, Immanuel, 32, 34, 38, 47, 53, 194, 196, 202

Lacan, Jacques, 18, 32, 44, 47, 48, 52, 65
Latour, Bruno, 83, 167, 182, 187, 202, 222

materialism, 17, 22, 24, 49, 54, 59, 64, 66, 68, 147, 149, 154, 167, 169, 237, 238
  new materialisms, 21–4, 77, 167, 177, 217, 222
  vital materialism, 60, 148, 151, 182, 186
Mbembe, Achille, 165, 215

microbiome, 124, 125, 128, 169, 227, 229, 243
Morton, Timothy, 4, 23, 147, 222

Nietzsche, Friedrich, 17, 21, 32, 38, 50, 53, 91

plants, 5, 59, 113, 115, 122, 142, 147, 149, 150, 151, 152, 153, 162, 230
posthuman
  antihumanism, 17, 33, 38
  critical posthumanism, 5, 16, 18, 19, 21, 34, 38, 47, 183, 209, 221, 224, 231, 239
  inhuman, 18, 36, 38, 197, 215, 216
  nonhuman, 7, 23, 37, 39, 40, 50, 63, 112, 123, 142, 148, 152, 154, 162, 167, 177, 179, 184, 186, 192, 196, 197, 198, 201, 204, 213, 220, 228, 232, 244, 248
Povinelli, Elizabeth, 151, 169, 217
Puar, Jasbir, 67–8

queer theory, 2, 22, 45, 54, 65–9, 161, 185, 242
  trans, 181

race, 16, 45, 54, 65, 68, 91, 111, 127, 161, 165, 178, 182, 183, 184–8, 206–18, 222
  racialization, 212, 214
rights, 16, 65, 113, 114, 162, 165

science and technology studies, 3, 4, 120, 164, 167, 170, 178, 183, 222, 237, 240, 248
  biomedicine, 121, 123, 125, 161, 236
Sedgwick, Eve Kosofsky, 18, 66
speculative fiction, 19, 92, 93, 97–101, 199, 200, 203, 220–32, 246
Stiegler, Bernard, 20, 40, 77, 78

technology
  biotechnology, 120, 126, 128, 167, 227, 240, 245
  nanotechnology, 20, 226
  synthetic biology, 3, 122, 227, 238, 244, 248
transhuman, 19–21, 78, 91–3, 97, 101, 107, 179, 225–7, 231

utopian, 20, 21, 44, 48, 51, 67, 221, 237

Vint, Sherryl, 18, 107, 115, 184

Weheliye, Alexander, 165, 213–16
Wolfe, Cary, 4, 16, 18, 78, 105, 109–11, 169, 208
Wynter, Sylvia, 2, 105, 106, 210, 213

Zylinska, Joanna, 62, 122